Genocide and Gross Human Rights Violations

Genocide and Gross Human Rights Violations

IN COMPARATIVE PERSPECTIVE

Kurt Jonassohn with
Karin Solveig Björnson

Transaction Publishers
New Brunswick (U.S.A.) and London (U.K.)

Copyright © 1998 by Transaction Publishers, New Brunswick, New Jersey.

All rights reserved under International and Pan-American Copyright Conventions. No part of this book may be reproduced or transmitted in any form or by any means, electronic or mechanical, including photocopy, recording, or any information storage and retrieval system, without prior permission in writing from the publisher. All inquiries should be addressed to Transaction Publishers, Rutgers—The State University, 35 Berrue Circle, Piscataway, New Jersey 08854-8042.

This book is printed on acid-free paper that meets the American National Standard for Permanence of Paper for Printed Library Materials.

Library of Congress Catalog Number: 97-35608
ISBN: 1-56000-314-6 (cloth); 0-7658-0417-4 (paper)
Printed in the United States of America

Library of Congress Cataloging-in-Publication Data

Jonassohn, Kurt.
   Genocide and gross human rights violations in comparative perspective /
Kurt Jonassohn with Karin Solveig Björnson.
      p. cm.
   Includes bibliographical references and indexes.
      ISBN 1-56000-314-6 (cloth : alk. paper) — 0-7658-0417-4 (paper : alk.
paper)
   1. Genocide—Case studies.   2. Genocide—History.   3. Genocide—
Research.   I. Björnson, Karin Solveig.   II. Title.
HV6322.7.J65   1997
304.6'63—dc21   97-35608
                                                                        CIP

To the twenty-first century:
May it be kinder than the last one!

for

Shlomo who passed away before
seeing this book or the twenty-first century

and for

Sarah and Michelle
Jake and Erika
who shall see both

For my parents,
Bernadette and Gerald

Contents

Part 3: Revisiting the Past

Acknowledgements

During the years when this book went through various stages of gestation I have been assisted, critiqued, and encouraged by many students and colleagues. I am particularly grateful to Christy Buchanan, Taylor Buckner, Frank Chalk, Norman Cohn, Helen Fein, H. David Kirk, Leo Kuper, Henri Lustiger-Thaler, and Jeff Rosen. Among those who are not even aware of their assistance I want to thank the students in the course on the History and Sociology of Genocide, the members of the Genocide Workshop, and the librarians in our library at Concordia University. A special thanks is due to Karin Björnson who started as a student, became a research assistant, and now is a collaborator and co-author.

All of the chapters in part 1 have appeared, in their first version, in the series of Occasional Papers of the Montreal Institute for Genocide and Human Rights Studies. Permission to reprint is gratefully acknowledged.

Parts 2 and 3 are the products of collaboration between Karin Björnson and Kurt Jonassohn and, except for the paper on the former Yugoslavia, have not appeared previously.

Finally, in the production process, we acknowledge our debt to the editing by Laurence Mintz of Transaction Publishers.

Preface

The title of this volume has been chosen to signal my position on one of the enduring debates associated with genocide studies. This debate ranges from the position that defines the Holocaust as a unique event to the positions that restrict the subject matter under investigation by adopting various definitions. It is not at all clear what these debates contribute to our understanding. Thus, the title of the book signifies the plan to include in our analysis many cases that may violate one or another definition—including our own—while meeting some of the terms of most of them. The variety of cases included in part 3 will give the interested reader an opportunity to examine and decide such definitonal matters for themselves.

Ever since I have been doing research on genocide I have been preoccupied by two questions. The first one is to explain how it is possible for ordinary people to commit unspeakable atrocities. My question is not about the relatively rare psychopathic criminal about whom psychologists have written. Instead I am concerned about large groups of quite ordinary people who become perpetrators not of foreign victims, but who turn on their friends and neighbours; on people with whom they have lived in the same communities and with whom they have worked, played, and even intermarried. These people, according to the evidence, continue to be loving spouses and parents, they continue to be kind to children and animals and, at the same time, they are able to commit the most horrendous atrocities and to kill their victims. I regret to have to admit that I have not found an answer to that question.

The other question concerns the attempt to understand the nature of gross human rights violations and genocides, and how to intervene in their execution. That search and its results are the subject matter of this book. It has led to the realization that one step toward understanding is the formulation of a typology that distinguishes events that have different origins, occur in different situations, and follow different processes. All of this work has been motivated by the optimistic hope that it might be possible to reduce the number of genocides and to intervene in those that do occur. Needless to add that contemporary events do not provide much support for these hopes. If they are to be realized it will be essential that we get better and more accurate reporting on what actually happens rather than the current misinformation and self-serving disinformation. We need more focused analyses that go beyond the politically convenient and the culturally acceptable. Thus, an analysis of the functions of humanitarian aid is overdue; so is an examination of the part played by power relationships with other countries and the associated arms trade.

An aspect that does not even seem to be on the agenda as yet is the role of population policy and population pressures. We have a great deal of statistical data on rates of population growth, on population density, and on the carrying capacity of the environment. What seems to be missing is a serious and scholarly inquiry into the effects that these factors have on social relations, social attitudes, the scale of conflict, and its escalation into hostilities.

The chapters in part 1 are summaries of the results arrived at so far. In the process of doing this research it has become clear that the appropriate methods often are not conducive to ascertaining the facts. For this reason, part 2 explores some areas of research methods that seem problematic. Finally, part 3 lists a number of cases from all periods of history and from all areas of the world that should serve to amplify the typology—insofar as sufficient evidence is available for making such categorization.

Introduction

During the winter of 1979–1980, while on sabbatical leave, I was travelling around Europe in order to interview former members of the executive committee of the International Sociological Association. My intention was to write an intellectual history of the Association. The result seems to have missed the pond entirely; at least it produced no ripples at all. However, all was not lost. Serendipity, working its usual strange transformations, came to the rescue.

I was travelling on a Eurailpass, usually at night, from interview to interview. These trips gave me plenty of time to think about what I was doing. The shaking up by the railroad and the changing social and natural atmosphere from one country to another eventually produced recurring preoccupations with genocide. Long before I returned home it had become clear to me that I wanted to teach a course on that subject. My early education and my later reading made it clear to me that genocides had occurred repeatedly since antiquity. When I got home, I prepared a proposal for submission to the various university committees that have to approve such initiatives.

Shortly after my return home I met with Frank Chalk, a colleague in the history department and an old friend with whom I had collaborated on a number of projects. As is usual, we brought each other up to date on what we had been doing and where we had been. When I told him about my plan for the new course on genocides, he asked me whether he could team-teach it with me. I immediately agreed and so a new course was born.

When, after the usual bureaucratic delays, we received the 'all clear' from the various curriculum committees we started to prepare for this new course in earnest. But we were in for quite a shock. One of my original rationales for offering this course was that it would deal with an important phenomenon that was dealt with in the curriculum of many universities and that our university needed to catch up on. Based on that assumption, we started to collect information on these other university courses. It quickly turned out that nobody at that time was offering courses on genocide; what they were offering were courses on the Holocaust that only rarely included material on the genocide of the Armenians.

Our conception had been from the start that genocides had occurred throughout history in all parts of the world. Therefore, the subject needed to be approached from a comparative and historical perspective. While each genocide is a unique event, as social scientists we could only assume that something is to be learned by seeing what these unique events have in common. Thus, we discovered that, far from catching up on what other universities had been doing for some time, we were pioneering something that nobody had been doing. This made the course preparation much more difficult and much more exciting. We did not find the body of literature that we had expected to be able to build on. One of the few exception was *Genocide: Its Political Use in the Twentieth Century* (Leo Kuper, 1981) which had just appeared. For the pre-twentieth-century materials we had to search far and wide because few histories have been interested in the fate of the losers. The result was that we amassed a whole collection of photocopies consisting of snippets from here and a few pages from there in order to build up a sample of cases.

Those were the materials that our first students had to work with. Of course, the collection changed from year to year as we discovered new cases and new materials. That is how we eventually consolidated the collection of cases that became part of a manuscript that was published as *The History and Sociology of Genocide* (Chalk and Jonassohn 1990). Of course, many other cases have occurred throughout history and some of these are assembled in part 3 of this volume. However, those dealt with in the 1990 volume are not repeated in this book.

The question arises: how did we cope for so long and so intensively with such an inherently depressing topic? One way in which we had planned such coping was to offer the course only every other year. But the course was too successful and too many students clamored to get in. So, with only a couple of exceptions due to sabbatical leaves, we have offered this course every year since 1980. The far better way of coping with its very depressing aspects was and remains our basic motivation for even tackling this topic: the hope that by research and study we shall learn enough to gain an understanding of the underlying situations and processes that will make it possible to prevent new genocidal events in the future, or at least find ways to intervene effectively. As it turns out, this activist orientation is also what motivates many of the students who enroll in this course.

While we had no delusions of grandeur, we thought that our modest efforts might contribute to these aims. Therefore, we formalized our efforts and established the Montreal Institute for Genocide Studies which would allow us to reach beyond our own classroom. We have done this in a number of ways. The traditional ones are publications and presentations at conferences. In addition, we have produced a series of Occasional Papers that has allowed for the more rapid circulation of ideas than was afforded by the usual publication delays; these papers have been distributed to other interested scholars and several of these papers are included here as part 1, albeit in edited versions. We have also organized periodic workshops to which interested colleagues and students from all four of the Montreal universities were invited. Initially, several of these workshops were chaired by Norman Cohn and other visiting scholars. Lately, they have been held every two weeks during term and were attended by our graduate students and research assistants who also took turns making presentations. We believe that our activities have materially contributed to the increasing interest in the comparative and historical study of genocide, as evidenced by the growing number of scholars, the spreading of courses at other institutions, and, most recently, the founding of the Association of Genocide Scholars.

The hope that the increasing frequency of genocidal massacres may be counteracted by people of good faith is the overriding motivation that provides the coherence for the chapters that follow. While they were not written in the sequence in which they are presented here, it will become clear that they share an underlying theme. These chapters represent my thinking since the publication of the book on *The History and and Sociology of Genocide* (1990). While earlier versions of some of these papers have appeared in journals or as chapters in books, all of them have first seen the light of day as Occasional Papers.

In the first group of three chapters I deal with some conceptual matters. Chapter 1, "What is Genocide?" tries to give an answer to that question that goes somewhat beyond that of the U. N. Genocide Convention. In chapter 2, "Stages in the Development of Genocide" I look at history from antiquity to the present in terms of the kinds of genocides that occurred at various times. In chapter 3, "The Consequences of Ideological Genocides and Their Role in Prevention" I try to demonstrate that ideological genocides were enormously costly for the perpetrator societies, regardless of how much some individuals may have enriched themselves. Furthermore, these societal costs were extremely long lasting while the individual benefits proved quite ephemeral. If these aspects of ideological genocides were more widely known and better understood they might well help to discourage future prospective perpetrators.

There follows a group of two chapters that might well be referred to as the "chameleon in hiding." Chapter 4, "Hunger as a Low-Technology Weapon" shows how hunger has been a tool of conflict from the earliest times. Chapter 5, "Famines, Genocides, and Refugees" elaborates on the theme of how genocides have been disguised as natural events. In addition, it makes a plea for a broader, more interdisciplinary perspective by showing how famines, genocides, and refugees are all connected phenomena that cannot be dealt with satisfactorily in isolation.

There follows a chapter that demonstrates how the understanding of events changes when their historical background is taken into consideration. The "Antecedents of the Holocaust Denial Literature," covers only one hundred years but it shows the extent to which accurate reporting and rational analysis are quite irrelevant to the defining of a national mission and a myth of common origins.

Chapter 6, "On Jewish Resistance" raises the question of why the quite voluminous literature on that topic is so little known. Even in the literature on World War II resistance Jewish resistance receives little attention.

The final group of three chapters represents the development of my thinking about prediction, prevention, and intervention. These ideas will presumably continue to change under the influence of critiques from colleagues and under the impact of events in the real world.

Parts 2 and 3 are the result of the invaluable assistance of, and collaboration with, Karin Solveig Björnson. The chapters in part 2 address a number of questions dealing with methods in comparative and historical research with particular emphasis on how they affect research on genocide and gross human rights violations. Part 3 gives very brief summaries of a large number of cases, each listing a few sources to assist readers who may be inclined to enquire further into the particulars of a case. The final chapter is a much longer exploration of the background to the events in the former Yugoslavia. It is intended to illustrate how a familiarity with the historical background can enhance the understanding and appreciation of current events.

Finally it should be pointed out that the interest in research on genocide and gross human rights violations is of quite recent origin. Thus, not only recent events but also our knowledge in these areas are changing very rapidly. In a published book, such as this one, there is no way of being up to date when dealing with contemporary events. For some readers this may be a serious lack. However, recent technological developments have come to their assistance. Publication on the internet is almost instantaneous and there are now many sources dealing with contemporary events and their interpretation. Therefore, we have included in the bibliography the addresses of internet web pages—where available—that deal with the cases mentioned here. Many of these web pages include bibliographies, sometimes annotated, and/or links to other relevant web sites. While the quality of these web pages is very uneven, and while we have made an effort to list the better ones when there is a choice, browsing them is often very rewarding. Now, that the web includes internet journals, books, book reviews, and many major newspapers, among other items, it is rapidly becoming an indispensable research tool.

It is our intent and hope of this book will contribute to the analysis and understanding of the tragic processes and situations involved in genocides and gross human rights violations.

Part 1

Thinking about Contemporary Concepts and Their Historical Background

1

What is Genocide?[1]

From the beginning of our collaboration, Frank Chalk and I have found that the definition of genocide contained in the United Nations Convention on Genocide, adopted in December 1948, was quite unsatisfactory for one very simple reason: none of the major victim groups of those genocides that have occurred since its adoption fall within its restrictive specifications. This seems to be true, regardless of whether we are thinking of Bangladesh or Burundi, Cambodia or Indonesia, East Timor or Ethiopia. The crux of this problem is contained in Article II of the U.N. Convention which limits the term genocide to "acts committed with intent to destroy, in whole or in part, a national, ethnical, racial or religious group" (Kuper 1981: appendix 1). Other victim groups—whether they be social, political or economic ones—do not qualify as the victims of genocide because they were omitted from that definition. The reasons for that omission have been discussed by Leo Kuper and are less relevant here than our need for a definition that would cover the planned annihilation of any group, no matter how that group is defined and by whom (Kuper 1981: ch. 2). Minimally, such a definition should include economic, political and social groups as potential victims. There have been a number of efforts to amend and expand the U.N. definition of possible victim groups—so far without success (Whitaker 1985).

This lack of success is all the more puzzling since the 1951 United Nations Convention Relating to the Status of Refugees specifies that a refugee is "Any person who owing to well founded fear of being persecuted for reasons of race, religion, nationality, membership of a particular social group or political opinion, is outside the country of his nationality" (D'Souza and Crisp 1985:7).

These two conflicting definitions, arising from the same organization, seem to produce the paradox that some people fleeing from a genocide are being recognized as refugees, while those unable to flee

9

from the same genocide are not acknowledged as being its victims. So, after many revisions, we have finally adopted the following definition for our own research:

> GENOCIDE is a form of one-sided mass killing in which a state or other authority intends to destroy a group, as that group and membership in it are defined by the perpetrator. (Chalk and Jonassohn 1990: 23)

The main difference between the United Nations definition and ours is that we have no restrictions on the types of groups to be included. This allows us to include even those groups that have no verifiable reality outside the minds of the perpetrators, such as "wreckers" or "enemies of the people"; while such groups may not fall within the usual definition of a group as used in the social sciences, the labeling of the group by the perpetrator suffices to define them. Our definition also allows us to include groups that may be recognized by the social sciences, but that had escaped the imagination of perpetrators before Pol Pot, such as the victimization of urban dwellers in Pol Pot's Kampuchea.

However, I must point out that this concern with post-World War II cases does not represent the complete range of our interests. On the contrary, we believe that we have evidence that genocides have occurred during all periods of history and in all parts of the world from antiquity right up to the present day. Our sampling of cases in the History and Sociology of Genocide was not meant to be exhaustive, because it is not possible to be expert on all periods of history in all parts of the world (Chalk and Jonassohn 1990: Part 2). We are quite confident that there are cases that we are not even aware of, not only because of our own limitations, but also because of the "collective denial" that has limited the reporting of cases during most periods of history.

We need to begin with a question: what elements do we look for in evaluating situations and events before determining whether we are dealing with a case of genocide? We used three major criteria: (1) there must be evidence, even if only circumstantial, of the intent of the perpetrator; (2) there must be a group whose victimization threatens its survival as a group; and (3) the victimization must be one-sided. We realized that these conditions can, in some cases, be problematic; therefore we recognized as "genocidal massacres" those events that seem to violate one of our conditions. Let me elaborate.

1. Of these three criteria, the first one, which requires that there be evidence of intent, is clearly the most difficult one to deal with. Researchers must not be misled by the Holocaust; it is the only case where

the perpetrators' leader wrote a book outlining his plans for the state he hoped one day to lead and where these plans were carried out (Hitler 1924: passim). Simon Taylor argues convincingly that the intention to annihilate the Jews physically was developed and stated publicly well before the Nazis came to power (Taylor 1985: 218). Not only that, Germany is also the only case where a successor government did not deny that the killing had taken place and agreed to make reparation payments to certain survivors. In most cases of genocide the evidence for intent and planning is more difficult to obtain. There are many reasons for this: (a) in many societies such materials are not written down, or are destroyed rather than preserved in archives; (b) many perpetrators have recourse to elaborate means of hiding the truth, controlling access to information, and spreading carefully contrived disinformation; and (c) historically, most genocides were not reported because, until the middle of the twentieth century, there appears to have existed a sort of conspiracy of "collective denial" whereby the disappearance of a people did not seem to require comment or even a mention. Just one example: the literature on antiquity is full of the names of peoples, cities, and empires that have disappeared without ever a mention of what happened to the populations involved. The main exceptions to this secrecy surrounding the most horrendous events in history are certain religiously motivated cases of genocide where the perpetrators proudly announced their "victories" over the nonbelievers, pagans, or heretics.

So, what can be done to ascertain the presence of intent and planning? This rather formidable-looking problem resolves itself on closer inspection into the problem of obtaining accurate and reliable information about killing operations. Once such information has been obtained and verified, it can usually be treated as circumstantial evidence for the intent and planning of the perpetrator. It is usually not plausible that a group of some considerable size is victimized by man-made means without anyone meaning to do it! This emphasis on intent is important because it removes from consideration in the study of genocides not only natural disasters, but also those man-made disasters that took place without explicit planning. Thus, the many epidemics of communicable diseases that reached genocidal proportions were often caused by unwitting human actions; but they could not have been intended because knowledge of the causes of these epidemics was not yet available.

2. The second criterion for considering a case as a genocide was that there must be a group whose victimization threatens its physical survival as a group. There are cases where the identity of a group is de-

stroyed without the killing of its members; this is the definition of ethnocide. But the threat to the physical survival of the group is essential if genocide is to be distinguished from other death-producing events such as rebellions and civil wars within states and wars between states. Sometimes these lethal events may involve genocidal massacres; but they should not be considered as genocides for several reasons. Rebellions and civil wars may produce considerable casualties, but they usually do not threaten the survival of either of the opposing groups. In antiquity, wars between states may well have threatened the survival of the losing side because many warring states were very small. However, modern wars have become total wars, which means to say that such wars are not combats between opposing military forces any more, but have become conflicts between much larger nation states that involve total societies. The intent of such warring states is not to annihilate a group, but to win the war. In any case, modern nation states are far too large for such an intent to be at all achievable, although some of them have not been above performing a genocide during a war if they thought that it might hasten a victory or in order to deflect the world's attention from it.

3. In order for a case to be considered as a genocide the victimization must be one-sided. This criterion is an essential part of our definition because we mean to exclude from our comparative analyses cases of conflict among more or less equally strong contenders. It also is an additional reason for excluding the casualties of wars between modern nation states. This does not imply that the victims of genocide must always be weak or defenseless, but it does mean that the perpetrator must be significantly stronger than the victims—otherwise a genocide cannot be carried out at all. Finally, nobody has yet shown that our understanding is enriched by comparing such unlike phenomena as wartime casualties and genocides. The fact that both produce massive casualties is a terrible commentary on man's inhumanity to man, but does not enrich our understanding of either phenomenon. We do not believe that there is anything to be gained analytically by comparing cases that have little in common, except that large numbers of casualties resulted. There are a great many things that happen in violation of the various U.N. Conventions on human rights and our own sense of human dignity and worth; but the causes of such violations will not be better understood by mislabeling.

Let us briefly turn to the instruments of genocide and how they have changed over time. Perhaps the most obvious observation is that they have often benefited from advances in technology. But it is easy to misinterpret such use of higher technology. The basic problem about killing very large numbers of people is that it is very hard on those who have to do the actual work, which includes not only the killing but also the rounding up beforehand and the disposal of the bodies afterwards. Modern technology is primarily useful in creating a distance between the killers and the victims. However, discipline among the killers seems considerably more important than technology. Thus, even in post-World War II genocides, the most primitive technology is still being used in very poor countries and is obviously still capable of annihilating very large numbers of victims. In both Kampuchea and Burundi, for example, the killers were instructed not to use bullets because they were too costly. And then there is a most horrible invention of very ancient vintage, but revived in the twentieth century, that uses a quite primitive technology: the man-made famine. It combines the advantages—for the perpetrators—of costing very little, while at the same time putting physical distance between the perpetrators and the victims. Stalin used famine in the Ukraine in the early thirties, and in the eighties it was being used in Ethiopia and in the Sudan.

I wish to expand this excursion into history by commenting briefly on the prevalence of genocide in the ancient and the modern world and to suggest a tentative explanation of its rise in the twentieth century. Chalk and Jonassohn (1990: part 1) distinguish two major types of genocides. The first type consists of genocides that were practiced in the maintaining and expanding of empires; they were committed in order to deal with actual or perceived threats, in order to terrorize real or potential enemies, or in order to acquire economic wealth. This type of genocide has played a major role in history and seems to have been associated with all empires. The evidence is quite difficult to gather because it used to be so taken for granted that often neither the perpetrators nor the victims commented on it. The perpetrators included it in their reports of victories and conquests, but they either forgot to mention what happened to the victim populations, or their fate was beclouded by semantics, such as the "razing" of a city—which could mean anything from tearing down its fortified city walls to its total destruction, such as in Carthage where the fate of its population is still a matter of debate among the specialists. The victims, on the other hand, usually accepted their lot as the fate of the losers. Besides, the victims did not usually record what had happened to them. The most famous exceptions are the victims of the Mongols under Genghis Khan and his successors; they left voluminous reports on the outrages committed by the conquerors.

Perhaps the easiest way to explain the prevalence of this type of genocide throughout history is to observe that it worked. It did, in fact, eliminate threats, terrorize enemies, and help to acquire economic wealth. It
has been on the decline because the age of empires has passed. Now it
occurs only where small indigenous populations control economic resources that more powerful neighbours want to acquire and exploit.

The second type of genocide first occurred in the Middle Ages and
was performed in order to implement a belief, an ideology, or a religion. It has become a paradigmatic type only in the twentieth century.
This much can be said simply as a statement of empirical fact. To provide an explanation is a much more difficult matter, in part because
most of the relevant research has not yet been done.

Perhaps it is easier to begin by mentioning those explanations with
which I disagree, although there will not be space to develop the arguments in this chapter. Psychological and psychiatric theories dealing
with hostility, aggression, etc. are unlikely to be relevant because such
drives or instincts surely occur among all peoples, and because large-
scale phenomena such as genocides are not likely to find their explanation in the attributes of individuals. Neither do explanations involving
advances in the technology of killing instruments hold much explana-
tory promise, as already indicated above. They may be relevant to what
some writers have referred to as "omnicide," that is, a global nuclear
war destroying humanity, but if that cataclysm were to come about,
then none of us would have to worry about theories and explanations.
And now to some more promising approaches.

Christina Larner, encouraged by Norman Cohn, worked out a hypothesis which related the occurrence of genocide to the need of new
states and/or new regimes to legitimate themselves and to their need to
impose a new discipline on a recalcitrant population (Larner 1981: 5).
This explanation seems plausible enough to warrant further research
because both genocides and new regimes and/or new states have become more frequent in the twentieth century. But the research to confirm or deny this hypothesis remains to be done.

Three other scholars should be mentioned briefly. A view, most recently expressed by Conor Cruise O'Brien (1989) has sought an explanation in the rise of nationalism, a view with which Hannah Arendt
strongly disagrees (Arendt 1958: 269–90). Their different interpretations seem in part to hinge on a semantic problem, that is, on the different ways in which they use the relevant terms. For O'Brien, nationalism
is a "terrestrial creed" that encourages the glorification of the in-group

and the devaluation of all out-groups; it has "proved to be the most effective engine for the mobilization of hatred and destruction that the world has ever known"; O'Brien holds it responsible for the Holocaust and many other genocides in the modern era.[2] For Hannah Arendt, the nation-states which replaced the earlier empires conferred citizenship rights on everybody; they were tolerant of the minorities within their boundaries; all citizens were equal and their rights were protected by the rule of law. For her, it was not the nation state nor the associated nationalism of its citizens that constituted a threat; rather, it was totalitarianism that was lethal; it led to the destruction of the nation state and to the victimization of its own citizens. Aristide Zolberg has expanded her analysis to explain the waves of refugees that these perpetrator states keep producing. He argues that "the secular transformation of a world of empires…into a world of national states" is accompanied by "a generalized political crisis, in the course of which victim groups are especially likely to emerge" (Zolberg 1983: 24–38). Just what happens to the members of such victim groups depends on the particulars of the situation. They may be discriminated against, or expelled, or annihilated, or all three.

Larner, O'Brien, Arendt, and Zolberg start out by trying to explain quite different phenomena—from the Great Witch-Hunt, to the Holocaust, to the rise of totalitarianism, to the generating of refugee flows. They arrive at very similar explanations. I have mentioned them here because such convergence indicates to me a very promising avenue of analysis to explore.

As scholars, it is of course terribly important to us to find a theory that will explain genocide. That would not only satisfy our scientific curiosity, it would also help us to predict the occurrence of genocide in the future. As concerned citizens we would find that even more important. But these two so very desirable aims of theorizing—explanation and prediction—seem to be eluding our grasp. If they are going to be achieved, it seemingly will not be in the immediate future. That prospect will not discourage the scholars because they are only too familiar with the need for patience in their scientific efforts. But to the concerned citizen in all of us that daunting prospect should cause us to look for other avenues leading to prevention. Fortunately, prediction is not a necessary precondition for prevention—a proposition that has not been adequately dealt with in the literature. It is quite possible to develop a variety of strategies that may help to prevent future genocides long before adequate explanations have been found. Thus, our best hope lies in the development and implementation of such strategies.

Notes

1. An earlier version of this chapter was presented at the Genocide Watch conference in New York, 22–23 May 1989 and published as chapter 2 in Helen Fein, ed., *Genocide Watch* (New Haven: Yale University Press, 1992).
2. Even more radical a view than O'Brien's is represented by Perlman who defines genocide as "the rationally calculated extermination of human populations designated as legitimate prey" and relates it to nationalism (Perlman 1984: 13). "The idea that an understanding of genocide, that a memory of the holocausts, can only lead people to want to dismantle the system, is erroneous. The continuing appeal of nationalism suggests that the opposite is truer, namely that an understanding of genocide has led people to mobilize genocidal armies, that the memory of holocausts has led people to perpetrate holocausts" (Perlman 1984: 28).

2

A Conceptual Perspective

Introduction

In our book Frank Chalk and I have tried to show that genocidal massacres and genocides have occurred throughout history in all parts of the world (Chalk and Jonassohn 1990: part 1). Robert Melson in *Revolution and Genocide* put it this way "...the capacity to commit genocide is not limited to one culture or one people but is an inherent potential of the human condition" (Melson 1992: xix–xx). We cited a number of cases to illustrate this argument. Since then we have continued to comb history for additional cases. This is an ongoing project because we believe that only an examination of the past will provide clues to an understanding of the present. We believe this for two reasons: the first one is the hope that the study of such clues will contribute to a better understanding of the processes that lead to massacres and to genocides.

The second reason is that we are dealing with processes that change extremely slowly—processes that some scholars have referred to as "long waves." Genocide seems to have been practiced since the earliest days of antiquity. It is still being practiced in our time. The changes it has undergone have covered time spans of hundreds, if not thousands, of years. The rapid expansion of scientific knowledge, the great developments in technology, and the speed of modern travel and communication have all led to a foreshortening of our time perspective and the apparent collapsing of history into just a few years. This ahistorical perspective is reinforced by the manner in which current events are reported in our mass media. When they provide background information and explanation at all, they usually do so in terms of contemporaneous events and conditions while ignoring the historical roots of current events. This accounts for the facile, but frequently erroneous or irrelevant, analyses that they offer. Such an ahistorical approach should not mislead us, since it clearly does not apply to processes that have been evolving for thousands of years, like gross violations of human rights and genocides.

The following pages will outline three aspects of these changes:

1. The origins and rise of utilitarian genocides from antiquity to their decline and relative scarcity in our own day.

2. The rise and the decline of slavery insofar as it is related to the outcomes of wars and the practice of genocide.

3. The third topic will cover the appearance of ideological genocides and their prevalence in the twentieth century.

This will be followed by some remarks on definitions and typologies and their bearing on the outcome of research. In the conclusion we shall offer some thoughts on the role of international organizations and international relations as potential agents in the possible control of gross human rights violations and genocides committed by sovereign nation states on victims within their own borders.

The Origins of Utilitarian Genocide

While the origins of genocide are lost in remotest antiquity, it is possible to speculate about their origin. In our book cited above we have suggested that the fertile crescent of the Middle East seemed a breeding ground for almost continuous conflicts between small city-states that wanted to expand their dominion over fertile land, primary resources, or trade routes. Similar conflicts arose between the settlers in the rich river valleys of China and India and their nomadic neighbours who coveted their wealth. Very often these conflicts were resolved only for short periods because the losers recovered and proceeded to train and equip another army in order to revenge themselves. It probably did not take very long before someone realized that one way to put an end to such a series of repeated conflicts would be for the victor to totally eliminate the defeated people (Chalk and Jonassohn 1990: 32–33). The resulting genocides were motivated by the desire to eliminate a real or perceived enemy, to forestall a real or perceived threat, or to acquire and possess economic wealth that could not be simply carried off by the perpetrators. All three of these motives were usually present in varying proportions, which is why such genocides are usually referred to as utilitarian genocides. These utilitarian genocides had certain features in common: they were committed in the founding and expanding of empires; they were always successful in the sense that they accomplished the perpetrators' intended goals; and they were directed at victims outside the perpetrators' societies. This type of genocide has declined dramatically in the modern era.

Baillet, writing about ancient Egypt, developed a hypothesis about how this happened. He argued that whole populations disappeared during the third millennium B.C. due to such destructive practices, but that these changed about a thousand years later. This was not due to any emergence of humanitarian sensibilities among the victors, but rather due to their realization that in a very labor-intensive culture the losers were much more valuable as slaves than as corpses (Baillet 1912: vol.1, 152–53). Thus, the practice of genocide declined in favor of slavery.

A similar change occurred in the thirteenth century when Genghis Khan invaded China. His armies did not receive regular pay. Rather, they were rewarded from the loot and tribute that ensued from a successful campaign. It seems to have been standard procedure to extract huge tribute from opponents that accepted Mongol rule without a fight, but to massacre whole populations after they had fought and lost. In that case, the loot was enormous, consisting of all physical wealth that could be carried off. Such portable wealth included selected craftsmen, artists, and savants whose skills the Mongols considered useful. One such captive was a young Chinese scholar who so impressed Genghis Khan that he was promoted to become his secretary. In this capacity he managed to convince Genghis Khan that it would be much more profitable not to massacre the Chinese so that they could be taxed every year. Thus, the profit motive saved several million lives, some to serve as slaves and others to become vassals.

In the late fourteenth century in India it was Firuz Shah (1397–1422) who realized that prisoners were more valuable than bodies. His use of slavery was described by Havell, as follows:

> Among his other administrative activities Firuz Shah paid great attention to the organization of the institution of slavery; partly, it would seem, to prevent the inhuman massacre of prisoners of war, partly to increase the supply of skilled artisans in Musalman cities, and partly to bring more infidels within the Muslim pale. No doubt the Muhammadan invasions and the unsettled condition of Hindustan in the previous reigns had driven great numbers of Hindu craftsmen to avoid forced labour under Musalman masters by emigration. Firuz Shah gave orders to his officers and feudatories that as many prisoners as possible should be taken in war-time, and that the best should be sent for the service of the court. "Those chiefs who brought many slaves received the highest favour, and those who brought

few received proportionately little consideration." The effect was that numbers far in excess of the Sultan's requirements were sent to Delhi, but the situation was met by distributing them over the different provinces. Some were employed in the Sultan's bodyguard and personal service, or in the army. Some were sent to study the Quran and the law of Islam at Mecca, or at the numerous Muslim colleges in India; others were apprenticed to tradesmen and taught handicrafts. In this way "12,000 slaves became artisans of various kinds." (Havell 1918: 321)

An Excursus on Varieties of Slavery

In contemporary Western culture our perception of slavery as a status in society is conditioned by the history of the American South where slaves were mainly used to work on plantations and to perform menial labor in the homes of their owners. Slavery has not always had this restrictive meaning. Therefore, it seems useful at this stage of our discussion to point out that slavery is an omnibus term that has denoted very different social arrangements in different cultures and under different regimes. These differences seem to be related to the particular needs of the victors. In labor-intensive cultures, prisoners might be enslaved to perform unskilled work in irrigation agriculture or in the building of palaces and temples. When the losers possessed skills that the victors hoped to acquire, they spared craftsmen, artisans, or scholars to serve them and to teach them their skills. When the victors were engaged in protracted warfare they would save the male prisoners to serve in their own army. On the other hand, if the loser's army was perceived as a potential future threat, the victors would kill all of the male prisoners and enslave only the women and children. In addition, it was not always the case that slaves were confined to the lowest social stratum; in many cases they could rise to honored and distinguished positions.

The wide range of social arrangements that are all subsumed under the term slavery is best illustrated by a few examples. In ancient Athens the status of slavery meant exclusion from participating and voting in the popular assembly; with that exception slaves could participate fully in economic life. They might be working in the mines as slaves, but they might also be the owners of these mines and of the slaves that worked them. The Mongols under Genghis Khan often selected for special treatment the people with skills or knowledge that they themselves lacked but wanted to acquire. They also introduced elements of a feudal system into a Central Asian tribal system that was based entirely on clan loyalties. This allowed them to incorporate conquered peoples not as slaves, but as equals provided they accepted loyalty to the Khan. The officers of such defeated armies might rise to very senior ranks. Of course, if the enemy refused to accept the divine rule of the Great Khan, they became the victims of genocide—with the exception of the craftsmen and artisans who the Mongols found useful. Thus, as feudal relationships became more common, prisoners of war stopped being enslaved. However, the status of the slave remained popular with rulers throughout the ages because slaves could be employed even in high office without representing a potential threat to the regime. This apparent contradiction is explained by the fact that such slaves usually exercised power without having their own independent power base (Coser 1974: 8–9 and chapter 3).

An exception occurred when slaves possessed or developed exceptional military skills. In states that were often at war such skills were of great value and might even be decisive in determining their future. Slaves were often used in the armed forces and sometimes even rose to the status of general of the army. Then their army became their power base and made it possible for them to topple the regime and to become the new rulers. Qutb-ud-din who had been a slave "succeeded Muhammad Ghuri as sovereign of the new Indian conquests, and from 1206 may be reckoned as the first sultan of Delhi...[t]he dynasty founded by Qutb-ud-din and continued by other princes of servile origin is consequently known to history as the Slave dynasty" (Smith 1958: 237). One of these other princes was Balban who started out as a slave and rose to become a general, then a statesman, and finally the sultan (Lane-Poole 1982: chapter 4; Joshi 1982). The last one was Mahmud whose death in 1412 ended the Turki slave dynasty which had ruled Delhi for a century (Havell 1918: 279).

Another avenue of influence presented itself when slaves became teachers in societies where that was considered a low-status occupation. Sometimes this also meant that free parents would not send their children to schools where they would have to sit before, and take orders from, teachers who were slaves. An example in the twentieth century is Niger where slaves became an educated elite. In the sixties, much of that country's government, including the prime minister's office, was staffed by people whose technical status was that of slave.

These examples illustrate both the diversity of forms of slavery as well as their popularity with the victors in conflicts. They also explain the decline in the prevalence of utilitarian genocides. While these two processes took place at different times in different parts of the world, an entirely new phenomenon appeared in Europe. The fact that this new phenomenon is also called genocide should not lead us to assume that it can be explained in the same way as the earlier forms of genocide. The term genocide is applicable to both phenomena because in both cases the perpetrator's intent was to annihilate a targeted victim group.

Modern Ideological Genocides

Utilitarian genocides were performed in order to eliminate a real or perceived enemy, a real or perceived threat, or to acquire economic wealth. They decreased in frequency when the enslavement of conquered peoples became a widely used alternative to killing.

Modern ideological genocides, on the other hand, have their origin in the religious persecutions of the late Middle Ages when the pope was both a worldly and spiritual power. Eventually, he was deprived of his worldly power and the principle of the separation of church and state became widely accepted in the West. The result was that instead of the church persecuting heretics and nonbelievers, the state persecuted racial, ethnic, and ideological deviants among its own citizens. But ideological genocides have reached their fully modern development only in the twentieth century. They have been increasing in frequency, they are performed in order to implement the imperative of a belief, ideology, or theory, and they victimize the perpetrators own citizens (Kuper 1981: 9).

A word needs to be inserted here about the Crusades which are traditionally seen as a Christian effort to free the Holy Land from the occupation by the infidels. The Christian warriors committed a number of genocides, including those associated with their conquests of Antioch and Jerusalem. They made few efforts to convert the infidels and to spread the Gospel, but they established a number of fiefdoms for the landless aristocrats who had volunteered to lead them. Thus, these cases seem to have more in common with utilitarian genocides than with ideological ones. This might also be said of the Albigensian crusade which, while persecuting heretics, also served to expand the realm of the king of France. However, it also played its part in the establishment of the Inquisition.

The activities of the Inquisition and the persecution of witches may be considered the precursors of modern ideological genocides. While these persecutions did not in themselves constitute genocides, many of the methods then employed are still being used today. The widely recognized and used manual for these persecutions of the witches was the *Malleus Maleficarum* which specified in great detail the methods of identifying witches, extracting proofs and confessions, conducting trials, and executing sentences (Institoris and Sprenger 1949, c.1928).[1] Written by two Dominicans and approved by the pope over 500 years ago, this volume has proven remarkably durable. In the twentieth century new editions have appeared in Latin, English, French, and German. In 1974 Caedmon issued a phonodisc of an abridged English version. The *Malleus Maleficarum* is still in print by several publishers and it carries a most remarkable introduction by the Reverend Montague Summers who was educated at Trinity College in Oxford, became an Anglican priest, and then converted to Catholicism. In 1946 he still thought the *Malleus Maleficarum* one of the two or three most important books and concludes his paean by assuring the reader that even now judges could not go wrong if only they followed the wisdom contained in the *Malleus Maleficarum*. It is very doubtful than many judges could now be found who would agree with him. Therefore, the history of this book can only serve as another example of how slowly changes take place in some areas. Unfortunately, the frequent printings and editions of this work give no reliable indication of how many readers are inclined to agree with the Reverend Summers.[2]

Ideological genocides have been committed in the name of a fundamentalist religion, a millenarian political theory, or the implementation of nationalist purity. The latter motive has been an increasingly frequent one in nation-states where ethnic groups develop chauvinistic ideas about their superiority and exclusiveness. This happened in many of the states that achieved independence after World War II.

While early utilitarian genocides were successful in the sense that they achieved their intended goals, modern, ideological genocides are costly failures in the sense that they have always failed to achieve the goals in the name of which they were perpetrated.[3] In view of these failures it is difficult to understand the increasing frequency with which ideological genocides keep occurring in the twentieth century. However, all indications point to the continuation of this state of affairs as a growing number of countries try to turn themselves into homogeneous nation states. This sober assessment is based on two observations. First, in order to outlaw a wide variety of human rights violations the United Nations as well as other international groupings have generated an impressive body of conventions, agreements, and resolutions. Since none of them are supported by an enforcement mechanism, they only confirm Dadrian's conclusion that crimes that are not punished only encourage their repetition (Dadrian 1988: 326–33). Second, the perpetrators of these human rights violation not only go unpunished, they are even rewarded. On the international scene they are accorded all the respect and courtesies due to government official. They are treated in accordance with diplomatic protocol in negotiations and seated in the General Assembly of the United Nations. When they are finally ousted from their offices, they are offered asylum by countries that lack respect for international law, but have a great deal of respect for the ill-gotten wealth that such perpetrators bring with them.

Notes

1. Additional issues in English were published: New York: Pushkin, 1948; New York: Dover, 1948 and 1971; London: Hogarth, 1969; New York: Bloom, 1970; Salem: Ayer, 1988; as well as on phonodisc by Caedmon, 1974.
2. One lawyer, when asked why he kept this book on his shelves, said that he needed it when having to deal with the lunatic fringe (personal communication).
3. For an elaboration of this argument, see chapter 5, "The Consequences of Ideological Genocides and Their Role in Prevention."

3

Hunger as a Low-Technology Weapon: With Special Reference to Genocide[1]

Introduction

Throughout most of history the great majority of people were considered successful if they were able to provide adequate food, clothing, and shelter for their dependents and themselves. But hunger, starvation, and famine have, in all ages and in all parts of the world, been the source of the greatest suffering. Food supplies, although essential to maintaining human life, have often been uncertain. Too much or too little water, too much or too little sun, as well as the whole gamut of natural disasters from earthquakes to volcanic eruptions have all had immediate effects on the availability of adequate food resources. Such natural events will not be dealt with in this paper, but the interested reader is well served by an extensive literature on these topics. Golkin (1987) provides a useful guide to that literature as well as a "Chronology of Famines" and a classified bibliography.

There exists considerable ambiguity as to the exact meaning of the word "famine." According to de Waal (1989: ch.1) its original meaning in English was "hunger" or "dearth." Its current meaning of mass death produced by starvation originated with Malthus who used it not as a description of empirical fact, but as a logical last step in his theory of checks on population growth (de Waal 1989: 17). Mass deaths as a result of crop failures seem not to have occurred in modern times whenever accurate statistics have been available to check on such reports. Even when people are dying, it tends not to be as a result of starvation, but rather as a result of the variety of diseases that accompany undernourishment and starvation. It will be the argument of this chapter that famines, in the sense of mass deaths, are unlikely to occur as a result of massive crop failures, but that they commonly do occur as the result of man-made starvation regimes leading to famines in the Malthusian sense of the term.

While there exists a vast literature on natural events that affect food supplies, there is a much more limited literature on such man-made famines. These are of two kinds: the first kind of man-made famine occurs as the result of the unintended consequences of economic, political, and social processes that aggravate rather than ameliorate an existing shortage of food caused by natural events (de Castro 1977; Dando 1976; Sen 1981). This is an important area of research that raises a host of questions, based on hindsight since these outcomes had not been anticipated. We must ask whether foresight can be improved to the point where social arrangements that potentially produce famines can be avoided. Is it possible to define a minimum standard of food production and distribution that must be maintained in any social system? These important questions will also not be dealt with in this chapter.

The second kind of man-made famine is the result of the age-old and intentional use of hunger as a weapon in conflict and warfare, and this is the main topic of the present chapter. The fact that human beings need food and water in order to survive has been a crucial element in the conduct of conflict since the earliest times. From the "to bed without supper" punishment inflicted by some parents on their misbehaving offspring, to the starvation imposed on beleaguered towns, the deprivation of nourishment has always been perceived as a method of enforcing superior demands. Although the existence of planned famines is often acknowledged in passing, the literature on intended famines is very limited (Dando 1976; Kane 1988: chapter 2). Dando, who writes mainly about man-made famines, does mention planned ones and is also working on a book that discusses such famines in connection with genocide (private communication). Mudge (1969–70) has examined the legality in international law of the starvation of a civilian population as an instrument of war. This question was raised for him in connection with starvation in Biafra; the results of his inquiry are inconclusive because they depend on whether the intent is to force a surrender or to kill the opponents. In a much more categorical vein, the World Food Conference (1974) adopted, and the U.N. General Assembly endorsed, the Universal Declaration on the Eradication of Hunger and Malnutrition which states that "Every man, woman and child has the inalienable right to be free from hunger and malnutrition." But available data provide ample evidence that these resolutions have not been respected during recent conflicts (Golkin 1987:143). The man-made famines in Ethiopia, Sudan, etc. are sufficiently dramatic to underscore this point.

The Question of Intent

During most of history, when the threat of starvation was used in order to force fortified places into surrender, there was no question of the aggressor's intent. It was to win the war at any cost. Neither was there any doubt that the famine eventually resulting from a refusal to surrender was a man-made one. If the city refused to surrender and forced a long siege, then it often happened that the final capitulation resulted in a genocidal massacre.

When food shortages occurred in peacetime, as they did with great frequency during most of history, they did not always escalate into famines. Crop failures were frequent enough so that many cultures had developed methods for overcoming such periods of shortage. However, the effectiveness of such methods was circumscribed by the available technology for storing, transporting, and distributing surplus food stocks. To the extent that famines did occur, the question arises whether they were brought about by some human agency, or solely by the vicissitudes of nature? If the former, were they the unintended consequence of other social processes, or were they intended as part of a larger plan of government? Such questions can be answered only by a careful examination of the circumstances surrounding each case.

Within the compass of this chapter there can be no question of examining all famines. Since starvation has frequently been used as a method in performing genocides or genocidal massacres, the focus here will be on the origins and history of that usage, as well as on the social situations that seem to have predisposed to its usage. In the cases selected to illustrate the argument, the question of intent is often very difficult to resolve. However, an attempt will be made to differentiate between man-made famines that were the unintended consequence of other policies, and those famines that were deliberately used as low-technology weapons in conflictual situations. Unfortunately, such differentiation will be difficult when these two conditions overlap; there are cases where the starvation was not intended, but, once observed, was allowed to continue because it was perceived as the just punishment for the victims' perceived failure to make a success of the policy of the ruling group.

An Abbreviated History

The earliest domesticated animals were found in the Near East about 8,000 B.C. and plants seem to have been domesticated about 1,000 years earlier than animals (Berger and Protsch 1973). It was only after such domestication had been introduced that people were able to regularly produce more food than they consumed. Such surplus food production was the basis for a division of labor that allowed specialists to concentrate on practicing their specialty without taking time off to produce food. This was the basis for a complex set of developments involving the collection of food stuffs from producers and their distribution to consumers in exchange for specialized goods and services. These processes were accompanied by developments in techniques of storage and methods of administration. Inevitably, this also implied a certain amount of centralization, and so the first cities were born shortly after the domestication of food production.

Almost by definition, these cities became depositories of wealth that attracted raids by neighbouring warlike peoples. Since such settlements were obviously not mobile, they were at a military disadvantage and almost from the beginning they developed fortifications. We know that Jericho, one of the oldest cities, was already a fortified settlement about 10,000 years ago (Watkins 1990). For thousands of years after their first establishment, cities had to be fortified to protect them from attack. It seems that from the beginning the technology of fortification was better than the technology of siege machines. Hackett (1990:16) cites archaeological evidence for the early building of massive fortifications, including storage provisions for food and water during a siege. Since the attackers usually were not able to take the city by storm, they relied on a siege that ended only when the defenders ran out of food and water. Thus, starvation became a weapon of warfare and it has remained so right up to the present day. "Surprising as the fact may appear to modern eyes, none of the classical military writers paid much attention to technology" (van Creveld 1989: 321).

The Bible, which is our best source on events in the Promised Land, reports several periods of starvation and famine. However, it contains evidence suggesting that famine was not a hazard in preagricultural systems. That hazard became a characteristic of semisedentary or sedentary agricultural systems with developed central places (Dando 1983: 242). Such early cities in the ancient Near East soon developed into states of two quite different types, the national state and the territorial state:

A territorial state is one where the people identify themselves as dwellers of a given territory. A national state, on the other hand, is one where the people are aware of their identity as a group on the basis of other factors than simple contiguity within the same territory. What are these factors? First of all, the conception of kin relationship among the members of the group: the people conceive of themselves as descendants from a common ancestor, and they trace their history back to him. This ancestor may have come from a territory other than the one where the people live at any given time of their history: thus their history is only accidentally the history of a country; primarily, it is the history of a people. The reverse is obviously true in the case of a territorial state.... It should be noted that the two terms are not exclusive, for, obviously, a national state is territorial, in that its sovereignty is limited by definite territorial boundaries. The choice of the terms is, therefore, a matter of emphasis, rather than one of opposition. (Buccellati 1967: 13–14)

A further distinguishing feature of the developing states in the ancient Near East was that in the national state the organization of the army was the same as that of the people, while in the territorial state the army was a professional militia. The participation of the people in war contributed to their consciousness of national solidarity. In the notion of the sacred war, "[w]ar becomes the intimate concern of God...[t]he two most characteristic features (of such sacred wars) are the maintenance of legal purity including sexual abstinence...and, in certain cases, the law of total annihilation of the enemy and his property. These practices are typical of the national state." On the other hand, such practices have not been observed for the territorial state, so that we may consider this another distinctive feature of the national state (Buccellati 1967: 106–17). This distinction is being introduced here because it helps to explain, in part, why some wars in antiquity resulted in genocide while others did not. (Needless to add that this distinction should not be generalized to apply to modern nation-states.)

The Assyrians invented a complex collection of devices for besieging fortified cities and carried a siege train with them on campaign as a matter of course (McNeill 1982: 14). Still, "faced with a formidable array of defenses, the besiegers often resorted to throwing up earth walls around the city and bombarding the besieged with propaganda, threats and demands for surrender. Anyone who emerged was turned back to his fate." (Wiseman 1990: 48). Such Assyrian sieges could last from a few weeks to three years. Under the Assyrian king, Sargon, "Everything was destroyed and the fertile region, with its crops, plantations and forests, fired to prevent support for human or cattle and preclude renewed rebellion" (Wiseman 1990: 51). But sieges were lengthy and arduous undertakings that the Assyrian kings preferred to avoid. If, however, they could not gain admittance by means of their siegecraft, and if time was of no consideration, they would resign themselves to a lengthy siege. "When at length the town yielded to the enemy, it was often razed to the ground, and salt was strewn upon its ruins, while the unfortunate inhabitants were either massacred or transplanted en masse elsewhere" (Maspero 1906–08, vol.6: 200–2). Thus, holding out under a long siege, unless successful for the townspeople, often enraged the besieging king so much that the entire population was killed. This meant that the inhabitants died either as a result of starvation or at the hands of the victors; in both cases we probably have here the first recorded cases of genocide.

The Greeks used similar methods. In addition, they are also recorded as being the first practitioners of chemical warfare in their efforts of dealing with fortified cities. McCarthy (1970: 3) tells us, albeit without citing sources, that Solon of Athens, 600 B.C., poisoned the enemy's drinking water, while Sparta burned sulfur and pitch to create sulfur dioxide over besieged cities. During the Peloponnesian War, city walls were very simple and barely sufficiently guarded; still, they seem to have been invincible. The Peloponnesians did not achieve their goal by means of their primitive siege methods and had to contend themselves with surrounding the city walls and thus starving the inhabitants (Delbrueck 1975: 153). Devine (1990: 120) tells us of the long siege of Tyre that "the storming of the city ended in bitter street fighting, in which the Macedonians gave little quarter. Tyre was burnt and the 2,000 surviving Tyrians were crucified to satisfy Alexander's rage." Peter Garnsey (1988: 37) makes a distinction between food shortages, which were quite common in the Hellenistic period, and famines. The three best attested famines were siege induced and therefore of relatively short duration. In contrast, both sieges and shortages were relatively frequent in the early period of Roman history.

The Romans not only developed siege technology to a high level but were also quite ruthless in ravaging the enemy (*vastatio*). "Crops were carried off or burnt, animals driven off or slaughtered, human beings were massacred or enslaved, buildings burnt" (Dobson 1990: 208). At the same time, they had strong opinions about proper and improper methods in warfare, in Julius Caesar's day, Roman jurists castigated the use of poison in war (McCarthy 1970: 3).

Similar tactics, based on the human need for food and water, were common around the world. In China, from the second millennium B.C until the fall of the Han dynasty in 220 A.D. the destruction of the enemy's grain supplies was a standard military tactic (Yates 1990). However, even in peace time crop failures due to natural causes were so frequent that between 108 B.C. and 1911 A.D. 1828 famines occurred, or one nearly every year in some one of the provinces (Mallory 1926: 1). This was so in spite of the fact that public granaries were maintained for much of that time in most of the provinces; while this did not prevent famines when crops failed over wide areas, it greatly mitigated the suffering of the people and in minor disasters these supplies were sufficient to meet the needs (Mallory 1926: 67–68). This plan, which was followed with conspicuous success by Joseph in Egypt, has been reported in many areas as a traditional method of insurance against the worst ravages of naturally caused crop failures.

The Middle Ages, particularly in Europe and the Middle East, witnessed the introduction of further refinements into the production of man-made famines so that they occurred not only among the besieged, but also among the besiegers. This was not at all uncommon and came about because the besieged destroyed the countryside before retreating into their fortifications. The purpose was to prevent the besiegers from being able to live off the land while the besieged were starving. When the Crusaders besieged Jerusalem in 1099, the Franks suffered more than the people inside the city. They starved until messengers could bring bread from their ships and they were forced to carry water in animal skins from a spring six miles away (*Gesta Francorum*, as cited in Peters, 1985: 284–85). Their suffering may help to explain the extraordinary fury with which the Crusaders massacred the population of Jerusalem once they entered the city (William of Tyre, as cited in Peters, 1985: 287–88).

During such sieges both sides engaged in quite extraordinary brutalities. From the Western European scene we know that when the defenders' food supplies started to run low, they often would evict everybody who was not an active defender: the young and the old, the women and the sick and the wounded. Sometimes these people were allowed to pass through the enemy lines; at other times they were stuck between the lines without food, water, or shelter and suffered a terrible death in full sight of the besiegers and the besieged (Warner, 1968: 133–34, 186).

The extent to which the starvation of the besieged population escalated into famine depended entirely on the combatants' calculation of their chances of success and the price they were willing to pay for such successes. These calculations were complicated because the deprivation of fresh food and water and the crowding inside the fortifications produced not only starvation, but also cannibalism and epidemics.

The use of deliberate starvation in the conquest of fortified places did not disappear until the modern technology of bombardment from the ground and from the air made the defense of towns impossible. However, the use of deliberate famine as a method in the conduct of conflicts has not disappeared because its basic appeal has remained unchanged: it acts on the basic survival needs of the enemy, it is a low-technology method that is easy to administer, and it is cost effective. As Cornelius Walford wrote over a hundred years ago:

> That war has been in the past, and probably ever will (while it shall exist) be productive of famines, seems to be a self-evident proposition. Not only does it draw from their employments those who would engage in the cultivation of the soil; but it withholds the labour necessary to gather in the crops already produced; while by devastating the plains, as also in its endeavours to starve out the enemy, it wastes and destroys at every step that which has been already garnered in. At sea it blockades and diverts cargoes from their destinations; on land it cuts off armies, cities, districts, from their supplies. Still further, war breeds pestilence; pestilence cuts down the population who have escaped from its ravages; the land lies uncultivated; the livestock dies; and desolation proclaims itself. Hence the sword, pestilence, and famine are now, as they have been in all times, the three associated deadly enemies of the human race. (1970: 107–8)

Another arena of conflict where starvation has been used with deliberate intent is the confrontation between indigenous peoples and their colonizers. In the late nineteenth century the U.S. encouraged the hunting to extinction of the bison in order to control the Indians of the northern Plains whom they had not been able to subdue militarily—a policy approved by Secretary of the Interior Columbus Delano in 1872 (Nash 1986: 577). By 1910 this policy had been so successful that only ten bison, out of an estimated mid-nineteenth-century population of sixty million, remained. Since the bison was the mainstay of the Indians' diet, its disappearance played a major role in their submission to the government's wishes. Impressed by their own success, the government continued to use the withholding of rations from recalcitrant Indians even after they had been confined to reservations (Wilson 1986: 15). The colonial policies of Germany in Southwest Africa at the beginning of this century were even more crudely stated and documented, and included depriving the Hereros of food and especially of water. When these policies were not carried out to their fullest extent, General von Trotha was sent to take over the command because he had already established his reputation in East Africa (Bridgman 1981: 124–32). When it finally came to a battle with the Herero, von Trotha deliberately allowed them to escape into the Omaheke Desert; then he sealed off the only avenues of escape and thus condemned them to die of thirst (Drechsler 1980: 155–56).

What seems to be new in the twentieth century is that most wars as well as most genocides are now directed at "enemies" inside the perpetrator society. In an age of nation-states that are extremely jealous of their rights to sovereignty, the persecution of groups inside the perpetrator society is relatively easy and free of risks. In an age of a highly developed, but also very costly, technology of aggression, famine is a low-cost and low-technology method that is available even to the poorest and most underdeveloped state. It requires neither sophisticated expertise nor elaborate bureaucracy in order to achieve its intended goal.

Twentieth-Century Famines

Stalin in the Ukraine performed the first carefully planned, large-scale famine in the twentieth century. He wanted to collectivize agriculture not only to eliminate the kulaks, but also in order to increase production. At the same time, he wanted to accelerate industrialization. The increased agricultural production was intended for export in order to pay for the import of the technology that was essential to his program of industrialization. He increased agricultural quotas beyond the capacity of the land to deliver. At the same time, he reversed an earlier policy that tolerated national cultures and languages. The Ukraine was particularly targeted by him because it was the bread basket of the USSR and also the seat of a strong, nationally self-conscious identity. Its borders were sealed off so that nobody could leave or enter, quotas were set impossibly high, and troops were sent in to confiscate food stocks that the peasants were accused of hiding. The facts of the resulting famine were hidden from the outside world, and denied when information leaked out. Offers of food shipments by humanitarian organization were refused (Conquest 1990). The result was that an estimated 5–7 million people died in the Ukraine. This was so clearly a famine that was meant to terrorize the Ukraine by the killing of millions of its citizens that the actual level of the harvest was quite irrelevant.

Hitler's Europe is perhaps the most dramatic case of hunger and starvation being used as a deliberate policy. The geopolitical fact that

Germany did not provide sufficient food for itself, and the ideological imperative of racism, were combined into a policy of using Europe's agriculture to maintain an adequate diet for the "master race." In the 1930s, before World War II, this was accomplished by a concerted drive to barter food imports for promised German industrial products. After the outbreak of the war, the food stocks of occupied countries were simply confiscated (Shub 1943: ch. 12). Hitler's nutritional policy divided the population of Europe into the well-fed, the underfed, the hungry, and the starving. The Germans were the only well-fed people.

> The collaborating peoples, who were engaged in tasks of vital or military importance for German security, received a diet that permitted them to maintain a certain degree of labor efficiency. Enemy countries were held to a regime of intense privation, so as to remove all will to resist, while certain racial groups, such as the Jews, were simply starved to death. (De Castro 1977: 418)

Or, as Reich Labor Leader Robert Ley succinctly put it, "a lower race needs less room, less clothing, less food than the German people" (quoted in Shub 1943: 38).

The genocide was, of course, carried out by several methods. But while the gas chambers of Auschwitz have received a great deal of attention in the literature, the famine deaths in the ghettos, the slave labor factories, and the concentration camps are much less well known. In addition, starvation took precedence whenever several policies conflicted. Thus, even when Jews were used as slave labor in war industries, it was more important that they die than that they produce war materials (see chapter 3).

After the end of the war, starvation continued in a Europe devastated by bombs and undermined by administrative disorganization and corruption. Recovery was very slow because even the American agricultural surplus could not feed all of Western Europe, and also because 1946 and 1947 brought droughts and frosts that damaged crops on an enormous scale. In 1947 the United States introduced the Marshall Plan as a "form of generalized economic aid to the European countries devastated by the war. The U.S.S.R. was invited to be one of the recipients, but the Soviet delegation at the Paris Conference declared that the plan was a device of American imperialism and left the conference" (de Castro 1977: 439).

The starvation imposed by Hitler was a clear case of the planned and deliberate use of famine as a weapon against specific groups. The postwar situation in Europe, on the other hand, was a clear example of famine being the unintended result of human actions, although it was aggravated by crop failures.

China has the dubious distinction of having produced the most devastating famine of the twentieth century. The massive famine that occurred between 1959 and 1962 is variously estimated to have caused 16 million to 27 million deaths above those that would have been expected during those years under conditions of normal mortality (MacFarquhar and Fairbank 1987: 598).

The causes of this particular famine seem to have been located in a political system based on rigid adherence to an ideology, extreme centralization, and totalitarian intolerance of debate, criticism, and empirical facts. The government tried to consolidate agriculture into giant communes; it engaged in large-scale dam construction which often did more harm than good; it tolerated a disorganized information system based on false reporting due to the intolerance of correct reporting that diverged from the Great Leap Forward. Thus, it "insisted that the peasants leave the land fallow in 1959 to avoid losses from not having enough storage facilities to handle the anticipated surplus" (MacFarquhar and Fairbank 1987: 318–19). Needless to add that the anticipated surplus never materialized, but the land that was left fallow contributed to the famine.

This famine fell much more severely on rural than urban areas because agricultural procurement quotas continued to drain the countryside of available supplies; these quotas were even increased to support the intense mobilization of resources for accelerated industrialization. The famine was also aggravated because self-sufficiency, which was an integral part of the ideology of the commune movement, inhibited the traditional interprovincial flow that used to make up for local shortages. This was particularly hard on regions that specialized in nonfood crops, such as cotton. Distribution by the government broke down because nobody wanted to report local failures and also because transportation was disrupted by the Great Leap Forward (Lardy 1987: 376–78).

Based on the still limited evidence available, it seems clear that originally there was no intent on the part of the government to decimate a specific group of victims. The government did want to implement its design for the Great Leap Forward, and it did enforce its new agricultural and industrial policies. Mao rejected critical reports from the field by insisting that the gains of the Great Leap Forward outweighed the costs (Kane 1988: 133). The most likely hypothesis is that the famine started out as the unintended consequence of a series of particularly inept political decisions, and that it was allowed to run its course because the government saw it as the just punishment for an uncooperative peasantry (Rummel 1991: chapter 11; Becker 1996).

Only a few years later, beginning in 1966, China was again ravaged by a major upheaval: the Cultural Revolution. The issue here was not hunger so much as the enforcement of orthodoxy to Mao's ideas of a permanent revolution. The resulting disorganization and dislocation produced enormous hardships, including starvation. While Chinese sources claim that 100 million intellectuals were victimized, estimates of the number of fatalities vary between one million and twenty million (White 1989: 7). No information is available on the proportion of the victims who died of disease, starvation, or at the hands of the Red Guards.

Here again, there was at the outset no intent to produce a famine, but the anarchy of the Cultural Revolution was encouraged by Mao's regime, although it was not tightly coordinated (White 1989: 331). Since, for quite a long time, no attempt appears to have been made to stop the rising toll of the Cultural Revolution, we must assume that Mao thought that the victims deserved their fate. Thus, we must conclude that both of these cases started out as the unintended consequences of policies designed to produce radical change in Chinese society, but ended up as the welcome punishment of those groups that were perceived as being less than fully cooperative.

Ethiopia is a large and fertile country that could produce enough food to export in appreciable quantities. Since 1974 it has been ruled by a communist regime that wanted to nationalize the property of the peasants and control their activities from the center. It has also had to deal with several liberation armies who controlled various amounts of territory. By 1984–85, these policies, plus a drought, had produced a massive famine (Clay and Holcomb 1986: ch. 10; Henze 1986). The details became well known around the world due to their intensive media coverage and appeals for humanitarian aid. What is hardly known at all is that the very same drought affected agriculture in Kenya in an even more serious fashion. But there was no famine and nobody starved, and therefore there was no news reporting. What happened was remarkably simple: the government of Kenya set up an interministerial 'drought response committee.' They consulted with foreign advisers and donors, and began ordering food imports through normal commercial channels. Although the drought and the threat of famine were a serious problem for Kenya, there was no crisis. The imported food and the donor contributions were distributed through normal sales outlets at normal prices.

> Since Kenya did not permit any of its people to reach the point of starvation, and since peasants did not flee from their normal living areas, the vast needs for emergency medical services and supplies of blankets, clothing, and elementary household goods that were required in Ethiopia, never arose. And since the framework of rural life was not disrupted, when the rains came again in 1985, farmers could go back to work on their land with no needs other than seeds to sow. (Cohen and Lewis 1986)

This is a perfect illustration of how a natural event, drought and the resulting crop failure, will have very different results depending on the actions of the governments of the affected territories.

Sudan, the largest country in Africa, is a neighbor of Ethiopia. While some parts of it have been affected by the drought, the famines have largely been a byproduct of the civil war between the Islamic North and the animistic and Christian South. One of the more bizarre aspects of this conflict was that the governments of the Sudan and of Ethiopia were mutually hostile to each other and therefore were willing to assist each other's refugees from famine areas more than they were willing to help their own citizens. There have also been reports that the Sudanese government was exploiting humanitarian aid funds in order to pay for the import of armaments. Lacville described one of the ways of doing this that violates the spirit but not the letter of the aid agreements:

> One greying Sudanese who works for an American charity then produced a chilling statistic: 'Every $1 you bring into Sudan to help feed internal refugees, you change it at the bank for 4.5 Sudanese pounds. That is the official government exchange rate. The real economic exchange rate on the "open" market is $1 = 80 Sudanese pounds. So every embassy, every American charity, every Canadian well-wisher for the refugees is in fact contributing 4.5 SP to the refugees, and 75.5 SP to the Government. And the military regime uses this money to buy ammunition to kill the people. That is why we do not want your charity in Sudan.' (Lacville 1991)

What makes the intentions of the government quite unambiguously clear is that it has refused access to several aid organizations who have been trying to get food into the famine areas. In this case, it is not only the government that uses famine against the people of the South, but the liberation movement in the South applies the same policy against the Northern occupation forces.

Finally, it should be obvious from any scanning of current events that starvation is still considered an appropriate tool in the conduct of conflicts. Whenever sanctions are imposed by one group on another, they often include the withholding of food supplies. This seems to be true regardless of whether victims are another country such as the recent instance of Iraq, a protesting group such as the Canadian Indians of Oka in 1991, or rebellious prisoners in jails almost anywhere.

Summary

The above cases illustrate the long history of man-made famines that range from those that occurred as the unintended result of unrelated policy decisions to those that were deliberately planned as weapons of conflict. Between these two extremes there occur cases that start out as the former and end up as the latter. This means that intent is not only difficult to ascertain, but also that it may evolve as events unfold.

The appeal of the use of hunger as a weapon goes back to antiquity and has persisted into the modern age. There seem to be a number of reasons for this. The first one is that it acts on one the basic needs of human beings. But equally important is the fact that it is a weapon that is cheap to produce, that does not require high technology or elaborate administrative structures, and that can be applied under the cover of a natural disaster. This latter subterfuge still works in many countries that do not want to disclose their real aims of persecuting a group of their citizens. Besides, this ruse allows them to receive large amounts of "humanitarian" aid that then can be used for many other purposes than the one for which it is intended.

What is to be Done?

In addition to being the result of conflict, hunger can also be the cause of conflict. One need only think of the bread riots that have so commonly been the result of food shortages in ancient Rome, early China, and medieval Europe. Kates and Millman made a good case for saying that we have reached a stage in our history that makes the abolition of food shortages possible:

> The demise of hunger may be attainable because for the first time in human history it is possible to contemplate the end of food scarcity, famine, and mass starvation. With the exception of its intentional creation or per-

petration as a weapon of war or genocide, a combination of effective famine early-warning systems, national and global emergency food reserves, and improved experience with distribution and food-for-work programs has brought the end of famine well within sight. (Kate and Millman 1990: 404)

Unfortunately, they make an exception for intentionally created famine, although in the twentieth century the majority of famine victims have been the result of just such intent. Thus, the real question is: what can be done to reduce or eliminate such lethal actions.

In order to address that question, it is important to examine the conditions under which these genocidal famines occur in the twentieth century. We live in an age of nation-states that jealously guard their sovereignty. Conflicts between states have been declining since World War II, but conflicts within states have been increasing dramatically. The latter have the advantage that other states are not expected to interfere in what the international community has agreed to define as the internal concerns of a sovereign state. At the same time there has appeared an increasing concern with human rights in many countries as well as within the United Nations. Now we seem to be entering a period in which much of the world is not any more prepared to remain unconcerned bystanders when gross human rights violations are committed by a country within its own borders against a group of its own citizens. Two recent events seem to support this optimistic view.

After the end of the recent "Gulf War" the Kurds in Northern Iraq came under attack by government forces causing the majority to flee to neighboring Iran and Turkey. At first, massive aid was provided for these refugees by many countries. But since the only long-term solution for the Kurds seemed to be a return to their former homes, the United Nations passed a resolution authorizing the presence of foreign troops in northern Iraq in order to protect the returnees.

Even more recently, conflict broke out in Yugoslavia over the attempt of several ethno-national groups to become independent. Although these conflicts were internal to the former Yugoslavia, several international organizations, including the United Nations, decided to become involved. They sent delegations to negotiate a peaceful compromise. A number of truces have been agreed to and broken; a number of peace proposals have been negotiated and rejected. At the time of writing, hostilities have been suspended, elections are being organized, and prospects for peace have improved. However, peacekeeping troops may have to continue their mission for some time yet.

Another case where outside forces are attempting to settle internal strife is Liberia where peacekeeping troops of the OAS are attempting to reestablish peace. So far, they have not succeeded.

These actions are cited because they represent a historic break with the consensus among the member states of the United Nations that their sovereign rights are beyond questioning. Thus, regardless of the success or failure of these efforts, these events seem to signal new attitudes with regard to the internal affairs of nation states that may result in limitations on their sovereign right to persecute their own citizens. Of course, there are also states that are impervious to such attempts to limit their sovereignty. The optimistic hope is that eventually they will not be able to hold out against an increasingly general consensus.

Note

1. This is a revised and expanded version of a paper read at the Annual Meeting of the American Sociological Association held on August 20–24, 1992 in Pittsburgh.

4

The Tragic Circle of Famine, Genocide, and Refugees[1]

Introduction

The attempt to understand the causes of genocide, the appearance of famines, and the generation of refugee flows has been seriously hampered by overspecialization. Each of these areas has given rise to a considerable body of literature that, however, rarely shows signs of familiarity with that of the others.

Genocides, including the Holocaust, have been written about very widely. Most scholars examine only one genocide, such as that of the Armenians or the Jews. Recently, a small but growing group of scholars has treated several genocides in a comparative fashion (Chalk and Jonassohn 1990; Kuper 1981). But neither group has paid enough attention to the deliberate use of hunger and starvation by the perpetrators. Nor has either group been much concerned with refugees although there have been escapes from all genocides.

Famines are an age-old phenomenon that has periodically savaged humanity. They have been studied and written about at great length. Most of the literature treats famine as the result of natural events, as was appropriate throughout much of history. It has only been since the middle of the twentieth century that the technology of storing, preserving, and transporting food stuffs in large quantities over long distances has been developed. The availability of this technology has made it possible to deal with natural disasters so efficiently that no further famines were to be expected. But famines do persist and continue to be blamed on natural events. Only a very small portion of the huge famine literature deals with so-called man-made famines (Sen 1981). Authors using this term deal with cases of famine that were the unanticipated consequence of misguided policies. Hardly anyone deals with the deliberate and intentional use of famine as a method of persecution or as a weapon in conflicts (Dando 1980; see also ch. 3). This seems all the more surprising since hunger, starvation, and famine have been used in this manner throughout history. The reader needs only be reminded of the many cases where a city that could not be taken by storm was beleaguered until it ran short of food and water.

Refugees have become an increasingly serious problem because their number has been growing dramatically. As a result, international and humanitarian organizations find that the demands on their resources keep escalating. At the same time, they are examining and exploring a variety of policies that might help them to cope with the growing numbers of refugees. However, there has been little awareness, until quite recently, that refugees fleeing from famines are not fleeing from natural events, but are the victims of persecution and even genocide (Clay and Holcomb 1986).

This chapter attempts to explore two related issues. The first issue raises questions about the possible ways in which understanding and explanation would be affected if we were to study genocide, famine, and refugees not in isolation, but as different aspects of the same underlying process. The second issue explores the ways in which our understanding would be changed if we were to treat refugees as the carriers of early warnings of incipient catastrophes. These two questions are, of course, intimately related: if we were to accept the news carried by refugees as factual, and if we were to develop a more complex understanding of the genocidal process, then the international community would at least have the opportunity of intervening. Whether anyone will take advantage of this opportunity will probably depend more on political and economic considerations than on humanitarian concerns.

Definitions

This chapter is based entirely on secondary sources. Since these sources are often at odds about definitions, it is essential that confusion about such differences be avoided. The simplest definition is that dealing with starvation and famine which are quite generally defined as the absence of sufficient food and water to sustain life. But even this simple definition has become problematic. As Kates and Millman (1990: 404) have pointed out, it is now possible to abolish famine, except when it is intentionally used as a weapon. This raises the question of whether an up-to-date definition of famine and starvation should not include a reference to the intent of the perpetrator?

The definitions of genocide and of refugee, however, illustrate the above-mentioned overspecialization. Both have been defined by the United Nations on separate occasions with quite conflicting results. The United Nations Convention on the Prevention and Punishment of the Crime of Genocide restricts the victims of genocide to members of "a national, ethnical, racial or religious group as such" (Centre for Human Rights 1988: 143). The Convention Relating to the Status of Refugees on the other hand, says that "the term 'refugee' shall apply to any person who…owing to well-founded fear of being persecuted for reasons of race, religion, nationality, membership of a particular social group or political opinion, is outside the country of his nationality" (Centre for Human Rights 1988: 295–96).

These definitions of genocides and refugees are unsatisfactory for many reasons that have given rise to much critical examination. When taken in context, two contradictions become apparent: the two definitions define different groups and the second one defines a geographical area, which the first one does not. The difficulty becomes clearer when we think of a group of refugees fleeing from genocide. They will be recognized as refugees only if they are outside the country of their nationality, and they will be recognized as victims of genocide only if they belong to one of the four specified types of groups. However, most observers agree that victims of genocide may belong to groups other than those mentioned, and that refugees may be found inside the country of their nationality.

Since it is not the intent of this paper to engage in a definitional debate, we shall treat as victims of genocide any group that a perpetrator tries to eliminate, and as refugee any person fleeing from life threatening violence.

Food Shortages as Evidence of Genocide

The major activity of the United Nations High Commission for Refugees and of most of the nongovernmental organizations (NGOs) dealing with famines is the supplying of food, shelter, and medical supplies to the victims. There is no question that these supplies are needed by the victims; but their need is often not the result of shortages, but rather the result of the deliberate withholding of available essentials. Often the problem is not shortage but distribution. Supplies go to those with the guns, not to those with the empty stomachs. In Bosnia the victims of "ethnic cleansing" were starving while Serbia was exporting food to Russia in exchange for technology and weapons. This tragedy was reaching comic proportions when it was announced that warships would enforce the embargo against Serbia by patrolling the Adriatic coast while it was generally known that violations of the embargo were taking place primarily via the Danube.

It is not our purpose here to review contemporary famines in detail. Yet, if we were to do so, it would become abundantly clear that most of them are the result of a planned campaign against a victim group and not the result of a natural catastrophe. In fact, this premeditated use of starvation has been a central part of many genocides. Its appeal to the perpetrators is manifold. It conserves food resources that may already be in short supply. It allows the perpetrators to hide their real motives behind an apparent natural disaster. Because it is a method that requires neither an advanced technology nor a highly developed bureaucracy it can be applied by even the poorest country. It weakens the victims physically and lowers their resistance to epidemics, while at the same time it undermines their morale and their ability to resist. And eventually it kills.

The understanding of this use of starvation as a form of persecution should and can have wide-ranging consequences for action. It forcefully underlines that humanitarian supplies reach the victims only rarely. In the majority of cases such supplies enrich the perpetrators through their sale on the black markets and through their barter for additional arms and ammunition. The alternative would require the international community to find ways of establishing enforcement mechanisms for the various United Nations conventions that were meant to deal with such human rights violations.

The bottom line is that famines are evidence of genocide and not of food shortages. It is, of course, quite possible to perform a genocide without first imposing starvation on the victims, but such cases have become quite rare in the late twentieth century. If there is an advantage to the victims, it is in favor of starvation because of the slowness with which it escalates to famine. That extra time creates at least the possibility of resistance, of outside help arriving in time, or of escaping. It is the information carried by such early escapees that ought to alert the world to the need for action.

Refugees as Sources of Information

The following remarks are meant to indicate how little we know about the onset of genocides and how difficult it is to obtain accurate information during moments of crisis. This particular quest for knowledge is not only inspired by scholarly curiosity, but rather by the desire to help the victims of persecution, and by the possibility—at least in theory—to intervene in the evil designs of the perpetrators. However, either possibility requires a base of accurate information on which to develop appropriate policies and actions. But such accurate information is remarkably difficult to obtain by conventional means.

In cases of incipient genocides the usual channels of information are almost always blocked or distorted. The perpetrator country usually denies its role in annihilating a group as well as any intention of doing so. Visas to enter such countries are often impossible to obtain, access to the relevant areas is predictably blocked, or only brief, stage-managed visits are arranged to convince outside observers that nothing out of the ordinary is taking place. Information from the perpetrator governments, if available at all, is full of distorted facts and/or denials. Other obvious sources of information are foreign diplomats, journalists, Red Cross workers, and other representatives of humanitarian aid organizations, as well as academic specialists. Unfortunately, their evidence is also suspect because they are likely to omit or distort information that might get them expelled from the perpetrator country, or denied entry in the future. Finally, there are those emigrés and refugees who have managed to escape in time. Their testimony is almost always considered equally suspect because of their obvious personal bias.

But none of this information reaches us directly; it is always predigested for us by the media and by the experts from academic and diplomatic circles who add their own biases and ideological interpretations. The results, thus distorted, are often responsible for much suffering and a very large number of deaths. Why is this so? Because reality gets lost in the process of transmission. The evidence from the perpetrator governments and their sympathizers receives credibility; ideological interpretations are accorded more attention than simple facts; and the evidence from the refugees is totally discredited. Thus, any conceivable policy or action is very likely to fail because it is based on deceptions, misinterpretations, lack of accurate information, or downright lies.

An early assessment of the accuracy of victims' testimonies comes from Marie Syrkin (1976). In the fall of 1945, after the end of World War II, she took the first ship from New York that sailed to the Middle East with civilian passengers. Her purpose was to interview survivors of Hitler's death camps and participants in Jewish resistance, the majority of whom then were to be found in the former Palestine. Her results were published in 1947 and reissued thirty years later. During that interval a great deal of documentary evidence became available, as well as much more testimony that had been carefully analyzed and verified by many professionals. However, Syrkin notes in her introduction to the new edition that these materials support the evidence of the witnesses whom she had interviewed as essentially accurate. She adds that there is little that she would omit, though of course there is much that she could now add. The important point is that these early interviews, with victims soon after their escape, yielded essentially accurate data.

Clay and Holcomb (1986) have illustrated dramatically how the lack of accurate information played a decisive role in the case of the Ethiopian famine. While the world was shocked into action by the news of mass starvation, nobody seemed willing to inquire into the causes of the famine. Humanitarian organizations poured in substantial quantities of money and materials without having a sound basis of information. Most of them accepted whatever the government said and they restricted their activities to those places to which the government gave them access. At the same time they refused to contribute any money at all to research designed to elicit accurate information because they were afraid of how the Ethiopian government might react (Clay and Holcomb 1986: see especially chapters 1, 10, and 11). Although their humanitarian motives were admirable, their actions were to a very great extent misguided in that they perpetuated the situation that had produced the starvation in the first place. Even their food distribution program was of limited assistance because only a little food reached those who needed it and then only in certain areas, specified by the government.

One of the important indicators that most helping organizations seem to have ignored is the meaning of the starvation that they have tried to alleviate. In the present stage of the world's development the presence of serious starvation in a group is one of the first sure signs that this group has been singled out for victimization. Starvation due to natural causes can now be dealt with by appropriate governmental action. Man-made starvation that is the unintended consequence of dysfunctional social organization or misguided social policies can equally be avoided if appropriate actions are taken as soon as it is recognized. We have available a most instructive demonstration in the crop failures due to lack of rain that hit both Ethiopia and Kenya in the eighties. No serious famine conditions occurred anywhere in Kenya because the government reacted to this emergency by importing food stuffs and distributing them through the established wholesale and retail channels, while the Ethiopian government used this opportunity to victimize its enemies (see chapter 3). The result was that the media did not even pay attention to the crop failures in Kenya. The Ethiopian famine, on the other hand, received worldwide attention without a discussion of its man-made origin and without the appropriate action that such a discussion might have prompted. Neither governments nor NGOs seem to have been aware of or drawn the obvious conclusions from the example set by Kenya.

The significant contribution of Clay and Holcomb consists in showing that a great deal of information can be collected in a quite short time at a very modest cost. They have demonstrated conclusively that it is possible to obtain very reliable information from refugees, in spite of the traumatic effects of their recent experiences. Whether governments and NGOs are prepared to accept such information and act on it is quite another matter. But in future they will not be able to discount the information obtained from refugees quite so cavalierly.

More recently, Bill Frelick has taken up this same issue in the World Refugee Survey (1988) because genocides are becoming more frequent and are responsible for increasing refugee flows. He addresses several significant issues—issues that have to be addressed if there is going to be any hope of international intervention. Even when the news leaks out, there is a need to break through the barriers to disbelief. In order to do so it would be important to produce evidence of intent, which is an essential part of the definition of genocide. The perpetrators only rarely declare their intent as openly as did Hitler in *Mein Kampf* or Hujjatu'l-Islam Qazai, president of the revolutionary court in Shiraz, did when justifying the destruction of Iran's Baha'i community. (The credibility that the world accorded the news of the persecution of the Baha'is contributed greatly to generating support and helped to interrupt the killings.) Therefore, other kinds of evidence of intent need to be examined. Here both the number of refugees and their testimony play a crucial role. Frelick suggests a variety of methods for obtaining this evidence and for establishing its credibility. Though most of these methods are the stock-in-trade of anthropologists and sociologists who engage in field work research, they are frequently ignored by journalists, diplomats, and the representatives of the various aid organizations. These methods include such elementary aspects as establishing the credibility of the interviewer, finding a private setting that excludes peer group pressures, establishing trust, using reliable translators, verifying the accuracy of the translation, and matching the sex of the interviewer with that of the interviewee. While such methods may appear elementary to the social scientist, they are often very difficult to implement in the field. However, they are absolutely crucial if the evidence collected from refugees is going to be accorded credibility by the world.

Summary

Studying refugee flows, genocides, and famines as isolated, independent phenomena can only lead to erroneous interpretations of results. Treating them as components of a larger process is an essential part of their problematic. It is only a part because it is the essential basis for intervention, but it does not insure that such interventions will in fact take place. For that to happen, international meetings and organizations need to acquire the willingness to act on their various pronouncements on human rights, instead of merely passing resolutions.

Note

1. A revised version of a paper published in *Society*, vol.30, no.6 (Sept./ Oct., 1993), 72–76.

5

The Consequences of Ideological Genocides and Their Role in Prevention[1]

Introduction

Jules Baillet reports that the Egyptian monuments depict the wars of the third millennium B.C. as totally destructive. Whole populations disappeared because they were either massacred, taken captive, or because they had fled across the desert. Even the land was rendered unproductive and uninhabitable, either by sword or by fire (Baillet 1912: 151–52). This pattern of warfare in ancient Egypt seems to have changed only about 1,000 years later during the conflicts that preceded the twelfth dynasty (1991–1786 B.C.). Baillet argues that the change was the unintended consequence of the dominant motives of the warriors—which was their greed for loot and ransom. That greed caused massacres to be replaced by enslavement and imprisonment, although the exacting of tribute did not appear before Egypt's asiatic conquests (Baillet 1912: 167–68).

The Old Testament contains a number of cases that today would be considered as genocides—not because of the casualties of warfare, but because of the killing of noncombatant women and children. Not all of these cases can be considered as factual, especially in view of the fact that the Amalekites seem to have been massacred several times over.[2] The importance of these reports lies in the manner in which these genocides are referred to, which would indicate that such behavior, far from being unusual, was considered customary at that time.

Westington tells us that the Romans committed routine genocide on cities that resisted them. It was the custom to massacre every living creature, man and beast. The earliest case he reports is from 494 B.C. (Westington 1938: 70,77). Only when labor was needed, were a certain number of slaves taken. Then the conquered city was razed to the ground and burned. The Gauls, who destroyed Rome in 390 B.C., used similar methods of dealing with their enemies and are said to have murdered all whom they captured, regardless of sex or age (Westington 1938: 71). Hannibal also adopted the same methods after the capture of Saguntum (Westington 1938: 73).

Since then genocide has been practiced throughout most of history in all parts of the world, although it did not attract much attention because genocide was usually accepted as the deserved fate of the vanquished.

In this century, we now have to deal mostly with ideological genocides that are performed to implement a theory, belief, or ideology. There are several significant differences that distinguish ideological genocides from the earlier types, and these differences have a bearing on the effects for the perpetrator society. First, their aim—to impose an ideological imperative—has never yet been carried out successfully. Second, the victim groups are part of, and located within, the perpetrators' societies.[3] Third, the costs to the perpetrators and to the victim groups are both borne within the perpetrator societies, except for those members of the victim groups that survived and were able to flee.

An empirical study of the relevant cases will show not only that the consequences of ideological (internal) genocides for the perpetrator societies are a burden of enormous costs, but also that it takes a very long time to recover from them. This is true notwithstanding the fact that individuals may enrich themselves during the very same genocidal process that imposes such huge costs on the perpetrator society. The following brief sketches are intended to convey an idea of the direction of the argument by presenting some typical cases. The list is not meant to be exhaustive.

The Albigensian Crusade

The Albigensian Crusade was the first ideological genocide and it is included here because it gave rise to the Inquisition—an institution that developed many of the techniques of persecution that are still in wide use today. The Albigensian Crusade took place in the first half of the thirteenth century in the Languedoc, an area that has no precise geographical boundaries, but generally refers to the south of France. The Languedoc at that time was distinct from France because the people spoke a different language and because it was much more highly developed. Politically, the region was highly decentralized—a state of affairs that greatly facilitated freedom and independence among its people. Resident aliens enjoyed full citizens' rights regardless of nationality or creed (Oldenbourg 1961: 24). Economically, it was a wealthy, mostly regional, economy that benefited from control over several trade routes. Culturally, the region was host to hundreds of troubadours who traveled from court to court (Wakefield 1974: ch. 3). Occitan was the language of poetry and of literature. Religiously, it was tolerant of all beliefs and of a host of itinerant preachers. But the Catholic Church was unpopular because the clergy's worldly affairs were more important to them than the spiritual well-being of their flocks. It was probably the richest area in Europe in terms of agriculture, trade, cosmopolitan culture, and the standard of living of its people—at a time when Berlin was just beginning to be founded. Several heresies flourished and found an interested audience even among the aristocracy and especially at the court of the Count of Toulouse. This tolerance was not shared by the papal authorities who called for a crusade to wipe out this threat to their authority. The king of France fielded the required troops and reaped the benefits of enlarging his kingdom.

The crusaders killed not only the heretics and their sympathizers, but also many innocent bystanders. After the fall of the city of Béziers in 1209 the abbot was asked by the crusaders how to distinguish the heretics from the good Catholics. His oft-quoted order—"Kill them all, for God knows his own!" (Lea 1955, vol. 1, 154)—may not be historically correct, but it is a critical comment on the Crusade and might well serve as a motto for any ideological or supposedly ideological genocide (Oldenbourg 1961: 116). The crusaders ravaged the countryside, looting and burning, cutting down orchards and vineyards, and poisoning wells. As a result, famine and sickness killed more people than actual battles. The crusade was too successful; it not only exterminated the heretics, it also ruined agriculture and commerce so thoroughly that the Languedoc has not fully recovered to this day and is still considered a depressed region.

The Albigensian Crusade was a transitional case in the sense that the victims were a group outside the perpetrator state (as had been true of earlier genocides) while the motive was to enforce conformity to a belief system (which makes it an early case of the transition to ideological genocides so common in the twentieth century). This case is included here to highlight the main argument of this paper. When the victims were located outside the perpetrator state, it was obvious that the victim society or state suffered enormously—this was so obvious that nobody seriously questioned it. It was also taken for granted that the perpetrator state reaped benefits in terms of wealth and acquisition of territory. However, when the victim group is located inside the perpetrator state a great deal of this cost and suffering does not simply disappear—it is now located inside the perpetrator state and cannot be confined only to the victim group. This phenomenon has received very little attention, although the proposition that a state can victimize and exterminate one of its constituent parts without damage to the whole seems on the surface implausible. This important point should become clearer by examining several cases where the perpetrator state victimizes one of its constituent parts. These cases occur most frequently in the twentieth century and involve most often an ideological genocide. But, before we get to the twentieth century, it is important to look at another transitional case because it developed and refined many of the techniques of persecution that are still in use today.

The Spanish Inquisition

The Spanish Inquisition is not usually considered a genocide at all because the nonbelievers could emigrate or convert to Christianity, and because the heretics could confess and abjure their errors. It is considered as a major genocide here because the most crucial part of any definition of genocide is that there must be an intent to destroy a group. While evidence of intent may be difficult to obtain in many other cases, the Spanish Inquisitors left no doubt about their aims (Llorente 1826: 77–78, 83–86). They wanted to destroy all traces of heresy, whether these were of Islamic, Jewish, or Protestant origin, or were deviations from orthodox Roman Catholicism, but they were less interested in individual deviations from orthodoxy than in collective deviations. This became quite clear through the requirement that confessions include the names of others who failed to conform. They enforced such orthodoxy by forcible conversion, imprisonment, penance, burning at the stake, or expulsion. But they went beyond Spain to propagate the true faith and to do battle with any group that believed otherwise. The Inquisition was established in Mexico and South America as well as in the Low Countries. In the latter it was introduced by Philip II in 1560 to cope with the growing Reformation movements. The resulting rebellion soon became mixed up with heresy to such an extent that, "for economy of effort, a decree of the Inquisition (confirmed by Royal Proclamation) condemned all the inhabitants of the Netherlands to death as heretics, save for a few specially exempted persons—a total of some 3,000,000 souls: the men being generally burned and the women buried alive" (Roth 1964: 173). Although the Dutch War of Independence intervened and prevented the carrying out of this sentence in its entirety, the Duke of Alva is said to have boasted that during his rule 18,600 persons were executed and many times that number were driven into exile.

The goal of the Inquisition was to create a homogeneous Catholic realm. The converts were, however, never fully accepted; even after several generations they were still referred to as "New Christians" and suspected of secretly adhering to their former faith. Since accusations of heresy were difficult to prove, the Inquisition asked citizens to report to it such suspicious behavior as: abstinence from wine or pork, traditional dances or songs at weddings, scrupulous regard for personal cleanliness, the use of Hebrew or Arabic language, or any observance of Jewish or Islamic law. Baths were destroyed, including those in the Alhambra (Roth 1964: chs. 6 and 7). Victims were severely punished, including burning at the stake, and their property was confiscated. Many had to flee for their lives. Before the expulsion of the Jews and the Moors and the persecution of the Conversos (or Marranos, as converted Jews were referred to) and Moriscos (converted Moors), Spain flourished, and not only economically. It was a seat of learning, of philosophy, and of the arts. Arabic, Greek, Hebrew, and Latin language and literature interacted through translation and enriched each other. Spanish culture and learning influenced much of the rest of contemporary Europe. But after the edict of 1567, on the anniversary of the surrender of Grenada, a huge book burning took place there and henceforth owning a book in Arabic was an offence that was severely punished. Andalusia, deprived of its skilled population, became a desert; the old system of irrigation fell into disrepair, and what had once been the garden of Spain is today still an underdeveloped area.

The expansion of trade and the establishment of colonies by both Spain and Portugal took place during this same period. Iberian ships sailed to the ends of the world. But even here the motives were not purely economic. While trade and the acquisition of wealth financed the journeys, spreading the Gospel and the saving of souls justified them. The proselytizing was done so successfully that in the early seventeenth century it caused Japan to enact several so-called exclusion decrees which effectively closed that country to the rest of the world until the nineteenth century (Sansom 1963: 36–39).

After the purification of Spain from all non-Catholic influences it began to stagnate. The Inquisition had exacted a terrible toll. In addition to the millions that were forced to emigrate, Juan Llorente, who was secretary general of the Inquisition before he too came under suspicion, gives us the following totals for the period from 1481 to 1820: 34,658 were burned alive; 288,214 were condemned to the gallows or prison (mostly for life); and 18,049 were burned in effigy (because they had escaped before they could be arrested) (Llorente 1826: 248). He ends with this summary:

> Not only has the Inquisition decimated the population of Spain by her autos de fe, but has considerably reduced it by provoking civil wars, revolts, and expulsion of the Jews and the Moors. More than five million of inhabitants have disappeared from the fine soil of Spain whilst the Holy Office has exercised its terrible administration, and we can say of this barbarous institution what Montesquieu said of an emperor of the East,—'Justinian, who destroyed sects by the sword and by laws, and who by compelling them to revolt, was obliged to exterminate them, rendered their provinces uncultivated. He believed he had augmented the number of the faithful: he did nothing but diminish that of men' ([Llorente 1826: 249] If Llorente's figure was at all close, it represented over one third of Spain's population.)

For a while, the wealth brought home from the newly acquired colonies kept Spain afloat economically. The cultural decline was much more rapid. In both areas Spain has not recovered to this day. Its economy is still one of the poorer ones in Europe; its cultural and intellectual life has still not produced a world-class university. It seems clear that the cost of enforcing conformity to its homogeneously Catholic society has been very high.

The Papal Inquisition was established in the thirteenth century and the use of torture was authorized by a Papal Bull in 1252. It was only in 1834 that the Inquisition was finally suppressed in Spain, although it had already become inactive in the late eighteenth century. But it was only in 1860 that the official and disabling distinction between Old Christians and New Christians was abolished in Spain, and that the certificate of *limpieza*, or purity of blood, was no longer required for certain careers. In 1869 the principle of religious toleration was incorporated into the Spanish constitution. It took until 1931 for religious equality also to became part of the Spanish constitution (Roth 1964: 268–69).

The Armenian Genocide

The Armenians were the victims of a genocide carried out during World War I by Turkey which then was an ally of Germany. The Otto-

man Empire had been declining for some time and Turkey was trying
to orient itself toward a nationalistic ideology centered on the image of
an ethnic Turkic state in which there was no room for a foreign, non-
Moslem group. While the Armenians were predominantly peasants,
they also played a major role in the skilled trades, commerce, and the
professions. Their elimination had both short-term and long-term consequences; the former became almost immediately felt during the war.
A couple of illustrations may suffice here.

The completion of the Berlin-Bagdad railroad, the construction of
which had been started long before the war, was considered to be of
prime strategic importance, especially since there were very few all-
weather roads in Turkey. The German embassy and the railroad
company's management were engaged in protracted negotiations with
the Turkish government because the project was in financial difficulties that threatened it with bankruptcy. To add to these problems, the
Turkish authorities were arresting and killing the Armenian construction crews; the result was that two-thirds of the originally scheduled
work was left undone (Trumpener 1968: chs. 7 and 9). The negotiators
tried very hard to convince the Turkish rulers that the completion of
the railroad was a top priority within the overall war effort—without
success. The majority of the workers were Armenians and they were
slaughtered. The result was that the railroad was not completed before
the war ended.[4]

Another illustration concerns the great demands for health care by
the Turkish army as well as the civilian population during wartime.
Although the demands for medical services were far beyond what could
be met by available resources, Armenian health professionals—both
doctors and nurses—were liquidated without hesitation and often with
the complicity of their Turkish colleagues (Dadrian 1968: 183).

The long-range consequences of the genocide of the Armenians by
Turkey are more diffuse and not quite as easy to measure. In addition
to losing the war, Turkey had also lost much of its skilled labor force,
its professionals, and its commercial and trading elites. This has dramatically retarded its economic development, the effects of which are
observable to this day. It also continues to suffer diplomatically on the
international scene because its present government continues to deny
that a genocide did occur; instead, it invests heavily in denial propaganda—both at the political level as well as by sponsoring scholarly
conferences and publications. These activities, together with its record
of continued human rights violations, are helping to bar it from admis-

sion to the European Community—a membership that its government covets.[5] Finally, there are a number of consequences for both national and international law that have recently been discussed by Dadrian, but that are too complex to be considered here (Dadrian 1989: 221–334).

Genocides in the Soviet Union

The people of the USSR experienced a great deal of persecution under Stalin's reign of terror, and it is quite easy to demonstrate the enormous costs of these genocidal campaigns to Soviet society (Conquest 1968; Mace 1988). In the 1930s Stalin decided to eliminate the so-called class of kulaks. Many were killed outright, many more died in the Gulag, and the survivors were forcibly converted to collectivized agriculture (Mace 1984; Antonov-Ovseyenko 1981: 55–68). The result: what had been an agriculture that without modern equipment like tractors and combines had produced a large surplus for export, became an agriculture that has not recovered to this day; the U.S.S.R. has been an importer of foodstuffs ever since.[6]

A little later Stalin decided that the military were not to be trusted. He proceeded to wipe out almost the entire officer corps (Antonov-Ovseyenko 1981: 182–90). When Germany attacked in spite of Stalin's pact with Hitler, the Soviet war effort was in the hands of inexperienced and rapidly promoted junior officers. It seems reasonable to suppose that there might have been fewer defeats and lower casualties if experienced senior officers had remained in command. Roy Medvedev writes that with better leadership the Soviet army would have defeated the Nazi aggressors sooner and farther west without the cost of 20 million lives (Medvedev 1973: 465).[7]

Industrial production also suffered severely because the purges fell heavily on the industrial elite: managers, technicians, scientists, designers, and so on. This led to extraordinary turnover rates. It was not uncommon for an enterprise to have five managers during the course of one year; of those who held key positions in the railroad system in November 1938 only 24 percent had been holding their jobs for at least one year (Katz 1973: 9–10). Barbara Katz tried to measure the negative impact of the purges and of the preparations for war on industrial performance during the period of 1938–1940. She found that the purges were more important in affecting the level of industrial output than the preparations for war (Katz 1973: 342).

Insofar as these purges focused on specific groups of people, they should be considered as genocides. The military, economic, political, scientific, and intellectual elites and the peasants do not qualify under the United Nations definition—which is the very reason why that definition is not very useful for scholarly purposes. The members of these groups were not targeted by Stalin as individuals; their associates, friends, and families shared their guilt, and though their accusations were spurious, the results were no less real for all that.

Even the authorities in Moscow in the last years of the Soviet period began to acknowledge the mass killings of the Stalin regime and the costs to their own society. Therefore, there is no need to go into the other genocidal persecutions of the Stalin era. Once a perpetrator country acknowledges the historical facts, the evidence to support the argument about the consequences of genocide becomes widely available. "Perestroika" as promulgated by Gorbachev can be interpreted, in this context, as an effort to make up for the expensive and long-lasting consequences for Soviet society of the genocides of the Stalin era.

Nazi Germany and the Holocaust

The case of Nazi Germany is a very special one, in this context as well as in others: first, because West Germany has openly acknowledged its guilt, and second, because West German scholars themselves have started to look at the costs for Germany. These costs may be roughly divided into those incurred up to the end of World War II, and those continuing to be exacted since then.

In the first category may be cited the loss of human resources in those areas where Jews excelled. Engelmann provides a list of notable Jewish men and women in medicine (Engelmann 1984: 333–53). Weinreich deals with antisemitism in the universities and its effects (Weinreich 1946). Müller-Hill also deals with science in academia (Müller-Hill 1988). All such accounts may be summarized briefly enough: before Hitler, Germany had several world-famous universities and collected a disproportionately high number of Nobel prizes; since World War II, Germany arguably has no outstanding university in either of its two halves and receives a disproportionately low number of Nobel prizes. But even when Jews were used only as slave labor in German war industry or in factories associated with concentration camps, it was more important to kill them than to let them work.

The I.G. Farben plants near Auschwitz provide a particularly bizarre case study; one of them was designed to produce gasoline and methanol and another one was to produce a synthetic rubber called 'buna.' Construction was started in April 1941 at that location because careful studies had shown that it would meet all important demands: water and rail transport were available and it would provide both labor and protection from Allied bombing (both of the latter two calculations turned out to be wrong). These plants almost immediately found themselves short of labor. Since there were not nearly enough people living in the area to provide an adequate labor force, the original Auschwitz camp was enlarged and several new camps were built. Because the great marching distance between the building site and the camps decreased the available time and energy for work, later camps were built closer to the actual work site (DuBois 1953: 156, 222). "The SS authorities in charge of the camp labor allocation were infuriated by the large number of Jews sent directly to the gas chambers" and "[a]s early as December 28, 1942, Himmler had ordered the death rate reduced" because of the reported labor shortage in the plants (Yavner 1984: 47, 49).[8] By the summer of 1944—the first Allied bombing raid did not take place until August 20, 1944—the synthetic oil plant had achieved a peak production of 3,000 tons a month, which was only half of I.G. Farben's original projections. The Allied bombing raids gradually reduced this output. Although buna rubber production was planned to start in the second half of 1943, not a single pound of synthetic rubber was ever produced. DuBois' scathing summary is worth quoting:

> In Agra, India, the sweat and toil of 22,000 slaves at least resulted in a beautiful building, the Taj Mahal. But Buna-Auschwitz was not only the most appalling failure in the history of modern industry—it had no parallel anywhere in history in the uneconomical exploitation of labor. Human beings were dissipated so unmercifully that after almost four years the construction was still unfinished.... At a human cost of 200,000 lives— plus a quarter-billion Reichsmark—not one pound of rubber was ever produced at I.G.Auschwitz! (DuBois 1953: 341)[9]

It has also been suggested that the extensive use of rail transport during the implementation of the Holocaust interfered with the sending of troops and materiel to the front. As to the troops themselves, their number was dramatically diminished by the implementation of Nazi racial policies and by the additional numbers that would have served if there had been no anti-Jewish policy. Though it may be difficult to agree on actual numbers, there is no doubt that this effect was considerable (Englemann 1984: ch. 6).[10] Finally, some have argued, though it could never be proved, that without the costs of the Holocaust Germany might have won the war—in part because it would probably have had the atom bomb first.[11]

In the second category of costs, those incurred after World War II, one would start with the enormous loss of talent and expertise that is clearly observable in those areas where the Jews had excelled. One might also point to Germany's loss of international prestige as the information about what had happened spread throughout the world. Additionally, most Germans consider the division of their country into the two Germanies to have been a major loss. Several German authors have written books about the many ways in which Germany and the world, particularly the Western world, would have been a different place had the Holocaust and its costs not changed it in so many ways (Englemann 1984: ch. 10; Haffner 1979: 99–145).[12]

These post-World War II costs were so dramatic and the economic state of West Germany was so appalling that the U.S. implemented the Marshall Plan. This rescue operation was so successful that the country, in short order, became one of the world's great industrial powers. The reunification of the two Germanies has put a considerable strain on that position. Another area in which the costs of the Nazi period not only occurred after the end of the war, but are still mounting, concerns the disposition of confiscated and stolen properties. Half a century later, the claims to real estate, gold, jewelry, money, and art works are still being negotiated. In fact, the losses have been spreading to countries that either profited from or assisted in hiding such ill-gotten gains.

The Cambodian Tragedy

Cambodia will be the last case to be considered. We have here an almost pure case of ideological genocide. In April 1975 the Khmer Rouge came to power in Cambodia and renamed the country Kampuchea. In a little over three and a half years—by January 1979 they were out of power—they attempted to achieve their special form of pure communism in one fell swoop, rather than gradually. The costs of this attempt were so devastating that some authors have referred to it as "autogenocide," seeing in it an analogy to suicide.[13]

When the Khmer Rouge came to power, Cambodia probably had a population of about 7 million people (Kuper 1981: 157). Since no reliable figures on the number of victims are available, Etcheson lists the estimates of a dozen authors (Etcheson 1984: 148). His own estimate is that, "[a]t least a third and possibly as many as one-half of the Khmer people have perished as a result of war, disease and starvation, and political terror" between 1970 and 1983 (Etcheson 1984: 149). Dramatic as these population losses were, their consequences were to inhibit even in the future almost all forms of development because the educated, the intelligentsia, the professionals, and the technicians were all targeted for immediate elimination because they represented the bourgeoisie and its foreign influences.

Soon after coming to power, the Khmer Rouge under Pol Pot emptied the cities by killing the members of the above-mentioned groups and by driving the rest of the population into the countryside.[14] They tried to build a new society from the ground up by destroying all linkages to the past. They abolished the traditional history of the country. They introduced a primitive barter economy that would function without money. They rejected all forms of specialized skill and knowledge, preferring to place their trust in the native ability of the uneducated peasantry. Much detail is not yet known and much may never be known because it was either not recorded or the records have been lost or destroyed (Chandler and Kiernan 1983: introduction).

The Khmer Rouge ruined agriculture by their rejection of traditional expertise and social organization. Irrigation projects suffered from faulty design and workmanship because the people with training in irrigation engineering had been eliminated; when they finally had to retreat in 1979, the Khmer Rouge sabotaged some of those irrigation works that were still working. All this resulted in widespread starvation; but the famine was eventually self-limiting as the surviving population decreased dramatically (Etcheson 1984: 213–14).

The imposition of a pure communism also destroyed industry, partly as a result of the radical rustication program, partly due to the rejection of technology and of machinery (except for war), and partly due to the abolition of money and of private property.

In the final analysis, the Khmer Rouge revolution succeeded in destroying Cambodian society and social organization, including its cities, its educational and health systems, and its economy and agriculture; but the Khmer Rouge failed entirely in creating the new society that their ideology called for. They were driven into remote border regions by the invading Vietnamese troops, who have since then relinquished their control to the results of the U. N. supervised elections. The future seems very uncertain for Cambodia, except for the certainty that nothing good has come from the genocide.

Conclusion

Finally, there is one consequence of genocide for the perpetrator society that all cases seem to have in common: an enormous increase in corruption. As life for the people in the perpetrator society, beset by restrictions and shortages, becomes increasingly difficult for most of its people—not only the victims of persecution—there will be more and more other people who will see this as an opportunity to enrich themselves. Unavailable goods and services will become available at a price. Once such practices become established, they are unlikely to disappear, and the perpetrator societies will continue to be subject to such practices long after the genocide has become history.

The list could be continued. But I think that the point is quite clear. Genocides that victimize a part of the population of the perpetrator country impose a huge cost on the perpetrator society. These costs are paid by many succeeding generations.

The lesson of history was, and still seems to be, that genocides produce material benefits for the perpetrator society. This was undoubtedly the case when the victims of genocides were a people outside the perpetrator society. But the process works differently in ideological genocides when the victims are located within, and are part of, the perpetrator society. In that case there are no benefits. Instead, there remain only enormous costs.

In attempting to make connections between historical events it is, of course, always difficult to establish proof. These examples of the deleterious consequences of genocides may have been the result of quite different factors. Thus, Strayer disagrees with the prevailing view of the consequences of the Albigensian Crusades and argues that "the economic depression of the fourteenth century and the ravages of the Hundred Years' War did more physical damage to Languedoc than the Crusades did." (Strayer 1971: 169). It can also be argued, to give another example, that the continued failure of Soviet agriculture is the result of collectivization. Since it is safe to say that all historical events are the result of multiple causation, it is probably the case that Stalin's massacre of the kulaks and the drive to collectivize were both factors in the failure of agriculture. Instead of proof, one has to rely on the weight of the evidence and the plausibility of the argument.

Afterword

For those of us who are committed to the prediction and the prevention of genocide the above argument seems to open up another possible avenue of action. If we can publicize such findings sufficiently, we may eventually be able to change the out-dated lesson from history about the benefits of genocide. That such lessons from history are not irrelevant is quite clearly illustrated by Hitler's reading of history. As Gulbekian has shown in his well-documented paper, Hitler's analysis of the uses of genocide was all positive and may be summarized by his often quoted question: "Wer redet heute noch von der Vernichtung der Armenier?" (Who today still speaks of the annihilation of the Armenians?) (Gulbekian 1988:1–14). The new lesson from history ought to be that genocides can be carried out only at enormous costs to the perpetrator society and that even the potential ideological benefits are never realized. Then, even if some future head of government were to follow Hitler's analysis, his people may refuse to go along with it or to remain passive bystanders.

Such analysis should be incorporated into the curriculum of the many courses on genocide and the Holocaust that are being established. In North America such course materials are being widely introduced into high schools, colleges, and universities. Curriculum proposals seem to generate heated debates about cases to be included or excluded. However, there is little debate about how to cover prediction and prevention—in part because as yet there is so little known in this area. Therefore, the above analysis should be added to the curriculum so that eventually this knowledge may attain the status of conventional wisdom and contribute to the prevention of future genocides.

It seems very likely that with such conventional wisdom in wide currency the incidence of genocides will decline dramatically. Even if potential perpetrators would be tempted to test this finding on their own society, their own people would not support them in such plans, and without a minimum of such support a genocide can hardly be carried out. This latter point is crucial for the prevention of future genocides; the carrying out of a massive genocide does not necessarily require the active support of the population, but it does minimally require the passive acquiescence of the bystanders (Langbein 1976: 21–

34)—and even that is hardly likely to be forthcoming when the prospect of the enormous costs has acquired the status of conventional wisdom.

Lest the above argument be misunderstood, let it be clear that these costs are not a reason for being opposed to genocide. Those reasons are based on humanitarian values that are much more important than any cost-benefit analysis. Surely, we should oppose mass killings even when there are material benefits. The enormous costs of ideological genocide to the perpetrator society are simply being employed here as one of the potential tools in our attempts at preventing genocides in the future.

Such efforts at preventing future genocides should have recourse to a wide variety of methods. We can never be quite sure which such efforts are going to be effective in a particular, concrete situation. Therefore, human rights activists and humanitarian organizations (not to mention governments) ought to be able to draw on a wide repertoire of actions to increase to probability of obtaining the desired results. It seems possible to develop strategies for such actions in the fields of education (including adult education), early warning research, publicity and public relations, economic sanctions, organizational and international pressures, and so on. The elaboration of such a repertoire of strategies and methods for potentially preventive actions will be the topics of the three chapters on "Prevention and Intervention."

Notes

1. Earlier versions of this paper appeared in the *Armenian Review*, vol. 42, no. 4/168 (Winter 1989), 1–16. This edited version is included here because the point it makes deserves to receive much wider attention in the context of preventing future genocides.
2. The Bible, Exodus, 17: 8–16; Deuteronomy, 25: 17–19; 1 Samuel, 15: 2–8; 1 Samuel, 30: 1–19.
3. This second difference may even be used as the basis of a new typology: external versus internal genocides. The genocides performed by Nazi Germany and the Soviet Union in occupied territories may appear to be external genocides. However, from the perpetrators' points of view they were not; both perceived these territories as having become part of their own realm as a result of conquest.
4. In July 1940, during World War II, the last unfinished section of the original "Berlin to Bagdad" railroad was finally completed, and through-train service all the way from the Bosporus to Bagdad became a reality (Trumpener 1968: 316).
5. "This Week," *Manchester Guardian Weekly*, vol. 141, no. 25 (December 24, 1989): 6.

6. Roy A. Medvedev tells us that "per capita grain production in 1953 was 19 percent lower than 1913" (1973: 486). See also Antonov-Ovseyenko (1981: 182–90).
7. Recent reports in *Pravda* (Moscow) put the figure at 26 million lives lost.
8. However, Himmler had no patience with humanitarian feelings and is reported to have said: "What does it matter to us? Look away if it makes you sick." Quoted from the Nuremberg trial records, in Borkin (1978: 139). Borkin's title "The Crime and Punishment of I. G. Farben" is somewhat misleading since there was a very great deal of crime and very little punishment.
9. This conclusion is confirmed by Borkin: "in the final tally, I. G. Auschwitz was a miserable failure. Despite the investment of almost 900 million Reichsmark and thousands of lives, only a modest stream of fuel and not a single pound of Buna rubber was ever produced" (1978: 127).
10. See also Haffner (1979: 126): "The extermination of...human beings... impeded the conduct of the war because thousands of SS men, who were fit for active service but who were engaged on this operation, were lacking at the front—all in all the equivalent of several divisions—, because the daily mass transports to the extermination camps, right across Europe, were depriving the fighting forces of an appreciable amount of rolling stock which was in short supply and which was urgently needed for supplies."
11. Engelmann is convinced that "both the United States' possession of atom bombs before the end of the Second World War and the failure to develop nuclear weapons in Hitler's Germany were an inevitable consequence, directly and indirectly, of Nazi 'racial' persecution" (1984: 205). Jungk (1958: 88), expresses the same judgment in a more nuanced way: "Four factors combined to frustrate the construction of a German atom bomb. In the first place the absence of the eminent physicists driven into exile by Hitler proved a severe handicap."
12. Haffner's sarcasm is worth quoting: "what one would not find in the whole of world history is a man who, with an unparalleled and gigantic effort, achieved, as Hitler did, the exact opposite of what he had hoped to achieve" (1979:100).
13. For instance, Mr. Boudhiba, the chairman of the U.N. Sub-Commission on the Prevention of Discrimination and Protection of Minorities, as quoted in Kuper (1981: 171).
14. "In Phnom Penh itself there is no drinking water, no post or telephone, no transport, no registry office, no money, no markets." Jean Pierre Gallois of Agence France Press reporting later, as quoted in Shawcross (1984: 96).

6

Some Antecedents of the Holocaust Denial Literature[1]

Introduction

Geoffrey Barraclough has argued that "the years between 1890, when Bismarck withdrew from the political scene, and 1961, when Kennedy took up office as President of the United States, were a watershed between two ages...it was then that the forces took shape which have molded the contemporary world" (Barraclough 1967: 10). In this perspective, it will be argued here that the roots of the rise of Nazi Germany did not begin with Hitler, but must be looked for much earlier or, as Hannah Arendt wrote in 1951:

> African colonial possessions became the most fertile soil for the flowering of what later was to become the Nazi elite. Here they had seen with their own eyes how peoples could be converted into races and how, simply by taking the initiative in this process, one might push one's own people into the position of the master race. (Arendt 1951: 206)

Since then, a number of authors have debated this proposition; some of them have agreed with it (Bley 1971: 282; Schmitt-Egner 1975; Stoecker 1986; Helbig 1988); and some of them have tried to refute it (Gann and Duignan 1977: xii, 226–29). This debate has become somewhat diffuse because some of these authors have misquoted Hannah Arendt in order to prove or disprove an assertion she never made. Thus, Helmuth Bley talks about the "seeds of totalitarianism" (Bley 1971: 282) while Gann and Duignan find no link between "colonialism and the emergence of fascism" (Gann and Duignan 1977: xii).[2] This kind of misquotation is taken to unusual lengths by Woodruff Smith who accuses Helmut Bley of accepting "Hannah Arendt's notion that colonialism was a precursor of twentieth-century totalitarianism" (Smith

1979: 241)—a statement that she never made, as far as I have been able to ascertain. Ludwig Helbig, without actually mentioning Hannah Arendt, argues that the methods of dealing with people, their legitimization through the ideas of a racist ideology, their grounding in laws and bureaucratic supervision proved to be a prelude to German fascist practices between 1939 and 1945 (Helbig 1988). That these debates are still alive after all these years is shown by Volker Ullrich (in German, 1994) and by Jon Swan (in English, 1991) both of whom affirm not only that genocide occurred in German South West Africa, but also that it had links to the Nazi's rule in Germany.

While Hannah Arendt's statement referred to Germany's "African colonial possessions," I shall limit my discussion to German South West Africa, as did Volker Ullrich and Jon Swan. The history of this colony and the arguments whether or not a genocide occurred there will be reviewed here only in a summary fashion.

The major purpose of this paper is to show that not only was South West Africa a "fertile soil" for the growth of the future Nazi elite, but that it also spawned the rise of a literature that first denied the genocide of the Herero, and later the facticity of the Holocaust.

A Brief History

Over the centuries a few missionaries from several European countries had come to the South West African coast. In the nineteenth century German missionaries became predominant. Since 1842 the German Rhenish Missionary Society had established several settlements. They conducted extensive trade there and even before 1878 this Society had applied several times for annexation of this area by Prussia (Stoecker 1986: 18–19). Already in 1870 they had established the "Rheinische Missions-Handels-AG" in order to finance their relatively important trade, of which the most profitable part was the sale of rifles and ammunition; this had the additional effect of creating close ties to a small circle of native customers (Kamphausen 1977: 20–29). However, the effects of the spiritual activities of the missionaries was negligible, and even their medical efforts could not compete with those of the indigenous witch doctors (Goldblatt 1971: 50–51). In 1879 Dr. Friedrich Fabri, inspector of the Rhine mission for twenty-seven years, a prolific writer in support of German imperialism, and a founder of the "West German Society for Colonization and Export" (1880), (Wertheimer 1971: 63) published a pamphlet "Does Germany Need Colonies?" that helped spark the public discussion of the pros and cons of German colonization (Stoecker 1986: 21).[3] Then, "In 1882 a rather disreputable German trader," F. A. E. Lüderitz of Bremen, tried to establish himself in Angra Pequena, a port on the desolate west coast of Africa (Taylor 1967: 23). He quickly discovered that instead of the instant riches that he had hoped to find he suffered large losses, and he therefore tried to sell out to any interested buyer.[4]

When that buyer turned out to be English, Bismarck in 1884 officially declared that the establishments of Adolf Lüderitz were under the protection of the German Empire (Stoecker 1986; 26–27). Then Lüderitz founded the Company for South West Africa in 1885, but he drowned soon afterwards in 1886 (Smith 1979:54). That company not only lost money, but was also "financially unable to support a government of any kind, to explore the interior, or to control the natives. For this reason, it continually refused to accept the charter conveying sovereign rights, with which Bismarck offered again and again to invest it" (Townsend 1966: 129). These charters are of particular interest because they help to explain the behaviour of German commercial enterprises in the colonies:

> The charter, or *Schutzbrief,* one of the only two which Bismarck succeeded in granting, is interesting as reflecting the plan which he was unable to carry out for all the colonies. It is extremely brief and notable for two characteristics. First, it imposed only one condition upon the company in return for the many privileges received. As if to emphasize the Chancellor's wish that the companies be as independent as possible, the charter conveyed 'all sovereign rights over the territories acquired by the company, jurisdiction over the natives and other inhabitants,' on the one proviso that the company remain German. And, in the second place, it omitted to enumerate many obligations common to the charters granted by other nations during the same period, such as the prohibition of trade monopoly, which even the English charters of the nineteenth century contained; the prohibition of slavery and sale of liquor; the duty of promoting the welfare of the natives, and the duty of building roads and harbors. These omissions may have been due to haste, to design, or to inexperience; but whatever their cause, they render the author, the Chancellor, partially responsible for the flagrant misgovernment and many abuses of which the companies were guilty. (Townsend 1966: 133–34)

In 1885 Dr. Heinrich Göring was sent out to German South West Africa as *Reichskommissar* (governor) and made protection agreements with those chiefs who could be persuaded to accept the protection of the German Emperor (Wellington 1967: 169): "Dr. Goering, (had) to take charge of the interior, since the company was only pretending to function on the coast.... the company grew ever weaker.... Dr. Goering then extended his imperial sway over the entire protectorate, and the company's political role ceased, never to revive" (Townsend 1966: 129–30).

Dr. Göring's term lasted five years and is of interest here mainly because his more famous son Hermann was Hitler's *Reichsmarshall* and head of the *Luftwaffe*. Dr. Göring, a widower with five children, had made a young woman pregnant and seems to have been quite content to leave Germany for a while. He stopped in London to get married before taking up his post in South West Africa. Upon the termination of that assignment his career deteriorated to the point where he accepted

an invitation from a castle-owning millionaire whose acquaintance the Görings had made in South West Africa and who was godfather to the Görings' second son, Hermann, to come live, rent-free, in a small castle near Nuremberg; the generous friend's undisguised use of Frau Göring as his mistress for fifteen years, during which time the adoring Hermann absorbed the godfather's passion for pseudo-medieval pomp and circumstance, and the former *Reichskommissar* consoled himself with drink, dying in 1913, one year before the outbreak of World War I and two years before the protectorate was wrested from the Germans by the Union of South Africa, in one stroke annulling everything he and his successors had accomplished, except for the killing and enslavement of whole tribes of people. (Swan 1991: 40)

A more direct link to the Nazi elite is found in the career of the scientist Eugen Fischer who in 1908 collected materials in South West Africa for his studies of the "Rehoboth Basters" (persons of mixed blood, born mainly of unions between Boer men and Hottentot women). In 1927 he was named director of the Kaiser-Wilhelm-Institute for Anthropology, Human Genetics, and Eugenics, and in 1933 he became rector of the University of Berlin. He represents the continuity between the Kaiser's colonial policy and National Socialist racial policy (Ullrich 1994). Fischer cited the Rehoboth Basters as evidence of the potentially harmful results of "hybridization" and the need to develop "a practical eugenics—a race hygiene." In 1913 he published his results in the book *The Bastards of Rehoboth and the Problem of Miscegenation in Man* in which he wrote that "free competition would lead to their decline and destruction" (Müller-Hill 1988: 8). In 1923 Hitler read the textbook by E. Baur, E. Fischer, and F. Lenz, *Menschliche Erblichkeitslehre und Rassenhygiene* (The Principles of Human Heredity and Race-Hygiene) while imprisoned in Landsberg, and later included racial ideas from that textbook in his own book, *Mein Kampf* (My Struggle). In that same text one finds the statement that "The question of the quality of our hereditary endowment is a hundred times more important than the dispute over capitalism or socialism" (as quoted in Müller-Hill 1988: 8–9).

The local link to Nazi philosophy was the theoretician Paul Rohrbach who was the head of the South West Africa Settlement Commission. He was the author of *German World Politics,* published in 1912 (English translation, 1915), where he developed a rationale for the extermination or expulsion of the native inhabitants of the colonies to make room for the white race (Swan 1991: 54–55). There he also formulated the racial concepts that formed the basis for the enslavement of the natives and that later became part of the plans for the conquest of the people of Eastern Europe (Ullrich 1994). Henning Melber is even more specific: he says that Rohrbach's writings became after 1933 part of the programmatic documentation of the Nazi party (Melber 1992: 101).

Some Domestic Sources of German Racism

These developments did not take place in a vacuum. The racial theories of Gobineau and Chamberlain were widely read and discussed in intellectual circles in Western Europe. A great variety of organizations formed in several countries by people with social, economic, or political concerns dealing with colonization, nationalism, and racism. The newly united Germany, being a latecomer to such concerns with nationhood and empire, experienced these debates with the added virulence of those trying to catch up. One of the leaders in these debates was one of the smaller organizations that made up for its lack of size with an extraordinary amount of activity on a wide variety of topics: the Pan-German League: "The captain of the Pan-German ship was Dr. Ernst Hasse...in 1885, he became a *Privatdozent* at the University of Leipzig and in 1886, *Ausserordentlicher Professor,* teaching statistics until 1888, when he instituted a course on colonial politics, the first regular university course on the subject in Germany" (Wertheimer 1971: 44). How widespread these concerns were among the intellectually active sectors of the population can be seen in the official *Handbuch des all-deutschen Verbandes* (Handbook of the Pan-German League) for 1914 which published a list of German associations and societies that contains eighty-four names (Wertheimer 1971: 237–39). They were not all equally active, but collectively they represented a considerable pressure group when the occasion arose. There exists a considerable literature on the activities of these organizations and their efforts to promote colonialism, nationalism, and racism. The Pan-German League in particular has been much written about because of its extreme and hyperactive presentation of the issues that it included in its platform. Among these was a strong anti-Semitic bias (Wertheimer 1971: 100)[5] and the advocacy of strong measures for the suppression of the Herero in South West Africa (Wertheimer 1971: 168). Wertheimer, in a careful analysis of surviving data, also shows to what extent the membership was made up of educated middle and upper occupational groups. In 1901, for instance, 85 percent of the membership consisted of academics, businessmen, and members of the liberal professions (Wertheimer 1971: 65).[6] Or, as Roger Chickering pointed out, "No feature of a German community more affected the vitality and shaped the character of a chapter of the Pan-German-League than did the presence of an institution of higher learning" (Chickering 1984: 145). It becomes clear that these groups were the targets of proselytizing theories directed at them by political parties and dedicated organizations through books, pamphlets, lectures, and meetings. By contrast, there exists very little research on how racist and colonial theories spread among those who did not read the theorists or joined these organizations.

Beginning with the enlightenment, Central and West Europeans had developed an increasing curiosity about the worlds outside their own countries. They became thus open to foreign influences that enriched their perceptions of themselves and humanity. This is an enormous topic that is beyond the scope of this chapter. Suffice it to point to the almost faddish penetration of Europe by Chinese and Japanese influences at that time. For many people this opening up of the world was brought home to them by the showing of exotic peoples at country fairs and exhibitions. The opportunity to see exotic people from different parts of the world, often in their realistically recreated villages, was a tremendous success that attracted huge crowds. A couple of illustrations will suffice: at the large Panama-Pacific Exposition in San Francisco in 1915:

> Apart from their national pavilions, many countries had also constructed native village settings.... There were vendors and dancing girls from 'The Streets of Cairo'; Igorrots from the Phillipines; Eskimos from northern Canada; Japanese Aborigines; Workmen from China; even 1,000 natives imported to give the massive eleven-acre Jerusalem concession its character. But most interesting of all was the living ethnological exhibit in the

Hall of Anthropology which contained everything from giants from Patagonia to pygmies from Africa. In fact between 15,000 and 20,000 people actually lived on the site during the exhibition. The health of these 'people of all climes and of varying degrees of civilization from savage to enlightened' had been of some concern to the organizers but the strict enforcement of health regulations stopped any contagious diseases gaining a foothold. (Allwood 1977: 114)

Similarly, the French exhibition of 1931 included a "North African village complete in every detail" (Allwood 1977: 138). At the same time, the traders who provided zoological gardens with animals experienced a slump during which they lost money. Noting the success of exhibiting people, they added people to their enterprise (Staehelin 1993: 30–32). Between the 1870s and 1930s it became commonplace for parents to take their children to the local zoo where they could admire real-life elephants, lions, tigers, and native tribes from several continents—all from a safe distance behind fences. Staehelin was able to trace twenty-two such exhibitions in the zoo in Basel, Switzerland between 1879–1935; most of these had several engagements before and after Basel in other European countries before returning to their homes (Staehelin 1993: 156–58). However, this fashion of classing human beings with animals was not limited to Europe. In 1906 the New York Zoological Park "exhibited a human pygmy in an enclosure in the monkey house" (Horowitz 1975).

A rather pathetic revival occurred during the Nazi regime under the aegis of the colonial section of the Foreign Office:

among other things it shielded from the Party's race fanatics a number of pathetic Africans, who, as former members of the German colonial military forces, had been exiled from their homelands. In order to enable them to make a living, the Foreign Office organized and subsidized a travelling "Africa Show," which went through various vicissitudes before the Party forbade all non-Aryans to appear as entertainers. Eventually, these loyal African subjects were supported by a dole which the Foreign Office arranged to have paid to them by the Kolonialkriegerbank. (Schmokel 1964: 43–44)

For about sixty years children absorbed this kind of unprogrammed race education with their entertainment. In a quite homogeneous society like Germany, where these children were most unlikely to ever encounter non-Germans in any other setting, these experiences must have formed a solid background for their adult attitudes towards other peoples.[7] However, unlike in the case of the educated classes, the for-

mation of these attitudes was not the outcome of deliberate proselytizing; rather it was the fortuitous byproduct of the search for profits by
animal impresarios and of the declining attendance that was producing
financial difficulties for zoological gardens.

The extent to which such attitudes could become generalized toward any stranger is illustrated in South West Africa by German hostility to non-Germans that was not limited to indigenous Africans. After
the "Herero Wars,"

> the *Luderitzbuchter Zeitung* asserted that "the only gratifying feature in
> the census return is the fact of the large decrease in the number of foreign-
> ers in our midst." Theoretically the German is friendly towards the Boer,
> colonially and commercially he regards him as an intrusive and competi-
> tive foreigner, while personally he cannot forgive him for the services he
> rendered the Fatherland in the subjection of the tribes from 1904 to 1908.
> "But for the assistance of British and Dutch Afrikanders," writes the Spe-
> cial Commissioner of the *Transvaal Chronicle* of some two years ago, "it
> is doubtful whether the Herero War would have been settled even in the
> long span of four years. There are Boers in the country today who have
> rendered splendid services to the Germans, but who have been treated
> shamefully ever since, and are now fast leaving the country.... Feeling
> between German and Boer is very strained. They do not understand each
> other. The German soldier envies those of another nationality who wear
> the Kaiser's medals for conspicuous bravery and deeds of valour on the
> battlefield, and to-day many an Afrikander wears the black and white rib-
> bon—a coveted order. The shooting of Marengo, on September 20th, 1907,
> by Major Elliott, of the C.M.R.— a corps, by the way, into which so many
> Germans would like to get—was another event which fanned the jealousy
> of the German officials. They had been on the track of Marengo for months.
> Major Elliott settled the matter in a couple of hours, and the coveted 'Kai-
> ser Medalle' went to him instead" (Calvert 1969: 31–32).

The detailed history of German colonial administration and its application as it occurred in South West Africa can not be dealt with in
this short paper. However, Bridgman's "Bibliographic Essay" provides
a useful guide to the literature on that history (Bridgman 1981: 175–
77). Suffice it to say that a series of conflicts between Germans and
Hereros eventually escalated in 1904 into what the German government considered its first major war since 1870. The German troops,
under the command of General von Trotha, had great difficulty in dealing with the Herero and Nama resistance. This so-called Herero war
lasted three years. Because the Germans victimized prisoners, women,
and children, it qualifies as the first genocide of the twentieth century.
For the details of these Herero wars, the major engagement at Waterberg,

the actions of German General von Trotha, their genocidal aspects, the racist legislation that followed them and applied to all of the indigenous peoples, the reader is referred to Bley (1971, 1967), Drechsler (1980), Katjavivi (1988), Stoecker (1986), Townsend (1966), or Wellington (1967). These sources will provide an entry into a vast literature. Thus, Spohr's 1969 bibliography of German publications, which did not include archival sources, covered 3,423 entries (Spohr 1968).

Robert Cornevin provides a pithy, though biased, summary of the trends in the literature on the German colonies in Africa. He argues that the general works on German Africa

> may be divided into two main categories according to their date of publication. Those published before 1914 are almost all by German authors and have essentially a documentary and didactic character. They aim at instructing the metropolitan country about the economic importance of these colonies, so rapidly acquired during the course of 1884 and 1885. Those published after 1918 are written by Germans, English, French, Americans and Belgians who are all more or less biased and pass moral judgements on German colonization in Africa. From 1945 onward the communist writers of East Germany come to confirm, in works written from the archives in Potsdam, the charges against German colonialism published between the two wars by English and French authors, and to utter a cry of alarm against the neo-colonialism of West Germany. (Cornevin 1969: 223)

We shall ignore here the work that was published before 1914 because the focus of this paper is on the revisionist denial literature that is still finding an audience to the present day.

Denials after World War I

As a result of losing the war Germany also lost all of her colonies. In the terse summary by Gann and Duignan:

> The war of bullets was followed by a war of books. German nationalists defended their country's record and levelled accusations against their former enemies, making a formidable though unintentional contribution to the critique of imperialism in general. (Gann and Duignan 1977: 223)

The first shot in this war of books was a report published by the British government that became known as the "Blue Book" (Union of South Africa 1918) which produced evidence of German abuses that had not been available until the German power in South West Africa was overthrown by the South African invasion of 1915. It was only then "that official records were examined and the Natives were encouraged to speak freely of their experiences" (Wellington 1967: 231). The German authorities replied with a "White Book" published in 1919 that accused the "Blue Book" of being propaganda, full of falsehoods, and mainly designed to prevent the return of her colonies to Germany. It refuted what became known as Germany's "colonial guilt" by citing events in British colonial history arguing that Germany did nothing that was not also done by the other colonial powers in Africa (Wellington 1967: 236–37). In defense of the "Blue Book" Wellington argued that,

> the fact remains that large parts of the 'Blue Book' are straightforward translations from German authors and from German official records which were captured in 1915 and were available for anyone's inspection. Provided the translations are correct and there has apparently been no suggestion that they were inaccurate such statements can certainly not be classed as tendentious and lying. (Wellington 1967: 231)

> the 'White Book' spotlights the worst events in British colonial history, alleging that they are as culpable as anything done by the Germans in South West Africa...but when England's treatment of the African Boers is likened to the German treatment of the Natives of South West Africa the accusation becomes somewhat absurd in view of the fact that the Report was authorized by the two Boer leaders who had fought with England in the war against Germany and who urged at the Peace Conference the confiscation of South West Africa. (Wellington 1967: 236–37)

These two books have set the stage for a debate that is still being conducted both inside and outside of Germany. The denial literature is based on disagreements about the facts, refutations of Germany's "colonial guilt," and assertions of Germany's right to her colonies (lately rephrased as the right to play a role in the third world). The historical literature is based on additional archival documentation concerning the contested events and explorations of the linkages between German colonial history and the rise of Nazism.

The "Blue Book" and the "White Book" were produced by their respective governments and represented their respective positions. However, the bulk of revisionist or denial literature is produced by individual authors. Since most twentieth-century perpetrator governments are deniers, there is no disagreement between them and the individual authors. In fact, they often cooperated and reinforced each other. The major exception is the West German post-World War II government which has admitted the reality of the Holocaust.

An early broadside in defense of German colonialism was published in English by Dr. Heinrich Schnee. He wrote a book to counteract the accusation of Germany's "colonial guilt" that, he argues, was spread by the Allied powers in order to deprive Germany of her colonies after World War I (Schnee 1926). According to a "Biographical Note," Schnee already as a young man sought an education preparing him for the colonial service, including learning the "Suaheli" language (Schnee 1926: 47–48). He rose through the ranks, became director of the Imperial Colonial Office in 1911 and was governor of German East Africa in 1912–1919. His book demonstrated that German administration compared favorably with that of other colonial powers, how individual excesses had also occurred in other colonies but had been promptly punished in the German ones, and how early mistakes were due to a lack of experience and were equally present in other new colonial powers. He ended by stating that "Germany claims the opportunity and the right to take her part again permanently in the civilizing mission of the white races" (Schnee 1926: 176). The author, whose argument was supported in a lengthy introduction by W.H. Dawson,[8] dealt quite briefly with an accusation of "three great rebellions, which were coupled with heavy loss of life to the natives.... These were the Arab revolt in German East Africa in 1888, the Maji-Maji revolt in 1905, and the Herero rebellion in German South-West Africa in 1904" (Schnee 1926: 115–16). It is worth quoting in some detail how this author dealt with the fate of the Hereros:

> In relation to the third revolt, that of the Hereros in German South-West Africa, this was occasioned through the gradual penetration of the white settlers, in whom the natives saw a menace to their continued possession of the land. In this respect it resembled the revolts with which white settlers had had to contend in North America, in Australia, and in South Africa. The Herero revolt began with a massacre of all German settlers who happened to fall into the hands of the rebels. The Herero developed unexpected powers of resistance, so that the despatch of considerable bodies of troops from Germany became necessary. They were defeated only after long and wearisome fighting, and it is true that a part of them fled into the sandy wastes, where they died of thirst.
>
> The British Blue Book misrepresents the facts to such a degree as to make it appear that the Herero tribes had been persistently and cruelly oppressed by the German colonists and that the crushing of the rebellion had been a mere war of extermination. These charges have been completely refuted by the before-mentioned German White book, which, nevertheless, does not attempt to conceal the fact that at times military methods were adopted in combating the revolt *which were not sanctioned by the*

German Government and were formally repudiated. These measures may be explained, if not excused, by the bitterness occasioned by the massacre of the German settlers. (Schnee 1926: 117)

As to the "repudiation" by the German government, the reader need only be reminded that it was this government that sent in General von Trotha whose methods for dealing with native uprisings in China and in German East Africa had earned him a well-known reputation.

The Hitler Period

Germany's attitudes to colonies and their associated denials seem to have been quite unaffected by changes in government. The indoctrination of schoolchildren which had been continuous since the time of Imperial Germany and through the Weimar Republic was intensified during the Hitler period. Teachers were to educate their pupils in the colonial spirit, to make a special point of refuting the "myth of Germany's colonial guilt," and to glorify Germany's "colonial pioneers" (Ballhaus 1986: 348).

The most popular novel of the period was published by Hans Grimm (1875–1959), who between 1897 and 1928 had been a port agent of the Ost-Afrika-Line in Africa (Grimm 1960: 5, 333). His publishing success led him to become a journalist after his return to Germany. His novel, *Volk ohne Raum* (People without Space), first published in 1926, advocated finding *Lebensraum* in the colonies rather than in Eastern Europe. The book became an influential bestseller and by 1935 it had sold 315,000 copies (Smith 1986: 224–25). However, the slogan "Volk ohne Raum" was first coined by Foreign Minister Gustav Stresemann during an address at the Berlin Colonial Week and Exhibition held from 30 March to 8 April 1925 (Rüger 1986: 315).

The German Colonial Society, too, had been established long before Hitler came to power to develop plans that could be implemented as soon as the German army reoccupied its former colonies:

In 1932, the Nazi Party formally made colonial demands part of its platform when Marshall Goering, whose father had been the first Governor of South West Africa, opened a National Socialist colonial exhibition at Frankfurt.... By 1934 the Society was a full-blown department of the Nazi Government. Hitler appointed as its chief General Franz Ritter von Epp.... He had helped to smash the Herero native rebellion in South West Africa.... Von Epp injected new life into the colonial movement. With Nazi Party funds, he organized nearly 7,000 local groups, enrolled more than 1,000,000 members.... Two German colonial schools were revived and several more were established. (James 1943: 321–22)[9]

However, such colonial schools had never quite disappeared in Germany, making it the only country that continued training colonial administrators even when it had no colonies.[10]

Other veterans from the colonial past, in addition to von Epp and Heinrich Schnee, who joined the Nazi party and held leading positions under Hitler, especially in the colonial movement, were: General Eduard von Liebert, former governor of German East Africa; Duke Adolph Friedrich zu Mecklenburg; Friederich von Lindequist; and Theodor Seitz, a former governor of German South West Africa, among others (Ballhaus 1986: 342).

Thus, during the 1930s the denial literature received a strong boost from Hitler's plans for world domination; the ground for these plans was quietly being prepared through the sponsorship of Nazi activities in its former colonies (Bennett 1939). For instance, Johannsen and Kraft in 1937 published a book in English in order not only to deny the accusations of Germany's "colonial guilt," but also to present arguments why its former colonies should be returned to Germany (Johannsen and Kraft 1937). In 1936 Dr. Paul Leutwein, the son of the major Theodor Leutwein who had succeeded Dr. Göring as governor, wrote a book containing six biographies of Cecil Rhodes, Karl Peters, Theodor Leutwein, Lettow-Vorbeck, Menelik, and Haile Selassie. He not only celebrated his father's career, but in the introduction also emphasized Germany's right to her colonies, refuted the lie of "colonial guilt," and advocated the timeliness of regaining her colonies peacefully through strong politics (Leutwein 1936). Paul Leutwein had followed his father to South West Africa in 1903 and had dedicated himself to colonial policy ever since (Leutwein 1936: 110). Parenthetically it is worth noting that Theodor Leutwein was a quite extraordinary character whom Hugh Ridley described as "one of the most fascinating political technocrats of nineteenth-century Germany. He had a cold, logical mind, trained and sophisticated, self-assured but not over-confident, versed in Hegel and Moltke, 'silent in seven languages', and yet with an amazing store of political naïvety" (Bley 1971: xiii–xiv). After the end of the Herero Wars he recorded: "At a cost of several hundred millions of marks and several thousand German soldiers, of the three economic assets of the colony, mining, farming, and native labour, we have destroyed the second entirely and two-thirds of the third" (Wellington 1967: 213).

Denials since World War II

The result of World War II was that Germany was divided into two countries. The new boundary was the result of the relative positions of the victorious armies at the end of the war and of the negotiations between the Allies. This newly created boundary between the two Germanies did not imply differences in their respective populations, nor did it permit mass migration. Nevertheless, West Germany continued to emphasize its achievements in its former colonies, to deny that there had been a genocide, and to stress its destiny to spread its civilizing influence to the less developed peoples of the third world. At the same time, East Germany convinced itself, and tried to convince the rest of the world, that its citizens were anti-Nazis and anti-colonialists, while all the Nazi imperialists were in West Germany. Equally paradoxical, West Germany acknowledged German responsibility for the Holocaust, while East Germany rejected responsibility for any part of it. This is the stuff of which national myths are created!

While the hope of regaining her former colonies had to be abandoned in this post-colonial age, West German pride in the achievements of her colonial administration and in her capacity to spread its culture into the third world remained unabated. These affirmations of German successes on the colonial scene and the denials of "German colonial guilt" were published and widely supported in West Germany.

> After 1965 the situation was such that a journalist who attacked the "Koloniallegende" (the positive legend of Germany's achievements in the colonies) on television received death threats, while someone who, while abroad, pointed out the parallels between the genocide of the Hereros and that of the Jews and the Poles had to cope with censorship threats by the foreign office. (translated by the author. Bley 1977: 2–5)

There is an additional irony in the fact that the reunited Germany has made the denial of the Holocaust a criminal offence, while the denial of the genocide in South West Africa seems to remain official policy.

One of the most elaborate denials was published in German in 1975 by Gerd Sudbolt, who had lived in South West Africa for several years and been active on the "Allgemeinen Zeitung" in Windhoek (Sudholt 1975). As the two Germanies were still separate countries at that time, and since the communist government of East Germany had no interest in rescuing the reputation of German imperialism, Sudbolt was denied access to the Archiv des Reichskolonialamtes in Potsdam where

Drechsler had done the work that so undermined that reputation (Drechsler 1980).[11] Ten years later Karla Poewe published her denial in English, substantially repeating Sudbolt's arguments (Poewe 1985). His main case rested on his claim that the famous battle at Waterberg, where the Hereros broke out of a German encirclement into the desert, was in reality a major failure for the German general. However, since this was the first war fought by Wilhelmine Germany, it had to be dressed up as a victory that could be celebrated at home. Von Trotha's use of the word *Vernichtung* (extermination) in his battle orders, he claimed, had been widely misinterpreted since it simply meant an order to break the Hereros' military ability to resist. He further tried to disprove that this was a genocide by citing the preparation of camps capable of housing 8,000 prisoners of war. Further, the number of Hereros gathered at Waterberg must have been vastly exaggerated because there simply was not enough water available there for them and their cattle; therefore the number of killed must also have been exaggerated. With respect to von Trotha's so-called "extermination order," he argued that it was issued eight weeks after the battle at Waterberg, that it was translated into the Herero language, given to prisoners before their release, and that its purpose was to discourage the attacks by small guerilla bands that had been inflicting serious losses on German troops (Sudbolt 1975: 181–89). These arguments are repeated point by point by Poewe (1985: 60–65).

However, further publications kept appearing that documented the already well-established history of Germany's maladministration of her colonies. Many of these were based on the government archives that had been opened in Potsdam. The most important of these are the several publication by Helmut Bley, Helmuth Stoecker, and Henning Melber.

The most recent denials have been published by Gunter Spraul (1988: 713–39) and Brigitte Lau (1989: 4–5, 8).[12] The latter seems a most unlikely source since she is the chief archivist of the National Archives of Namibia. Although her denial appeared in a quite obscure source, it generated a heated exchange in the London *Southern African Review of Books*. The first reply was by Randolph Vigne, the honorary secretary of the Namibia Support Committee in London, who accused Lau's arguments of being both unsound and unoriginal because they could all be found in Sudbolt, Poewe, and Spraul (Vigne 1990: 31). Lau replied by questioning the number of victims involved, emphasizing the German casualties, and arguing, *inter alia*, that the term "genocide" is not applicable in this case (Lau 1990: 31). This elicited a further reply by Vigne and an additional letter from Henning Melber who wrote from Kassel University in West Germany to reject any argument based on the numbers. Lau terminated the exchange with a brief note complaining about "editorial distortion of its substance by deletion and substitution" of a single word (Vigne et al. 1990: 23).

The level to which this debate has sunk may be indicated thus: Lau accused Vigne of citing numbers from Drechsler that, she wrote, occurred neither in Drechsler nor anywhere else; whereupon Vigne responded by citing the exact page references where Drechsler discussed his estimates of the losses suffered by the Herero and the Nama.

At this point, there is little to be added to a quote from General S. L. A. Marshall who said: "Many years ago in the course of my work as a soldier and writer, I discovered pretty much on my own that the one thing more difficult to refute than a final truth is an utter absurdity" (Rhoodie 1967: preface). Amen.

Conclusion

Recent publications have provided supporting data for Hannah Arendt's assertion about the origins of the Nazi elite. They have also provided additional evidence for the importance of historical and comparative analysis. The major oversight in these recent studies is that they did not also include data on the lively and voluminous denial literature that was generated by German colonialism in general and by the genocide of the Herero in particular. That this denial literature still flourishes so long after the event, illustrates not only how memories can be manipulated, but also the crucial role such memories play in shaping national identities—as well as being shaped by them. In the case of German nationalism, a central component of these memories consists of the roots of racism and their role in shaping the myths of national identity. That some of these roots have been repressed from conscious memory adds to the challenges that face researchers in this area. In fact, one of the things that makes the study of nationalism so fascinating is that the memories that underlie a national identity consist both of those that continue to be celebrated, as well as of those that have been suppressed or repressed.

Notes

1. An earlier version of this paper was presented at the XXXII Congress of the International Institute of Sociology on July 3–7, 1995 in Trieste, Italy.

A further revision was published as "Before the Holocaust Deniers" in *Society,* vol. 33, no. 2 (January/February 1996): 31–38.

2. However, on 226–27 they write that, "Arendt's interpretation has some merit."

3. Hillebrecht points out that the second largest collection of materials on South West Africa—after the governmental archives in Potsdam—is the Archiv der Vereinigten Evangelischen Mission in Wuppertal (the archive of the United Evangelical Mission in Wuppertal) which includes the materials of the Rhenish Mission (see: Melber, et al., eds., 1984: 187–88).

4. On the rather byzantine relations between several companies that sought to exploit economic resources in South West Africa and the economic and diplomatic relations between Germany, Great Britain, Portugal and South Africa, see Voeltz (1988).

5. "the Pan-German League continued to play an active role in the politics of the Weimar republic" where its platform presaged the practices of Nazi Germany (see Chickering 1984: 3).

6. See 65–72 for additional details on membership data.

7. The apparent naiveté of Germans interested in the educational functions of zoological gardens is quite amazing. In 1953 appeared a book on the zoo in Leipzig that was commissioned by the department of publuc education of the city of Leipzig. In that volume, Alfred Lehmann, "Schaustellungen im Leipziger Zoo" (pp.72–92), stresses the educational functions of exhibiting peoples, how these exhibits enlarged the spectators' view of the world without having to travel, and how this living education in geography and ethnology gave children an advantage in their school work (73). Karl Max Schneider, the director of the zoo, in his paper "Vom Werden und Wandel des Leipziger Zoo's in rund 70 Jahren." (pp. 3–64) does raise the question of whether such exhibitions of peoples will recur in the future. He suggests that this depends on the spirit in which it will happen. But he is quite sure that it will not happen if these exotic peoples are again made into objects to be stared at together with the animals (38) (Schneider 1953).

8. This is the same W. H. Dawson who at the request of the Foreign Office wrote *German Colonization* for use at the Peace Conference. He continued to support the justice of Germany's cause into the Nazi period. See his letter to the editor of *The Times* (November 4, 1936) which is reprinted as pp. 95–96 in Johannsen and Kraft (1937). This small book deals only with the demographic and economic effects of Germany's loss of her colonies after World War I. Dawson, in the above-cited letter, refers to many tributes of praise and admiration for Germany's colonial work, and then continues: "In the early years mistakes were made, excesses committed, and in one case a rebellion was quelled by drastic measures. But was it different with any other Colonial Power, and was the suppression of the Hereros of South-West Africa by the Germans harsher than the suppression of the Matabele and Mashonas?"

9. For additional details, see chapter 24 "Axis Plans for Africa."

10. "The Kolonialschule at Witzenhausen, which trained young men for various positions in colonial and overseas areas and had its origin in the 1890s, was supported throughout the Weimar and Nazi periods by Reich funds, either through the Foreign Office or the Ministry of the Interior. It remained, however, a private institution and still exists, under a different name, at this time. The Koloniale Frauenschule at Rendsburg, on the other hand, was founded in 1926 under the joint aegis of the Reich Ministries of the Interior and of Education and was supported entirely by these agencies" (Schmokel 1964: 44–45).

11. This is the major indictment of German colonial policy, based on access to the archives in Potsdam, that has been used by a number of writers as a source of previously unavailable data.

12. Lau published in *Migabus*, a publication that was quite hard to trace because only two numbers of *Migabus* were published in Windhoek by an independent editorial collective (personal communication).

7

On Jewish Resistance:
An Essay on Perceptions[1]

Introduction

During the late 1950s, when I was a graduate student in sociology, Everett Hughes was the guru of Canadian students at the University of Chicago. He not only provided us with a welcoming atmosphere, but also with a quite unique perspective on sociological research and analysis. Two features of that perspective have stayed with me ever since and have shaped my own thinking to a considerable extent. The first one was his insight that a great deal might be learned by comparing groups that at first blush seem to have nothing in common. The second one was his urging us to look for what is not there. It was this second injunction that made me wonder why there was so little attention being paid in studies of the Holocaust to the resistance of the victims? This question is even more puzzling when considering the volume of literature devoted to Jewish resistance.

My original intent was to add to this paper an exhaustive bibliography of relevant works in English. This language restriction seemed essential to making this project manageable. I was already aware of the fact that most of the relevant literature is published in other languages and is much more voluminous than the part available in English. The attached references will indicate that I actually started on this task. Fortunately, I soon stumbled on to the "Bibliography on Holocaust Literature" by Edelheit and Edelheit (1986) which lists over 9,000 items, all in English and organized into subject categories. The category labeled "resistance" contains 1,020 items. Two supplements, published in 1990 and 1993 respectively, more than double the total number of citations and increase those listed under "resistance" by an additional 490 items. I recommend their perusal to all who are under the impression that there is little literature on Jewish resistance.

This frustration with the relative absence of awareness of Jewish resistance is not confined to the English-speaking world. Hermann Langbein, writing in German, shares this perception and contributes a very detailed account of resistance actions in order to show that they are deserving of our attention (1980: 8). Among other details, he gives the known number of escapees from Auschwitz by year of occurrence; his total is 647 of whom 270 were caught, however (Langbein 1980: 274). This information should be particularly impressive to those who were under the impression that escape from Auschwitz was impossible. He adds a bibliography with over 400 entries, mostly in German, which does not seem to have impressed a wide readership in that language. The only country where such awareness seems to be widespread is Israel.

In addition, it seems that Jewish resistance has been relegated to footnote status in many histories of the Holocaust. Such footnote treatment has been sometimes positive and sometimes negative. But in either case such treatment has undoubtedly contributed both to the general ignorance about Jewish resistance and to its misinterpretation.

This assessment agrees with the findings of Glickman and Bardikoff that resistance is all but ignored in the treatment of the Holocaust in history and social science textbooks (1982: 23–24). Even in university courses dealing explicitly with some aspect of the Holocaust only about one half seem to give prominence to resistance. Shimoni (1991) has collected the course outlines of twenty-six courses taught in seven countries. Even though Israel is overrepresented in his sample of countries, there is no mention of resistance in thirteen of these course outlines. At the extreme of nontreatment are, of course, authors like Jørgen Hæstrup who has managed to write a "complete history" of European resistance movements without so much as mentioning even the Warsaw ghetto uprising (1981).

Such treatment stands in marked contrast to Henri Michel's assessment that "Jewish resistance wrote one more magnificent page of history to prove the fighting qualities of the Jewish race and its will to live" (1972: 180).

Jewish Resistance to Nazi Victimization

The German Jews were the first victims and they were faced by a situation that nobody could have predicted. They were also living in a state where the possession of arms was a crime and where even going into hiding was not a realistic possibility, partly because in such a densely populated country there are few places to hide, and partly because the law specified that everyone had to report their address to the police, and changing one's address without notifying the police was in itself already a crime. Under these circumstances the only kind of resistance possible was emigration which was limited by the scarcity of countries that were willing to accept an adequate number of Jewish immigrants.

In spite of such difficulties, there have been instances of Jewish resistance in Germany. Perhaps one of the most dramatic was the successful effort of large numbers of Jews to hide and to survive in Berlin. They managed to do this in spite of Goebbels' declaration of 10 June 1943 that Berlin was now *judenrein* (cleaned of Jews) (Benz 1988: 753).

While Jews were involved in resistance activities in all countries under Nazi influence, they were normally members of the national resistance organizations of their home country. There were minor exceptions to this, as for instance in occupied Paris and in Berlin. The major exception occurred in Poland where widespread anti-Semitism prevented such integration, except on a quite minor scale. The result was that Jewish resistance in Poland differed from other resistance movements in several important respects: it received no support from its national government, nor from their allies; it had to rely on itself, with only minor exceptions; and it often had to defend itself against non-Jewish resistance movements. In addition to the serious difficulties that these conditions created, it also had to face a language problem of major proportions. Many Polish Jews did not speak a fluent Polish that would have allowed them to either pass undercover as Poles or to collaborate with the Polish underground. In addition, Jews from all Nazi-occupied countries were being sent to ghettos and concentration camps in Poland. To the extent that many of these Jews were Jewish only by the definitions of the Nuremberg racial laws, or were secular assimilated Jews who spoke neither Yiddish nor Hebrew, they often had no means of communicating with their fellow Jews, or with the Polish population, or perhaps even with their Nazi captors.

In spite of handicaps that no other resistance movement had to face, Jewish resistance in Poland achieved many successes and was a thorn in the side of the German authorities. In addition to the Warsaw ghetto uprising, some resistance activities took place in almost one hundred ghettos (Bauer 1989a: 133) and most concentration camps, as well as in the forests of eastern Poland (see Kowalski 1985, Krakowski 1984, and Suhl 1975, among many others). These activities ranged from the destruction of killing facilities in several camps, to the smuggling out of information to the Allies, to the disruption of railway lines, to the maintaining of contacts between resistance groups in different parts of Poland, to the forging of papers and helping escapees and to the maintenance of cultural, religious, and social activities.

But one of the greatest successes is probably the least known. The purpose of concentrating the Jews in ghettos seems to have been to control their access to food and to starve them (de Castro 1977: 424). The rations allotted to the Jews in Warsaw, for example, had an official caloric value of 220 (Bauer 1989b: 247). If the Jews had lived only on these rations they would not have survived long. But they quickly developed gardening and smuggling operations as well as methods of producing artificial food stuffs that supplemented these starvation rations. The death rate from starvation remained enormous and accounted for more victims than either the firing squads or the gas chambers (de Castro 1977: 424). But, thanks to the gardeners and smugglers, many Jews managed to survive much longer than expected. As a result the Germans were forced to change their plans; they had to devote significant resources to the transportation of the Jews to specially built killing camps.

The wide range of resistance activities need not be expanded on here because they are well-documented in a large and growing literature. What remains a puzzle is why this literature has remained largely unknown, even to some people with a serious interest in the history of the Holocaust:

> the world knows little or nothing about the other side of the Holocaust picture: Jewish resistance—how the Jews struck back at their tormentors. The epic Warsaw Ghetto uprising is famous, but it is not generally known that in practically every ghetto and in every labor and concentration camp there existed a Jewish underground organization that kept up the prisoners' morale, reduced their physical sufferings, committed acts of sabotage, organized escapes, collected arms, planned revolts, and, in many instances, carried them out." (Suhl 1967: 1)

This was written thirty years ago, and it seems just as true today.

The Warsaw Ghetto Uprising

The Warsaw ghetto uprising demands our special attention because it is the one instance of armed Jewish resistance that is widely known, and because it has generated a very large body of literature. That lit-

erature illustrates many of the biases that have minimized and deval-
ued Jewish resistance and partisan activities. It is therefore instructive
to take a closer look at that literature.

The Warsaw ghetto uprising started on 19 April 1943 in response to
the German order to liquidate the entire ghetto in three days. The ensu-
ing struggle has been widely celebrated and memorialized. These events
have been well-documented from several perspectives. From the Jewish side we have several ghetto accounts as well as those from the
Jewish National Committee; from the German side we have the official Stroop report by the commander of the German forces that were
ordered to subdue the uprising; and from the Polish side we have several reports issued by the Home Army and the Department of Internal
Affairs of the Polish Government Delegacy (Krakowski 1984: 183).

The detached reader might have expected that these sources would
have been used to construct a fairly factual picture of what happened,
and a few authors have, in fact, attempted to do so. But that detached
reader would be very disappointed because it turns out that the German version of events, as recorded in the Stroop report, is given the
greatest credibility in much of the literature. One can only speculate
about the possible reasons for this undue attention. The fact that the
author was the commanding officer of the German forces, that he produced this document as his official report, that the German reputation
for accuracy, efficiency, and reliability preceded him—all of these may
have played a role in this unwarranted attribution of credibility. It is
unwarranted for several reasons. One reason is that a German officer is
likely to emphasize the successes of his troops and to play down those
of the enemy—especially when that enemy has long been characterized as vermin that does not belong to human kind, as exploiting others, as cowardly, and so on. Another reason why such attribution of
credibility is unwarranted is that the Stroop report contains much information that is contradicted by other sources, as well as by internal
contradictions. Some of these discrepancies have been analyzed by
Yisrael Gutman (1982: ch. 14) and by Shmuel Krakowski (1984: ch.
10). A few examples will illustrate: the Stroop report includes a list of
the units under his command that fought in the ghetto. It also reports
the use of howitzers and a list of casualties. But none of the units listed
were equipped with howitzers (Krakowski 1984: 185) and some of the
casualties belonged to units that were not listed as involved in the ghetto
fighting (Krakowski 1984: 192). Stroop's own adjutant confirmed the
use of the units mentioned by Stroop, but reports much higher num-

bers of personnel in these units (Krakowski 1984: 186). Also, Stroop never mentioned the use of the air force although this has been confirmed by many eyewitness reports (Krakowski 1984: 185). Another example illustrates the point even better. Stroop declared on May 16 that the campaign had been successfully concluded and he entitled his report "The Jewish Quarter of Warsaw is no More" (Milton 1980). But he forgot to tell this to those resistance fighters who were still inside the ghetto and who had decided to hold out to the bitter end. A small number of Jews kept fighting for many months more. We know this from reports of shooting in the ghetto and of further bombing by the Germans (Gutman 1982: 400; Taylor and Shaw 1987: 347). Finally, it is worth quoting Ber Mark (1975):

> The last recorded report of a Jewish fighting group wandering through the ruins of the ghetto is dated June 1944. The Polish underground publication, *Eastern and National Information,* wrote on July 7, 1944, that in June of that year a Jewish group attacked a detachment of gendarmes that happened to pass the ghetto area in broad daylight, killing three Germans. The Germans immediately ordered a round-up. They caught and shot twenty-five Jews. (Mark 1975: 114)

That a small group of untrained resistance fighters with few and partly homemade weapons should have been able to stand up to the might of German arms deserves to be celebrated in the collective memory of all people and especially the Jews—and it really is not terribly important whether that stand lasted one month, or one year, or even longer. What is important is to credit the Jewish partisans in the forests and the Jewish resistance fighters in the ghettos and the concentration camps with a true measure of their achievements. Much of this has been done by Gutman (1982), Krakowski (1984), Suhl (1975), and others—but unfortunately their work is not widely known.

Finally, it is worth quoting Albert Speer who was Hitler's minister of war production. He was not at all concerned with the fighting in the ghetto and does not even mention it directly. His only concern is that "in this situation, there was a greater danger that fleeing Jews would join the partisan movement, which had long since brought catastrophic confusion to the supply lines for the German army" (Speer 1981: 269).

Reasons Why Jewish Resistance is So Little Known

A full answer to the question posed in this paper will have to wait for further research and analysis. There seem to be a fairly large number of reasons why so little is known about Jewish resistance, only a few of which can be briefly mentioned here.

Historically, Jews have not been allowed to bear arms in most of the countries of the diaspora. Therefore, when they were attacked, they were not able to defend themselves. In some situations, their protector would defend them. If not, they only had a choice between hiding and fleeing (Hay 1992). This is the origin of the anti-Semitic canard that Jews are cowards. It may also be at the root of the Jewish self-criticism that asks why they went like lambs to their slaughter. This is a peculiarly Jewish question that has been attacked unmercifully by Yehuda Bauer as a form of self-hatred. He points to the tens of millions of non-Jewish Russians, Ukrainians, Poles, and other nationalities who were killed by the Nazis without offering any resistance and none of whom were accused by their compatriots of having gone like lambs to their slaughter (Bauer 1989b: 219–20).

Much of the literature on the Holocaust and on Jewish resistance relies on German sources. There are several reasons for this. The Germans kept voluminous records, many of which survived the war in spite of the Nazis' order to destroy those dealing with anti-Jewish activities to prevent their falling into enemy hands. These records have often been accepted as the authoritative statements of events due to the long-established reputation of Germans for efficiency, thoroughness, and bureaucratic orderliness. What was often not taken into account were the rather obvious sources of bias in the reporting on Jewish resistance. The Nazis underreported all kinds of resistance, for obvious reasons. But Jewish resistance was especially damaging, considering that it came from the very people whom they had branded as subhumans incapable of resisting their superior racial endowment.

Prominent Jewish writers on the Holocaust have dismissed Jewish resistance as very limited and ineffectual, as have quite a number of non-Jewish sources. They arrived at such conclusions by applying definitional standards to Jewish resistance that they did not apply to non-Jewish resistance. The former they considered only when it was armed and inflicted significant defeats on the enemy, while non-Jewish resistance needed to fill neither criterion. Instead, a great many ancillary activities, from hiding people to monitoring illegal radio transmissions and producing false identity papers, counted as being an appropriate part of resistance activities. Clearly, application of such a double standard leads to the denigration or ignoring of Jewish resistance.

The inattention to resistance for about a generation after the events was probably part of the general reluctance to talk or write about the

Holocaust. There were, of course, exceptions; but they are a very small part of the volume of Holocaust literature that has appeared since then. We still have no fully satisfactory explanation for this extraordinary reluctance to address the Holocaust for about a generation after the event. Many of the explanations that have invoked psychological variables are not adequate by themselves. After all, it took the Library of Congress until 1968, fully twenty-five years after the news of the Holocaust had reached the West, to introduce the category "Holocaust" into its classification system; and the Library of Congress can hardly be accused of being affected by the same psychological variables that produced a similar time lag among Jewish authors. But our question remains unanswered: why did Jewish resistance share in this period of embarrassed silence rather than become part of the general resistance literature that appeared so much earlier?

There are, of course, other reasons that could be cited. For instance, why is it that a major Jerusalem institution like Yad Vashem celebrates the contributions of Righteous Gentiles, while the celebration of Jewish resistance fighters is left to a kibbutz north of Acre, Lohame Hageta'ot (the Ghetto Fighters House)? Do we really prefer to remember the victims of the Holocaust as lambs that were led to their slaughter?

One might also point to the fact that much of the relevant literature is not published by large, well-known publishers who are able to invest heavily in publicity and marketing. A glance at the references cited below will confirm this point. But perhaps enough has been said to prove that Jewish resistance deserves to be much better known and also that it deserves a greater place in the history of the Holocaust.[2]

Conclusion

It is probably true, as has been claimed by Hilberg and others, that resistance did not substantially affect the outcome of the war. Individual actions often were successful in the sense that they achieved what they set out to accomplish. But in an age of technological warfare, involving tanks and planes, no amount of underground and partisan activity was likely to change the final outcome. In fact, if it had done so, it would hardly be called a resistance movement. If it had changed the final outcome we would now be talking about a revolution, a civil war, or a counter offensive.

But there is another perspective in which to examine resistance activities. They represent a way in which people in occupied countries could express their disagreement with the oppressor; they could affirm that they were not just unimportant slaves doing the bidding of the master race; they could express their human dignity, both individually and collectively. This affirmation of their freedom and their dignity is what earned the resistors a place in the collective memory of future generations. Thus, occupied countries continue to remember and honor their resistance movements; their literature celebrates them and their special nomenclature has become a part of their language.

This brings me back to the question that started this paper: why is Jewish resistance, with the glowing exception of the Warsaw ghetto uprising, quite unknown among most of us and almost forgotten? Is it because the Jews did not have a country, that they were not entitled to make resistance part of their collective memory? Or is it because Jews were perceived as, and saw themselves as, the perennial victims of persecution, that they are not entitled to affirmations of their individual and collective dignity? Or is it because Jews have internalized the anti-Semitic view of their own inferiority, that they are unable to celebrate affirmations of their ability to deal with crises of survival?

Or does the explanation lie in the motivations of the authors and their readers? The majority of the authors who celebrate Jewish resistance in their writing are themselves survivors who participated in or benefitted from the activities of resistance movements. They have good reasons for wanting to celebrate the achievements of resistance because they want the truth to be known and because they want to counteract the canard about the lambs going to their slaughter. However, the majority of the Jews in the Western world have lost members of their families in the Holocaust. Thus, when they read about the Holocaust they are mourning the loss of their relatives and are trying to understand what cannot be understood. Reading about resistance does not help them in their mourning nor in their understanding; therefore it recedes into the background.

Finally, a colleague offered the suggestion that this memory lapse may be the result of a perceived incongruity. He suggests that the overwhelming image of the six million who died is so deeply embedded in modern consciousness that it does not leave room for resistance. After all, if there was that much resistance, then why did six million die? He thinks that the reports of widespread Jewish resistance undermine the credibility of the enormous losses and are therefore pushed out of memory.

I still do not know the full answers to these questions, and perhaps I shall never know them. But instead of waiting for someone to produce such answers, let us make the questions irrelevant by acknowledging with pride the enormous efforts and sacrifices that Jewish resistors have made during the Nazi years in order to affirm their dignity and ours.

Notes

1. Revised version of a paper read at the 31st International Congress of the International Institute of Sociology held on 21–25 June 1993 at the Sorbonne in Paris, France.
2. The items cited in the text and below represent only a sampling of the literature on resistance that is available in English. Additional literature exists in the languages of all of the countries that were occupied by Hitler's troops, as well as in Hebrew and Yiddish. Much further material can be expected to be published as scholars begin to work on the archival materials in Eastern Europe that have only recently become available and accessible. Additional information may be found in: Ainsztein (1974), Arad (1987, 1981), Balfour (1988), Ball-Kaduri (1959), Bauer (1979), Benz (1988), Donat (1964), Duraczinski (1987), Eckman and Lazar (1977), Foot (1976), Gutman and Zuroff (1977), International Conference on the History of the Resistance Movements (1960), Levin (1985), Muszkat (1974), Novitch (1980), Steinberg (1978), Syrkin (1976), Wiener Library (1978), and Zuckerman (1971).

8

Prevention without Prediction[1]

*"The destruction of memory is both the function
and the aim of totalitarianism."*
—Milan Kundera as quoted
in Shawcross (1984: 12)

*"Sober perseverance is more effective than
enthusiastic emotions, which are all too capable
of being transferred, with little difficulty, to
something different each day."*
—Václav Havel (1990: 111)

Introduction

This chapter addresses a number of issues of importance to that
intrepid band of activists who believe that it is possible to prevent
genocides in the future. They have assumed that this requires the
knowledge to predict such events, based on a number of indicators
that would serve to activate an early warning system. That system
would then alert the world to the impending disaster and arouse it to
preventive action.

However, prediction in the social sciences requires much more
knowledge than we presently have—if it is at all possible. In the past,
when change was much slower and much less frequent, prediction had
a certain amount of prestige. But that prestige was usually based not
on the quality of the predictions, but rather on their having been forgotten long before experience had falsified them. Lately, the pace of
change has accelerated so dramatically that many predictions are remembered only too well by the time they have been falsified. That also
means that it now takes much more courage to commit a prediction to
the written record because it may have been contradicted by events
even before it has appeared in print.

This state of affairs has very serious implications for those of us who are interested in social policy and social action because many of us have assumed that prediction is a sine qua non for prevention. It is the purpose of this paper to show that this is not necessarily so. But assuming, for the sake of argument, that well-grounded predictions were to become available, they would probably create a whole series of new problems. These would be of three kinds. If the prediction were to prove correct, and if it had been made inside the perpetrator country, the authors of that prediction might well become its first victims. (In Burundi in 1994, the minister of information warned of the genocidal potential of the internal conflicts and was one of the first victims of that genocide). If, however, a correct prediction were to be made outside the country, and if preventive actions were to prove successful, then it would be difficult to prove that a genocide had been planned; those who made that prediction would then seem to have accused the potential perpetrators unfairly. On the other hand, if the prediction turns out to be incorrect, it would very likely undermine the credibility of the source of the prediction as well as of the activity of predicting.

Thus, a prediction, by definition a long-range statement, in order to be useful must be credible, and must be accepted by actors who are willing to act on it. Both conditions are quite questionable at this time. So, if we lack the means to make predictions credible and the actors who will rely on them as guides to action, then we need preventive measures that do not require a prediction. It is the purpose of this paper to show that prevention and intervention are, in fact, possible without the necessity of prior prediction.

Early Recognition

Until we can predict when and where a genocide will occur, we cannot set up an early warning system. But we certainly can recognize a genocide once it has started. Several authors have attempted to sort out the beginning stages of genocide, based on the observations of past genocides. Stanton (1989) says that these stages consist of: classification, symbolization, vilification, identification, and finally extermination. Hilberg's stages are: definition, expropriation, concentration, and annihilation (1979: 31). The differences in their schemes may be due to their being derived from events in quite different culture areas. With a little more research it should be possible to specify a set of broad stages that apply across culture areas. The reason for doing this re-

search is that mass killing does not ever occur without some prelimi-
naries that can be used to recognize when a process of genocide is
unfolding. The point here is that the early recognition of such prelimi-
naries should be taken seriously as signals of impending disaster.

In addition, there is a variety of other precursors to the actual killing
that may not be observed in every genocide, but whose occurrence should
lead to an early recognition of human rights violations that have the
potential of escalating to genocide. The human rights violations here
referred to are not all of those codified in the United Nations Declaration
or the Helsinki Accord; instead we are limiting the discussion to only
those human rights violations that are a direct threat to the life of persons
and of groups, such as torture and killing. McDougal et. al. refer to such
human rights violations as the final or extreme deprivation of well-being
(1980: 27, 576, 639). Among the precursors that should alert us to the
early recognition that a genocide is in its incipient stage are:

• Official statements of lethal principles and plans, and of actions
already taken (Iran issued both) should be taken seriously because it
may still be possible to intervene in a process that may lead to the
annihilation of a victim group.

• The appearance of refugees ought to be taken very seriously; it is
the best indicator because people do not leave their home without their
possessions, their family, and their friends unless they have genuine
reasons to fear for their survival. In addition, these refugees are usually the first as well as the most reliable source of information (Clark
1989). If they are interviewed by competent researchers who know
how to gather and verify data, they will prove to provide the most
accurate information on what is happening in their country of origin.
In the past, their witness has not carried much credibility because they
were accused of being biased observers; thus, much information and
insight was ignored (Clay and Holcomb 1986: ch.1; Frelick 1989).

• Government regulations and other documentary evidence, where
available, should also be taken seriously. Most revealing are new or
amended laws that circumscribe some human right. But lesser changes
should not be ignored, such as orders-in-councils, travel restrictions,
currency controls, etc. Such documents by themselves may not mean
very much; they need to be evaluated in context.

• The appearance of false news, denial of news, and biased or ideologically slanted statements, ought to arouse suspicion among outside
observers, especially if they have prior specialized knowledge that allows them to interpret such news in an objective manner.

Of course, early recognition of an incipient genocide may be generated by tragedies other than genocide, and refugees may be fleeing from disasters other than mass killings. Leon Gordenker suggests that "early warning ought to concern itself with movements of people who are subjected to severe deprivations that they could not avoid and did not themselves cause" (1985: 69).[2] Such deprivations should not be ignored; instead they ought to lead us to extend our attention to all forms of human rights violations and to collaboration with other human rights organizations. In fact, genocide early recognition systems could probably be much more easily implemented if they were part of more general warning systems of refugee flows. Such integration into larger and preexisting efforts requires careful attention to possible conflicts of emphasis. Thus, most organizations interested in predicting refugee flows want to know how many refugees will require their assistance, while early recognition of genocide is less concerned with the number of refugees than with the situation that caused them to flee. The demand for assistance to large numbers of refugees has, however, increased an interest in the possibility of preventing the causes of such flows. This was one the reasons for the recent creation of the Office for Research and the Collection of Information (ORCI) within the United Nations Secretariat. Whether ORCI will be any more effective than other relevant United Nations bodies remains to be seen.[3]

The early recognition of incipient genocides is essential for two important reasons. First, if such early identification is based on carefully collected and verified data, it avoids the possibility of launching an accusation and preventive action against a perpetrator who may be entirely innocent. As was noted above, this possibility of a false accusation is one of the dangers inherent in basing such action on prediction instead of on early identification. Second, the early recognition of incipient genocide or genocidal massacres is crucial if preventive action is to be effective in saving the lives of potential victims. That the saving of lives is important to the readers of this book is self-evident. Unfortunately, it is not equally self-evident that the saving of lives is a consideration in the councils of the United Nations or in the affairs of states.

The rest of this chapter will explore some suggestions for a variety of measures, applicable in different institutional areas of every society, that may contribute to the early recognition and prevention of future genocides. It is unlikely that any of these measures will be effective by themselves; each of them should be evaluated as part of a concerted campaign. The list is not yet exhaustive, nor are all of these suggestions new or original; but this seems to be the first time that such a listing has been assembled.

Education

The term genocide is now widely misused to denote almost anything that an observer is violently opposed to, whether or not anyone is being killed. In that usage it carries a strong negative burden without corresponding to any accepted definition. At the same time, the topic of genocide is surrounded by a veil of silence that often expands to collective denial. Both ought to be dispelled as part of any educational program that proposes to deal with the subject.

In order not to trivialize the subject it is important to counteract the misuse of the term genocide. It is in this context that the discussion of definitions becomes relevant. The term genocide has been used to embrace anything from urban planning to environmental pollution to family planning methods. Students of policy options ought to recognize that such misleading use militates against any hope of successful prevention.

Collective denial also needs to be discussed in detail because it amounts to saying that "what must not be, cannot be"; also, that which is denied need not be prevented. Therefore, it is important to counteract all forms of denial and to keep the memories alive. At present there exists a great deal of social science and history literature that deals with empires from ancient Egypt to Rome to those of the twentieth century without ever a mention of what happened to many of the people that became the victims of these empires.

It is equally important to counteract the destruction of memory. To give just one example, according to Adalbert Rückerl, the head of the Central Office of the Land Judicial Authorities for the Investigation of National-Socialist Crimes, over 110,000 legal prosecutions have been initiated since the end of the the war in what was then Hitler's "greater Germany" (FRG, GDR, Austria) (Rückerl 1980: 72, 74, 117). We have no similar figures for the Soviet Union, Poland, Japan, and all the other countries where criminal proceedings arising from wartime activities were held. For the present argument it is not important to consider the outcomes of the proceedings; they ranged all the way from death penalties to dismissals due to lack of evidence or due to inability to locate the accused. What concerns us here is that these events have received very little attention—with the exception of the Nuremberg trials. We know little about these cases and even less about the effects they may have had on the accused or on their communities. Of course, no comparable judicial proceedings were instituted against the perpetrators of all the genocides that have occurred since then and, as Dadrian (1989: 326–29) has pointed out, an unpunished crime encourages its repetition. The result is summarized by Kuper in one of his blackest moods: "the sovereign territorial state claims, as an integral part of its sovereignty, the right to commit genocide, or engage in genocidal massacres, against people under its rule, and.... the United Nations, for all practical purposes, defends this right" (Kuper 1981: 161) and "One can only ask—is genocide a credential for membership in the General Assembly of the United Nations?" (Kuper 1981: 173).

In order to prevent genocides in the future, it is futile to rely exclusively on the United Nations or on its member governments. Instead, it is imperative to educate a generation of citizens who will not be prepared to be passive bystanders to the violation of human rights, but who will actively criticize and/or oppose their governments when they want to engage in such violations. That it is possible to do this without themselves engaging in violence is adequately demonstrated by the American citizens' protests that helped to end the war in Vietnam, as well as by the recent events in Eastern Europe.

The following topics might be considered in courses that deal with genocides and human rights:

• The U.N. Genocide Convention: its origins, its pros and cons (especially Whitaker 1985), its effects, and the way some scholars have proposed to revise its definition. This unit should include a discussion of the legislation relating to the Convention, to hate mongering, and to human rights in the students' own country.

• The occurrence of genocide through the ages, emphasizing the roles of the various participants: those who gave the orders, those who carried them out, those who were their victims, and those who were bystanders (active or passive).

• The struggle for human rights, both individual and collective. The role of the culture of various countries in facilitating or inhibiting the acceptance and protection of human rights. It may be useful to emphasize that having the same right is desirable, while being homogenized is pernicious.

• The importance of realizing that genocide is the ultimate human rights violation. While the right to life should make this self-evident, very few human rights organizations concern themselves with genocide. This could be misinterpreted to mean that human rights do not include protection from genocide, or that genocides are not a problem any more. Both conclusions are evidently false.

• The consequences of ideological genocide for the perpetrator society should be discussed in some detail. It should be emphasized that the costs for the collectivity are both enormous and long lasting, in spite of the fact that there are always individuals who enrich themselves in almost any situation (see chapter 5).

• The differences between democratic and authoritarian regimes. These ought to be dealt with in terms of decentralized versus centralized control; the rule of law versus the arbitrary use of law; the relative valuations of the individual versus the collectivity; the encouragement of initiative versus the enforcing of conformity; and the separation of church and state.

This kind of education is, of course, based on the optimistic assumption that an informed citizenry will not allow a genocide to occur in its own country and will also be willing to assist in preventing it in other countries.

Finally, a basic pedagogical question needs to be explored. Is it enough to insert these topics into the curriculum at several levels of schooling? Or is it also important to allow young people to encounter serious issues outside the medium of their school experience. One such medium is television; although there has been much research done on the influence of television, it is still not clear whether and when young people take it seriously or perceive it simply as entertaining fiction. One suggestion is to take a closer look at the effects of books like Carol Matas' *Lisa's War* (1989), which in a children's book deals with the "adult" problems of Jewish survival in Nazi-occupied Denmark without talking down to the readers. In order to achieve a similar effect in the classroom, instructors might consider using role-playing sessions on the pattern of the model U.N. parliament sessions so popular in some areas; members of a class would first research and then debate the roles of specific actors associated with a particular genocide, with the rest of the class acting as critics.

Publicity

The important and positive role that publicity has played in reducing the persecution of the Baha'i in Iran (in addition to important diplomatic initiatives) and in easing the famine in Ethiopia should remove any doubt about the value of such publicity. However, not every bit of bad news will receive public attention, or will even be reported. If publicity is to play a significant role in stopping serious violations of human rights and in recognizing and arresting a developing genocide then some preconditions need to be attended to.

• For publicity concerning impending mass killings to work and to be spread it is crucial that the credibility of the news be established beyond doubt. Unless that can be done, such publicity will either be ignored or will be interpreted as hostile propaganda. In both cases it will only do harm to the cause of prevention.

• Credible reports are certainly much more likely to receive wide press coverage in the important media, in addition to their restricted circulation in the obscure newsletters of humanitarian organizations. Therefore, reports should include not only the salient facts, but also the reasons for believing them to be accurate.

• Wide coverage will also be easier to obtain if it is demanded and/ or supported by prominent individuals and prestigious organizations. This may be much more difficult to arrange than it sounds because there often are influential and/or powerful interests that prefer to keep such news out of circulation. One needs to think only of the ongoing persecutions of the Kurds and of the people of East Timor which are most of the time being widely ignored by the press and the United Nations; in these two cases the reasons for such ignoring of ongoing persecutions and massacres are fairly obvious: the costs in human lives and suffering are considered small compared to the economic and strategic benefits derived from maintaining friendly relations with the perpetrator countries.

• The different communications media will require different approaches and will also have different effects on quite different audiences. This subject will require a good deal of attention if the message is to have its intended effects. This means that human rights activists need to pay much more careful attention to the relationship between the media of communication and the audiences that they are attempting to reach in order to intervene in a specific case.

Economic Sanctions

If a particular situation represents a serious enough case of persecution, it may be possible to organize an economic boycott. Such action

can be imposed by governments through legislation, or by nongovernmental groups through the organization of campaigns against buying
the country's exports or against investing in its enterprises. Such campaigns can be organized only in exceptional cases, and even then there
is some debate as to whether they really work at the economic level.[4]
But even if that debate were to be decided in the negative, economic
sanctions remain a very potent weapon due to their enormous impact
on publicity and on the political relations of the offending country.

An additional feature of economic sanctions is that they inevitably
will involve organizations and interest groups that ordinarily have no
great concern with humanitarian issues. Their involvement requires a
good deal of skillful attention exactly because they are not interested
in issues of human rights, but will be concerned with economic or with
political issues. They may be reluctant to get involved unless their
primary interests are likely to suffer, or they may even get involved in
defensive and denial activities to protect their own interests.

In the quite rare cases where it is possible to organize a boycott that
affects the economic, political, and social life of the offending country, it
is very likely to prevent the most serious human rights violations. The
events in the Republic of South Africa that preceded the ending of apartheid seem to support this argument. It remains to be seen whether current economic sanctions of Myanmar (Burma) will have a similar effect.

Organizational Linkages

One area in which a tremendous amount of work remains to be done
concerns the relationships between the many organizations that already
are active on some aspect of human rights. Very often their various activities are not coordinated, sometimes they work at cross purposes, and
occasionally they may even negate each other's efforts. This is not an
argument for establishing another umbrella organization with its own
bureaucracy, but rather a suggestion that they might be more successful
if they communicated more among themselves (Cohen 1990). To implement such a suggestion would require that they agree among themselves
to assign a higher priority to their human rights activities than to their
commitments to ideologies, to influential power groups, to protecting
their own turf, or even to their various ego building tendencies.

Since different organizations may require different approaches, the
following grouping of relevant organizations is suggested. This grouping is not intended as a typology, but merely suggests which organiza-

tions might respond to like approaches when seeking their support for the prevention of genocides.

• The United Nations and its various organizations, such as the U.N. Educational, Scientific, and Cultural Organization (UNESCO), the U.N. High Commissioner for Refugees (UNHRC), and so on. While they have done very significant work in helping refugees, they have hardly addressed the causes of refugee flows. Neither have refugee issues been associated with human rights issues. As Roberta Cohen (1990) has shown, there is a great deal of room for improving the agendas of these organizations.

• Human rights organizations, such as Amnesty International, Cultural Survival, Peace Research institutes, and so on. These have a great deal in common, but they rarely exchange information with organizations concerned with refugees (Refugee Policy Group, May 1989). They might be convinced to cooperate in a common network among themselves and with other organizations in order to share information and to plan concerted actions. Modern technology facilitates the establishment of such networks. If this could be done with the cooperation of most human rights organizations it would quickly become a major means for collecting as well as disseminating data on incipient genocides. In addition, the sponsorship of these organizations would make it less likely that such dissemination of news of an incipient genocide would be ignored by the media, the United Nations, the sponsors of the Helsinki accords, as well as all the other groups that have in the past expressed concerns about man's inhumanity to man.

• Various "green" groups. Some of these have primarily political interests while others are more concerned with immediate aid to the environment. What they do have in common is their concern for safeguarding the natural environment; they might be open to expanding their interests to the human environment and to saving the people for whom they are preserving the natural environment.

• The "ethical" mutual funds and industries. These have arisen only recently. Some of them are engaged in debates about the meaning of "ethical" in the context of their activities. They ought to be encouraged to include the violation of human rights in their definition of "ethical."

• Various governmental and nongovernmental organizations that deal with refugees. As already mentioned, most of them are primarily concerned with helping these refugees; they usually pay little attention to the causes of these refugee flows. This sometimes prevents them from diagnosing the situation appropriately. Thus, the UNHCR sees repatriation as the preferred solution to the refugee problem (Zolberg et al. 1989: 268) without apparently taking note of the fact that refugees from genocide will find this the most unacceptable solution to their plight. At the same time, most of these organizations are extremely reluctant to say or do anything that might offend the refugee-producing country for fear of having their assistance activities banned. However, their activities and their prestige give them a particularly strong base from which not only to assist refugees, but also to recognize the causes of refugee flows; this also puts them into a strong position from which to assist in the prevention of these causes.

The Law

Unfortunately the law is only marginally relevant in matters of prevention. There are several reasons for this. The perpetrators of modern genocides are collectivities, and it is much harder to prosecute a collectivity than an individual. These collectivities are almost always states that victimize their own citizens. Thus, a case would have to be brought before a court in the perpetrator country. However, countries that permit suits against their own government are most unlikely to be the perpetrators of genocide.

The U.N. Genocide Convention, in Article VI, foresees an "international penal tribunal" before which a case of genocide shall be tried. Such a tribunal has never been set up and none of the contracting parties have accepted that such an international tribunal might have jurisdiction. Hurst Hannum (1989), who is the executive director of the Procedural Aspects of International Law (PAIL) Institute, has examined the case of the Cambodian genocide in some detail. He argues that the International Court of Justice could hear such cases, and concludes that the fact that no government has been willing to invoke international law on behalf of the victims of genocide is less an indictment of the law than of governments.

Such cases as have been tried before a court of law have accused individuals rather than regimes. After World War I, Turkey tried and condemned the leading figures that had been responsible for the Armenian genocide, several of them *in absentia*. Very few of the sentences were carried out. After World War II, war crimes trials were held in many countries, those in the two Germanies and in Austria being the best documented ones. These courts dealt only with individuals and relatively few of the sentences were carried out (Rückerl

1980). Considering the many human rights violations in the world since those days, it would be very difficult to maintain that such trials, held long after the events, have had a widespread deterrent or preventative effect.

More recently, prosecutions for genocide have been initiated in Rwanda and in The Hague. It remains to be seen what results they will produce and what effects they will have.

Another problem with judicial processes is that an individual can be charged only after a crime has been committed. At that stage he is not likely to be prosecuted in his own country. In theory, one ought to be able to bring a case to court in another country; in practice, few other countries would be willing to do this. Even if they were prepared to engage in such actions, there is no judicial authority for such a procedure, and if the defendant were tried *in absentia* the sentence could not be carried out.

So, why discuss the law in the context of prevention? The main reason is that one can always hope that the law will have a deterrent effect if, but only if, applied more forcefully and consistently within the country where an offense is committed. As more and more countries are willing to enact human rights legislation and enforce it without undue delay, a day may soon come when potential perpetrators will be so widely perceived as moral outcasts that they will hesitate to engage in activities that the law, as well as the communities, have rejected as uncivilized.

There is an administrative, quasi-judicial procedure, however, that ought to be used more frequently: the refusal of visas to perpetrators who have been overthrown in their own country. In the majority of cases of serious human rights violations, including genocides, the perpetrator regime is overthrown, albeit after the fact. Many of the individual perpetrators then seek an asylum to escape the treatment that the new government may have in store for them. If more countries were to refuse entry visas to such criminals, it might contribute to a deterrent effect and it might expose the remaining countries of asylum to international censure. This administrative procedure has the additional advantage that it is much easier to implement than a legal proceeding.

Conclusions

The above discussions lead to three conclusions: First, efforts to develop indicators that will allow us to predict massive human rights violations, including genocides, are not likely to produce results in the near future. Without such indicators it is not possible to develop reliable early warning systems. Second, such massive human rights violations and genocides do not appear on the world scene full-blown, without preparations. We do know a great deal about the preparatory and initial stages of such events. Thus, while we may not be able to predict them, we can recognize their occurrence in their very early stages. Third, our efforts, therefore, should be directed towards the early recognition of the stages of incipient genocides as soon as they occur. This provides much less lead time than a reliable prediction, but in the present stage of knowledge we do not have a choice. Because the lead time may be quite short, it will be important to obtain reliable and verifiable information and to mobilize all possible means to prevent and/or to arrest the looming disaster.[5]

Notes

1. Revised version of this paper has appeared in *Holocaust and Genocide Studies,* vol.7, no. 1 (Spring 1993), 1–13.
2. Gordenker clearly uses the term "early warning" in the sense of recognizing a process already under way, not in the context of predicting future events.
3. Since this was written that hope seems to have evaporated.
4. Whether economic sanctions can be effective is largely a matter of imagination and inventiveness. For example, several states in the U.S. have passed legislation that prohibits their departments and state supported organizations from purchasing anything from enterprises that have economic relations with Burma (Myanmar). Since the domestic business is in almost all cases greater than business with Burma, such legislation has proved remarkably effective.
5. For additional discussions of these issues the reader may consult, among others: Clark (1989), Clay and Holcomb (1986), Cohen (1990), Dadrian (1989), Gordenker (1985), McDougal et al. (1980), Zolberg et al. (1989), as well as the publications of International Alert, African Rights, and so on.

9

Rethinking the Conceptualization of Genocide and Gross Human Rights Violations[1]

"If we could learn to look instead of gawking,
We'd see the horror in the heart of farce,
If only we could act instead of talking,
We wouldn't always end up on our arse.
This was the thing that nearly had us mastered;
Don't yet rejoice in his defeat, you men!
Although the world stood up and stopped the bastard,
The bitch that bore him is in heat again."
—Bertolt Brecht[2]

I want to discuss several aspects of the "rethinking" in the title of this paper—each of which deserves a fuller treatment than space allows here. I trust that the brief discussion devoted to each of these aspects will sufficiently spark the readers' interest in exploring these issues further.

The first major rethinking concerns the limits that we seem to have imposed on areas of study. These limits are far too narrowly drawn to allow us to come to grips with the phenomenon that we claim to be our focus of attention. Let me illustrate this problem by referring to what usually are considered three quite separate fields of inquiry: famines, genocides, and refugees. Each of these fields has generated a considerable body of literature—each being quite separate from the others.

There exists a large literature on famine, most of which treats famine as caused by natural catastrophes, such as too much rain or floods, too little rain or drought, earthquakes, crop diseases, invasions of grasshoppers or locusts, and so on. A quite small part of that literature does deal with man-made famines in the sense that they are caused by the unanticipated results of misguided social arrangements and policies. However, with one or two exceptions, none of that literature deals with famines that are caused by the planned use of starvation as a tool of conflict or persecution. What seems particularly odd about this state of the literature is that the intentional withholding of nourishment has been practiced since the establishment of the first cities about 10,000 years ago. It seems that the methods for defending a city were almost always better than those for attacking them. This only changed in the nineteenth century with the advent of long-range guns. Since cities, from the earliest ones, were always attracting raids on their wealth, they built ever stronger defenses. Therefore, determined attackers usually had to resort to a protracted siege in order to starve the defendants into surrender. What makes starvation and famine such attractive tools to perpetrators of genocides is that they are cheap and require neither sophisticated technology nor an elaborate bureaucracy. In addition, they can be disguised as caused by natural catastrophes.[3] For this reason it seems important to maintain for research purposes a more restrictive definition of the kind cited in chapter 1 above or by Horowitz (1997: 80–91).

Similar statements can be made about the literature on genocides. It rarely discusses the role of starvation (except with reference to the Ukraine) in spite of its widespread use during the Armenian genocide and the Holocaust as well as in the more recent cases in Ethiopia, Sudan, and Somalia, among others. Neither does the genocide literature have a great deal to say about refugees, in spite of the fact that all genocides have produced refugees. In fact current estimates indicate that the great majority of today's refugees are fleeing from genocides. Needless to add that the refugee literature is no broader. It pays very little attention to famines and almost none to genocides.

If we take a little time to think about these three areas, we realize that they are closely connected and that treating them in isolation distorts what is going on in the real world. Famines, genocides, and refugee flows are related processes and the study of their relationship cannot but help enrich our understanding.[4]

My second aspect of rethinking concerns the time frame within which we locate our studies. My own bias has led me to start in antiquity because I have been repeatedly impressed with the slowness with which some processes change. On the other hand there are some recent studies that have restricted their time frame to post-World War II genocides. Between these two extremes there is a lot of room for debate, but only the results of research can decide which time frame produces the most important results. In spite of that reservation, it strikes me as a mistake to start only after World War II. Doing so eliminates three major genocidal periods from consideration: Turkey during World War I, the USSR during Stalin's reign, and Nazi Germany. I find it hard to see how their omission can improve research results, especially since the consequences of these genocidal periods are still with us. Or, as Daniel Chirot puts it, it is important to study Stalin and Hitler because they served as "models for a century that produced many others like them" (Chirot 1994: 25).

Let me give you an illustration of how the findings of these studies of post-World War II cases have led to a dubious conclusion: they found that democracies do not commit genocides (Fein 1993: 79–106). This is a dubious finding for two reasons. The first one is that such a finding is surely redundant if we accept the notion that the form of government that we call democracy is based on the consent of the governed. Since most genocides in the second half of the twentieth century are victimizing groups of the perpetrators' own citizens, it is safe to assume that they did not give their consent to their own victimization.[5] Thus, a democratic state would have to become something else before it could commit a genocide. The crucial question then should be: how does a democratic state turn into a nondemocratic one? In this context the exclusion of Nazi Germany becomes significant because it is a case study of how a democracy became a dictatorship. It is not good enough to say that Weimar Germany was a pretty shaky democracy since that would only force us to define when a democracy is not shaky any more. That exercise might have forced us to look at Bangladesh, Brazil, Burundi, Egypt, Greece, India, Japan, Turkey, Rwanda, Sri Lanka, Yugoslavia, etc. in order to decide which ones are shaky and which ones are not. Those found not to be shaky would then be presumed to be free of the risk of experiencing a genocide in the future. I wonder how many serious scholars would be prepared to stick their necks out that far?

This leads me directly to the third aspect of rethinking which raises the thorny question of the extent to which features of a research design will have an effect on the research results. Thus, the dissatisfaction with the definition of genocide has now reached the point where cases that clearly do not qualify as genocides are included by labeling them as democides, omnicides or politicides. It is not at all clear that broadening the data base in this way will contribute to better explanations.[6]

For this occasion it seems important to maintain for research purposes a more restrictive definition of the kind cited in chapter 1 above or by Horowitz (1997: 80–81). While all of the gross human rights violations included in these broader terms are to be fought against, ignoring the differences among them is not likely to lead to greater insight. Even more important, ignoring these differences obscures the fact that they must be fought against or prevented by using quite different methods. Without being facetious, let me take Amnesty International as an example. They have been very successful in doing a great deal of admirable work defending victims of house arrest, imprisonment, and torture, but it should be clear that their campaigns of letter writing, faxing, and prison visits are not likely to have any effect on the perpetrators of genocides.

Rummel developed an expanded definition which led him to coin the term 'democide' (1994: chs. 2 and 3). While this allows him to include a wider range of cases, he insists that intent and actual killing must be part of the definition. The latter condition is essential in distancing his treatment from that of Lemkin as well as that of the United Nations. Both include in their definition other conditions such as the prevention of births. Rummel is also one of the few authors in this field who deals, albeit briefly, with pre-twentieth-century genocides.

The fourth aspect of rethinking concerns a paper that I published last year on "Prevention Without Prediction" (see ch. 8). In that paper I tried to point to some areas that might provide opportunities for contributing to concerted efforts at intervening in the early stages of a genocidal process.[7] Briefly, these areas dealt with education, publicity, economic sanctions, organizational linkages, and the law. In my discussion of the latter two categories, I still believed that the United Nations had a significant role to play during efforts at intervening in and outlawing genocides. Recent experience throws renewed doubt on this misplaced confidence. Or, as a senior relief official in Sarajevo said in October 1993: "If the UN had been around in 1939, we would all be speaking German."[8]

On rethinking my discussion in that paper I became convinced of a serious omission in my argument. The steps leading to intervention that were outlined in that paper provide patchwork relief at best. While these may provide help for some of the victims, they do not prevent the perpetrators from committing further obscenities. Such prevention can be achieved only by a massive, grass roots protest coming from the people of many countries. Whether such protests will ever

be aimed at the perpetrators of genocides I have no way of predicting. But recent experience demonstrates quite convincingly that it is
possible to raise popular consciousness even in this blasé age. Thus,
the war in Vietnam was eventually stopped, not because the government thought this the better part of wisdom, but because—among
other causes—the American people protested against it in huge numbers. Similarly, it has been possible to arouse international outrage
on behalf of seal pups and rain forests, among other causes. Nobody
can predict whether such widespread concern will be mobilized on
behalf of human lives. But it seems clear that without such massive
opposition from their people neither sovereign countries nor international organizations are willing to stop the victimization of millions
of human beings in all parts of the world. How and by whom such a
consciousness raising will be set in motion and whether it will mobilize a mass outcry against the perpetrators of genocides, remains to
be seen. All I can do is express the devout hope that it will happen
sooner rather than later.

However, in order to appraise the chances of raising the consciousness of large numbers of people it is essential that we acquire a better
understanding of their attitudes toward those who in some relevant
respects are different from themselves. If it is true—and it obviously
is—that both individuals and collectivities discriminate invidiously on
the basis of a wide variety of characteristics, then we need to know
more about the nature of such discrimination. We are here not concerned with the kind of discrimination that allows us, for instance, to
distinguish one person from another. Rather, we are concerned with
the kind of invidious discrimination that various international instruments on human rights have attempted to define and to outlaw. The
extreme forms of such discrimination are often referred to as racism
and have often led to various expressions of hostility that in the polar-
ized cases have escalated to genocide.

In order to come closer to an understanding of these processes we
need to ask whether the discrimination or the racism is self-conscious
or unselfconscious. By self-conscious racism we mean the intellectually articulated position that advocates the hierarchical reordering of a
nation state or of all of humanity on some characteristic defined by
some ideological imperative. Since people who subscribe to that position tend to represent a proportionally small part of the population,
they also tend to oppose the rule of law and popular democracy. In
order to increase their base of support they tend to rely on sophisti-

cated and massively produced propaganda. One reason why such propaganda is so often surprisingly successful is that there is a much larger part of the population who are unself-consciously racist. These are people who would violently reject any accusations of racism. Some of them may even be active in the work of human rights organizations and publicly defend the rule of law and the equality of all people, regardless of their particular characteristics. These are people—the great majority of the world's population—whose youth was spent within a homogeneous culture that fostered the unquestioning acceptance of its own worldview. This is not deliberate indoctrination, but rather the acceptance of what that particular culture defines as the obvious. Children raised in such a culture absorb such definitions and these remain the unself-conscious baselines of their perceptions of the world in which they live. This creates the odd situation where we can study people's attitudes by questionnaire or interview and find them to be tolerant and nondiscriminatory. If, however, we study their behavior instead, they are found to treat—without being aware of it—members of certain minority groups in a discriminatory manner. This may mean that they will treat such people worse that their peers; but it may also mean that they will make a deliberate effort to treat them better than their peers—in order to atone for the difficulties to which their minority status exposes them.[9] In either case, such behaviors are indicators of an unself-conscious racism. This is one of the mechanisms that explains why attitudes often are not good predictors of behavior.

The interesting question, an important question to be investigated, is whether such people are more or less receptive than others when they are exposed to discriminatory or racist propaganda. Another question concerns the effect such people may have on the subjects of the discriminatory behavior. While the unself-conscious discriminators may be quite unaware of the meaning of their behavior, the subjects of these behaviors are likely to be very much conscious of the slight—intended or otherwise—and their reactions may well contribute to an increase in hostilities. To the extent that the members of the offending group reciprocate against what they perceive as unprovoked humiliation, both sides are now embarked on a vicious circle of insult, hostility, aggression, and escalating violence. In this way, a much ignored phenomenon may in time contribute to a horrendous result—which is the reason why those interested in prevention ought to become aware of it.

Notes

1. An earlier version of this chapter was presented at the Annual Meeting of the American Sociological Association, held on 5–9 August 1994 in Los Angeles.
2. Bertolt Brecht. *The Resistible Rise of Arturo Ui,* adapted by George Tabori (New York: S. French, 1972) epilogue, p. 128. Little did Brecht know just how fertile she would turn out to be!
3. For a detailed discussion, see chapter 3.
4. I made a modest beginning in that direction in chapter 4.
5. While it is true that victim groups usually are in the minority, it seems very unlikely that in a democracy any significant number of votes would be cast in favor of genocide.
6. Helen Fein has dealt with this issue in her paper "Genocide, Terror, Life Integrity and War Crimes: The Case for Discrimination" (1994).
7. Note that I carefully avoided the phrasing "humanitarian intervention" which has acquired a specific meaning that makes it an oxymoron.
8. As reported by Thomas G. Weiss in "UN Responses in the Former Yugoslavia: Moral and Operational Choices." *Ethics and International Affairs,* vol. 8 (1994): 1.
9. For example, in several countries in which native populations have been displaced by European settlers, the natives are often considered to represent a lower form of civilization who need to be "protected" as wards of the state. However, when equal rights advocates insist that they are treated as equals, they are expected to compete with the majority population on even broader terms. Not having had a share in equal preparation, they still find themselves in a discriminatory situation.

10

On the Prevention of Unpunished Crimes[1]

Introduction

To engage in research, writing, and teaching about genocide is a very depressing enterprise; one can only keep going by placing one's faith in the hope of finding means of preventing such abominations in the future. Of course, I am not the only one who is motivated by the hope for a better future, even though all the contemporary evidence seems to point in the opposite direction. This is shown by the growing body of literature dealing with prediction, prevention, early warning systems, international law, trials of the perpetrators, and humanitarian intervention.[2]

A significant body of scholarly opinion holds that "humanitarian intervention" represents our best hope for the future. For those who are not familiar with the semantics of this debate, I should point out that there is nothing humanitarian about the proposed intervention. The term is meant to reassure critics who oppose gunboat diplomacy, no matter how cleverly disguised. The advocates of this policy still believe problems, including genocide and gross violations of human rights, can be solved by sending in the armed forces. They hold to such a view in spite of the lack of evidence in its favor. At the time of writing, there has not been a case of military intervention that would support their claims.[3] The evidence seems to indicate that humanitarian intervention mainly achieves an increase in the number of the dead. Thus, for soft-hearted critics like myself, there must be other methods for eliminating genocide that do not rely on additional killing.

It was for such reasons that a few years ago I, too, was moved to publish a paper on prevention (see ch. 8). In that paper I explored some areas that might contribute to intervention in the early stages of genocide. Briefly, the areas dealt with were: education, publicity, economic sanctions, organizational linkages, and the law. Ever since I wrote that paper, I have sporadically thought about why this effort left me feeling dissatisfied. One reason was that its recommendations relied entirely on formal organizations for the implementation of preventive mechanisms. Since then, I have modified my views and have presented a paper which made the case for the participation of an aroused citizenry as an essential element in putting pressure on formal organizations and governments (see ch. 9). It seemed to me then, and it still does, that if a citizenry's consciousness can be raised in support of seals or trees, then it ought to be possible to mobilize their support in favour of people. However, my feelings of dissatisfaction have continued and have led to further thinking and exploring of this theme. Therefore I offer this further installment on the same topic.

Who is the Perpetrator?

Almost half a century ago, the General Assembly of the United Nations approved the "Convention on the Prevention and Punishment of the Crime of Genocide." Although it defined the crime, it failed to put in place the judicial and enforcement mechanisms for the prosecution and punishment of the perpetrators of such crimes. Thus, none of the perpetrators of the many genocides committed since then have been either tried or punished by the United Nations. Most commentators have blamed this state of affairs on the fact that the United Nations is a club of sovereign nation-states who are unlikely to agree to the impeachment of one of their members. While there is evidence accumulating that sovereignty is losing some of its aura of legitimacy, this is not the focus of this paper. Instead, I propose to raise some questions about the meaning of the term "perpetrator." Because it has been used to denote both collectivities as well as individuals, I propose to explore some aspects of this dichotomy insofar as it is relevant to the prevention of genocides and gross human rights violations.

The Collectivity as Perpetrator

The United Nations' inability to act on its own Convention does not require further comment at this time. What is even more discouraging, however, is that international relations among countries allow equally small room for hope. They may make "politically correct" statements about human rights, but they are unlikely to act on such statements unless their interests in power and/or wealth are served at the same time. As a Canadian politician recently said when interviewed about his trip to China, if we suspended trading with all the countries that violate human rights, we would have very little foreign trade.[4] The international trade in arms and war-related technology is a good example. While some of these suppliers may disapprove of the human rights records of their customers, they excuse their actions by arguing that others would pick up the business if they refused it. Since the advent of the economic recession, the weapons trade has become increasingly significant in countries with a large war industry. To prevent their poorest customers from deserting them, several of these countries are now making their foreign aid dependent on weapons purchases.

Other pressures apply to members of the international community: diplomats, journalists, human rights workers, or research scholars whose observations on human rights violations are reported in too much detail and too accurately, are asked to leave perpetrator countries and are denied visas in the future. To avoid such situations, much information is either suppressed or distorted. When the people who are exposed to these threats accept such strictures, they usually have an interesting rationalization. They argue that a boycott of economic and diplomatic relations would not work and might even convince the perpetrator of the rightness of his ways; even more important, such boycotts would deprive democratic countries of the opportunity to exercise a liberating influence. They do not usually provide evidence for the effectiveness of such influence, nor do they refer to the cases when their influence was in support of right-wing totalitarian alternatives. Without going into much detail here, it seems that there is little to be expected from the actions of governments, NGOs, or multinational corporations that might reduce the frequency of gross human rights violations. In other words, perpetrator governments or organizations have little to fear from the self-appointed defenders of democratic freedoms.

The Individual as Perpetrator

"Those who were fortunate enough to survive must assume responsibility for fighting the silence and the shadows which impunity seeks to cast over society—or else become its accomplices."—Luis Perez Aguirre (1992: 111)

"[T]he goal of prosecution is to discourage the recurrence of such abuses, as well as to strengthen the Rule of Law, and thereby demonstrate to those invested with state authority that they are ultimately responsible for their actions."—Adama Dieng (1992: 21)

While genocide and gross violations of human rights are always committed by governments or quasi-governmental organizations, it is also true that within these collective bodies there are individuals who make decisions and give orders. In addition to giving orders that threaten the survival of victim groups, these individuals also enrich themselves in many illegal ways. The sad fact is that the vast majority of these individuals are never prosecuted and held accountable for their actions.

However, it is in this area that one can locate hopes for prevention, provided that large parts of the public can be motivated to join in an outcry against such individuals. Such a process might go through several stages, from ostracism to arrest and punishment.

Ostracism would deprive such individuals of diplomatic immunity and legitimacy. If widespread enough, it would prevent such perpetrators from travelling outside their country and from receiving distinguished visitors in their own country. The recent history of Kurt Waldheim, whose crime was a much lesser one, proves that ostracism can be a very effective punishment.[5]

A further step would become possible if there were some international agreement on how such perpetrators should be arrested and tried. This will require revisions to the international aspects of human rights legislation and to extradition treaties. However, in the meantime, it is often possible to prosecute perpetrators even in the absence of such revisions. A recent example concerns Kamal Bamadhaj who, carrying a passport of New Zealand, was shot three years ago by the Indonesian army in a massacre carried out during a peaceful demonstration in East Timor. General Sintong Panjaitan, who was at the time in charge of the army in East Timor, and who is now a senior adviser to the Indonesian minister of technology, was ordered by a U. S. federal court to pay $14 million in punitive damages and for causing pain and suffering to the family. Since the general has no assets in the U. S. and cannot be arrested as long as he stays out of that country, this sentence is not likely to be carried out. But it represents a symbolic victory of tremendous value.[6] Unfortunately, this case received very little publicity. If more countries were to hold such trials more frequently, and if such trials received more publicity, the perpetrators would increasingly be perceived by the general public as scofflaws.

This case is also a dramatic illustration of the behind the scenes management of publicity. One would have thought that a judgment handed down by a U.S. federal court had sufficient credibility and legitimacy to be reported in the media of the day. However, no mention of this case was found in several newspapers such as the *New York Times*, the *Washington Post*, or the *Chicago Tribune*. At the same time, there was extensive coverage of the economic summit that took place in Jakarta.

Many other cases could be cited where the media published distorted coverage or no coverage at all. An example of the former was the widespread refusal of the media to report the 1984 Ethiopian famine as a deliberately planned, man-made weapon against groups opposing the government. An example of no coverage is the plight of the East Timorese which received widespread coverage only when, after fifteen years of victimization, a massacre took place in the presence of foreign journalists.

Most discouraging is the almost total silence of the media about those cases where an effort is being made to bring individual perpetrators to justice. At present, only a few such individual criminals have been tried or are being tried. For example, two Treblinka trials were held in Düsseldorf in 1964–65 and in 1970, and there were three Auschwitz trials in Frankfurt between 1963 and 1966. Ethiopia has over a thousand men in the Addis Ababa jail awaiting trial for war crimes. The Yugoslav War Crimes Tribunal has prosecuted its first case, against a Bosnian Serb, Dusan Tadic, under arrest in Germany since December 1994. In November 1994, the U.N. created an international tribunal to try those responsible for genocide in Rwanda.[7] Unfortunately there appears to exist a conspiracy of silence about such proceedings. I am not even willing to guess at the components of this conspiracy, but I am pleased to notice that it seems less efficient with regard to the recent tribunals in the former Yugoslavia and in Rwanda.

The final step in dealing with individual perpetrators would be to prevent them from enjoying a golden retirement when their regime is finally overthrown. This would require, (1) new controls on the transfer of stolen wealth and (2) pressure on those countries that are inclined to provide safe havens for such criminals.

In short, we are facing two interrelated problems in following this course of discouraging future potential perpetrators. The first one is to bring the offenders to justice; not only the relatively minor ones, but also those in charge. But it is not sufficient to bring them to justice if most are pardoned and only a few receive modest sentences. That would only continue to send the message that gross violations of human rights may be committed with impunity. The second problem is to bring such judicial proceedings to the attention of the widest possible audience. So far, the media have largely refused to do this. That makes them co-conspirators in the continuing massive violations of human rights in so many countries that have sanctimoniously signed the relevant conventions outlawing them.

As long as none of these things happen, there is nothing to discourage future perpetrators. Quite on the contrary, they can look forward to a rich and successful career. To confirm that this is so we need only look at the careers of some of the more prominent perpetrators in recent history. Idi Amin of Uganda is reported to be living off his ill-gotten gains in great luxury in Saudi Arabia. Mengistu Haile Mariam of Ethiopia is reported to enjoy similar privileges in Zimbabwe. Suharto of Indonesia remains in full control of his government, as do a large number of other perpetrators of human rights violations. Perhaps the most egregious example in recent history comes from Haiti where the military dictatorship was finally forced out of office by a threat of military intervention from the United States. However, this success was severely tarnished when the same United States used its own aircraft to fly Cedras and his family with their ill-gotten wealth to retirement in Panama, and flew the rest of his entourage to retirement in Miami. There was no suggestion that any of them would be held accountable for their misdeeds.[8]

In the case of the former Yugoslavia, we were treated to the spectacle of the perpetrators being received with diplomatic courtesies at peace negotiations where they agreed to cease-fires they had no intention of observing. The case of Rwanda is even more curious. The United Nations has activated an international court in The Hague to deal with cases from the former Yugoslavia. It has not yet done so for cases from Rwanda. In the meantime, the postgenocide government in Rwanda is proceeding with its policy to punish the perpetrators. While they have arrested over 75,000 people, imprisoned in badly overcrowded facilities, they have barely started to set up courts to try them. The trials will have to wait until a legal infrastructure is in place that can conduct fair inquiries. At the time of writing, the first handful of cases are being processed.

In my current state of thinking, the most important step toward the prevention of future gross human rights violations is the prosecution of key individuals in responsible roles. Although it should be self-evident, it must be stressed that the targets of such prosecutions should be the people at the top—not those at the bottom, as is so often the case.

In order for such prosecutions to take place we should not rely on governments and NGOs to take the initiative. Such initiatives will become meaningful and effective realities when grass roots outrage will reach a crescendo that cannot be ignored. How such an awakening of grass roots consciousness is to be stirred up is a practical problem. Perhaps we should study the techniques employed so successfully by

Greenpeace. If they can rouse such outrage in support of saving seals and trees, we should have little trouble mobilizing similar support for saving people.

Conclusion

In modern genocides, the perpetrator society can almost always be shown to incur serious and long-lasting losses. This self-inflicted punishment would act as a deterrent if it were widely recognized and understood. For this reason such societies should not be prosecuted[9]—even if such prosecution could be undertaken and its results be enforced. Instead, the scale of their losses should become widely known and understood. However, this could happen only if massive popular outrage were to force educational institutions and the mass media to deal with these aspects of genocide.

While societies incur collective costs, individual perpetrators enrich themselves in entirely illegal ways at the expense of the victims. In addition, if they live that long, they are now allowed to enjoy their ill-gotten gains in luxurious retirement. It is such individuals who should be tried and punished in highly publicized ways.

If the costs to the perpetrator society and the punishment of the individual perpetrators were properly documented and widely publicized, then there would be some hope that genocides and gross human rights violations would decrease—perhaps even disappear—in the future. How these goals are to be achieved is the question that this paper challenges you, and our newly founded association, to answer.

Notes

1. From a paper read at the founding meeting of the Association of Genocide Scholars, June 14–16, 1995, at the College of William and Mary at Williamsburg, Virginia.
2. For one of the best recent discussions of these topics see: Yves Ternon *L'état criminel: Les génocides au XXᵉ siècle* (Paris: Editions du Seuil, 1995), cinquième partie, "Problématique de l'intervention." especially. 396–403.
3. India's intervention which led to the founding of Bangladesh may be considered an exception. However, the circumstances were quite unique and are unlikely to be duplicated.
4. Premier Harcourt of British Columbia.
5. The role of the Vatican probably did more to damage its reputation than to enhance that of Waldheim.

6. Letter to the editor, *Manchester Guardian Weekly*, vol. 151, no. 21 (November 20, 1994): 2.
7. Colin Tatz, *Reflections on the Politics of Remembering and Forgetting*. The First Abraham Wajnryb Memorial Lecture, 1 December 1994. North Ryde, NSW, Australia: Centre for Comparative Genocide Studies, 1995: 26–31. While several cases are before the Tribunal, all but Dusan Tadic remain at large. There may well be additional data since this was written.
8. It has been argued that this solution saved a great many lives that would have been lost if the government of Haiti had been changed by military action. This is almost certainly so, but it unfortunately remains true that what happened looked remarkably like rewarding those who had been responsible for the misdeeds of the previous regime.
9. Such prosecutions of perpetrator societies can, in theory, take many forms: from censure by the United Nations, to prosecutions in the world court in The Hague, to punitive treaties imposed after military intervention, to withdrawal of foreign aid and technical assistance, to economic boycotts, and so on.

11

A Summation

There are two ideas that have motivated me to spend so much time and energy on such a depressing topic as genocide. The first one is the firm conviction that there must be an explanation for a phenomenon that has such a long history in all parts of the world. The second idea consists of the optimistic hope that in the future genocides can be either prevented altogether or at least "nipped in the bud."

The Past

In our book and in my papers we have tried to show that genocides or genocidal massacres have occurred since the beginning of history in all parts of the populated world. Until modern times, these genocides have almost always been of the utilitarian types that we have categorized in terms of their motives as those intended to eliminate a real or potential threat, to spread terror among real or potential enemies, or to acquire economic wealth that could not be carried off in the form of loot. These types of genocide were employed in the building and expanding of empires and they were always successful in the sense that they achieved the ends to which they were the chosen means. In addition, they achieved these ends at relatively minor costs to the perpetrator society—minor when measured against the ends obtained. It was these successful outcomes that have ensured genocides their continued popularity.

A decline in the popularity of genocides set in when it occurred to some perpetrators that their victims were much more valuable to them as slaves than as bodies. This idea occurred quite independently at least three times: first to the Ancient Egyptians, then to Genghis Khan during his conquest of China, and finally to the Moghul conquerors of India. Such slaves were valued either as workers in labor-intensive societies or as artisans who brought skills that were in short supply in the perpetrator society. The resulting increase in the popularity of slavery produced a corresponding decline in the frequency of genocides. Slavery became the preferred means in the building and expanding of empires. This period came to an end with the decline of empires and with the phenomenal success of the antislavery movement.

However, these processes did not lead to the disappearance of genocides. Instead, the world saw the invention of and a gradual increase in ideological genocides: those performed in the implementation of a belief, ideology, or theory. The early cases of ideological genocides were an effort to enforce adherence to a religious belief; later they were employed to enforce conformity to a political theory; in the twentieth century they are most frequently used to in support of an ideology of ethno-nationalism. The enormous increase in the frequency of ideological genocides, in the scale of their casualties, and in the number of refugees they produce, have caused grave concerns for human rights organizations and humanitarian aid groups. However, the urgency of the problems they daily face causes them to be preoccupied with daily emergencies that leave very little time and very few resources for considerations of how to intervene in emerging genocides or how to prevent them in the future.

The Future

In spite of the strenuous efforts of futurologists, the future remains a closed book. That is probably as it should be and it should stay that way. If the future were predetermined, and if we could obtain access to its plans, we almost certainly would not like what is in store for us. In addition, we would all become fatalists because we are unable to change what is to come. As long as the future remains a closed book we have to take some responsibility for it.

In the case of genocides our responsibility as citizens is clear enough. To the extent that we are not completely immersed in the material world of consumerism and have some sense of civic obligations left, we must take some responsibility for the fate of decent people and the future of the world.

None of the following actions will by themselves prevent future genocides. But several of them implemented together ought to succeed in preventing genocides, or at least in intervening when gross violations of human rights are reported—no matter where they are observed. These actions, in summary form, are:

• Education, at all ages, should include the teaching about human rights, about the enormous losses incurred by genocidal societies, and about the impermanence of the illegitimate gains accumulated by individual perpetrators and their friends.

• The abolition of impunity and the introduction of appropriate laws, judicial tribunals, and enforcement mechanisms in order that perpetrators be punished and their stolen wealth be returned to the people from whom it was looted.

• Media organizations that report not only the suffering of the victims, but also the prosecution of the perpetrators. It should become part of common knowledge that there are no gains to be derived from ideological genocides for the perpetrator society or for the perpetrating individuals.

• Finally, we need a human rights movement, analogous to Greenpeace and Amnesty International, that is able to raise the popular conscience to such a degree that governments would find it increasingly difficult not to act in favour of peace and human well-being and against those who want to commit or already have committed crimes against humanity.

These four areas seem to be the crucial ones, although other relevant areas like stopping the international arms trade, the degradation of the environment, etc., certainly should not be ignored.[1]

A final word: There is another method for abolishing genocides, gross human rights violations, as well as a number of other evils. While there seems no chance that this method will be seriously considered by anyone in the near future, it seems worthwhile to conclude this discussion with an excursion into utopia.

This conceptually simple method consists in spreading the earth's wealth to the poor in all parts of the world. This is not a subversive plea for some kind of socialism. On the contrary, it ought to appeal to every thinking capitalist. If everybody could partake in a reasonably comfortable lifestyle, it is unlikely that anyone could muster participation in, or support for, genocide or similar atrocities. Unfortunately, this method appeals neither to potential perpetrators, nor to public or private bureaucracies or corporate elites because their policy decisions are heavily influenced by lust for power, greed, and the inability to think up imaginative solutions. The interesting aspect of this reluctance to raise the living standards of the developing world is that it runs counter to self-interest. While it is true that raising them would make the armament industries[2] suffer, every other economic activity would flourish. The consumer market of the world would expand exponentially. Population growth rates would decline significantly. And intergroup friction would not escalate into violence because everybody would have too much to lose. The self-interest of the majority of people would be directed toward maintaining their lifestyle, their children's prospects for the future, their homes, and their comforts. The minority whose interests run in the other direction would be ostracized or criminalized. In either case they would be unable to create much mischief.

Notes

1. For an excellent, recent discussion of intervention, see: Yves Ternon, *L'état criminel: Les génocides au xxe siècle* (Paris: Editions du Seuil, 1995) *cinquième partie* "Problématique de l'intervention." especially 396–403. Ternon is also one of the few authors who includes demographic considerations in his discussion.
2. While the bulk of arms are exported by industrial countries, the bulk of imports is into developing countries. But while the same industrial countries spend $1,082 per person on health care, developing countries can spend only $17 per person on health care. Ruth Leger Sivard. *World Military and Social Expenditures 1996* (Washington, D.C.: World Priorities, Inc., 1996): 13.

Part 2

Methods in Comparative Research on Genocide

12

Preliminary Considerations

Some Specifics of Genocide Research

The comparative study of genocide is a very curious field. The events under investigation have occurred throughout history while their study has only begun in the second half of the twentieth century. The methods, assumptions, and analytic frameworks developed in other areas of comparative research apply equally in this area. However, the subject matter imposes its own particulars that inevitably modify any preconceived set of methods. It is these modifications that will be the focus of the following chapters. The summaries of cases in part 3 will illustrate their particular impact on the applicable methods of research.

A word about assumptions: the first one underlies all research. It is the assumption that the phenomenon under study can be understood and explained. It is important to make this assumption explicit because in the case of genocide there are people who do not think that this is possible at all. If we were to share their view, then there would be no point in doing this research. In more technical language, the search for explanations should be a linkage between research and theory.[1]

There is another assumption that needs to be made explicit. It concerns the belief that the events that have been defined as genocide have features in common whose comparison will provide clues to their understanding and explanation. Again, without this assumption there would be no point in doing comparative research. But, at the same time, it must be remembered that by abstracting those features that several cases have in common, the very uniqueness of each case escapes our attention. That uniqueness is of great importance and is the proper subject matter of several disciplines outside the social sciences. Insofar as the social sciences attempt to analyze and generalize they require sets of data, no matter how much violence the assembling of such sets does to the uniqueness of each case. Of course, that violence can be justified only if it does, in fact, produce the results that the comparative method promises.

However, producing such results is only likely when some formidable difficulties have been overcome. One of these is that no agreement has yet emerged on the definition of genocide, that is, we have yet to agree on what it is that we propose to study. Similarly, there is no agreement on a typology, in spite of the importance of there being one (Lenski 1994: 1–2; 21–22).

Another stumbling block for causal analyses is that the data available for comparative analysis are typically cross-sectional, that is, they are collected at one time period. What is really needed in order to unravel the dynamic processes involved, are repeated observations over time (Williams 1994: 73).

For a much more detailed discussion of the problems of comparative research than would be appropriate here see, among many others, the volumes by Armer and Grimshaw (1973) or Øyen (1990). The papers in these volumes deal almost exclusively with comparisons across space and ignore the additional complications introduced by comparisons over time.

For a discussion of the more limited range of problems encountered in dealing with first-person accounts, Totten's "Introduction" will also be helpful (Totten 1991).

When such historical dimensions are introduced, the problems of data collection and analysis multiply. In the particular case of gross human rights violations and genocide, an additional complication arises from the fact that nobody feels indifferent about them and that everybody wants to present their own view of the data. Thus, there are many reasons that help to explain the many ways in which data can be and are distorted. At the collective level, we have to deal with deliberate misinformation, denials, censorship, legislation against unfavorable reporting, denial of access to relevant places, closed archives, among other ways of distorting the truth. At the individual level, the data may be distorted by culturally defined attitudes, deficient memory, deliberate falsification, or disinclination to testify. In addition, victims are often disinclined to report anything good about the perpetrators or anything bad about the victims, while the opposite tendency is often observed among perpetrators.

Another way in which data can be distorted arises out of the qualifications of the investigators. In attempting to deal with cases garnered from all parts of the globe and all periods of history, an investigator has to accept a certain amount of incompetence. Thus, nobody could possibly be an expert on all of the societies and the cultures that produce these cases and that form the context within which they should be interpreted. There is no way to avoid this situation short of having each case treated by an area specialist—and that would lead to several other problems. The compromise adopted in this work is to limit the reporting of each case to the performance of the genocidal killings without attempting to interpret these within the cultural context in which they occurred. While this compromise allows the presentation of a large number of cases (part 3), it is important to remember that a more intensive study of a case requires an understanding of the context in which it occurred (see ch. 34).

These are some of the aspects of data collection for comparative research on genocide that will be explored in the following chapters. While the collection of such data will receive quite detailed attention, the methods available for their analysis will only be listed here.

At the outset of research it is important to decide whether to use the individual or the collectivity as a unit of analysis. This distinction often is a source of confusion although its consequences are quite dramatic. Thus, the two questions, why did Hitler commit genocide, and why did the Germans commit genocide, produce quite different results.

Relevant quantitative data are rarely available; when they are available descriptive and analytical statistical methods will be useful. In the majority of cases only qualitative data will be available, requiring content analysis, checks on reliability and validity, and triangulation by several methods. Readers who are looking for detailed discussions of these techniques are referred to the standard texts on research methods. The reason for this unequal treatment of data collection and analysis is that the special difficulties associated with research on genocide are largely confined to the acquisition of data, while the methods for their analysis are quite standard. However, before proceeding, a few more parameters need to be discussed.

A Note on Definitions and Typologies

Attempts to eliminate entire groups of people have been a part of human conflicts for the past 5,000 years. However, it is only since the 1944 publication of Raphael Lemkin's book *Axis Rule in Occupied Europe* and the passing of the resolution by the General Assembly of the United Nations in 1946 that such massacres have been defined as crimes against humanity. That redefinition, and the new word "genocide" that Lemkin coined for it, has been of tremendous importance for the development of human rights codes; but it has done little for the burgeoning field of comparative research.[2] Like other scholars in this area, Frank Chalk and I found that this definition contained in the U.N. Convention on the Prevention and Punishment of the Crime of Genocide was unsatisfactory for research purposes. Therefore, we have formulated a definition of genocide that we are still finding useful in our own attempts at comparative research.

> GENOCIDE is a form of one-sided mass killing in which a state or other authority intends to destroy a group, as that group and membership in it are defined by the perpetrator. (Chalk and Jonassohn: 1990: 23)

For similar reasons, a number of other scholars have proposed their own definitions without being able to reach a consensus. Helen Fein has summarized most of these various efforts to define genocide, including a critique of our definition (Fein 1993: ch. 2).

The most recent critique of our position may be found in the first volume of a projected three-volume work by Steven Katz (Katz 1994: 125–74). In order to prove that the Holocaust was a unique event in history, Katz examines a large number of cases showing that none of them qualified as genocides. In order to accomplish this he formulates his own definition of genocide which is so restrictive that its literal application would also exclude the Holocaust. The result is that Katz now has a definition according to whose terms there is not a single case that meets its requirements:

> I shall employ the notion of Genocide as applying to, and only as applying to, the actualization of the intent, however successfully carried out, to murder in its totality any national, ethnic, racial, religious, political, social, gender or economic group, as these groups are defined by the perpetrator, by whatever means. (Katz 1994: 131)[3]

> the intent to murder a group in its totality (possibly linked to a variety of national, utilitarian, political, ideological, racial, retributive, religious, sexual, social and economic ends) is a necessary condition, per definition, of genocide. (Katz 1994: 133)

It is quite clear that Hitler did not intend to murder the Jews in their totality. There were many exceptions to this intent. Yehuda Bauer has collected and examined several of them (Bauer 1994).

At this point it may be useful to be explicit about the role of definitions and typologies in research. They are emphatically not exercises in mindless neatness or compulsive pedantry. If that were their valid interpretation we could easily discard them and their loss would not be mourned. However, they play a much more important role in research. A definition is an essential tool that tells us what phenomena are included in that particular research. Typologies order these phenomena into subcategories that ensure that only phenomena with similar characteristics are compared with each other. Thus, we are dealing here with tools of research that are neither good nor bad in themselves; they are good tools only insofar as they assist us in producing research results, and they are bad (i.e., inappropriate) tools if they fail to do so.

The U.N. definition of genocide was never intended as a research tool, but as a legal instrument that emerged from a political compromise (Kuper 1981: ch. 2). It has a number of supporters because it has the legal credibility that all the other definitions lack. The alternatives proposed by various academics fail to attract wide support for several reasons. Perhaps the most important of these reasons is that the subject matter to be defined has been shifting. Chalk and Jonassohn include the entire span of recorded history (Chalk and Jonassohn 1990). Others, especially Leo Kuper and R. J. Rummel, have restricted their recent work to the twentieth century (Kuper 1981; Rummel 1992: 1–10). And lately we find that scholars like Fein, Gurr, and Harff are restricting their attention to post World War II cases—but cases of what?[4]

The cases that these latter scholars include in their analysis are a very mixed lot, partly due to varying definitions, and partly due to their expansive typologies. They include a number of cases that should by no definition be called genocides. Instead they employ terms like democide and politicide that allow them to include cases of gross human rights violations of various kinds. For these cases they do not find it necessary to insist on the perpetrator's intent nor on his aim in eliminating the victim group. But what qualifies a case for inclusion is not clear. If the criterion for inclusion as a genocide or a genocidal massacre is the commitment of gross violations of human rights that involve large numbers of deaths, then one wonders why some cases are in while very similar ones are out. Cases reported from Armenia-Azerbaijan, Bangladesh, Burma (Myanmar), India, the former Yugoslavia, among others, are omitted while cases reported from Afghanistan, Angola, Sri Lanka, Uganda, among others, are included (Fein 1993: table 2b, 91).

It is too early in the very short history of genocide research to decide which of the various definitions and typologies that have been proposed as tools will prove to be the most useful. However, it seems unlikely that giving in to the prevailing trend toward ahistorical research will yield significant results. There are many reasons for this. One is that it is hard to see how the process of inquiry is advanced by defining relevant cases in such a way that the major cases of genocide in the twentieth century are excluded. The Armenian genocide of 1915, Stalin's man-made famine of 1933, Hitler's attempt to eliminate Jews, Gypsies, and several other groups in the 1930s and 1940s are such paradigmatic cases that their omission seems unlikely to contribute to knowledge. Another reason why the exclusion of pre-1945 cases is most likely to interfere with the production of significant results is that it, albeit unintentionally, reinforces the position of the so-called revisionist historians. Some of these people deny the facticity of the Holocaust. This denial has been gaining credibility due to the ambivalence of the German government's policies: on the one hand they have criminalized the denial of the Holocaust while on the other hand they de-emphasize its history in favor of reestablishing the reputation of German culture, industry, and respectability (Bialystok 1993: 1–2; 4). Other revisionist deniers include the government of Turkey, which not only officially denies that the Armenian genocide ever happened, but also sponsors academics who are willing to support its policy in scholarly publications. Similarly, the USSR, under its communist government, used to ignore or deny accusations of genocide; since its demise, Russia has incrementally revealed documentation confirming events that formerly had been denied. It seems clear that denials of well-established and verified facts are becoming increasingly acceptable in many parts of the world.

Another consequence of omitting the Holocaust from a comparative analysis of genocides is that it satisfies those scholars who have argued that the Holocaust was a unique event that cannot and should not be subjected to comparative analysis. While it certainly was unique in a number of ways, it must not be excluded from analysis. In many respects it not only can be compared to other cases of genocide, but it even highlights some of the underlying processes. Or, as Yehuda Bauer (1993) has put it, how can you know that it was unique unless you do comparative analysis? The cases described in part 3 will serve to reinforce that perspective.

The most comforting finding from these studies is that democratic states do not commit genocides. This is a very important finding and it seems to hold up, if we make allowances for minor exceptions. This finding adds urgency to the defense of functioning democracies and to the need to spread the kind of government that is based on the consent of the governed. Unfortunately, the warm feeling that comes from knowing that one lives among the "good guys," does not last long. The reason it disappears is twofold. The first one is the sudden recollection of genocidal massacres and "politicides" that have been committed in countries that claim to be democracies, like Bangladesh, India, Northern Ireland, Sri Lanka, and Turkey. Fein may consider that these are not "stable" democracies. That would get us into the awkward position of having to decide when a democracy is a democracy—and that is not likely to be a very rewarding exercise. The second reason why that briefly warm feeling disappears so quickly is that the finding sounds more tautological the longer one thinks about it. Yes, democratic states do not commit genocides because, if they did, we would not call them democratic. And then we remember what these authors conveniently defined outside their area of research: the Holocaust. There can be little argument that the Weimar Republic was a democracy before Hitler came to power. Thus, the researcher now needs to decide when a democratic state is stable enough to prevent it from becoming a perpetrator. Since that question is likely to end up in another tautology, I propose a more challenging question: in what situations and by what processes does a democratic state turn into a totalitarian state? This is not a purely academic question. Recent history has witnessed the rise of right-wing movements with totalitarian aspirations in several democratic states, such as France and India. That rise seems to be facilitated by growing popular impatience with the inability of the democratic process to deal promptly with the major problems of popular concern. Clearly, much research needs to be done on those processes that facilitate the rise of undemocratic political movements, and its results will need to be distributed for discussion to a much wider audience.

Finally, the concept of the "nation" requires attention. This concept creates confusion within a single language, and even more so when translated. Since this is not the place to review that vast literature, nor to enter into the debates on that subject, Johan Galtung's definition will be used in this volume when that concept becomes relevant.

For several reasons, the word "nation" has attained two, even three, quite different meanings, all of them relevant for the general subject of comparative studies (meaning studies comparing nations). The three meanings are:

1. "Nation" in the sense of country, a political entity in territorial space, autonomous in the sense that ultimate political control over internal power relations is made in the country (e.g. with the particular organization referred to as the "state"). A country is also often called a state.

2. "Nation" in the sense of ethnic group, a socio-cultural entity in non-territorial space (as it may be scattered anywhere), characterized by some kind of shared culture, for instance, carried by language, religion, way of life, shared history and/or racial (anatomical) characteristics.

3. "Nation" in the sense of a nation state, meaning a "state" (country) populated (almost) only by members of the same "nation" (ethnic group).

To give some rough orders of magnitude: there are about 150 nations in the first sense of the term in the world today (although the autonomy of many of them is a matter of dispute), about 1500 nations in the second sense of the word, whereas the number of nation-states must be in the order of magnitude of 15.

Most countries are today multi-ethnic, and the "minorities" may even, singly or combined, be majorities—"minority" being a power term (meaning powerless), not a statistical, numerical expression. (Galtung 1982: 17)

This distinction is becoming important to comparative studies of genocides because most modern genocides are ideological and, among these cases, ideologies concerning the nature of the state, the nation, and ethnicity are predominant.[5] It is, however, only when such ideologies become the defining characteristic of a totalitarian state that they are likely to lead to gross abuses of human rights and even genocide. One reason that they do so is that in the hands of a totalitarian regime they come to define the range of acceptable behavior and expression in all areas of human existence. The ideology becomes elaborated to define levels of pollution and purity. This applies not only to race and ethnicity: language is purified of "foreign" elements; the arts of music, painting, poetry, etc. are freed of "decadent" influences; the sciences are purified of "foreign" knowledge; and human relations from friendship to kinship to family behavior are redefined to conform to the new model of purity. These are features of all ideologies in their orthodox or fundamentalist form; they become serious threats to human rights when they become the identifying feature of a totalitarian regime.

It turns out that the concepts of nation and nation state, and the realities that they describe, are not at all new. Buccellati, in his study of the ancient Near East, makes a distinction between the territorial state and the national state that seems as insightful now as it did then (Buccelatti 1967: 13–14). He argues that already in antiquity these two types of states can be clearly distinguished: the territorial state was identified by the territory over which it ruled, while the national state was characterized by the ethnic identity of its citizens. And it was the latter that was likely to commit genocide. A twentieth-century adaptation might argue that the aspiration to become a national state frequently leads to genocide. That aspiration arises out of a rapidly spreading ideology that defines the ethnically homogeneous state as an ideal to be achieved.

The relevance of these factors is particularly striking in view of the fact that ethnically homogeneous states are very rare. That fact helps to explain the contemporary popularity of nationalist ideologies. That is not to say that it helps to explain to increasing number of genocides. We still lack an adequate explanation of why interethnic hostilities escalate to genocide in a few countries while they do not do so in the vast majority of others.

That failure is at least partially due to our looking at the wrong variables. When dealing with "nations" or "ethnies" (A. Smith 1986: ch. 2) we most often focus on their ascribed characteristics, such as their language, their religion, and their common past. While these characteristics may help to define the group, they do very little to explain the relations between the several groups in a country. Except under conditions of dictatorship or a greatly disproportionate distribution of power, that relationship is more likely to be illuminated by looking at those institutions that define the country as encompassing all of its constituent groups more or less equally. There are many such quite mundane institutions that become more significant when they are missing than when they are present, and they become most significant when they are present in regional rather than in centralized forms. Thus, we need to ask whether a given country has a national currency, a national postal service, a national army, a national travel system (of roads, railroads, and airline), a national communication system (telephone, radio, television, and press), a centralized system of social services (medical, hospital, unemployment insurance, old-age pensions, etc.), a centralized legal system (police, courts, prisons, etc.), and so on. Perhaps the institution that is extremely influential without the reinforcement of the others is education; decentralized school systems are the most likely to teach and reinforce regional differences that encourage interethnic conflict. Individually, such details among different institutional areas may seem unimportant. Many of them taken together convey a symbolic message about the nature of the country and about the relations between its constituent groups. The more atomized these institutions, the more conflictual the groups within a state are likely to be. The more centralized these institutions, the more they are likely to convey the message of a collective identity and solidarity.

These statements should not be taken as findings—they probably oversimplify a very complex area and they have not even been tested yet. They are advanced as hypotheses here in order to alert the reader to some of the questions that ought to be asked when reading the materials on comparative methods and on the cases that follow.

Notes

1. Gunnar Myrdal, "The Beam in Our Eyes." in Donald P. Warwick and Samual Osherson, eds., *Comparative Research Methods* (Englewood Cliffs, N.J.: Prentice-Hall, 1973), 89–99. This is still the most succinct statement on the interplay between method and theory.
2. One of the first sociologists to deal with genocide explicitly was Brewton Berry in *Race and Ethnic Relations* (Boston: Houghton Mifflin, 1965 [1951]). Already in the 1950s he included several pages on it in his text. While he treated it comparatively, he not only used the United Nations definition, he was still optimistic about the United Nations' ability to implement the provisions of the Convention, 156–62.
3. The large number of adjectives seems redundant since Katz makes it quite clear that he sets out to prove that the Holocaust was the only genocide in history.
4. Helen Fein, "Accounting for Genocide after 1945: Theories and Some Findings," *International Journal of Group Rights* 1 (1993), 79–106. This is the most recent version of this approach. Her discussion and bibliography contain the relevant citations to the work of Ted Gurr and of Barbara Harff.
5. For a more nuanced view, see: Uri Ra'anan, "The Nation-State Fallacy," 5–20, chapter 1 in Joseph V. Montville, ed., *Conflict and Peacemaking in Multiethnic Societies* (Lexington, Mass.: Lexington Books/D. C. Heath and Company, 1990).

13

The Language of Data

In considering the problems and pitfalls encountered in doing comparative research on genocide, the mistakes and misuses of language surely rank very high. In exploring some of these problems and pitfalls it is not our intention to present solutions for them. Instead, we would consider it an achievement if we succeeded in making all researchers aware that they exist. Of course, not all of the following aspects of language will apply in the study of every case. However, we suggest that one needs to be aware of them before one can decide which of them do or do not apply.

A New Word for an Ancient Crime

While genocides have occurred since antiquity and throughout history, the term "genocide" first came into use in 1944 with the publication of Raphael Lemkin's book. He was well aware of the existence of appropriate terms in most languages, but felt that a new term was needed to denote the virulence of the Nazi killing program:

> New conceptions require new terms. By "genocide" we mean the destruction of a nation or of an ethnic group. This new word, coined by the author to denote an old practice in its modern development, is made from the ancient Greek word *genos* (race, tribe) and the Latin *cide* (killing), thus corresponding in its formation to such words as tyrannicide, homicide, infanticide, etc. (Lemkin 1944: 79)

It acquired wide usage as a result of Lemkin's success in lobbying for the December 1946 resolution of the General Assembly of the United Nations and the December 1948 adoption of its Convention for the Prevention and Punishment of the Crime of Genocide (Kuper 1981: appendix 1).

Scholars of comparative genocide studies soon applied this new term to genocides that had occurred since antiquity. This practice was objected to by some less than inspired critics on the grounds that a phenomenon could not exist before it had a name. That a phenomenon first has to have a name in order to exist is too ridiculous a proposition to require further rebuttal. However, what does make the critique of some interest is that words for that phenomenon did actually exist in most of the relevant languages. The use of "genocide" became quickly so widespread that few people remembered the earlier terms.

We are grateful to a number of students and colleagues who have made us aware that there is an equivalent term available in their mother tongue. At first, none of them provided documentation in support of their assertions. Since then, we have been able to trace appropriate terms for genocide in several languages.[1]

In English "the murder of a nation" is the heading of a chapter by Henry Morgenthau describing the suffering of the Armenians in Turkey (Morgenthau 1918: ch. 24).

In French, Gracchus Babeuf used the term *"populicides"* for the massacres in the Vendée during the French Revolution.[2] "Populicides" is an artificial word meaning the killing of a population.

In German, the poet Graf von Platen-Hallermünde coined the term *"Völkermord"* in 1831 which he applied to the brutal suppression of the Polish revolution by the Russians.[3] It simply means the murder of a people.

In Polish we find the term *"ludobo'jstwo"* which also means the killing of a people. (We have not traced its origin.)

In Armenian we have been able to trace *"tseghasbanoutiun"* in print, which means the killing of a race.[4]

In Greek the word *"Genoktonia"* is apparently of ancient origin and translates literally as the killing of a nation or the death of a nation.

This semantic enquiry is particularly interesting because these languages have available, since World War II, two terms for the same phenomenon. However, in recent literature, English and French seem to prefer using 'genocide', while German seems to prefer using "Völkermord." Presumably the reason for using the new term is that it has become enshrined in several documents of the United Nations, and thus obtained an international currency and a legal status that the alternatives lack. The usage in other countries remains to be investigated, as does the reason for either choice.

The sources consulted so far do not go back further than the French Revolution. Therefore it is not clear whether any of these terms were in use before that time. However, it is not surprising that the revolutionary emphasis on equality and the "rights of man" created a new perspective on mass murders. Because these were increasingly perceived as massive violations of the rights of man, authors required a new word to describe this phenomenon.

Translation

Among the difficulties in studying genocides are problems of translation and transliteration. Such problems are not new to historians or social scientists, but pose special difficulties for those in the field of genocide studies. For example, scholars of the Holocaust should master at least German, Polish, Russian, Yiddish, and Hebrew in order to do serious work in that field; otherwise they must rely on translations. Genocide scholars, dealing with a wide variety of cases, are faced with an even more insurmountable problem, because learning all the languages involved is quite impossible and forces the researcher to rely on the work of translators.

However, translations always represent additional risks for researchers. As few researchers have the linguistic skills to verify the quality of a translation, they are forced to depend on the reputation of the translator and/or the scholarly acceptance of the translation. It is only when different versions of one text appear that one realizes the enormity of such problems. The best-known illustration of such difficulties concerns the Bible. In the seventeenth century Baruch Spinoza, the Dutch philosopher and theologian, challenged the orthodox view that the five books of Moses had been dictated by God on Mount Sinai. For his trouble, he was excommunicated by the Jews and condemned by the Inquisition. But ever since his pathbreaking studies, scholars have analyzed and debated the meanings of the five books of the Torah. (Their task was complicated by the fact that the official Hebrew version does not include vowels.) The results of such investigations have only become obvious to the layman when their work resulted in new translations. Thus, the translation published by the Jewish Publication Society[5] is full of footnotes that warn the reader that the meaning of the original Hebrew is "uncertain" or "obscure."

And no one realizes better than the committees responsible for the new Protestant and Jewish versions how the number of such caveats could readily have been doubled and trebled, and more. (Orlinsky 1963: 249–64)

There are several ways in which the use of translations becomes problematic. First of all, the user of translation does so because he/she requires full access to the content of a text in an unfamiliar foreign language. That also means that the user is not able to assess the quality of the translation. Secondly, since translating no longer has the high status it once enjoyed among social scientists, it is now often performed by translators who are not familiar with the specialized vocabulary that may be required. In addition, since translation is rather costly, publishers are not often prepared to spend additional funds to have someone check the quality of a translation. Finally, there is the problem of secondary or tertiary translation, where a translator does not work from an original text whose language may not be familiar, but rather from an earlier translation into a language that he/she does know.

Verifying the quality of a translation becomes increasingly difficult when the text in question is a translation of a dead language. An example of such a linguistic quagmire is ancient Mongolian. The only surviving record of Chingis Khan's reign that the Mongols themselves produced is the *Secret History of the Mongols*, a text originally written in ancient Mongolian. Since no copy of the original has ever been found, our knowledge is based on a text that was transliterated into Chinese during the Ming dynasty (1368–1644). The scribe who wrote this text intended to phonetically represent the Mongolian original and added a gloss of the meaning in Chinese. After the Mongols were driven out of China, Mongolian texts were destroyed; it is thought that the main reason why this text survived at all was because it was written in Chinese characters. Its Mongolian origin could become apparent only after careful examination.

The transliteration of the text was discovered by scholars in the nineteenth century, and it was soon translated into Russian, Japanese, German, French, English, Hungarian, and modern Mongolian. In addition, the translators were faced with the task of rendering a medieval language into a modern one, even if they were fully knowledgeable of ancient Mongolian and ancient Chinese.

The English translation of this text was completed by Francis W. Cleaves in the 1940s, but was not published until 1982. This text has then been adapted and interpreted by Paul Kahn, a scholar who readily admits that he has never looked at the original text, because he has no knowledge of Mongolian or Chinese. *The Secret History of the Mongols* poses another problem, as it was written in verse. As factual recordings of events are easier to translate than poetry, one must ask in this case how much of the translation is an interpretation of the original text (Kahn 1984: xi–xii).

This example also draws attention to the many difficulties created by variations in writing systems. Within the range of those languages that use alphabets there are enormous differences in the number of letters used (e.g., Armenian uses thirty-six letters), whether vowels are written (e.g., Arabic and Hebrew), and the number of forms that each letter can take (e.g., Amharic).[6] If these variations look intimidating, other writing systems that use hieroglyphics, ideograms, etc. pose even greater problems. Of course, the individual researchers will be concerned only with those languages associated with the particular cases that they are studying.

Another problem faced by a translator is that there are untranslatable concepts in every language, untranslatable even between languages that share the same cultural and linguistic background. Illustrations from English are particularly interesting since it is a language with a very large vocabulary. Even so, it has adopted French terms like "coup d'état" or "double entendre," German ones like "Weltanschauung" and "Blitzkrieg," African expressions like "mumbo jumbo", such Spanish words as "matador" and "guerilla," and Italian terms like "dolce vita," and "mafia," to name but a few examples.

Perhaps more troublesome are concepts that are only imperfectly translatable. Thus, while English has one verb 'to read,' there are at least twelve different verbs in Polish that distinguish different kinds of reading from one another. Much more important is the inability of English to render a distinction found in many European languages. In spite of its shared linguistic heritage, English employs a single verb "to know" for the distinction in French of *connaître* vs. *savoir*, in German of *kennen* vs. *wissen*, and in Spanish of *conocer* vs. *saber*. The inability of English speakers to easily make this distinction may have had serious consequences for methodological thought in the social sciences in general and in comparative genocide studies in particular (Deutscher 1973: 171).

An example more directly relevant to genocide studies is the "perpetrator" concept which has the great advantage in English that it can denote either an individual or a collectivity. There is no term in French that can take both meanings. While the verb *"perpétrer"* is in current usage, the noun *"perpetreur"* was in use in the sixteenth century (Huguet 1961: 734), but has fallen into disuse. As a genocide researcher, it was easy to resurrect the noun because its meaning is obvious since the verb is familiar. In German the situation is different: while there is no equivalent for "perpetrator" (*"Übeltäter"*), its meaning can be approximated by using the plural.

A similar dilemma is associated with the term "bystander." In English, the verb "to witness" means to observe an event. The term itself does not indicate whether the person who witnessed the event was an accidental bystander or an interested spectator. In German, the verb is more specific. *"Wegsehen"* means to look away, while *"zusehen"* means to watch (a person or an event) (Duden Oxford 1991: 1358, 1393). The English "bystander" is usually translated as *"zuschauer"* which means "spectator" (where *"schauen"* is the southern form of *"sehen"*). Thus, the English notion of "bystander" who may or may not be looking away is not translatable into German without an explanation, one that the researcher may not be aware of. The French translation of "bystander" is *"spectateur"* which also excludes the neutral or the "looking away" meanings.

That such distinctions matter may be illustrated by the reactions of Yves Ternon upon reading the French version of Raul Hilberg's new book (Hilberg 1994). Ternon disagrees with the translator's rendering of "perpetrator" as *"exécuteur"* (Ternon 1995: 123). For the translation of "bystander" as *"témoins"* he substitutes 'spectateur' in order to emphasize the passivity of someone who is present (Ternon 1995: note 51, 413).

When two languages are closely related due to common origins, they sometimes trip up the unwary by what professional translators call *les faux amis* (false friends). This term refers to cases where the same word is found in two languages, but does not mean the same thing. For example, when genocide researchers are interested in the effects of persecution on reproduction in a victim population, they should know that "fertility" translates into French as *"fecundité"* and that "fecundity" translates into French as *"fertilité"*. Otherwise, these faux amis might be responsible for producing some very odd findings.

When one is dealing with unrelated languages and/or cultures, such problems intensify. Not only are there concepts and expressions that are untranslatable, but the cultural points of reference can sometimes be so different that even descriptive translation becomes difficult. For example, in Hindi, the past and present tenses are very simple and easily translatable. However, the future tense is very complicated, as it implies degrees of obligation. For instance, since it is culturally unacceptable to turn down an invitation, the only recourse is to agree, using a grammatical form that implies the possibility of negation. If one were not aware of this particularity of Indian usage, the future tense could lead to many misinterpretations.[7]

In *The Chinese Chameleon*, Raymond Dawson addresses this issue, centering on the translation problems between Chinese and European languages. He states that problems related to translating Chinese into a European language are to a certain degree exacerbated by the contrast between Chinese characters and the common heritage of an alphabetic script which all European languages share. Such problems have nothing to do with the peculiarity of Chinese grammar, however, as there is no truth to the notion that ideograms express ideas rather than words, and that Chinese has no grammar comparable with that of other languages. The main problem is that in translating Chinese, one is trying to translate from a language with different cultural values, experiences, and terms of reference. The translator from French, or even Latin or Greek, can assume a common cultural background that is familiar to the educated reader. That translator has the two-dimensional job of converting languages belonging to the same culture area. The translator from Chinese into English, however, has the three-dimensional job of translating for a readership that, except in specialist journals, is usually unfamiliar with Chinese culture. This raises all kinds of problems for the translator unless the material in question is of a modern international character. The translator's task, therefore, does not end when a satisfactory English equivalent for the Chinese text has been found: the translator must visualize a hypothetical general reader and devise means of converting the material into something within the reader's range of experience without doing too great harm to the original text. When dealing with anything unfamiliar the translator always has to decide whether to trust the reader's knowledge, explain in a footnote, or convert the text into more familiar terms (Dawson 1967: 121–22).

This raises certain questions for the genocide scholar when dealing with a translated text. For example, when the Romans used the word "*devastato*" when referring to the destruction of a city, what exactly were they referring to? Did they physically destroy the city, did they kill its inhabitants, or were the people sent into slavery?[8] If there is confusion with regards to vague words in languages which are related, then there may be even greater confusion between languages that are not related. As most translators are not familiar with the peculiarities of genocide studies, the genocide scholar should view any reference to destruction and killing with some suspicion. For example, when one examines the story of the Romans spreading salt over Carthage so that nothing would ever grow there again, one must wonder whether there was enough salt available to the perpetrator to actually do this. As salt was an expensive commodity during that time, it seems more likely that a little salt may have been sprinkled ceremoniously over a patch of earth.[9] It is very possible that this myth became so entrenched in our history books as a result of an error in translation: the original meaning of spreading the earth with salt, which most likely referred to a ceremony, was eventually lost and then translated literally.

Evolution of Language

Languages evolve with time, and it is not always easy to recognize whether the translator has taken such change into account. *The War of the Conquest: How It Was Waged Here in Mexico* (de Sahagun 1978) is an example of a text which raises several questions concerning the reliability of the translation. It consists of collected accounts of the Spanish conquest of the Aztecs, as given to Fray Bernardino de Sahagun, a Franciscan missionary, circa 1555, by Aztecs who had witnessed the conquest thirty years earlier. The text was originally recorded in Nahuatl, the Aztecs' own language. Sahagun had learned their language in order to teach them Christianity. The book is useful in that it is one of the few written documents to provide an account of events by the victim group, describing both how they felt about their conquerors and various instances of Spanish cruelty.

But the questions are: was Sahagun's grasp of Nahuatl adequate enough to fully grasp what the witnesses were saying? As the book itself was then translated from Nahuatl into English, did the English translators have a sufficient understanding of this language and of Aztec culture to identify errors which could have been made by the Franciscan? Did the translators take into account the fact that Nahuatl may have changed considerably since 1555? Because the text itself is a remarkable primary source, it is unfortunate that the quality of the translation is so difficult to evaluate. Scholars need to be aware of similar problems and raise similar questions whenever they deal with reports of cases written in other languages and translated by nonspecialists.

Cultural Points of Reference

Even within the Western culture area cultural points of reference will change over time so much that their meaning can get lost. For example, in 532 A.D., the Byzantine emperor Justinian I ordered the massacre of 30,000 horse racing fans, called Blues and Greens, who had rioted in response to the emperor's order to execute two men said to be members of the Blue and Green factions. In his book *Circus Factions: Blues and Greens at Rome and Byzantium*, Alan Cameron asserts that these sports fans, called factions, represented one of the last means of popular political and social expression in the late Roman Empire, and rose to such a degree of power that they actually posed a threat to the Emperor (Cameron 1976: 3).

In evaluating this case as possibly one of genocide, the meaning of sports fan in antiquity becomes problematic. Not only is the definition of the victim group uncertain, but also its membership. When Roman soldiers were ordered to slaughter the Blues and Greens, were they targeting all horse racing fans or just those considered particularly fanatical? As almost everybody in a city like Constantinople (or any large Roman metropolis) could be considered a Blue or Green fan, it seems likely that the fans who were targeted were those who posed a physical threat, such as those who regularly brought weapons and armour to the games. However, even if only the most militant fans were targeted, it does not seem likely that all of the 30,000 victims could be categorized as such.

On the surface, this would appear to be a case of rioting sports fans, similar to soccer hooligans in England. But on closer examination, the definition of a horse racing fan soon begins to blur. Was a sports fan in antiquity the same as a sports fan today? As our cultural points of reference inevitably change over time, such problems in historical research are quite common.

Place Names

A more common problem related to language and translation is represented by place names, due to their having changed over time, due to being translated into different languages, or due to places long ago destroyed and forgotten. Several of the cities that are reported to have been destroyed by the Mongols have, for such reasons, not yet been identified. Place names often vary from language to language, so it is not always obvious to the reader that one is dealing with the same place. Thus, Jerusalem in Arabic is called al-Kuds. Another example would be Germany, which in German is Deutschland and in French is Allemagne. While this example is very well known, it illustrates the fate of more obscure place names which are different in other languages. Is it obvious to scholars today, or will it be obvious to scholars in 500 years, that Aix-la-Chapelle is the same place as Aachen? The practice of translating place names may easily confuse genocide scholars, as they are not always dealing with familiar territory, and rarely know all the languages of the peoples they are examining.

Place names may also be deliberately changed as a result of conquest, revolution, or nationalist revivals. For example, Ceylon became Sri Lanka, Rhodesia became Zimbabwe, and Burma became Myanmar. With the rise of the Soviet Union, thousands of cities, neighbourhoods, and streets suddenly changed names. Now that there is no longer a Soviet Union, many of these names are changing again, either reverting back to their old names or changing to new ones. It is easier to know about such changes today, as they are usually standardized and chronicled by official bodies, such as the United Nations. But when one is studying a period or a place in history where no such standardized recording existed, recognizing place names and their location can sometimes be very difficult, or even impossible.

The changing of place names can sometimes give us clues as to the fate of the people who lived there. For example, after the Danes invaded England in the ninth and tenth centuries A.D., many place names were changed. In *Kings and Vikings: Scandinavia and Europe, A.D. 70–1100*, Sawyer suggests that the disappearance of former place names in the northern British isles indicates that "few natives survived and that those who did were reduced to a very inferior status" (Sawyer 1982: 101). Although most scholars are aware that place names do change, few have been willing to give such changes much importance. However, in a cases where little research has been done and much of the work relies on speculation, like the Danish invasion of England, the changing of place names does become a clue of some significance.

Writing Systems and Transliteration

As languages and place names can disappear over time, so can writing systems. But problems relating to such systems are not only associated with those that are lost. Even modern systems pose certain difficulties for genocide scholars. How much of the original text is lost when it is transliterated into another writing system? Surely certain nuances or meanings of the original language disappear in this process. This must also be true of instances where hieroglyphs are transliterated into alphabets.

The main problem of transliteration occurs when the goal language has no exact equivalents for sounds in the source language. This usually leads to several renderings that all remain in use until agreement is reached on a commonly accepted version. But even such widely accepted conventions for transliteration have only a limited life span, as was most recently demonstrated by the Chinese capital Peking becoming Beijing.

There are cases where the writing system of the group in question has not yet been fully deciphered or where no writing system existed, such as with most of the natives of the Americas. As there exists so far no archaeology of genocide, much is left to speculation with regard to the fate of some of these peoples. For example, much of what we know of certain native groups no longer in existence stems from Europeans who often had no knowledge of native languages and sometimes had no contact with the groups they are describing, relying on second- or even third-hand information. When the natives themselves had no writing system, we are left with source material from a perpetrator or bystander group. In addition to their imperfect language skills, these perpetrators or bystanders came from a very different culture which often accounted for their misunderstanding or misinterpretation of observed events. An additional source of confusion may occur when such languages without a writing system are written down by outsiders. The transliterations by several outsiders may produce widely differing versions of the spoken language.

Manipulation of Language

In addition to words whose meanings change over time, we must consider the deliberate manipulation of meanings in order to obscure ongoing events. The Nazis used the term "final solution" when referring to their plan to destroy the Jewish people. It is not clear by looking at the term that it has such a terrifying meaning. Now that it is widely recognized as one which refers to the destruction of Europe's Jews in the Holocaust, will this term always be used as such? Will scholars centuries from now recognize this term for what it is? It is quite possible that such terms in other languages, especially in ancient or extinct languages, escape the translator and the modern scholar. As translators are not generally specialists in the field of genocide, are they even looking out for such terms?

What of terms used during Stalin's regime? Thousands were executed after being labeled as "traitors" or "enemies of the people," but who were, in fact, innocent of such charges. Will such manipulation of language be recognizable to historians in the future? Certain pre-twentieth-century cases are characterized by the same gerrymandering of language as has been used in the various dictatorships of this century, such as the Inquisition's "new Christians" and "witches." Such labels of potential victim groups as well as of other outsiders have often (if not always) been derogatory. The ancient Greeks, for example, referred to anyone who was not Greek as a barbarian. Researchers need to be sensitized to the existence of such terms so that they may be addressed and recognized whenever possible.

This raises the issue of how language reflects the intentions of its user, either to report facts or meanings, to hide facts and meanings, or to spread disinformation. Codes or other systems of hiding information are meant to be clear to insiders and are meant to keep others in the dark. Are scholars always aware, particularly those researching antiquity, that the sources they are examining should not always be taken at face value? Historians researching cases in the twentieth century are aware of such linguistic alterations, such as "final solution" or "enemies of the people," but is this true of those examining earlier periods?

A more subtle manipulation of language occurs when people are sent into the field and report on events without being familiar with either the local language or culture. These problems are of equal relevance to foreign service officers, diplomats, journalists, peacekeeping forces, human rights workers, and so on. This situation is intriguing because its consequences are unintended: believing that "everybody" speaks English, such personnel never speak to those local people who do not speak English; should they attempt to do so, they are dependent on local translators who may have their own restrictions and/or biases. Not being familiar with the local language or dialect, they are then not able to evaluate the quality of the translators' work or their mastery of English. Although it is obvious that someone knowing the local language will be able to obtain more and better information, such skills are only rarely required for such jobs.

While many of the problems discussed in this section increase as events recede into the remote past, they are not negligible even in the present. Scholars engaged in cross-cultural and comparative research have documented the difficulties of translating questions so that they mean the same thing to respondents in different cultures.[10] But we should not be discouraged to discover that some of these problems require compromises because no solutions seem to be available.

Notes

1. I am particularly grateful to Michal Horoszwicz for guiding me to the following sources.
2. Émile Littré. *Dictionnaire de la langue française* (Paris: Gallimard-Hachette, 1962). "Neologisme du language révolutionnaire." Tome 6, 113 gives Babeuf as source. See also Gracchus Babeuf, *La Guerre de la Vendée et le système de dépopulation.* Introduction, présentation, chronologie, bibliographie et notes par Reynald Secher et Jean-Joël Brégeon, (n.p.: Éditions Tallandier, 1987), 98.
3. Kurt Böttcher, Karl Heinz Berger, Kurt Krolop, Christa Zimmermann. *Geflügelte Worte: Zitate, Sentenzen und Begriffe in ihrem geschichtlichen Zusammenhang* (VEB Bibliographisches Institut Leipzig, 1981), 466. See also Jacob Grimm and Wilhelm Grimm, eds., *Deutsches Wörterbuch* (Leipzig: Verlag von Hirzel, 1854), vol. 26, 510.
4. Mandiros Sarian, *Le fait accompli*, published in Armenian in Paris in 1933 and quoted by Yves Ternon, *Enquête sur la négation d'un génocide* (Marseille: Éditions Parenthèses, 1989), 218.
5. *Tanakh: A New Translation of The Holy Scriptures According to the Traditional Hebrew Text.* (Philadelphia: The Jewish Publication Society, 5746, 1965). Tanakh is an acronym for Torah (the five books of Moses), Nevi'm (The Prophets), and Kethuvim (The Writings).
6. Thus, the researcher may be forgiven for finding Amharic, the language of Ethiopia, rather daunting. Its alphabet consists of thirty-seven characters which may take either four or seven different forms, depending on whether the context is male or female, affirmative or negative, singular or plural, or the polite form. This means that the thirty-seven characters may be written in 247 different ways! Semena Woldegabir, *Amharic for Foreigners*, fifth edition (Addis Ababa: n.p., 1994; first ed. May 1966).
7. Personal communication with Professor John Hill, History Department, Concordia University.
8. When *"devastato"* is translated as "razing," we still do not know what they actually did to the city. We have simply found a way of translating one vague term into another vague term.
9. For a discussion of this myth, see R.T. Ridley, "To Be Taken With A Pinch of Salt: The Destruction of Carthage." *Classical Philology* 81 (April 1986): 140–46.
10. Michael Armer and Allen D. Grimshaw, eds., *Comparative Social Research: Methodological Problems and Strategies* (New York: John Wiley & Sons, 1973), especially chapter 4 by Joseph W. Elder "Problems of Cross-Cultural Methodology: Instrumentation and Interviewing in India."

14

Sources of Data

While genocides and gross human rights violations have occurred throughout history, there has been no reliable recording of such events, nor was there available an appropriate terminology for dealing with them. The sources of data on genocides have varied greatly throughout history and may divided into those originating with the perpetrators, the victims, and the bystanders.

Looking at cases of genocide throughout history raises a question that at first sounds somewhat "off-the-wall": What do we mean by "history"? That meaning changes over time. This is not the place to enter into a detailed semantic analysis. However, for the purpose of our research we need to distinguish three broad periods that are characterized by three different meanings of "history." In the ancient culture of Egypt, and in such of their contemporaries as Assyria, Babylon, Sumer, etc., reports were not intended to record facts, but rather to reaffirm that everything was right with the world. As Norman Cohn summarizes it:

> What was expected of the king did not and could not change, and it determined what was claimed for him. Rameses III (1198–1166) did not hesitate to claim for himself the astounding victory that Rameses II was supposed to have had over the Hittites—even though by this time the Hittites no longer existed as a political power.... Tutankhamen (1361–1352) who died at the age of eighteen, was portrayed as victorious over peoples south and east of Egypt, although he is known never to have campaigned against them. To call such accounts falsifications of history is to miss the point. Their factual accuracy or inaccuracy was irrelevant: their intention was to show that the pharaoh in question had indeed fulfilled his allotted role, had indeed affirmed and strengthened cosmos. (Cohn 1993: 17)

The next period is what we usually include under the heading of antiquity: Greece, Rome, and their contemporaries. The records of this period placed great emphasis on the factual accuracy of extraordinary events. Hannah Arendt cites Herodotus, the father of Western history, who "tells us in the first sentence of the *Persian Wars* that the purpose of his enterprise is to preserve that which owes its existence to men...and thus to make their glory shine through the centuries" (Arendt 1993: 41).

> What is difficult for us to realize is that the great deeds and works of which mortals are capable, and which become the topic of historical narrative, are not seen as parts of either an encompassing whole or a process; these single instances, deeds or events, interrupt the circular movement of daily life.... The subject matter of history is these intense interruptions—the extraordinary, in other words. (Arendt 1993: 42–43)

The third period begins with the scientific inventions of the sixteenth and seventeenth centuries. It is characterized by an overriding emphasis on process. "The modern concept of process pervading history and nature alike separates the modern age from the past more profoundly than any other single idea.... nothing is meaningful in and by itself ....certainly not particular occurrences.... or specific historical events" (Arendt 1993: 63).

The reason for even mentioning these ways in which the meaning of "history" has changed over time is that they become important when dealing with pre-twentieth-century cases. Since even historians have not always been aware of these differences in meaning, their reporting and interpreting of past events may need to be questioned. A classic example of the kinds of misinterpretation that this may lead to is the already mentioned case of Rameses' "victory" over the Hittites: the Egyptian reports of the battle and its outcome were accepted as factual until the discovery of the capital of the Hittites in the nineteenth century. Archeologists unearthed the royal library that contained thousands of clay tablets. They were perfectly preserved because they had been baked when the royal palace was burned. In that library was discovered, in three languages, the peace treaty that was signed between the Egyptians and the Hittites after what appears to have been an inconclusive fight.

Similarly, there seems to be a difference of opinion among archeologists about how to read Assyrian inscriptions. Some of them take these inscriptions as a king's accurate report of events under his rule. Others read them as royal reports on their stewardship to the god whom they represent on earth, reports that were designed to enhance the king's status and that were not meant to be read by earthly contemporaries.

In the modern conception of history, the total range of information could, in theory, vary from no information at all to all possible information. In practice, neither of these two extremes is ever reached in the real world. At one extreme of this distribution we find authoritarian structures that attempt to suppress all information. Fortunately, the fallibility of human nature and the imperfections of technologies make sure that this goal has so far never been reached and is likely to remain beyond reach. At the other extreme is the goal of complete information. Unfortunately for this goal, the scope of all relevant information is even in theory infinite. In practice, it is severely limited by the time and space available for collecting and recording, by the demands of the information consuming groups, and most importantly by what the various sources consider relevant and important within their own frame of reference.

Historically, perpetrators have been proud of their utilitarian genocides and recorded them as victories. Whether such records actually survived depended on whether the perpetrator society was literate, whether the written records survived the vagaries of nature and the destructive urges of their enemies, and whether the travelers, historians, or archeologists of some bystander power contributed to the preservation of such records.

This way of thinking changed in the twentieth century, when most perpetrators no longer boasted about the atrocities they committed, choosing instead to deny the events and hide the evidence of genocide.[1] The notable exception was, of course, postwar West Germany which, while certainly not boasting about the Holocaust, did admit that it occurred and even agreed to make reparation payments to certain groups of surviving victims. In spite of this well-known exception, most perpetrators continue to deny their guilt. Either way, this poses several problems for scholars who wish to use perpetrator documents. Such scholars must always be aware that the documents they are using could very well be affected by the perpetrator's concern for hiding the true nature of the events in question.

Even perpetrator documents which make no attempt to hide genocidal actions and which have traditionally been perceived as credible can result in deceiving the scholars who use them. One example is the German commander in charge of the destruction of the Warsaw ghetto who reported that the ghetto no longer existed whereas some fighting still continued a year after the date of that report.[2] That report was a deliberate attempt to mask the truth in order to show how successful the Germans were in crushing their enemies. Nazi documents are usually viewed as reliable data because of the German reputation for meticulous record keeping. This examples illustrates that even data normally considered "reliable" can sometimes be biased and should be verified with other, independent sources.

When considering perpetrators as sources of data we also include those who assisted them in executing their evil designs. For this purpose it is not relevant whether they volunteered or whether they acted under constraints—except insofar as it affects the quality of their testimony. The disadvantage of such perpetrators as sources is that throughout most of history they considered ordinary people so unimportant that even their massacre was not worth reporting unless it occurred in the context of an important victory. Furthermore, their reports were often less concerned with recording events than with affirming the rulers' virtue and fame and the victims' status outside the universe of mutual obligation.[3] In the twentieth century some perpetrators went one step further. They not only omitted the reporting or recording of genocidal massacres—they actively denied that they happened.

The victims, during most of history, shared the prevailing view that their losses were hardly worth reporting. With a few notable exceptions, such as several of the victims of the Mongols in the thirteenth and fourteenth centuries, victims have not provided much source material on their own fate. This attitude changed dramatically in the aftermath of the Holocaust whose Jewish victims felt most strongly that they themselves must create the record of their fate. Thus, this is the first genocide for which we have a large volume of diaries, autobiographies, and memoirs produced and collected by the victims themselves.

The bystanders are a large and varied group. For our purposes we need to distinguish between interested observers, uninterested or indifferent watchers, and deliberate away-lookers. In addition, there are the professional bystanders such as diplomatic personnel, employees of humanitarian NGOs, and professional reporters.

Finally, in addition to perpetrators, victims, and bystanders, major sources of information in the modern era are the various national and international news services. While they collect and disseminate a huge amount of data, none of them are unbiased sources. Their output is influenced not only by their own definition of what is newsworthy, but also by the attitudes and interests of their owners, their host governments, various pressure groups, and the technology for recording and disseminating their product.

More will be said about all of these sources below. Here we need to mention briefly two of the effects that operate on all of these sources. The first one is the passing of the U.N. Convention which established genocide as a crime in international law. In spite of its ineffectiveness in prosecuting and punishing this crime, this redefinition assured in one stroke that the killing of groups of people became a newsworthy event that could not be ignored. The second effect that operates on all sources of information is that in each society there are shared norms and values that are usually observed by its members. These include behaviors that are considered beyond the pale, opinions that must not be voiced, and group loyalties that are violated only at serious cost. The details vary, of course, from society to society and with the role of the source. Thus, while all groups think of themselves as superior, perpetrators will report mainly positive matters of themselves while they degrade the victims, whereas victims are unlikely to find anything good to report of their tormentors or much bad about their fellow victims. An example of behavior that is only very rarely reported, by either perpetrators, victims, or bystanders, is cannibalism—in spite of the fact that it often does occur in situations of extreme food deprivation. In other words, when doing comparative research it is important to be aware of the cultural and moral imperatives in a society that will lead otherwise reliable sources of data to practice a form of self-censorship that will make the reported data incomplete and therefore less useful.

Such "black holes" in our sources of data exist in every culture so that the researcher needs to be alert to what is not there. In the second half of the twentieth century a quite extraordinary change has taken place in the Western world due to the introduction of bills of human rights in many countries. These human rights have also been codified by the United Nations with the result that their violations get reported in great detail. The effect of such reporting is dramatic in two respects. The first one is that everybody may be included in such reporting regardless of social standing and no matter how unimportant they are in other respects. The second effect is that matters get reported that used to disappear in culturally defined "black holes." Thus, rape was probably part of warfare throughout history; but with rare exceptions, such as the famous case of the Roman rape of the Sabines, it was not considered important enough to be mentioned. The feeding and housing of prisoners only rarely deserved recording. Most importantly, for our purposes the fate of conquered people remains obscure in many accounts because it is either not reported or hidden under such vague terms as the "razing of a city."

Our sources for current events are more detailed and more varied than ever before. At the same time, their control by interest groups, government agencies, and the news-consuming public, is using increasingly sophisticated methods of news management and censorship. Therefore, the use of these sources for research purposes also requires increasing skill and sophistication.

Notes

1. For a detailed discussion of the variety of reactions from denial to acknowledgement, see Stanley Cohen, *Denial and Acknowledgement: The Impact of Information about Human Rights Violations* (Jerusalem: Center for Human Rights, The Hebrew University, 1995).
2. For a more detailed discussion of that case, see part one, chapter 7.
3. Helen Fein, *Genocide: A Sociological Perspective* (London: Sage Publications, 1990), vol. 38, no. 1, of *Current Sociology/La sociologie contemporaine*, 27, 36, et passim. A somewhat expanded version of this volume was published by Sage in 1993.

15

Kinds of Data for Contemporary Cases

As will be seen in part 3, data for pre-twentieth-century cases are usually quite limited and often come from only one of the possible sources. They often do not provide sufficient information on which to base an analysis. The reason for this separate heading is that data for contemporary cases tends to be voluminous, often coming from most or all of the possible sources.

Governments, in addition to their almost daily news releases, provide a great variety of useful information. This includes the records of various government departments and their archives, law codes and the judicial records showing how they were interpreted and applied, and transcripts of discussions and debates in those bodies where the relevant decision making was located. However, many of these records may not be accessible until years later.

The United Nations and its many agencies collect a great amount of information, most of which is published. One example is the Social and Economic Council and its committees which are engaged in monitoring the interpretation and implementation of the many resolutions and conventions on human rights. Another is the High Commission on Refugees which monitors the number and location of refugees and organizes aid to them. Unfortunately all of these bodies tend to be subject to political pressures from members states. The users of their information need to be aware of these presssures and of the direction in which they tend to bias the data.

A quite special case are the so-called war crimes trials. By definition, they take place only after the violations have ended. The information they produce may thus become available only much later. How much later will depend on the particular circumstances of each case. The trials taking place in The Hague are producing or confirming information on the events in the former Yugoslavia while the agreements meant to terminate these conflicts are still being implemented (at the time of writing). In Kigali, where accused perpetrators of the Rwandan genocide have been arrested, the trials have only just started due to an acute lack of staff and facilities. In Addis Ababa, on the other hand, the trial of Colonel Mengistu and forty-six members of his Dergue (ruling council) has already produced much evidence, including details on the until now mysterious death of Haile Selassie in 1975. Further information helpful to researchers will undoubtedly continue to be uncovered by such trials.

There also exists a great variety of nongovernmental organizations (NGOs), some of which will be found to be involved in any particular case of genocide. These will range from those dedicated to providing disaster assistance, to those defending human rights, to those dedicated to the prevention of famine or the providing of medical services. All of them are likely to produce records, field reports, and financial statements that may or may not be readily accessible. In addition, they issue news releases and appeals for funds that, by definition, are public documents.

For the purpose of this discussion, the so-called media include not only the usual print media, plus radio and television, but also the newsletters and bulletins of various special interest groups, regardless of whether they are distributed in print or via the Internet. These special interest groups make available a great deal of very detailed information, that is not usually available in the mass circulation media, often originating from well-informed professionals.

Finally, there is a great variety of material that is not easily classified and that may be relevant in a particular case of genocide. This amorphous group can include interviews with individuals who may have specialized knowledge, such as aid workers, diplomats, or refugees. Other individuals may have produced histories, memoirs, diaries, paintings, photos, or even sculptures that reveal relevant materials. In special cases, inscriptions on buildings, walls, doors, etc. may be useful. Finally, there may be sites such as prisons, labor camps, cemeteries, etc. that tell their own stories.

16

Quality of Data

Introduction

It should be evident from some of the above discussions that the quality of data is almost always difficult to assess and thus presents a major difficulty in the process of doing comparative research on genocide. The particular nature of such difficulties varies with the specifics of each case and the time when it occurred. But it must be pointed out right at the beginning of this chapter that these difficulties of assessing the quality of data have vastly increased in the contemporary period. There are two major reasons for this.

The first reason lies in the exponential growth of available information. At first this seems like a contradiction. However, while it certainly is true that we have far more information on contemporary cases, it is also true that the knowledge of propaganda, of public relations, and of the management of information control has vastly increased in scope and sophistication. These methods have been used to great advantage by totalitarian regimes to control the flow of information at home and abroad. But they are not exactly unknown in other societies as well. Their usefulness is not restricted to the management of news about genocides, but extends to all areas where a government wants to present itself in a positive light—positive in terms of its own major interests. These same methods are equally useful to any other group that has the relevant expertise or has the funds to hire such expertise.

The second reason why it has become more difficult to assess the quality of data lies in the enormous and continuing developments in the area of communication technology. These developments started with the invention of radio and then television. These were rapidly followed by computers, miniaturization, communication satellites, computerized data bases, and the Internet. These developments have vastly increased the volume and the speed of data transmission. This is usually considered to be a good thing. Here we encounter the second contradiction: many of these new technologies also make it more difficult to know the real source of the data, who has tampered with it in what ways, and what part of it is really authentic. To give just one fairly recent example: it is now possible to edit photos while they are being transmitted via computer. Unlike the earlier darkroom editing of pictures during the production of photos from negatives, there seems no way that computer editing can be detected; one reason is that there exists no negative from which the process starts. Thus, the authenticity of a photo must be inferred from extraneous evidence rather than from the integrity of the production process.

Cross-cutting both the exponential growth of available information and the impressive and continuing developments in communication technology is the question of ownership and control. The rulers of totalitarian regimes have always controlled access to information to a greater or lesser extent—depending on their interests and priorities. In more democratic regimes control becomes an aspect of ownership which, in the majority of cases, is located in the private sector. The growth of multinational corporations and their tendency to buy out their competitors has resulted in a great centralization not only of ownership, but also of control. Such control may be biased only in the direction of maximizing profits and in maintaining the system that produces such profits. But it may also be exercised to support or to suppress a particular world view or a favored regime. Needless to add, as the centralization of information industries continues, buying into them becomes increasingly costly. Since they control such a great share of the information flow, some of these multinationals have become very attractive to authoritarian states that can marshall the wealth required to take them over. Thus, the researcher may also have to ascertain the nature of the ownership before arriving at conclusions about the accuracy of information distributed by any particular organization.

The quality of data, while always an overriding concern, tends to vary with the sources that produced them. We shall, therefore, present our comments according to the originating sources.

Journalists' Reports

In reports of genocide, researchers must be aware of the possibility of bias or inaccuracies, and that even the best of intentions can lead to misinformation or disinformation. Furthermore, certain factors that are intrinsic to the way journalists operate affect the way such information is presented. The obvious point is that information appearing in the public domain is not guaranteed to be either true or unbiased. This applies to both historical and contemporary cases. While we recognize and appreciate the fact that many dedicated journalists have risked or given their lives in order to get information out to the world, we hope that by exploring some of these factors, we can raise scholars' awareness of the need to be cautious when using their reports.

The Western Media

Living in the information age has enabled us to learn about world events while they unfold. Never before has it been so easy to communicate across vast distances or to cross linguistic and cultural barriers. Thanks to communication technologies such as satellites and fax machines, news of world events can reach us instantaneously. But while new technology has helped the media to disseminate news and information more rapidly, it has not brought more accuracy in news reporting. This is especially true of reports of foreign conflicts. The following examples of media disinformation and distortion will illustrate this point.

Foreign Wars, War Correspondents, and the Cutting Room Floor

The Western media have long been in the business of reporting foreign wars to a news hungry public. The first war correspondents to report a foreign war to a civilian population at home were used in the Crimean War (1853–56) by such newspapers as the *Morning Post* and the *Times* of London (Knightley 1975: 4). Although these reports were often embellished descriptions of the valor and bravery of British soldiers, best illustrated by William Howard Russell's famous description of the charge of the Light Brigade, they were fairly accurate accounts of the battles of the Crimea. These war correspondents were either supporters of the war and therefore unlikely to criticize it, or were careful not to lose their positions by angering their employers.

The Crimean War set a precedent for journalism: when the American Civil War broke out five years later, there were 500 war correspondents there to cover it (Knightley 1975: 17). Although the techniques for covering wars have changed dramatically since that time, there are still certain aspects of early media coverage that have remained with us to this day. Correspondents still want to please their employers, and are sometimes less apt to report things they know will remain on the cutting room floor. What is surprising is the extent to which today's media comply with restrictions on the press. For example, during the American invasion of Panama in 1989, pool journalists who arrived there found themselves kept away from areas where there was continued fighting. The pool's main sources of information were CNN broadcasts of Pentagon briefings from Washington, the first demonstration of the network's potency as a media and military instrument. The media were able to paint Operation "Just Cause" as largely free of casualties and virtually unblemished in its execution, in spite of the fact that twenty-three American servicemen were killed and 265 wounded, a detail that only later became public. No eyewitness accounts, photographs or films of these battles found their way into the American media and requests for official military footage were mostly denied (Lloyd 1992: 52).

Censorship and the Western Media

It seems that since the war in Vietnam, the American military has become all too aware of the power of the media and their effect on public opinion, and thus become determined to keep the media in the dark. When one looks at the coverage of the Gulf War, one realizes the extent to which the Western military establishment has become successful in doing this. In Vietnam, journalists were free to move about and were thus able to prove the falsity of certain military reports. In the Gulf War, reporters not only had their work censored, they were also subject to severe controls in terms of movement and were prevented from visiting front areas without military escorts (Nohrstedt 1992: 119). The armed forces also set up a pool of journalists, enabling the military administration to limit the number of journalists at the front. Journalists who did not comply with the rules were threatened with losing their accreditations and with deportation.

The official reason behind the restrictions on the press was to prevent the disclosure of sensitive information that might endanger the security of the coalition or get into the hands of the enemy. Information about the size of military units, movements and destinations, and weapons were not to be revealed. Another purpose behind these rules was to stop pictures of wounded or dead soldiers from reaching their relatives through media channels. However, above all, restrictions on the media were designed as a propaganda tool to guarantee and to prolong public support for the war by America and its allies (Nohrstedt 1992: 120).

While the restrictions on the front were fairly straightforward, what of those imposed on the media at home? With few exceptions, the media did its own self-censorship and did this most efficiently. The American media, for example, did not report the fact that the Gulf War was widely opposed in such countries as Japan and Spain, or that there were protests against the war in Egypt. Also unreported were the views of Asians, Africans, and Latin Americans. Most telling about the role of the American media has been its lack of concern with the number of Iraqi casualties suffered due to incessant bombing and, in the waning hours of the war, due to the killing of retreating soldiers (Schiller 1992: 24–25). It is difficult to understand why the media have been willing participants in the military's propaganda machine, or why they have complied with press restrictions like those imposed during the invasion of Panama and the Gulf War. While we recognize that there has been criticism of those restrictions, there is no indication that it had any effect.

Censorship is not the only reason why the media have difficulty in reporting conflicts. William Kennedy argues that the press fails to adequately cover military conflict, not because of censorship, but because its training and organization are inadequate (Kennedy 1993). He argues that the press was unable to make an adequate assessment of events in the Gulf long before any restrictions were implemented. Not only did they fail to read military publications, such as *Army News*, which illustrated the American military's position in the Gulf months before the conflict took place, but the media also had little historical knowledge of the region and could not fully grasp the meaning of events as they were unfolding (Kennedy 1993: 11).

Many foreign correspondents work in areas of the world where there are severe controls on the press. Why do the Western media comply with such restrictions? If one considers the fact that few correspondents know the language of the area in which they are working, then one has to wonder how accurate their information is, especially in areas of the world where the press is quite restricted. Foreign correspondents regularly rely for their information on guides and translators who are usually provided by the local government. If the correspondents are working in a region with severe restrictions on freedom of the press, it is unlikely that the information provided by a translator or guide would be critical of the government. In Serbia, for example, there are no laws restricting freedom of the press, but the government routinely uses a variety of nonlegal means to control and punish critics. Any Western journalist who works in Serbia has to be aware of those controls and knows that the guides and translators the government provides are also subject to those same controls (Thompson 1994: 58). Meanwhile, Croatia has used the war as a means of controlling the media by adopting strict laws that punish unapproved reporting with jail sentences; several independent journalists have been bullied into giving up their profession.[1] The Western media rarely mention press restrictions when they publish reports from Belgrade or Zagreb, even when such restrictions apply to both local and foreign correspondents.

Another example of censorship of the media occurs in Sudan, a region that has been experiencing civil war for more than twenty years and where the man-made famine that raged there in the 1980s was meant to assist the efforts of the North to subdue the South. Sudan offers a good example of the Western media's complicity with censorship in the international arena. The Associated Press (AP), one of the world's largest news agencies, has no clients there, largely because the Sudan News Agency, which distributes news to the local media, lacks the hard currency to buy the satellite-beamed AP world service report. Local media are not credible as news sources because they are subject to official controls and the AP cannot economically justify maintaining a full-time correspondent in Khartoum. In spite of its knowledge that local media are not reliable, AP covers Sudan by using local journalists who may work for the government; periodically AP does send a staff correspondent to Sudan to check the background of a story or to cover something AP deems particularly "newsworthy." Therefore, the largest nation in Africa goes mainly unreported by the world's major news agency and what reports do get out are often provided by someone who works under strict censorship laws and who may be working for the Sudanese government (Hachten 1992: 40–41).

Another example illustrating the complicity between media and censorship is China, which imposes strict controls on news gathering within its borders as well as on the importing of foreign news. China's State Council has recently ordered foreign economic news agencies to submit to control by the Communist Party's New China news agency and has threatened to punish them if they release information that "slanders or jeopardizes" the country's national interest. This policy has had an immediate impact on information agencies, such as Reuters and Dow Jones, which have been selling economic information services to Chinese banks, trading companies, and security firms. These news agencies have complied with China's State Council order, in spite of their belief that this will have a detrimental effect on China's ability to compete internationally and to join the World Trade Organization.[2] One may speculate that noncompliance with China's State Council would spell the arrest of these agencies' reporters and/or shutting out their access to one of the largest markets in the world. Either way, the agencies are bullied into compliance, and do not protest (at least not too loudly) at China's measures to control their flow of information.

Censorship and Compliance: The Case of Walter Duranty

One of the most famous cases of a journalist complying with censorship laws is that of Walter Duranty, a correspondent working for the *New York Times* in the 1930s who won the Pulitzer Prize for his coverage of events in the Soviet Union. In spite of strong evidence that a famine was taking place in the Ukraine, a famine which resulted in the deaths of millions of people, Duranty insisted to his readers that "there is no famine or actual starvation nor is there likely to be."[3] When reports of the famine in the Ukraine became more widespread and it became impossible to deny the evidence, Duranty chose to play down those reports. Again and again, he argued that reports of famine in the Ukraine were exaggerated and/or examples of anti-Soviet propaganda. In exchange for his compliance, Duranty was able to hold personal interviews with Stalin, maintain a rather extravagant lifestyle while in Moscow, win the Pulitzer Prize, and gain a high level of personal prestige (although this, at least, did not last).

In spite of Duranty's reports to his newspaper, there is evidence that he knew about the famine and had witnessed some of its most horrific effects in the North Caucasus, the Lower Volga, and the Ukraine (Taylor 1990: 220–21). After he had left the Soviet Union in 1933, he estimated to the British embassy that it was possible that as many as 10 million people had died of starvation in the Soviet Union. In spite of the fact that it was already known that a famine had indeed taken place, Duranty's false reports had damaged the public's perception to such a degree that, thanks, in part, to his favorable appraisal of Stalin's regime, the United States recognized the Soviet Union in 1933.

Whatever Duranty's motives, there is another disquieting aspect of this story that raises questions about the reliability of newspaper data and foreign reporting. Although one can castigate Duranty for his actions, the responsibility ultimately lay with the decision of the editor of the newspaper to carry his stories. James William Crowl notes that it was impossible for foreign correspondents in the USSR to report anything that might be viewed as critical of the communist regime during the Stalin era (Crowl 1982). If a story proved objectionable, the reporter could be reprimanded and denied the use of press department facilities. There was the possibility that repeated violations would bring expulsion from the country. In spite of the fact that the *New York Times* and other American newspapers knew about travel restrictions and the censorship of their reporters, they failed to raise any objections to Soviet policy toward the press.

Crowl also raises the point that Western newspapers failed to properly inform their readers about events in the Soviet Union during this period. Only the most conservative newspapers carried stories of the famine in the Ukraine. Crowl states that the *New York Times* was no different from any other newspaper of that period in that it was more interested in gathering news than in making a determined effort to uncover the truth. He argues that American newspapers of that era, deeply affected by the isolationist mood after World War I, abdicated their responsibility for informing their readers about developments abroad (Crowl 1982: 196–200). As the *New York Times* is often viewed as a chronicle of world history and widely used as a source by social scientists, one must ask whether they realize that it has printed false reports such as those of Walter Duranty.

Editorial Bias

The *New York Times* is also not above reflecting Western society's dominant ideology. Researchers should be aware that editorial decisions in the selection and omission of disseminated information can produce, reproduce, and reflect this ideology. In a study of the *New York Times*, Lisa Klein argues that its coverage of the famine and civil war in Somalia from 1990 to March 1994 reflected the racism and sexism of Western society. Moreover, this racism and sexism is so subtle that it begins to seem natural and often escapes attention (Klein 1994).

While Klein's work is interesting in that it explores some of the ways the *New York Times* has fallen into the trap of wearing Western blinders, it is most telling when she examines the issue that led her to study this particular subject. Klein had originally wished to examine the war rape of Somali women as her research topic. She states that over one thousand rapes are estimated to have been perpetrated in and around Somalia, at the exact time that the U.N. Security Council was establishing the War Crimes Tribunal, in order to offer international redress to the survivors of just such abuse in the former Yugoslavia. This led her to question why she had not heard of the Somali rape victims, especially since these rapes occurred at the same time that the Bosnian rapes were beginning to be featured every day by the international media (Klein 1984: 4). What Klein discovered was that the *New York Times* mentioned the rape of Somali women only once, in its coverage of Somalia (Klein 1984: 44). In light of the fact that the Western media had become very interested in the issue of mass rape, it is very telling that the *New York Times* chose to give such little coverage to this case.

Stephen Hess has examined the more general question of how the U. S. media deal with international news coverage (Hess 1996: 70–78). In addition to discussing the pervasive economic and technical difficulties so often cited, he also points to editorial indifference and consumer apathy as contributing factors in explaining the inadequate coverage of international events.

False Reports

Perhaps as a result of certain characteristics intrinsic to the way in which the media operate, false reports still find their way into headlines and onto our televisions. One recent example is the widely reported statistic of 200,000 Muslim dead in the war in Bosnia. This figure was quoted by all major news organizations and by many policy specialists whose work directly affected Western foreign policy toward the Balkans. In his April 1995 article "The Bosnian Calculation" in the *New York Times Magazine*, George Kenney, a Washington writer who resigned from the State Department's Yugoslav desk in protest over the United States policy in Bosnia, states that the charge that the Serbs have committed genocide is a serious one and that it merits the effort to try to get the facts right. He argues that the figure of 200,000 Muslim dead, which he believes to be grossly exaggerated, was partly a result of the expectations of Western journalists and American and U.N. officials that Bosnia would turn into the world's next killing field. Revelations of ethnic cleansing and images of skeletal Muslim men in Serbian camps made it all the more plausible.

Kenney states that the Bosnian government's use of such inflated statistics was in its best interest, as it enabled it to gain political support in the West, as well as much needed donations from the Muslim world in order to buy weapons on the black market. It is not surprising that the Bosnian government would exaggerate its situation in order to garner support for its cause, but what is disturbing about Kenney's article is that the Western media and policy makers were so willing to accept such inflated figures (Kenney 1995). Kenney illustrates that researchers should be suspicious of data that becomes available during an ongoing war. Whether his comments have any factual basis is difficult to assess at the moment, illustrating that even if his viewpoints are not accurate, it is not possible to ignore them at this time. Without entering the debate about the number of victims, the researcher should ask questions about the sources of such numbers: Who did the counting? Were any records kept? By whom?[4]

An example of false reporting, this time of a nonpolitical nature, is Janet Cooke of the *Washington Post* who invented a story of an eight-year-old heroin addict for her paper's "Metropolitan" section in 1980. In spite of protests from Washington's black community and widespread searches for "Jimmy," the child Cooke invented, the paper stood by its reporter and recommended her for several journalist prizes, including the Pulitzer, which she was awarded. While it is true that no newspaper can erect an airtight defense against a lying reporter, the *Washington Post*'s editors and the Pulitzer Prize committee might have approached Cooke's fabricated tale with a higher degree of skepticism. While her Pulitzer was rescinded and she was fired from her job as a reporter, the reasons for Cooke's fabrication still remain, as there will always be young reporters who seek fame and glory no matter what the price (Kurtz 1992: 120–21).

This case is cited, not to accuse the press of false reporting, but rather to stress the researcher's need to verify the veracity of reports before citing them as evidence. It is simply not realistic to expect an editorial staff of a daily paper, no matter how competent, to verify every report they print. Therefore, researchers must take responsibility for the use they make of such reports.

The media also rarely provide the historical background needed to fully understand the reasons for foreign conflicts. This can be seen in the way in which the media reported the war in the former Yugoslavia. Until recently, the media blamed the conflict on antagonisms that arose during the Tito and post-Tito era, ignoring some of the historical grievances that each side has used in order to arouse hatred in the population. If any background information was provided, it rarely was detailed enough to allow the public to fully grasp the weight of history in the region. (For our attempt to provide such historical background, the reader is referred to chapter 22 in part 3.)

Ownership and Censorship

Another factor that can sometimes affect freedom of the press is media ownership, and this is true in both print and broadcasting. In his *Jerusalem Report* article "If You Can't Beat' em, Buy' em," Joshua Teitelbaum examines how Saudi princes are influencing the media in the Arab world (Teitelbaum 1995). He argues that the Saudi regime, having learned from the collapse of totalitarian regimes in Eastern Europe that the modern media and broadcasting across closed borders are a major threat to dictatorships, is determined to control the flow of information to its citizens. It has done so by banning satellite dishes within its borders (without strictly enforcing this ban) and by allowing foreign channels to be transmitted only through the government's own cable network. It is relatively easy for a dictatorship to control the media within its borders, but the Saudis have an added advantage of having enough capital to be able to control much of the media outside its borders by buying newspapers and satellite networks. Among the newspapers owned by members of the Saudi royal family are: the Arab world's two most widely distributed dailies, the *Al-Hayat* and *Al-Sharq al-Awsat*, as well as the major weeklies, *Al-Wasat* and *Al-Majallah*. Members of the royal family have also bought three satellite networks: Middle East Broadcasting Centre (MBC), Arab Radio Television (ART), and the Orbit Communications Company. Teitelbaum argues that the Saudi regime has attempted to shape Arab opinion of its government by buying much of the Arab world's media and that the Arab media's coverage of the Saudi kingdom often resembles news releases from the Saudi government's Press Agency. A recent example of Saudi censorship which supports Teitelbaum's theory is the BBC's Arabic language service's coverage of Saudi dissident Mohammed al Mas'ari which was repeatedly censored by a Saudi-owned satellite relay station.[5] Since then, they have cancelled their subscription to the BBC Arabic service.

The Saudis have also paid close attention to the Western media, placing full-page advertisements in the *New York Times* and *Washington Post* lauding Saudi Arabia, none of it labelled as advertising copy. Sheikh Walid bought United Press International several years ago

(Teitelbaum 1995: 48). To what extent Saudi capital has affected Western reports of the Saudi regime has not yet been the subject of a serious research effort.

What the Saudi example demonstrates is that media ownership can affect reporting and the way the news is presented. Social scientists who use the media as a source of data for their research should be aware of who owns the source they are using and who advertises in that source. Although the censorship of stories by the owners of print and broadcasting media may not always be as blatant as in the Saudi case, it is important to be aware of those cases where it is applied.

Western Culture and the Western Media

It should not be forgotten that the Western press is also affected by the culture in which it operates and the biases and prejudices that are present in that culture. For example, the way in which Africa is represented in the Western media often reflects Western misconceptions and assumptions about this continent and its people.[6] Chief among those misconceptions is the notion of Africa as a culturally homogeneous continent, ignoring the many nations and diverse cultural histories and traditions of Africa. For example, the Western media use the term "black-on-black violence," "tribalism," and "black factionalism" to describe conflicts raging in certain African countries. The media do not describe political disputes among white people as "white factionalism" and when these disputes turn violent, they do not refer to them as "white-on-white violence." Western ethnicity, political divisions, and nationalism are accepted at face value and are not called into question when conflicts occur between different ethnic, political, or national groups (Hawk 1992: 8–9). The use of a particular vocabulary to describe African peoples and conflicts has implied that describing Africans requires a different vocabulary than describing others. Beverly Hawk argues that implicit in this type of vocabulary is the notion that "African events do not follow any pattern recognizable to Western reason" (Hawk 1992: 7).

It is important to recognize that getting the story out of many regions of Africa is not easy. Reporters must often contend with sources reluctant to speak for fear for their own safety, difficult travel conditions, censorship, and inadequate communications facilities that make transmitting stories in time very difficult. Furthermore, media organizations must make large financial commitments in order to maintain a correspondent in Africa. When the media do cover Africa, their stories are often largely event-based and crisis oriented (Fair 1992: 110).

Alex de Waal, argues that the quality of coverage relating to problems in such countries as Ethiopia has declined in the last twenty years. The growth of telecommunications has shortened deadlines, increasing a demand for news that is more current, resulting in a decline of reporting from places that are less accessible to journalists: "[p]laces which are difficult to reach become subject to censorship through the very fact of their being inaccessible to the media" (de Waal 1990: 106). De Waal also contends that rapid travel has meant that newspapers and television have replaced their specialist long-term foreign correspondents with media "flying squads" who rush to wherever there is believed to be a newsworthy story; and without pictures an event is not considered newsworthy for television coverage. This has resulted in a loss of expert knowledge of low profile developments. In Ethiopia, this was one of the reasons why the media failed to recognize early signs of famine (de Waal 1990: 106–7).

The case of Ethiopia is particularly telling in terms of the media's failure to get the story straight. Not only did the media fail to recognize the early signs of famine, they also chose to blame the starvation of hundreds of thousands of people on drought and soil erosion. There was no discussion of the Mengistu government's deliberate use of starvation as a method of warfare against its enemies, of the forced migration of people to areas that were drought-stricken, or the government's failed agricultural policies.[7] This is partly due to the fact that the Ethiopian government enforced strict censorship concerning the causes of the famine (de Waal 1990: 110) and to the unwillingness of nongovernmental organizations (NGOs) to publicize the reasons behind the famine and risk expulsion. In fact, it was not until Médecins Sans Frontières (Doctors Without Borders) made a public stand concerning the Ethiopian government's resettlement of people in Wollo, which they maintained resulted in over 100,000 deaths, that the media began to pay attention to other factors which led to famine in Ethiopia (de Waal 1990: 112).

Another underlying reason why the media failed to recognize the causes of the famine in Ethiopia was their unwillingness to believe the testimony of refugees. Jason Clay and Bonnie Holcomb demonstrate that refugees are a valuable source of information. Prevented from doing research in Ethiopia itself, their only source of information were refugees who had reached Sudan. The refugees not only proved to be accurate in their accounts of events surrounding the famine, but the authors were also able to collect their information very rapidly (Clay and Holcomb 1986). One hopes that Clay and Holcomb's work will lead to greater acceptance of refugees as sources of information.

A more recent example of the Western media's failure to understand the nuances and complexities of African society is the genocide that took place in Rwanda in 1994. The Western media portrayed the killings as a manifestation of tribal animosity resulting from environmental degradation and/or centuries of tribal conflict. Again and again, journalists, particularly in the American media, used the term "tribal war" or "tribal bloodletting"[8] when describing the genocide in Rwanda, taking it for granted that there have always been divisions between Hutu and Tutsi, and that the animosity between the two groups has been present since precolonial times.

An example of a journalist who was particularly taken with the idea of tribal warfare and its inevitability is Clifton R. Wharton, Jr. who stated in an op-ed piece in the *New York Times* that the only heritage certain tribes or cultures could hold onto was warfare, and that the violence in Rwanda was just "the latest convulsion in decades of ethnic warfare." He then went on to argue that the only way to suppress this type of violence was through a brutal dictatorship and that "we cannot push democracy faster than it can be assimilated" (Wharton 1994: A21). Not only did Wharton ignore the role of the Hutu political elite and its fear of losing power, he also chose to turn a blind eye to the role of that same elite in masterfully engineering a massive propaganda program within Rwanda. By depicting this conflict as "tribal" and arguing that the hatred between Hutus and Tutsis was "centuries-old," and therefore inevitable and uncontrollable, the media have subjected Rwanda to widespread misunderstanding, and overwhelmingly failed in presenting the complexities that produced the genocide. To understand cases like Rwanda, one must examine all the issues motivating the conflict's actors.

Conclusion

One may ponder over whether it is possible to accurately report a conflict while it is under way, as journalists often comply with the censorship restrictions placed upon them and just as often lack the historical and/or linguistic training to make an accurate report in the first place. Another disturbing facet of the issue of accuracy is the

Saudi case, which brings the power of money and media ownership into the picture. As circumstances are often outside the media's control during a time of conflict and facts may remain hidden from view until many years have passed, it is the responsibility of serious researchers to be cautious when using data that was never meant to be used by them in the first place. We hope that the cases we have presented raise awareness among scholars interested in the study of genocide that inaccuracies and falsehoods appear all too frequently in the media, especially during times of conflict. Journalists' reports should be viewed with a certain degree of caution and should not be treated as research reports.

Site Visits

A visit by a qualified and impartial observer has often been considered as most reliable when reports of human rights abuses needed to be verified. The results of such site visits may be acceptable when the observer has been given free access to the country and unhindered opportunity to travel within it. But such conditions rarely exist. In the great majority of cases the human rights abuses are denied and the requests for visas are either ignored or refused.

When diplomatic and/or economic pressures make it impractical to continue such denials and refusals, the perpetrator governments attempt to carefully stage-manage such visits. The term "stage-manage" is appropriate because such visits are as carefully planned as a good opera production. The overall purpose of such productions is to hide what is really going on and to create an impression of respect for human rights. This is done in several stages. First of all the potential visitors are not allowed to come at their own convenience; instead they are told when they are expected and what their itinerary will be. Since the visitors have a choice only of accepting the terms offered or of not making the visit, they tend to opt for the visit on the perpetrators' terms. This seems to be true regardless of whether the potential visitors are the Red Cross, other NGOs, or journalists.

The second stage of preparation concerns selecting and instructing the people the visitors shall meet. This means that officials, translators, and guides are carefully selected and trained. It also means that prisons or camps are carefully selected and that their inmates are warned not to talk to the strangers. This usually poses no problems because the visitors are unlikely to know the local language, the inmates are only too aware of the punishments if they disobey, and potential visitors who do know the language are likely to be refused a visa.

The third stage of preparation is the cleaning up of the actual site. This may involve a fresh coat of paint, new prison uniforms for the inmates, and special provisions for the kitchen so that the visitors may be impressed by the quality of the meals. It also involves the cleaning up of the living quarters and the grounds so that no trace of mistreatment is in evidence. The guards will be issued proper uniforms while inmates who might spoil the desired impression will be temporarily relocated. Thus, under age children may disappear, obviously ill inmates will be relocated in a hospital ward, and "troublesome" inmates may be sent to another location.

Under both Stalin and Hitler these types of visits were perfected to such an extent that the visitors were taken in by the favorable impression that had been prepared for the day. Perpetrators who do not possess the requisite skill and/or resources for the elaborate preparations of such a visit tend to simply refuse permission and visas.

Other Sources of Data

There are many providers of information apart from the media and the journalists. Among the major ones to be briefly considered here are the United Nations with its many agencies, governments and their departments, a variety of non-governmental organizations, and a large number of humanitarian aid and human rights organizations. All of these produce many kinds of records and reports of varying quality and utility to a researcher. However, none of them have as their primary objective the providing of the latest news to the largest number of people. Only the reporters in the field, the representatives of the media par excellence, make this their primary motive, an objective for which they are prepared to risk discomfort or mistreatment, or even life and limb. Considering the number of journalists that have been abducted, imprisoned, tortured, or even killed in recent years, it is even surprising that many of them still accept such dangerous assignments.

The only other groups that have as their major goal to try to verify the facts are the international war crime tribunals who indict individual perpetrators. To the extent that such trials are held at all, they occur only after significant delays that may affect the quality of the data that they obtain.

In considering the usefulness of data sources there are several questions that a researcher may want to consider:

1. Who owns or controls the source of the data? This will usually determine who will get access, for what purpose, and under what restrictions.

2. What are their interests or commitments? It is very rare to find that those who own or control the sources of data are committed to the free flow of all of the information. Their interests, their ideology, or their relation to other power wielders will usually lead to bias, distortion, or even blocking of access. That is why it is important to ask:

3. For what purpose were the data collected? Only among the media do we occasionally find a disinterested approach to reporting all the "news." All other organizations collect and report selected information for a specific purpose that has to be congruent with their agenda, their policy, their relations with their intended clientele.

4. Who collected the data with what qualifications? This questions really breaks down into two aspects: the qualifications of the first-hand source, and the qualifications of the collector of that data. The qualifications of the first-hand source include acquired as well as inherent ones. Observational skills, languages, etc. can be acquired, while inherent ones like age, sex, colour, ethnicity, etc. are givens. Both may have an effect on the way data are perceived and acquired. The people who collect the information need to be aware of these qualitative aspects, while their own qualifications will have an effect on how they interpret it, how they assemble it into reports, and how they impose their own slant on it.

5. Why are they available, to whom, and at what time? None of the various data sources are equally available to everybody all of the time. Therefore, researchers need not only cope with these restrictions, they also need to ask why they are imposed and in whose interest.

These very general comments will be amplified below as they relate to several types of data sources.

National and International Governments

From a researcher's point of view the United Nations, regional organizations, and national governments have several features in common. Not only are they governmental structures that are central parts of the political institutions of society, they also have a number of interlocking relationships that tie them to each other. Their bureaucracies produce enormous amounts of paper, much of it classified. The reason for the great amount of classified materials lies in the nature of bureaucratic reward systems. There are no punishments for classifying materials, no matter what their content. However, there are serious punishments for those declassifying materials that someone else would have preferred to remain classified. The researcher brave enough to look for useful materials in the archives of these bureaucracies should consider these questions:

1. What diplomatic considerations have introduced what bias? Is it possible to balance such bias by consulting other sources?

2. What political parties and/or theories are involved? How does their particular view of the world distort the information and/or suppress some aspects of it alltogether?

3. Are there professional pressure groups that were involved? Is it possible to disaggregate their particular effects?

4. How do special interest constituencies introduce a bias? To what extent was a simple awareness of their existence sufficient to produce particular effects, without their active intervention?

5. Are there interdepartmental rivalries involved?

In addition, all the usual reservations about the quality of the data need to be kept in mind. These governmental sources only rarely give first-hand information. Usually they have collected data that others have observed. Often they do not query the quality of such data. Thus, they do not ask about the language skills of the observers. When estimated numbers are reported they do not question the observer's skill at making such estimates. When assessing the veracity of an observer they often give more weight to their own bias, and accord more veracity to members of their own group and suspect members of other groups of being biased.

Humanitarian Aid NGOs

This category includes a great variety of organizations. They vary in their aims, their personnel, their funding, their record keeping, and their reporting. Not all of those that do produce reports make them public. But even the published ones are often of limited use to the researcher. There are several reasons for this:

1. Their reports tend to focus on their activities, what they did, and what effect they believe they have had.

2. Their reports are often composed with the intent to impress actual or potential donors and sponsors.

3. They tend to be very careful not to offend their sponsors, their country of origin, or their host governments, lest it might affect their ability to carry out their often self-appointed mission.

4. Only rarely does one of them carry out, or support, or sponsor research into the background and dynamics of the situation they are attempting to ameliorate.

5. Since their personnel usually are unfamiliar with the history or the language of their intended beneficiaries, their understanding of the situation that they are attempting to improve is often deficient.

Human Rights NGOs

Some of these organizations are international and some are national though they too will deal with regional or international issues. Many of them publish very useful reports at frequent intervals. They are likely to be based in investigative reporting and/or careful research. Their usefulness to the researcher is very great, but may sometimes be affected by a narrow focus on a single issue or a commitment to a particularistic perspective. Unfortunately, many of them circulate only in specialist circles and may be hard to locate.

A useful contribution would be a widely available listing of all of these organizations, with their addresses, and a list of at least their major reports. An increasing number of them can now be found on the Internet.

Notes

1. Mark Thompson, *Forging War: The Media in Serbia, Croatia and Bosnia-Hercegovina* (London: Article 19, International Centre Against Censorship, 1994), 143–44; 198–200. Thompson lists a number of cases where reporters have been jailed for "spreading false information" or "false rumours" when reporting Croatian attacks on Serbs or their property.
2. Steven Mufson, "Move to Curb Financial News Firms," *Manchester Guardian Weekly*, January 28, 1996: 15.
3. Walter Duranty, quoted in Robert Conquest, *The Harvest of Sorrow: Soviet Collectivization and the Terror-Famine* (New York: Oxford University Press, 1986), 319.
4. For more examples of inaccurate reporting in the former Yugoslavia, see David Binder, "Anatomy of a Massacre." in *Foreign Policy*, no. 97 (Winter 1994–1995), 70–78; and Peter Brock, "Dateline Yugoslavia: The Partisan Press," *Foreign Policy*, no. 93 (Winter 1993–1994), 152–72. While Brock's argument was fervently refuted by journalists in the field (see Letters to the Editor, *Foreign Policy*, no. 94 (Spring 1994), these criticisms do not diminish his overall argument that the Western press dem-

onstrated such a strong anti-Serb slant that their ability to examine the conflict impartially and accurately was often severely diminished.

5. "In Brief," *Manchester Guardian Weekly*, January 21, 1996: 11.
6. For a more in depth examination of the way Africa is reported in the Western media, see Paul Harrison and Robin Palmer, *News Out of Africa* (London: Hilary Shipman, 1986).
7. For a more in depth discussion of famine and genocide, see chapter 4.
8. To name but a few examples of references to the use of such terms, see Jerry Gray, "2 Nations Joined by a Common History of Genocide," *New York Times*, April 9, 1994: I6; Donatella Lorch, "Anarchy Rules Rwanda's Capital and Drunken Soldiers Roam City," *New York Times*, April 14, 1994: A1, A12. Keith B. Richburg, "Rwanda Wracked by Ethnic Violence," *Washington Post*, April 8, 1994: A1.

Part 3

Revisiting the Past

Introduction

The cases presented in part 3 are meant to illustrate our contention that gross human rights violations, including genocide, have occurred throughout history in all parts of the world. They extend the range of cases that have been presented in Chalk and Jonassohn (1990). As was the case in that volume, these cases cover the range of human rights violations from massacres to genocide. Each case is accompanied by a brief list of sources that may assist the interested reader in further exploration.

Our emphasis on the historical aspects of gross human rights violations is based on the conviction that such dramatic events require the presentation of their historical background before an analysis and explanation can even be attempted. When dealing with cases in antiquity and the Middle Ages, this is often an impossible task because required documents have either not been discovered, did not survive, or did not exist. In modern cases the opposite problem usually faces the scholar: the volume of documentation is enormous, though some of it may not be accessible or easy to interpret.

If this is a problem for scholars, it is even more difficult for the educated citizen to get a grasp on the meaning and explanation of such events. We offer two contemporary examples.

First, gross human rights violations have occurred in the former Yugoslavia, up to and including genocidal massacres. This case continues to receive (at the time of writing) extensive coverage in the mass media, albeit without an adequate presentation of its historical background. The last chapter in part 3 is an attempt to present this historical background as briefly as possible without blatant omissions and distortions. It is meant to help the reader make sense of the daily media coverage.

Second, the so-called civil war in Sudan has been going on for much longer. It receives only sporadic mention in the mass media although it has been characterized by human rights violations from slavery to genocidal massacres. When the media do report on it, they usually present it as a conflict between the Islamic north and the animistic or Christian south. However, an investigation by African Rights demonstrates that areas in the north are also being victimized, including the victimization of some Muslims and the burning of their mosques (African Rights 1995) Instead of attempting to present this complicated case in this volume, we refer the interested reader to three chapters in Montville's 1990 volume.[1] Together with the African Rights report they provide a detailed description of the cleavages in this country of over one hundred languages, as well as summaries of its recent history.

However it is also true that there are many cases where we shall never have enough information for a definitive analysis. Several of such cases are included below. Let us cite one additional case to illustrate this problem.

Sybaris, a Greek city-state in the south of Italy, was destroyed by an army of the neighbouring city Croton (Bullitt 1969). The army of Sybaris was defeated and withdrew within the city walls. After a siege of seventy days the Crotoniates entered the city. They took no prisoners and killed all who were unable to escape. After looting and probably burning the city, they "conducted the river over it and submerged it" (according to Strabo as quoted in Bullitt 1969: 82) Since the killing was not limited to members of the army, we can call this a genocidal massacre. But since all we have is quite partial information from Strabo and Deodorus, there is no evidence about the number of people who managed to escape, and thus no basis for accepting or rejecting a verdict of genocide.

In this connection we must remember not to apply contemporary criteria to events in antiquity. Before the growth of empires, political units were very small. City states consisted of a city that would not exceed an area of two square miles plus a modest area for agriculture surrounding it. Thus, it was possible for a large number of such city states to exist in the same general area. Perhaps the contemporary reader can best appreciate the scale of societies in antiquity by thinking of a world in which most states were no larger than today's Andorra, Lichtenstein, or Monaco.

The very opposite situation—that is, a plethora of information and analyses—can be noted for Rwanda which has not been included as a separate case for that very reason. The recent genocide in Rwanda is remarkable in a number of ways. It produced a large number of victims in a very short time. It accomplished this with a very modest amount of bureaucracy and a minimal amount of high technology. It also produced an enormous number of refugees. From our point of view, it is remarkable in another way. Immediately following the genocide serious analyses have appeared. This is unusual as it normally takes years and much pouring over documents before any good scholarly work is produced on any given genocide. For example, Raul Hilberg's *The Destruction of the European Jews* (1961), the first comprehensive scholarly examination of the Holocaust, was published more than fifteen years after the Holocaust ended. In the Rwanda case, the background history, the precipitating events, and the details of the perpetrators' actions have already been analyzed and published by competent scholars. Rather than summarizing their findings here, the interested reader is referred to the sources listed below.[2] While no doubt additional details may be revealed in the future, the work of these authors seems destined to be definitive.

All of the information presented below has been extracted from published sources. In a strictly academic sense every sentence would require documentation. To avoid this extreme of pedantry the sources used are indicated in parentheses and endnotes. In addition, for all cases, several encyclopedias have been consulted. References have been included in the text only when it seemed important to document a particular event or process.

It is not our intention to present here an analysis of each case, nor to produce general verities about the genocidal process.[3] It will probably take much more time and the detailed work of many more scholars before these efforts will produce cogent analyses and explanations.

The case summaries that follow are arranged in a more or less chronological order so that the evidence may be assessed in the light of the three styles of reporting history. In part 2, chapter 3, we have discussed how these styles may have affected the reporting for particular historical periods.

As already indicated, the cases presented below are not meant to be an exhaustive listing, but rather to illustrate an aspect of history that has often been ignored. They cover a great variety of what today are considered serious infringements on human rights—although that was not how they were defined by their contemporaries. Some cases have been omitted because not enough information was available. Other cases have been omitted because they were included in the volume by Chalk and Jonassohn (1990). Finally, a number of contemporary cases have been left out because the relevant information is not readily available. Thus, Ethiopia, Sudan, and Tibet, for instance, certainly are cases where gross violations of human rights have occurred, but where sufficient data for analysis and reliable conclusions have not yet become available. This is particularly disconcerting in the case of Ethiopia because trials are being held there to bring Mengistu and his collaborators to justice; these trials are barely even mentioned in the press.[4] Finally, a number of cases in Central and South America, Africa, and Asia will have to await a future publication.

Notes

1. The three chapters are: chapter 20: Francis Mading Deng, "The Identity Factor in the Sudanese Conflict;" chapter 21: Nelson Kasfir, "Peacemaking and Social Cleavages in Sudan;" and chapter 22: John O. Voll, "Northern Muslim Perspectives." Perhaps it should be stressed that all statements dealing with the present refer to the time of writing—which inevitably is earlier than the time of publication. However, the interested reader may find more up-to-date information on some of the Internet web sites referred to below.
2. For some very useful information and analyses on Rwanda, see especially: Braeckman (1994), Prunier (1995), Verschave (1994), Steering Committee of the Joint Evaluation of Emergency Assistance to Rwanda (1996), and *Human Rights Watch/Africa* (1994).
3. However, for an early attempt, see part 1, chapter 2.
4. We repeat: all statements dealing with the present refer to the time of writing—which inevitably is earlier than the time of publication. However, the interested reader may find more up-to-date information on some of the Internet web sites referred to below.

17

Pre-Twentieth-Century Perpetrators

Case 1: The Destruction of Greek City-States of Selinus and Himera in Sicily by the Carthaginians, 409 B.C.

The Greek city-states of Himera and Selinus played an outstanding role in the battle for supremacy fought among the Carthaginians, the Athenians, and the Sicilian cities of Syracuse and Segesta in the sixth and fifth centuries B.C. Himera was situated on the northeastern coast of Sicily at the mouth of the river Himeras Septentrionalis and founded in 648 B.C. Selinus was located on the southern coast of western Sicily and established itself around 630–623 B.C.

The growing power of Syracuse and her allies (notably Segesta, Acragas, and Gela) in Sicily during the fifth century B.C. threatened Carthaginian possessions. The attempts by Syracuse to dominate other Greek city-states in Sicily after escaping an attack by Athens (415–413 B.C.) caused these cities to invite the Carthaginians in to help them against Syracusan aggression.

Punic armies, under the leadership of Hamilcar, came in great force and almost overran all the eastern part of Sicily. Theron of Acragas, an ally of Gelon of Gela, was trapped within Himera. In 480 B.C., with Gelon's assistance, the Carthaginians were repelled, Hamilcar was killed and thousands of Carthaginian soldiers were taken prisoner and enslaved. So complete was this victory over Carthage that Gelon's brother Hiero was able to complete the triumph of Syracuse by defeating an Etruscan fleet, and his court became a flourishing cultural center of many philosophers and writers, including Pindar, Simonides, Bacchylides, Aeschylus, and Xenophanes.

The Carthaginian onslaught was only temporarily postponed, however. In 409 and 408 B.C. Selinus and Himera were destroyed by Hannibal, the son of Hasdrubal and grandson of Hamilcar. Selinus was the first to be attacked and was quickly defeated: "its inhabitants were slaughtered and its splendid walls levelled with the ground" (Smith 1878, 49). Almost none survived this slaughter.[1] Although the city was eventually rebuilt, Selinus never recovered from the blow. It was reconquered by the Carthaginians in 250 B.C. during the first Punic War; the surviving inhabitants of the second destruction were deported to Lilybaeum (present-day Marsala) on the western coast of Sicily.

In the year following the defeat and destruction of Selinus, the Carthaginians attacked Himera. Diocles of Syracuse, knowing that the Carthaginians far outnumbered Himera's forces, persuaded the inhabitants to leave the city. Half the inhabitants were put on a Syracusan squadron and sailed for Messana, while the remainder were to hold out until the ships returned. While the ships were again in sight, Hannibal's troops broke through the city's walls and began a massacre of its remaining inhabitants.[2]

One of the reasons advanced by Hannibal for a war in Sicily was to avenge the death of his grandfather, Hamilcar, during the battle of Himera in 480 B.C. After destroying the city, Hannibal refused a Syracusan offer to pay a ransom for those inhabitants who survived the slaughter. He declared that he wanted to keep the survivors as slaves, but changed his mind: "in an outburst of fanaticism, half family and half national, he slaughtered 3,000 prisoners in cold blood on the spot on which his grandfather had fallen" (Smith 1878: 49).

The following year the few remaining inhabitants of Himera were allowed by the Carthaginians to settle into a new town the conquerors had founded, not far from the site of the older city. Himera itself was never rebuilt and the only visible traces today are ruins of a Doric temple.

It is clear that the Carthaginians had the intent to destroy Selinus and Himera in order to destroy enemies that had caused them difficulties in the past. Not only did these cities bear witness to the mass killing of their citizens, the few inhabitants who survived were either enslaved, displaced or, as in the case of the people of Selinus in 250 B.C., eventually deported. The destruction of these cities and of their populations is a clear case of genocide since it goes well beyond the casualties caused by warfare.

Case 2: The Defeat of Numantia in 133 B.C.

Scipio Aemilanus Africanus, known as "Scipio the Younger" was the Roman general who destroyed Carthage in the Third Punic War. The younger son of L. Aemilius Paulus, the conqueror of Macedonia,

Scipio derived his name from his adopted grandfather, Roman general Scipio Africanus, who had distinguished himself in the Second Punic War at the battles of Cannae in 216 B.C. and Zama in 202 B.C. At the outbreak of the Third Punic War in 149 B.C., Scipio went to Africa where he gained enough fame to be elected consul. In 146 B.C. Scipio returned to Rome in triumph, having destroyed and levelled the city of Carthage.[3] Following repeated Roman disasters in Spain, Scipio was again called to the consulship in 134 B.C. and, after a year-long siege, destroyed the city of Numantia in northeast Spain.

Numantia had successfully resisted Roman forces for twelve years, despite being greatly outnumbered. Moreover, the city had little support from their Celtiberian allies and only had 8,000 troops in 144, before the renewed attacks caused new casualties. In 139 B.C., for example, Roman general Pompeius, whose forces outnumbered those of Numantia four to one, failed to take the city either by assault or by siege. Although the city had negotiated peace with Rome several times, none of the agreements were honored by the Roman senate and the Numantians were forced to face a series of Roman invasions, miraculously remaining undefeated until 133 B.C.

From the start Scipio decided to take the city by siege rather than by assault, a decision most likely influenced by the caliber of the troops he had at his disposal. Scipio and his troops arrived at Numantia in the autumn before the harvest, just in time to forestall the Numantians from replenishing their grain stocks. In October 132 B.C. Scipio ordered the complete circumvallation of the town with a full circle of walls and intermittent towers. To house his 60,000 men, seven camps were constructed. Numantian attempts at negotiation having failed, the city still refused to surrender. As famine spread through the city some of its inhabitants resorted to cannibalism. Many of the 4,000 defenders slew themselves rather than surrender to Rome. Numantia, "after a heroic resistance, had been overcome, not by sword but by famine" (Schulten 1930: 322).

Without waiting for senatorial permission, Scipio burnt the city to the ground, "as a red layer of burnt material still bears tragic witness" (Scullard 1980: 305). Most of the survivors were sold into slavery and Numantia never again emerged as a living community. This is clearly a case of genocide as the perpetrator had the obvious intent to destroy the city and its inhabitants, using hunger rather than assault as the tool for success. It may be argued that the city might have survived if it had surrendered before famine set in. Considering the Romans' record of dealing with people who tried to resist them, this seems most unlikely. In fact, it was probably the knowledge of Roman policy that inspired the Numantians to such desperate resistance.[4]

Case 3: The Asian Vespers of 88 B.C.

Mithradates VI (132–63 B.C.) was king of Pontus, an area on the south shore of the Black Sea. In 110 B.C. he overthrew his mother, who had murdered his father. He then added Crimea to his expanding kingdom. His territory was separated from Roman Asia and Cilicia, on the western and southern coasts of Asia Minor, by two buffer states, Bithynia and Cappadocia. Mithradates had invaded parts of both kingdoms, but Rome, to whom Bithynia and Cappadocia looked for protection, had forced him to withdraw his troops from those areas that he had occupied (circa 95 B.C.).

Due to the civil conflict between Romans and Italians in the Social War (also referred to as the Italian War, 91–88 B.C.), there were few Roman troops in Asia Minor at that time. This provided Mithradates with the opportunity to invade Bithynia and Cappadocia in alliance with the Tigranes of Armenia. Everywhere in Asia Minor, Mithradates was hailed as a liberator. The Roman provinces had been seething with hatred toward Rome for some time because of its tax collection, and it was not difficult for Mithradates to receive popular support. The king saw himself as a defender of Greek civilization and found much support among Greeks, who also saw the Romans as oppressors. Athens and much of mainland Greece quickly joined forces with Mithradates; Piraeus became his chief naval base in the Aegean.

In 88 B.C. Mithradates issued his orders from Ephesus in Asia Minor, where he had set up his headquarters, stating that all Romans and Italians, adults and children, free men and slaves, should be put to death. Their bodies were to be cast out unburied, and their property divided between the slayers and the king. Secret instructions were sent to the satraps and to the city governments for a simultaneous massacre of all Romans and Italians throughout the province. "Refugees were torn from sanctuaries and butchered" (*Cambridge Ancient History* 1932, vol. IX: 242). The killings took place in several Asian city-states, including Ephesus, Pergamum and Cos. In Rhodes, "children were killed before the eyes of their parents, then the women, and lastly the men" (Duggan 1958: 62). The entire Italian speaking population in Asia Minor and mainland Greece was wiped out; eighty thousand people were killed in a single day.[5]

The Asian vespers introduces the important question of what sections of society supported or opposed Mithradates: "It is usually assumed that the massacre was carried out by 'the rabble' and it has been argued that Mithradates represented the 'lower' classes in a great war against their Roman and 'upper' class repressors" (McGing 1986: 113). However, this act of genocide was aimed at anyone who spoke Italian and no particular attention was paid to status. It is possible that the population perceived anyone who spoke Italian as a representation of the Roman ruling elite. This was the first time Greeks ever murdered people because they spoke a different language.[6]

Mithradates' intention is quite clear since he stated it explicitly in his orders, and his motivation was the elimination of an enemy or rival by destroying the entire Italian-speaking population in Asia Minor. It would be an error, however, to interpret this genocide as racially or politically motivated because he saw the Italians only as a stumbling block to his expansionist ambitions.

Case 4: Diocletian's Persecution of the Christians

From its beginnings, Christianity was perceived by the Romans as a foreign religion and Christians were persecuted under the Roman Empire. However, this persecution was sporadic and not part of the state's agenda until the Emperor Decius' edict in 250 A.D. required "all free inhabitants of the Empire, men, women, and children, to sacrifice to the gods of the Empire, pour a libation, and taste sacrificial meat" (Frend, 1967: 302). The penalty for refusing to comply with the edict was death.[7]

Under Valerian, the persecution of Christians continued, although it is not known to what extent the state was involved. Gallienus was the first emperor to grant official toleration of Christianity. Under his rule until Diocletian's "Great Persecution" in 303, Christianity prospered throughout the Empire.

The Emperor Diocletian (284–305 A.D.) brought a renewed level of security to the Empire. He reorganized the army, much enlarging it, and using more men originating outside the Empire as soldiers. Frontiers were greatly strengthened; the legions, reduced in size, now were stationed farther back from the frontiers for defensive purposes. Diocletian also instituted tax reforms, eventually curbing a once-rampant inflation that poorly run wars of the past had helped to create.

Diocletian held power and survived by making himself an absolutist, not only by use of his armies, but symbolically through ceremony, court practice, and even dress. His chief lieutenant, Maximian, was made a partner and given the name Augustus; he controlled much of the Empire. Each of them then had a second in command called a Caesar; these men, Constantius Chlorus for Maximian and Galerius for Diocletian, also had separate courts and areas of command. The government of the Empire became a tetrarchy, divided between four rulers. Diocletian and Galerius held the eastern half of the Empire, while Maximian and Constantius held the west. Each of the tetrarchs had his own capital; none ruled from Rome. Diocletian's headquarters was at Nicomedia in Asia Minor; Galerius chose Sirmium on the lower Danube; Maximian, Milan in northern Italy; and Constantius, Trèves in northeastern Gaul. The two Caesars did everything but lead armies; they provided the money and the supplies, controlled the bureaucracies and supervised the administration of justice.

Although Diocletian had brought about these widespread and remarkable reforms, he placed an equal emphasis on traditional Roman values. Diocletian was a religious man who, like many Roman emperors before him, subscribed to the idea of emperor worship. Proclaiming himself a descendant of the gods and therefore divine, he called himself Jovius and gave the name Herculius to Maximian. The restoration of the traditional Roman religion became an extreme priority to Diocletian, as it was generally felt that recent troubles in the Empire were caused by the neglect of the rightful Roman gods. Moreover, recent military victories in Persia had convinced the emperor that the growth of the Empire was "by favour of the gods" and in 299 Christians were purged from the army (Fox 1987: 594).[8]

Throughout the winter of 302–303 Diocletian and Galerius discussed the so-called "Christian problem." According to Lactantius, Diocletian maintained a resistance to a bloody solution, unlike Galerius and certain magistrates and officers who were consulted on the subject.[9] Diocletian was said to have agreed to a "solution" on the condition that bloodshed be avoided. On February 23, 303, the festival of Terminalia, the new church of Nicomedia was destroyed, marking the beginning of a bloody, albeit sporadic, persecution. The doors were forced, the scriptures burned and, within hours, the church was levelled to the ground. The next day Diocletian's first Edict was posted.

The Edict ordered all Christian churches to be destroyed throughout the Empire, all written materials pertaining to the Christian faith publicly burned and Christian assemblies prohibited. Christians who refused to offer sacrifice to the Roman gods would lose their rights and position in the State. For Christians, to sacrifice to the gods was to forfeit one's salvation. Although at least one Christian was killed while resisting the Edict, most complied with the order and there were few executions.[10]

Diocletian did not want to create martyrs for the Church and only those who openly defied the Edict were killed. A split between moderate and more fanatical Christians began to emerge: the moderates gave up their books (scriptures) to the authorities, while the more zealous regarded this as treasonous and believed it was a Christian's duty to resist the law and face death. Diocletian had hoped that this split would fester and that the more moderate Christians would return to the fold.

A short time after the first Edict the imperial palace at Nicomedia caught fire twice within fifteen days. Diocletian's own rooms were burned. There is some speculation that the fire was deliberately set by Galerius in order to push Diocletian to take more drastic action against the Christians (Lactantius 1984: 14, 2) But regardless of how the fires started, the Christians were the natural scapegoats and were immediately blamed. It was at this point that the persecution of Christians intensified.

The imperial palace was immediately purged of any Christian influence. Every Christian member of the palace was ordered to sacrifice, including the emperor's own wife and daughter. Sacrifice was the ultimate test of loyalty: those who refused were immediately under suspicion. Two of Diocletian's most trusted servants refused to sacrifice and were summarily tortured and executed. The emperor's attention was not solely directed at the palace:

> So now the emperor began to rage not just against the members of his household but against everyone.... Eunuchs who had once enjoyed great power, and on whom Diocletian himself and the whole palace depended, were killed; priests and deacons were arrested and condemned without any proof or confession and then led off with all their dependents. People of every age and either sex were seized for burning, and since their number was so great, they were taken not individually but in groups and then encircled by flames. Members of the household had millstones tied around their necks and were drowned in the sea. The persecution fell with equal violence on the rest of the population, as the judges, sent out around all the temples, compelled everyone to perform sacrifice. (Williams 1985: 179) [11]

A second Edict was issued shortly after the fires in the summer of 303. All Christian clergy were to be arrested and imprisoned. The prisons being filled created more problems for the state, as there was no room for legitimate criminals. Thus a third Edict was quickly drawn up to replace the second. This Edict was a sort of amnesty, granting the release of the imprisoned clergymen on the condition that they sacrifice to the Roman gods. Those who refused would be tortured and killed. It is likely that the state knew that most would refuse to sacrifice and viewed this as a better solution than overcrowded prisons.

Persecution was not the same in all areas of the Empire. Just as Christians varied in their defiance, so the authorities differed in enforcing the Edicts. In northwestern Asia Minor, for example, both clergy and laity were arrested and tortured, mainly because an over-zealous and cruel governor took the Edicts most seriously and hired squads of sadists to enforce them. Other governors and magistrates acted differently. Many could not afford the labour or equipment to demolish churches or the prison capacity to make mass arrests. Some were simply humane.

The tetrarchs themselves were split regarding the enforcement of the Edicts. Constantius and Maximian barely enforced the first Edict, and there was little bloodshed in the Gallic provinces and in Italy. In contrast, Africa was the scene of the most brutal persecution. Christians there would openly defy the law and all but dare the authorities to arrest them and the authorities seem to have had few misgivings about enforcing the Edicts.

In the East, where Diocletian and Galerius were influential, the persecution quickly turned bloody. This was particularly true after a fourth Edict was issued in April 304, ordering all Christians to sacrifice to the gods upon pain of death. Although the persecution was initially aimed only at the Christian clergy, it soon incorporated all Christians as potential threats to the state. Christianity was declared a *religio illicita*— no longer a permissible religion in the Roman Empire.

The Church took a clear stand on the issue of sacrificing to the gods, referring to the command made in Exodus, "Whoever sacrifices to any god, save to the Lord only, shall be utterly destroyed" (Exodus, 22.20). Persecution naturally led to martyrdom and to an increase in fanaticism on the part of the Christians. Many were eager to become martyrs and believed that by doing so they would go to heaven. Eusebius illustrates the magnitude of the slaughter and how some Christians actively sought martyrdom for their cause:

> Some of the victims suffered death by beheading, some by fire. So many were killed in a single day that the axe, blunted and worn out with slaughter, was broken in pieces and the executioners periodically relieved one another. But always I observed a wonderful, truly divine enthusiasm in those who put their trust in Christ. No sooner had the first batch been

sentenced, than others from every side would jump up to the platform in front of the judge and proclaim themselves Christians. (Eusebius 1953: 8)

In theory the fourth Edict sentenced millions of Christians living in the Eastern Empire to death, but the reality was quite different. The worst affected provinces were Bithynia, Syria, Egypt, Palestine, and Phrygia where Christians were numerous and where persecutors zealously enforced the Edict. Entire towns were wiped out:

> A little Christian town in Phrygia was surrounded by soldiers, who set it on fire and completely destroyed it, with its whole population—men, women, children—as they called on Almighty God. Why? Because every one of the inhabitants, including the town prefect himself and the magistrates, all declared that they were Christians. (Eusebius 1953: 8)

On the other hand, there are many cases where judges and magistrates refused to comply with the Edicts and, even when provoked by the Christians, were committed to avoiding bloodshed. They would simply record that the Christians had sacrificed whether they had done so or not. Sometimes only those Christians who shouted that they had not sacrificed were maltreated, often being driven into exile. What this demonstrates is that the Edicts were enforced sporadically and that there was no cohesive organized destruction of Christians.

The persecution of Christians continued after Diocletian's death in 305, as the cycle of violence and resistance became difficult to stop. Galerius, who succeeded Diocletian in the east, was still committed to wiping out Christianity. The persecution ended with the conversion of Emperor Constantine, the son of Constantius, in 312. He established toleration of Christianity throughout the empire and defeated the eastern emperor in 324, setting up his capital in Constantinople.

It is clear that the initial intent of the perpetrator was not to exterminate all Christians, but rather to terrorize them into submission by murdering members of their group, especially the clergy. However, the fourth Edict certainly demonstrates that the state pursued a genocidal policy toward the Christians in wanting to eradicate all those who refused to renounce their beliefs in favour of Roman gods.[12]

Case 5: The Fourth Crusade, 1202–1204

Initiated by Pope Innocent III, the Fourth Crusade was largely composed of French and Italian soldiers, many of them nobles. In the original agreement, the Venetians had promised to transport the French crusaders to Palestine and to provide them with military equipment and provisions. When the French soldiers arrived at Venice, they were too few to pay for the contracted amount: only twelve thousand of the thirty thousand warriors came. The Venetians, who had constructed ships and who had assembled provisions for the original number, proposed that the French make up the deficit by assisting them in attacking the seaport of Zara. Zara (also called Zadar), a major port city on the Dalmatian coast of Yugoslavia south of Zagreb, was ruled by the Christian king of Hungary and was the greatest Adriatic rival of Venice during this period. The original plan of the crusaders to use Egypt as a military base for an attack on Palestine was postponed. When Pope Innocent heard of the Venetians' proposal, he prohibited the expedition; when it was undertaken in spite of him, he excommunicated all participants. The crusaders ignored the pope and attacked Zara in November 1202, thoroughly pillaging the city and killing all its inhabitants.

Following the sack of Zara, the Venetians then suggested that the expedition now direct its efforts to Constantinople and restore the dethroned Byzantine emperor, Isaac II Angelos. They made a good case for the diversion: if the Crusade restored the deposed emperor, he would guarantee the manpower which the French had failed to provide, as well as providing money and supplies for the Egyptian expedition.

Pope Innocent again issued a reprimand to the crusaders, which they again disregarded, and on April 13, 1204 they captured Constantinople. At least 2,000 Byzantines were deliberately murdered after the capture of the city by Italian soldiers who were allowed to avenge themselves for previous grievances. The crusaders, both French and Italian, then began ransacking and raping, sparing neither church, noblewoman, nor nun. The army was given permission to go on a three-day rampage, initiating an "indiscriminate slaughter" that was so widespread that rivers of blood flowed down the city's streets for several days. During these three days, the invading Latin army was not subjected to any control, and it spared neither age nor sex: "women and children were not spared the sword...the army, hardened and embittered by penury and war, was transformed into a mob driven by hate." (Queller 1977: 149)

The crusaders, afraid that the Greeks who had survived might try to attack them, deliberately set fire to the city. So extensive was the fire, which burned all night and until the next evening, that...more houses were destroyed than there were in the three largest cities in France

"...the number of dead said to be *sans fin et sans mesure*" (Pears 1886: 351). There are no exact figures with regard to the number of dead, but few survived the slaughter. Although there is mention of an uncertain number of refugees streaming out of the city, it is clear that once the city had been burned very few had survived. The city's population was almost completely destroyed.

Once the Byzantine capital had been ravaged and ruined, the crusaders restored order. Since both the deposed emperor and his son had been killed in the interim, the crusaders established a Latin empire and selected the count of Flanders as its ruler. This empire lasted until 1261, but never ruled all of Byzantium; it was comprised of most of the land of Thrace and Greece, where French barons were rewarded with feudal fiefs. For their contributions, the Venetians obtained the harbor rights in Constantinople and a commercial monopoly throughout the empire and the Aegean islands.

The Fourth Crusade never reached the Holy Land and did nothing to weaken the Muslim Empire's power. Although Pope Innocent believed that the union of the Greek and Latin churches under the Roman papacy would remain permanent, the establishment of the Latin Empire only further perpetuated the rift.

Constantinople was so ravaged as a result of the destruction wrought by the Fourth Crusade that the Turkish conquest in 1453 was a rather "hollow affair" as "vast acres of it were in ruins long before the Turkish army swept through the breached walls. Vegetable gardens, trees and sown fields grew over the sites of forgotten palaces, roads had reverted to dust tracks, and churches were deserted and roofless" (Bradford 1967: 10).

The Venetians clearly intended to destroy their trading rivals. They themselves had no need for a greater labor force and Europe at that time suffered from overpopulation. Therefore, they had no interest in taking prisoners and instead did everything in their power to ensure the mass slaughter of their rivals.[13] The destruction of Zara and Constantinople are both cases of genocide.

Case 6: Vlad III of Walachia

Vlad III, Prince of Walachia, is perhaps better known today as Dracula. So notorious was his reign of terror that legends about this historical figure have persisted throughout the centuries in Romanian, German, Turkish, and English folklore. Most contemporary images of

Vlad III are derived from Bram Stoker's *Dracula* (1897) and from the hundreds of films adapted from that novel. Although the real figure behind the myth was no vampire, there is little doubt that Vlad III, known also as Vlad Tepes (the Impaler) was certainly monstrous. Under his rule, tens of thousands of civilians were the victims of a genocidal massacre.

The region of Walachia is now the southern region of Rumania and consists largely of the fertile plain of the lower Danube basin. During the reign of Vlad III, this region was under the suzerainty of the Ottoman Empire. Although Walachia was expected to pay tribute to the sultan, it was not under direct Ottoman control at that time.

As long as the Walachians continued to pay their annual tribute, Sultan Mehmed II left them in peace. Indeed, the sultan had helped Vlad to defeat rival claimants to the throne, taking Vlad's younger brother Radu as a hostage to the Porte. But once Vlad securely held power, he stopped paying tribute and refused to send the Porte the children demanded for the Janissary corps.

Vlad then began to infringe on Ottoman territory and to massacre the local Ottoman population. In the winter of 1461–1462 Vlad's army crossed the Danube and devastated Ottoman-held territories, burning every last village to the ground and massacring the defenseless population, including women and children. In a letter sent to King Matthias of Hungary on February 11 1462, Vlad stated that 23,884 men had been slain in this campaign. It was possible for him to give such a precise figure because their heads had been carefully collected, "not including those who were burned in their houses and whose heads were not presented to our officials" (Vlad II, quoted in Giurescu 1991: 18).[14] Vlad had also killed an envoy from the sultan, ordering that his turban be nailed to his head.

In response to this news, Mehmed II assembled an army of 150,000 men. The sultan himself chose to join his men on this mission. The size of Mehmed's army indicates that he intended to take complete control of Walachia, as he had of Serbia and Greece; he wanted more than to just bring about a change in princes.

Despite the size of the Ottoman army, Vlad had certain advantages over the sultan. The Ottomans were accustomed to campaigns in territories with powerful fortresses and walled cities. A decade earlier, Mehmed's forces had successfully taken Constantinople. Although capturing a city could prove difficult, once it had surrendered, the sultan could be fairly sure of controlling the surrounding countryside as well. Walachia was different in that it had few cities and those few were situated at the foot of the Carpathian Mountains. The plains were inhabited chiefly by peasants and shepherds. The Walachians practiced a scorched earth policy in facing off the invader: Vlad had ordered the peasants to burn their crops and to withdraw their cattle and movable goods to the dense oak forests nearby. These forests also served as cover for Vlad and his army of 10,000.

Vlad pursued the Ottoman army, harassing it with minor skirmishes, but never making a decisive attack. When Mehmed's army reached the Walachian capital of Tirgoviste, the city's doors were open and it appeared deserted. Leaving the city, the sultan and his men came upon a most gruesome sight: for half an hour the road leaving Tirgoviste was bordered by the impaled corpses of 20,000 Bulgarians and Ottomans. On the tallest stake and clad in ceremonial dress was Hamza Pasha, the commander of Vidin.

Vlad's initial success against the Ottoman army was rather short lived, however. After months of small skirmishes, Vlad withdrew to Moldavia, leaving behind a small force of 6,000 men. This detachment was almost wiped out entirely by the forces under the commander of the right wing of the Ottoman army, Turahanoglu Omer Bey. He laid the heads of 2,000 of these Walachians at the feet of the sultan and was subsequently rewarded by being reinstated as governor of Thessaly. Mehmed II was ultimately victorious. When he returned to Constantinople in July 1462 he appointed Mihaloglu Ali Bey as governor of Walachia with instructions to install Vlad's brother Radu as ruler. Radu, in contrast to Vlad, was a rather weak and ineffectual leader and would pose no threat to Ottoman rule. As for Vlad, he was captured by King Matthias of Hungary and imprisoned at Visegrad, where he remained for twelve years. He did succeed in recovering his throne in 1476, however, usurping the Walachian Prince Laiota Basarab. His reign was short lived, as Basarab returned only a month later and killed him.[15]

This case should be considered as a genocidal massacre. Certainly, Vlad's intent was to destroy the Ottoman population, both within and outside Walachia. The right bank of the Danube, from the mouth to the city of Zimnecea, was pillaged and burned leaving almost no survivors. The victims were both soldiers and civilians, and included men, women, and children. Although massacres were certainly not uncommon during this period, the methods of torture used by Vlad, namely the impaling of his victims, and the pleasure he seemed to have derived from it, have obviously left a very lasting impression.

Case 7: The Conquest of Mexico, 1519–1521

The Aztecs were an aboriginal people who settled in Mexico in the late twelfth century A.D. They were originally a hunting and gathering nomadic people from a region north of Mexico forced into the valley lake area by hostile tribes. By the time the Spanish arrived in Mexico, the Aztecs had become a powerful people living in Tenochtitlan (now Mexico City), a city that they had built on an artificial island in the valley lake.[16] Sources vary on the population of Tenochtitlan before the conquest, although 100,000 seems to be a generally accepted figure. Cortes remarked in his second dispatch to Charles V that the city was "the same size as Seville or Cordoba...and in the market sixty thousand people meet to buy all kinds of goods" (de Sahagun 1978: xvii). It is clear that the Aztecs were very advanced culturally, having developed a highly sophisticated style of architecture and sculpture. Aztec society was based on a caste system and a polytheistic religion involving human sacrifice.

The Valley of Mexico, home to the Aztecs and their allies, is a fertile basin about 120 kilometres long and almost as wide, surrounded by mountain ranges and containing an abundant water supply and several volcanoes. Later expansion by the Aztecs and their allies carried them into regions with more tropical climates. By the time Cortes and his small Spanish army landed in Mexico in 1519, the Aztecs and their allies had conquered much of present-day Mexico outside of the western and northwestern states, the southern part then occupied by the Mayas, and the small territory of Tlaxcala, a traditional enemy of the Aztecs. The Aztecs and their allies, together with the Tlaxcalans and many other groups in Mexico, spoke Nahuatl.

Although the Aztecs had been living in the Valley of Mexico since the twelfth century, they were not dominant militarily until the fifteenth century. The Aztecs and the people of Tlacopan were invited by the state of Texcoco to form an alliance. Aztec conquests were actually the work of all three allies, although the Aztecs soon dominated this alliance. In the process of conquering and subjugating their neighbours, the Aztecs developed a brutal military state that waged aggressive warfare against surrounding tribes. They subdued most of Mexico, moving into warmer climates where they found many products not available on the high Mexican plateau. However, because of the Aztec custom of human sacrifice and the Aztec demands for tribute, they did not gain the friendship of the peoples they conquered. As a result, when the Spanish arrived, they were not only aided by the Aztec's enemies, but also by many tribes the Aztecs had conquered and made part of their dominion. It was easy for the Spanish to turn native political conditions to their advantage.

Cortes, the leader of the Mexican conquest, came from the Estremadura region of Spain and had settled in Hispaniola in 1504. He rose to prominence in Cuba after 1512 and was commissioned by Diego Velazquez, the Spanish governor of Cuba, to establish full contact with the emperor Montezuma. Disassociating himself from Velazquez, Cortes moved by sea to the coast of Mexico and then overland to the elevated central valley near the Aztec state. Along the route, Cortes formed alliances with native peoples already enemies of the Aztecs (notably the Tlaxcalans) or with those who sought to free themselves from Aztec control.

Cholula was one of the few cities in the Valley of Mexico that was unaligned. Because of a recent altercation with Tlaxcala, the city tended to favor the Aztecs, but it was not part of the Aztec empire. There is some indication that the Tlaxcalans asked the Spaniards to destroy Cholula because its people were "evil" and friends of the Aztecs (Leon-Portilla 1962: 40). According to some sources, the Cholulans attempted to test the invading Spaniards to see whether they were mortals or gods. The people believed that if they were mortals or false gods, the wrath of the God Quetzalcoatl would destroy them (Brundage 1972: 258–62). Other sources point to an Aztec-Cholula alliance, believing that Montezuma's forces had planned to ambush the Spaniards (Gibson 1966: 27). Before they could do so, however, the Spaniards and their native allies (mainly the Tlascalans) overpowered the Cholulans in the main square: "For two terrible days destruction was wreaked upon the city, and it was that long before the vultures dared to descend into the embers to find their food" (Brundage 1972: 261). Cortes had "waged a cruel war in which vast multitudes were slaughtered, as is recorded in the chronicles" (Leon-Portilla 1962: 40). The Cholulans who survived the massacre "were taken to distant lands in expeditions or as colonizers" or lived on encomiendas (Reed 1966: 152). All were living in virtual slavery.

Several hundred Spanish soldiers, reinforced by many thousands of natives, arrived at Tenochtitlan in the autumn of 1519. Montezuma greeted the Spaniards and welcomed them to his city. Soon after, the emperor was taken prisoner, enabling Cortes to rule through him as a puppet emperor. Relations between the Aztecs and the Spaniards re-

202 Genocide and Gross Human Rights Violations

mained superficially agreeable until the spring of 1520, when, during Cortes' absence from the city, the Aztecs rose in rebellion. Despite Cortes' return and his effort to halt the uprising, Tenochtitlan reverted to Aztec control in June of 1520. The Spaniards found refuge with their allies in Tlaxcala. In the summer of 1521, they launched their final attack on Tenochtitlan. The Spaniards focused their land assault on the causeways to take over the city, sparing neither women or children: "the enemy's policy was of calculated terror and total destruction" (Brundage 1972: 286). Over 100,000 Aztecs and close allies were killed and drowned in the siege. "Over 40,000 bodies floated in the canals or remained stacked in rain soaked piles in designated buildings for lack of burial ground" (Brundage 1972: 286). Many more were dying of starvation and disease. Cortes states that after the fall of Tenochtitlan, "those left in the city stood and walked on piles of dead bodies" (Cortes 1962: 226).[17]

It is clear that the conquests of Cholula and Tenochtitlan were both cases of genocide, as Cortes and his allies had the clear intent to destroy these cities and their inhabitants. The Spaniards, with limited resources and far from home, could not afford to risk protracted warfare against a far more numerous enemy. Therefore, after having been attacked, they opted to destroy the enemy once and for all. In their aim of expanding the empire, they were eminently successful.

Case 8: The Sack of Novgorod in 1570 by Ivan the Terrible

Novgorod is a city north of Lake Ilmen on the Volkhov river, roughly fifty kilometres southeast of St. Petersburg. From the ninth to the early sixteenth centuries, Novgorod was a powerful commercial city of great wealth and importance. During the thirteenth and fourteenth centuries, Novgorod reached its zenith as a key city for Hanseatic trade in Northeastern Europe. Having at one time a reported population of 400,000, it was the wealthiest and most progressive of medieval cities in Russia. It had the highest degree of democracy and religious and political autonomy in the region. Princes and archbishops were elected by members of the Novgorodian merchant class and nobility.

Because of its wealth and political independence, Novgorod was always suspected of plotting with its Western trading partners against the growing power of the ruling families in Moscow. In the fifteenth century, there were also rumors that Novgorod wanted to sever its ties with Russia and place itself under the protection of Poland. The commercial rivalry between Moscow and Novgorod only served to increase the tension between the two cities.

In 1471 Ivan III (Ivan the Great) marched on Novgorod as a move toward a more unified Russia, breaking much of the city's political independence. Hundreds of nobles and merchants were forcibly exiled to Moscow. Whatever political and commercial power was left in Novgorod after 1471 was completely destroyed by Ivan IV in 1570.

Russian tsar Ivan IV, generally known as Ivan the Terrible, was born in 1530 and acceded to the title of grand duke of Muscovy at the age of three after the death of his father Basil III. The following fourteen years were marked by a violent struggle for power among the feudal aristocracy, the boyars. Only when Ivan IV became tsar in 1547 did the "time of troubles" cease.

Ivan was then under the influence of the Chosen Council headed by Alexis Adashev and the priest Sylvester. Ivan agreed with the reforms carried out by the Council, namely the centralization of government. But he despised its members for their opposition to his policy of conquest of neighbouring Livonia, for their hostility toward the Romanovs, the family of his first wife, and for their treachery in 1553. During his illness in that year, the Council supported another candidate to the throne and refused any allegiance to his infant son.

In 1564 Ivan abdicated the throne and left Moscow after the death of his general and councillor Prince Kurbsky. He returned within the same year, forming a special court (*Oprichnina*) consisting of thousands of hand-picked men who would become the commanders and administrators of the state and also the tsar's executioners and secret police. The Oprichnina enforced Ivan's policy of rule by terror: entire boyar families were killed.

In 1570 Ivan turned his attention toward Novgorod. Its independent spirit was a direct threat to the tsar's totalitarian ideology. There were also rumors that the leaders of the city, including the archbishop, were plotting with Poland to overthrow the tsar. These rumors were used as an excuse to destroy Novgorod, although the plan to invade the city had been in effect long before there was word of a conspiracy. Ivan ordered a large military force, mainly comprised of Oprichniki, to march on Novgorod in January 1570. His resolve was to destroy the city, to "virtually exterminate this centre of monstrous treachery" (Grey 1964: 178).

The first indication of what was in store for Novgorod was the closing down of the monasteries by the army and the seizure of all priests. Each cleric was ordered to pay a sum of twenty rubles. Those who could afford to pay the money were released; those who could not were flogged, often to death. Ivan and his party, comprised of some 1,500 Oprichniki, arrived in the city a week later. On the way, they burned the city of Tver and killed a large number of its citizens because the tsar suspected they were allies of Novgorod. Similar attacks took place in other cities and towns because the tsar wanted his campaign to be kept secret. On the road between the town of Klin and Novgorod, for example, "as far as the eye could see there were burned houses and fields and hundreds of corpses lying in the snow" (Koslov 1961: 197).

Once the tsar and his forces arrived in Novgorod, the punishment of the city began in earnest. The city's inhabitants are said to have been butchered at a rate of 500 to 1,500 a day: "Wives were forced to witness the quartering of their husbands; husbands were forced to see their wives roasted alive; babes in arms were put on the execution blocks together with their mothers" (Koslov 1961: 198). Men, women, and children were brought before the tsar, one hundred at a time. Because he wanted to identify disloyalty, they "were put to the question, roasted over a slow fire by some new and, as it would appear, particularly ingenious process, and then condemned, for the most part, to death, and sent out to be drowned" (Waliszewski 1966: 252). When formal executions proved to be too slow, the tsar ordered a series of daily mass drownings in the Volkhov river. People were tied to sleighs and pushed into the river. Soldiers in boats would then survey the river making sure no one could escape. The slaughter had also spilled over into the surrounding countryside for a radius of more than 250 kilometres. Farmers were murdered, their crops and houses set on fire and their cattle slaughtered. The tsar wanted to ensure that nothing would be left of what was once a rich and fertile region. The killing was said to have lasted more than five weeks.

In the second week of February, on the Monday of the second week of Lent, the tsar, said to be tired of the slaughter, called an end to the carnage in Novgorod. He then ordered that one male survivor per street be brought before him; only a handful could be found. He then made a speech, telling the survivors, "…You must not now grieve over all that has happened. Live honourably in Novgorod" (Ivan IV, quoted in Grey 1964: 181).

Just surviving in Novgorod was difficult enough. The clearing of the Volkhov river of bodies, severed limbs, and heads was only completed six months after the slaughter had ended. The spring and summer brought disease and plague to Novgorod. Moreover, because the crops had been destroyed and there was no money to buy food, the few remaining survivors were further decimated by famine. Novgorod was so thoroughly depopulated that it never regained any semblance of its former power. It became an unimportant little town, indistinguishable from other provincial towns in Russia. Estimates of the number of people killed range anywhere from 15,000 to 60,000. There are no available figures as to the population of the city in 1570 before the slaughter took place, although an estimate of over 50,000 is generally accepted.[18]

The lack of reliable statistics makes this case difficult to define. If one were to accept that almost no one survived the slaughter, the sack of Novgorod would be classified as a genocide. If one accepts the lower estimate of 15,000 murdered, however, and knowing that the population of the city certainly was triple that number, this case would be classified as a genocidal massacre. The perpetrator unquestionably had the intent to exterminate the power and the people of Novgorod because he perceived them as potential enemies. In the implementation of his design he paid little attention to either age, sex, or class and stopped only once he felt secure in the knowledge that the city could never again pose a threat to either himself or any future tsar.

Case 9: The Wars of the Vendée

The Vendéan wars have been relatively ignored by professional historians. Of an estimated 15,000 relevant publications, only a small proportion have been written by professional historians (Secher 1986: xi). The reason behind this is the view, which until recently was widely respected, that the royalist counterrevolution was regressive and that reports of wide-scale killing were exaggerated by the Vendée in order to gain sympathy. It was not until the publication of the work of Babeuf and Secher that the victims of this genocide have gained credibility.

The territory affected by the counterrevolutionary uprising, referred to as the "Wars of the Vendée" covers an area of roughly 10,000 square kilometres. The term "Vendée" does not, in this case, apply solely to the department of the Vendée in France, but refers instead to all the regions in France that rose against the French Revolutionary régime and acted as havens for refractory priests. In 1793 the rebellion spread throughout northern Vendée and Deux-Sèvres, and the southern regions of Maine-et-Loire and Loire-Inférieure. Although these areas have little common history and do not share the same natural resources, they do have a common geography: much of the region affected by the counterrevolution is heavily wooded. It has been argued that wooded areas would favor more traditionalist, proclerical sentiments. Their peasants, priests, and seigneurs would likely form more closely knit social groups because of their scattered populations and the poor communication between regions: the geography of these regions directly influenced their role in the insurrection.

One of the most striking differences between the uprisings characteristic of the French Revolution and those of the Vendée is the contrast between social alliances. Instead of a bourgeois-peasant alliance against the feudal system, this was an alliance between the peasantry and the nobility against the bourgeoisie. Parts of the Vendéan peasants' contempt for the bourgeoisie were related to their suspicions that the latter was taking too large a share of the recently nationalized wealth. Denied their share of the spoils and feeling that the revolution would only worsen their conditions, they returned to the seigneurs and the Church for protection.

The Vendée had made far fewer gains from the Revolution than had other regions. The abolition of seigneurial dues was of little consequence in areas where the burden was light and the lords distant, as in the departments of the Vendée and Sarthe. The opposition of such regions as a whole was made plain in the massive refusal to take the oath to the constitution. Many priests refused it under strong pressures from their parishioners, who wanted to send a clear signal to Paris. When the government was determined to treat these priests as counterrevolutionaries, it succeeded in making them into just that.

Britain's economic blockade of France and the war against Belgium, Austria, and the Netherlands led to severe shortages throughout France. Although the Vendée had already shown hostility toward the government in Paris and were even more prone to show that hostility when food shortages became more widespread, in the end it was conscription that provoked the Vendée into armed revolt against the government. Furthermore, resistance to the government, particularly at a time of war, was the equivalent of treason, and it was known that the government would treat it as such. There was little to lose in taking resistance all the way and waging war against the government in Paris. The rebels called themselves a royal and Catholic army, and looked to the nobility for leadership. The *emigrés* were more than happy to help the rebels and put all their efforts and hopes in armed insurrection. It is important to note that not all the leaders of the revolt were nobles; members of the peasantry did act as leaders in battle.

The widespread resistance to conscription and the armed rebellion that ensued, was met by severe measures on the part of the government in Paris. The constitutional decree of March 19, 1793 made it illegal to partake in counterrevolutionary activities or protests. On the 27th of the same month, a law was passed against all members of the nobility and anyone else deemed an "enemy of the Revolution." The penalty for being labelled as such was death. These laws clearly violated the government's own constitution and are clear examples of how much brutality the Jacobin dictatorship and the Terror would bring to the nation.

As hostilities continued, the government in Paris felt increasingly threatened. The idea to exterminate the population of the Vendée was already discussed by certain generals in April 1793 (Secher in Babeuf 1987: 22). Jean Baptiste Carrier, the deputy from Nantes, repeated to anyone who would listen that he would rather turn France into a cemetery than fail the Revolution.[19] On August 1, 1793 the government passed a decree prescribing a policy of total destruction (*terre brûlée*). The same government became increasingly frustrated by the continued fighting and passed an order on October 1 to exterminate the people of the Vendée.

One of the tactics employed by the revolutionary army was to purposely sacrifice their troops by sending them, often untrained and in small numbers, to fight the Vendée. This tactic, which Babeuf defines as part of a "system of depopulation" was designed by the revolutionary generals Ronsin, Rossignol, and Léchelle to prolong the war. They were not interested in ending the war in the Vendée, having already become used to the spoils of that war, and chose instead to ignore the government's orders to bring a quick and decisive end to the rebellion. This tactic also gave the people in the Vendée a false sense of security, making those who would not normally show their hostility to the government feel secure enough to do so. An example of such a tactic can be seen in the actions of General Léchelle in western France, who allowed the rebels to take Craon, Ancennis, and Laval and then sent eight hundred men, a minimal force hardly able to fight such a growing revolt, to attack the Vendéan troops. Tens of thousands of revolutionary soldiers were purposely sent to their death. Such actions led Pierre Philippeaux, a revolutionary lawyer sent to western France by the government and later executed with Danton, to state that Léchelle sacrificed his own troops to the rebels as if he had been ordered to do so.[20]

The government clearly showed its intent to destroy the inhabitants of the Vendée. In October 1793, it declared that all Vendéan "brigands" would be exterminated before the end of October.[21] Another decree was passed ordering the destruction of all mills and homes in the area. The revolutionary army finally set these decrees into motion in 1794, marking the beginning of a wide-scale genocide of so called "enemies of the Revolution" that would claim the lives of over 117,000 people, over 14 percent of the population (Secher 1986: 253). Men, women, and children were massacred, often in their own homes: women and children, even infants, were just as likely to be killed as men. One of the reasons the killing was not more widespread was that the army made more concentrated efforts in the countryside, destroying everyone and everything in its path. Luckily, many of the towns escaped such widespread destruction.[22]

The wars of the Vendée differ from most genocides because the rebels armed themselves and inflicted considerable casualties on the revolutionary army. Therefore these conflicts have many features of a civil war. The reason we consider this a case of genocide is that the exterminatory intent was clearly stated in the orders of several generals as well as in several decrees passed by the government.

Case 10: Bulgarian Atrocities, 1876

A great power in the Middle Ages, Bulgaria experienced almost five hundred years of Ottoman rule which began in 1393 when the Ottomans conquered Turnovo, then the capital of Bulgaria. Although they did tolerate a certain amount of religious and cultural freedom, the nature of Ottoman rule was quite exploitative. Despite general acceptance of Christianity, a number of Bulgarians were forced to convert to Islam during the centuries of Ottoman rule. When their empire was strong, the Ottomans were fairly tolerant of Bulgarian religious or cultural expression, but as their empire grew weaker in the eighteenth and nineteenth centuries, Ottoman oppression grew worse.

Although the Bulgarians were crushed politically and economically by the Ottoman empire, they were exploited religiously and culturally by the Greeks. The Ottoman rulers formally recognized the Greek patriarch of Constantinople as the exclusive spiritual representative of all Christians in their empire. As a result, the Bulgarian church was fully subordinated to the Greek. Greek priests were placed in the highest ecclesiastical offices, and a deliberate program aimed at Hellenization of the Bulgarian people was put in place. For centuries the Greek clergy used all possible means to eradicate Bulgarian culture. Greek clergy replaced Bulgarians; monasteries and schools became centers of Greek learning; libraries of important Bulgarian works were destroyed; and the Cyrillic alphabet and Bulgarian language were forbidden and replaced by Greek. Monks in the monastery of Mount Athos were the only figures of authority who continued to use Bulgarian.

During the Russo-Turkish War of 1828 a Bulgarian nationalist movement began to arise. At first, the struggle centred on educational and cultural freedom and was led by the emerging religious and secular intelligentsia. Foreign inspiration and support from both Russia and Western nations contributed to the movement. In 1835 Ottoman authorities succumbed to pressure and agreed to the opening of Bulgarian schools. In 1870 they also allowed the reestablishment of the autonomous Bulgarian church.

In the wake of this cultural revival came the struggle for political freedom. However, while the Ottoman regime had yielded to pressure with regard to religious and cultural reforms, it had no intention of allowing political reform. In response to this unwillingness to allow more political freedom, Bulgarian nationalists began preparing for revolution. By the 1860s they had formed underground organizations in Romania, as well as several local "committees" within Bulgaria itself.

In 1876 a large-scale revolt broke out against the Ottoman regime. Inadequately armed and lacking sufficient unity, the rebels were ruthlessly subdued by Ottoman forces a month after the uprising had began. The Ottomans did not immediately react to the revolt: the rebellion in Bosnia and Hercegovina and the threat of war from Serbia and Montenegro meant that the Ottoman government had few troops on hand in Bulgaria. By the beginning of May, Ottoman authorities began to react, sending five thousand soldiers to supplement local forces.

On May 7 one thousand Ottoman soldiers attacked the town of Klissura where the inhabitants had thrown up some hasty fortifications. By the end of the day more than two hundred persons, mostly women, children, and old people who had been unable to flee, lay butchered and not a single house was left standing. That same day another groups of five thousand Ottoman irregulars attacked the town of Perushtitsa, where there had been no uprising whatsoever, and began a siege. By the end of the day, more than four hundred men and women were taken prisoner, presumably to be sold as slaves, and the rest of the town's inhabitants, numbering over a thousand, lay dead.

On May 9 the town of Batak suffered a similar fate. There was no revolt in Batak, but an old litigation between the inhabitants of that town and a neighbouring Muslim village over the possession of land had made the Muslims hostile toward the Christians. As soon as the disturbances began in the area, a certain Achmet Aga appeared before Batak with three thousand irregulars (known as bashi-bazouks). The fighting went on for four days, during which Aga swore that he would protect the Christians if they surrendered. When they did this, his soldiers began to plunder the town and to slaughter its inhabitants. The thousand men, women, and children who had sought refuge in the town's church found no safety: burning timbers were thrown into the church and the people there burned to death. The total number of dead in Batak is said to number over five thousand, almost its entire population.

By the end of May 1876 the Ottomans announced the end of the rebellion and conferred decorations on the chief participants in the suppression of the revolt. Although there is little proof that the Ottoman high command ordered their soldiers to massacre civilians, the fact that the perpetrators of those massacres were decorated demonstrates that the Ottoman government certainly condoned these actions.

The fate of Klissura, Perushtitsa, and Batak are typical of fifty or more other towns. The number of dead remains uncertain, with most estimates at around fifteen thousand. Bulgarian historians, however, estimate the number at between 30,000 and 60,000.[23] This case does have its deniers, however. In *Reform and the Ottoman Empire,* Roderic Davison argues that reports of Bulgar casualties were exaggerated and Russian inspired (Davison 1963: 323 n. 58). He states that Turkish sentiment regarded the revolt as a massacre of helpless Turks by Bulgar rebels incited by Russia (Davison 1963: 323). He neglects the fact that most of the reports of the massacres came from British sources, many of them from British citizens living in Bulgaria.

While these gross human rights violations do not amount to genocide, the case is interesting in that it is the first time that public opinion abroad affected events within the Ottoman Empire. The British statesman Gladstone condemned Ottoman actions, which he referred to as "Bulgarian horrors" and he, along with the British press, was responsible for bringing Western opinion to favor the side of Bulgaria. Detailed accounts of the massacre were published in British newspapers, bringing moral indignation to bear on British foreign policy. A conference of Great Powers was held in Constantinople demanding that the Ottomans withdraw from Bulgaria. When they refused, they were denied their customary support from the British. With Britain out of the picture, Russia, the Porte's greatest enemy, invaded the Balkans.

This case is also interesting with regard to another perspective: it contributes to the Ottomans' long record of massacres of Christians within their empire.[24] The "Bulgarian atrocities," like so many other cases of Christian victimization and massacre within the Ottoman empire, serves as a precursor to the repeated massacres and eventual genocide of the Armenians.[25] The step from committing massacre to committing genocide can be a relatively small one.

Case 11: Argentina, 1878–1885

Patagonia is a region of southern Argentina, southernmost Chile and Tierra del Fuego, consisting of the eastern Andes and arid plateaux stretching to the Atlantic. Its primary exports are wool and petroleum. Patagonia is also one of the most sparsely populated regions of South America. In Argentina, for example, only two percent of the population (roughly 300,000) live in Patagonia, despite the fact that the region covers 28 percent of Argentine territory. The pampas is a region in eastern central Argentina, characterized by treeless plains. It is also the agricultural heart of the country, exporting wheat, corn, and beef.

The end of the nineteenth century was a period of rapid economic and social change for Argentina. The industrial revolution and the advent of the railway transformed this primarily pastoral country into a modern nation, attracting hundreds of thousands of immigrants from Europe, mostly from Italy and Spain. One of Argentina's greatest assets at this time was its vast reserve of prime land, much of which was still inhabited by thousands of autonomous Araucanian, Puelche, and Tehuelche Indians. The Indians who occupied Patagonia and parts of central Chile and the Argentine pampas had successfully held back European settlement for almost three hundred years by waging a constant war against any European attempt at colonization. Indian warfare took the form of attacks on the *estancias* and villages. One such Indian attack in 1876 penetrated to within 360 kilometers of Buenos Aires, departing afterward with a reported 300,000 cattle and 500 white captives. The hunger for land, combined with the advent of modern firearms, especially the Remington rifle, created a new European willingness to attack and eliminate the Indians. This took the form of an organized military campaign. General Ignacio Fotheringham had no illusions about the reasons for his success:

> The remington came, and with the remington, the offensive, the Indians were finished and the desert was conquered. (General Ignacio Fotheringham, quoted and trans. Bodley 1975: 47)

One illustration of the Indians' inability to match European weaponry is an 1878 incident, when a lone trooper with a rifle killed six Indians and captured nine.

By the early 1870s, a semi-static defense system had evolved to protect the expanding agricultural settlements from attacks by Indians. It consisted of a continuous line of ten major forts and nearly seventy smaller forts stretching 1,600 kilometers. Included in the line were 370 kilometers of walls, and trenches three meters wide and two meters deep, which were designed to impede the passage of Indian horsemen. When Indians were detected in the vicinity of the forts, cavalry troops were quickly dispatched to intercept them; if the Indians could be caught, they were usually slaughtered.

This "defense" network remained neither static nor defensive, as it aggressively moved forward conquering more and more land. Indians who surrendered were forced to sign treaties recognizing the sovereignty of Argentina. The situation changed when many national leaders, dissatisfied with the slow pace of the advance, began to call for a more aggressive approach. Not only were they concerned with taking land away from the Indians, they were also worried about Chile's claim to parts of Patagonia, still almost completely unoccupied by Argentina.

By 1878 the government had approved a plan involving five columns of 6,000 soldiers each, under the leadership of General Julio G. Roca, to depart from Buenos Aires (two columns), Córdoba, San Luis, and Mendoza. Within six months the frontier had been advanced some 640 kilometers to the south until it stood on the south bank of the Rio Negro. Although there are no exact figures with regard to the number of Indians killed, the campaign had reduced the Indian population to such an extent that they could never again threaten European settlement. Argentine President Nicolás Avellaneda called the campaign "a great work of civilization" and a "conquest for humanity" (as quoted in Bodley 1975: 48).

The campaign continued unofficially until 1885, when the general in charge of the forces south of the Rio Negro, proudly reported:

Today not any tribe remains in the field that is not voluntarily or forcibly reduced; and if any number of Indians still exist, they are isolated wanderers, without forming groups worthy of consideration. (General Lorenzo Wintter, quoted and translated in Bodley 1975: 48)

Indian settlements were indiscriminately destroyed and looted in the campaign. The few who were not killed were taken captive and removed to uncertain fates; many of the women were forced to marry European soldiers and settlers. This had a devastating effect, particularly on the Tehuelche who, by 1913, numbered less than a hundred. The Puelche were killed in such large numbers that by 1925 they no longer existed a separate people. The Araucanians apparently survived in greater numbers, but their total military defeat left them thoroughly demoralized and willing to accept the authority of the government. There is no doubt that the Argentine government demonstrated the intent to eliminate the Indians of the Pampas and Patagonia in order to acquire the nonmovable resources that immigrant settlers coveted for their own benefit. The intent of the government changed from a purely defensive posture to an aggressive one: in both cases, the army was used, first to protect the settlers, and then to eliminate the Indians as a competitor for valuable land, once and for all time.[26] This clearly was a case of genocide.

Case 12: The Brazil Backlands, 1886–1897

During the latter half of the nineteenth century, Latin America was witness to a number of millenarian movements. Religious in content and advocating a radical change in the world, millenarianism rejects the present and expresses hope only in the future. Followers of these movements believe that the present world will come to an end and, due to divine intervention, will be replaced by a better society.

One of the most famous of such movements took place in the desert backlands of Brazil's state of Bahia, where the mystic Antonio Marciel (also referred to as Antonio the Counsellor) and his followers established a flourishing agrarian community. Marciel's following grew as tens of thousands flocked to the settlement to hear him preach. The Canudos colony, as the settlement became known, was founded in 1883 in the poorest region of Bahia where people had long been cut off from the Atlantic seaboard and were centuries behind contemporary civilization. Marciel gave these people hope for a better future and a way of venting their frustration with the poverty and despair they were experiencing. In return, he received a fiercely loyal and determined following.

Marciel soon came into conflict with the Brazilian government after ordering his followers to stop paying taxes. Moreover, some of his conservative ideas closely resembled monarchism, a fact that did not sit well with Brazil's new republican government. The government was not alone in its animosity toward Marciel. The Church, being suspicious of his influence over the masses, had repeatedly denounced him, and local landlords were resentful because he drained their supply of rural workers. A campaign to destroy the colony was quickly organized, but Marciel's enemies failed to consider the determination of his followers: it took four military campaigns to defeat this movement. Although there are no exact figures with regard to the population of the Canudos colony, it is estimated that Marciel's followers numbered in the tens of thousands at the time of the Brazilian army's final campaign.

That campaign, directed by the minister of war, was fought literally house to house. Women and children took an active part in the fighting. On the last days of the battle, the Brazilian army bombarded the settlement: "the inhabitants no longer had any barriers or sheltered nooks which might afford them protection...the irrepressible screams were heard" (da Cunha 1944, 460–61). Many of Marciel's followers preferred to die rather than surrender: "Women hurled themselves on their burning homes, their young ones in their arms" (da Cunha 1944: 475).

In *Rebellion in the Backlands,* da Cunha asserts that 300 prisoners, mostly children and old women, surrendered before the end of the battle (da Cunha 1944: 472). However, most sources argue that there was no surrender, and the battle was fought until the population was completely destroyed. There was no one alive to be taken prisoner (Bello 1966: 155–56).

It is clear that the Brazilian government intented to destroy the Canudos colony. It is also true that Marciel's followers refused to surrender. Since women and children participated in the struggle, the Brazilian troops spared neither. Even infants were put to death. This makes it a clear case of genocide.

The Canudos colony, located in a very remote region, represented a minor threat to the central government, but quite a major threat to the local land owning elite. They shared an interest in eliminating this threat to the maintenance of the established order. The resulting genocide was performed mainly to protect economic interests.

Notes

1. In contrast to the more accepted view that few survived the slaughter in Selinus, Picard and Picard (1969: 102) argue that some of the inhabitants of Selinus were able to escape to nearby Agrigentum and were granted permission to return once the Carthaginians were secure in their victory.
2. For additional information, see Bury (1975), and *The Cambridge Ancient History* (1964, volume VI).
3. For a detailed discussion of this genocide, see Chalk and Jonassohn (1990: 74–93).
4. For additional information, see Appianus of Alexandria (1913), Astin (1967), Astin et al. (1982), Boucher (1914), Keay (1988), Livy (1959), Scullard (1980), Sutherland (1939), and Wiseman (1956).
5. In his notes, David Magie argues that Velarius Maximum and Memnon's estimates of 80,000 dead are more reliable than Plutarch's 150,000 figure. Magie believes Plutarch took these figures from Sulla, who inflated the number of dead to rouse his troops against Mithradates, and are therefore not reliable (D. Magie 1950, vol. 2: 1103, note 37).
6. For additional information, see Magie (1950) and Rostovtzeff and Ormerod (1932: 211–59).
7. The reason this study focuses on Diocletian rather than Decius is due only to the availability of source material. Little material is available to shed light on Decius' motives for persecuting Christians.
8. Fox also states that despite the purge, there is evidence that some Christian officers continued to serve in this period.
9. Lactantius (1984: 11, 3–8). Williams does not agree with this hypothesis, however. In *Diocletian and the Roman Recovery* (173), he states that Diocletian was seriously ill when the last and bloodiest Edict was set in place and was no longer in complete control.
10. Eusebius (1953: 8, 5) states that one man who tore down the Edict on the same day it was posted was subsequently tortured and burned alive.
11. Williams also states that small towns rarely enforced the Edicts as it was difficult to regard "these reserved but inoffensive" people as criminals. Often local magistrates would make a token gesture, such as closing down a church, to demonstrate that they were indeed enforcing the law.
12. For additional information, see also Jones (1970), Sordi (1983), and Wilken (1984).
13. For additional information, see Bradford (1967), Clari (1966), Rodd (1907), and Villehardouin (1908).
14. Giurescu states that the Turks were so struck with terror that even the inhabitants of Constantinople were prepared to leave the city, fearing that Vlad would succeed in reaching that far. A contemporary chronicler states that, "The multitudes (of Turks) were so terror stricken that those who could cross to Anatolia considered themselves fortunate."
15. For additional information, see Cazacu (1991), McNally and Florescu (1972), and McNally (1989).

16. The name Aztec sometimes includes other Nahuatl native groups in southern Mexico of the same culture who had allied themselves to the Aztecs in Tenochtitlan before the conquest. This summary will use the term "Aztec" when referring to the people of Tenochtitlan.
17. For additional imformation see Diaz (1963), de Madariaga (1942), and Todorov (1984).
18. For additional information see Graham (1968), Platonov (1974), Riasanovsky (1984), and Troyat (1984).
19. Carrier stated during the revolution "Nous ferons un cimetière de la France plutôt que de ne pas la régénérer à notre manière et de manquer le but que nous sommes proposé" (Quoted in Babeuf 1987: 53).
20. See Pierre Philippeaux, quoted in Babeuf (1987: 132) who states that Léchelle "sacrifiait en détail nos phalanges républicaines, et favorisait en tout les brigands, comme s'il eût reçu l'ordre secret de favoriser leurs succès."
21. The government declared: "Soldats de la Liberté, il faut que tous les brigands de la Vendée soient exterminés avant la fin du mois d'octobre. Le salut de la patrie l'exige, l'impatience du peuple français le commande, son courage doit l'accomplir; la reconnaissance nationale vous attend à cette époque" (Babeuf 1987: 140).
22. For additional information see Doyle (1989), Furet and Richet (1970), and Jurés (1924).
23. For a discussion of sources and the different casualty estimates see Harris (1939: 22).
24. In *Gladstone and the Bulgarian Agitation* (22, n. 3) R.T. Shannon estimates Christian casualties in the Ottoman empire in the nineteenth century at well over 200,000. Shannon uses K. Behesnilian's *Armenian Bondage and Carnage* (1903) as his main source regarding the number of victims, but states that his figure of 209,000 dead is an understatement.
25. For additional information see Harris (1939), Hozier (n.d.), and Shannon (1975).
26. For additional information see Cooper (1963), Crawford (1884), Graham (1968), Grey (1987), Perry (1972), Rennie (1945), Rock (1985), Scobie (1962), and Zimmerman (1945).
27. For additional information see Davis (1968).

18

Perpetrators in India

Introduction

We have found only a few relevant cases in Indian history before the Muslim and Mongol invasions. There are two reasons for this. The first reason is that materials for the early history of India are very scarce and quite unsatisfactory for our purposes. There is, for instance, the conquest of the Kalinga region by Asoka in the third century B.C. Asoka's brutality in slaughtering not only his enemies but also ninety-nine brothers has become legendary. His own remorse is cited to explain his conversion to Buddhism which then also became the official religion of his empire. It is not at all clear to what extent these events correspond to historical fact or serve instead to provide a dramatic explanation of his conversion.[1] This is a case that needs to be interpreted in terms of the three periods of history writing that were discussed in part 2, chapter 3. Unfortunately, the authors' interpretation was limited by their lack of the relevant linguistic skill and by their having to rely on some quite dated sources.

It seems that Indians were not particularly interested in recording their history—unlike the Muslim conquerors who seem to have considered it very important. Some sultans recorded their own history and most of them encouraged the work of their court historians.

The second reason is that in the warfare and rebellions of the Hindu states, noncombatant women and children seem not to have been involved . However, they were routinely victimized during conflicts in Central Asia, from where most of the invaders came. Vincent A. Smith quotes the historian Zia-ud-din Barani who gave a full account of the reign of 'Ala-ud-din Khilji (1296–1316) and of his crafty cruelty as saying that "Up to this time no hand had ever been laid upon wives and children on account of men's misdeeds" (Smith 1958: 245). Whether that was in fact so, we have not been able to verify. However, that innovation, introduced by the Muslim and Mongol invaders, accounted for the sudden appearance of genocides in India. E. B. Havell argues that the conflicts that resulted in widespread cruelties and genocides were not primarily about religious and ethnic differences, but rather about wealth and power.

> The sovereign in both Hindu and Mohammadam political systems was the representative of divine justice, but in the opinion of most Muhammadan writers of the period a liberal and fair distribution of the spoils of war among the elect covered a multitude of moral failings. The stain upon Mahmud of Ghazni's character was not that he massacred tens of thousands of non-combatants, but that he kept too much of the spoil for himself. The grave offence of the Raja of Vijayanagar was not that he was an infidel, but that being such he was more wealthy and powerful than any Muhammadan ruler in the Dekhan. He was also a high-caste Hindu whose social etiquette was a standing offence to the feelings of the Musalman freeman, however much he might try to avoid hurting them.
>
> The quarrels between the different Musalman rulers had as little to do with sectarian differences of the mullas.... The great problem of Musalman statecraft in the Dekhan was to reconcile the conflicting interests of the different military factions, rather than to steer straight between Sunni and Shiah sectarians. (Havell 1918: 405)

The following cases will illustrate this point. But one of these cases seems to have introduced a different element: the genocide of the "New Muslims" by 'Ala-ud-din. These were local people who had converted to the religion of the conqueror. While many of them made careers in the conqueror's administration, they were never considered completely equal and trustworthy. This discriminatory attitude was institutionalized in their being labeled as "New Muslims." Historically, such distrust was often attached to people who were forcibly converted. A similar case occurred in Spain in the sixteenth and seventeenth centuries where converted Jews and Muslims were for many generations referred to as "New Christians." 'Ala-ud-din's massacre of the "New Muslims," who were citizens of his country, rates as an early case of ideological genocide.

In what follows, we present very brief sketches of several cases without even indicating their historical background or their cultural significance. They deserve a much more detailed treatment—especially since many sources on Indian history do not even mention them. This is another instance of conquests being reported without any mention of what happened to the ordinary people. We have neither the training nor the space to rectify this omission here. However, these omissions are the reason why we were forced to base ourselves on only a few sources.

Case 13: The Persecution of the Jains

The first case to be mentioned here is the persecution of the Jains of of the Pandya kingdom in the eleventh century. Due to the conversion of the king, the Hindu faith became the only religion that the king would tolerate in his realm. The Jains who refused to follow the king's example suffered terrible persecutions, with 8,000 of them being impaled. The memory of this genocidal massacre is still being celebrated by the Hindus of Madura (where it took place). They have a festival (*utsava*) to celebrate the anniversary of the impalement of the Jains (Smith 1958: 227).

Case 14: The Fate of Ghazni

The destruction of Ghazni was the result of a blood feud between Ghur and Ghazni. 'Ala-ud-din Husain, an Afghan chieftain, captured and sacked Ghazni in A.D. 1151. The city was set afire and burned for seven days and nights, during which "plunder, devastation, and slaughter were continuous. Every man that was found was slain, and all women and children were made prisoners. All the palaces and edifices of the Mahmudi kings which had no equal in the world" were destroyed, save only the tombs of Sultan Mahmud and two of his relatives (Smith 1958: 233).

Case 15: The Conquest of Bihar

This conquest of the rulers of the eastern kingdoms was effected with astounding facility by Qutb-ud-din's general, Muhammad Khilji. The Muslim general, after completing several successful plundering expeditions, seized Bihar in 1193, and thus occupied the capital of the province of that name. The prevailing religion of Bihar at that time was a form of Buddhism, which had received liberal patronage from the kings of the Pala dynasty for more than three centuries. A Muslim historian, indifferent to distinctions among idolaters, states that the majority of the inhabitants were "shaven-headed Brahmans," who were all put to the sword. He evidently meant Buddhist monks, as he was informed that the whole city and fortress were considered to be a college, which the name Bihar signifies. A great library was scattered. Many monuments of the ancient civilization of India were irretrievably wrecked in the course of the early Muslim invasions. The remnants of the Buddhist sanctuaries at Sarnath near Benares still bear witness to this dstruction. These invasions were fatal to the existence of Buddhism as an organized religion in northern India, where its strength resided chiefly in Bihar and certain adjoining territories. The monks who escaped this massacre fled, and were scattered over Nepal, Tibet, and the south. After 1200 A.D. the traces of Buddhism in upper India are faint and obscure (Smith 1958: 235–36).

Case 16: Balban's Persecution of the Meos

The Meos were suppressed by Balban in 1260. He attacked the Meos south of Delhi because they had invaded the approaches to the capital and had ravaged the Bayana District. In a twenty-days' campaign they were slaughtered and subjected to a variety of cruel punishments. Some were taken to Delhi for execution. Others were cast under the feet of elephants, while the bodies of others were cut in two. Others "met their death at the hands of the flayers, being skinned from head to foot; their skins were all stuffed with straw, and some of them were hung over every gate of the city." In spite of the horrors of these unusual tortures a second campaign was needed, in July 1260, when Balban fell upon the insurgents unawares, and captured them all —12,000 men, women, and children—whom he put to the sword (Smith 1958: 240–41).

Case 17: Terror under 'Ala-ud-din

Khilji (1296–1316) ruthlessly killed off everybody who could be supposed to endanger his throne or threaten internal security. Being informed that some of the chiefs of the "New Muslims" he had enlisted in his army were disaffected and plotting revolt, he determined that "the whole of that race settled in his territories should be exterminated." Between 20,000 and 30,000 of them were accordingly massacred. "After these punishments," Havell quotes a Muslim historian, "breaches of the peace were never heard of in the city" (Havell 1918: 302–3).

'Ala-ud-din proved the efficiency of his war machine by repelling several formidable Mongol invasions, and by carrying on a successful campaign in the Dekhan under the command of his general Malik Kafur. The latter was a Hindu slave who had embraced Islam, and being attached to the imperial bodyguard had speedily risen to a high position at the court, much to the disgust of 'Ala-ud-din's Turki and Afghan retainers (Havell 1918: 306).

Case 18: Timur's Conquests

In 1398 Timur invaded India. Amir Timur (1336–1405) was a Barlas Turk, whose father was one of the earliest converts to Islam. For political reasons his court genealogists gave him a pedigree which made him a pure Mongol and a descendant of Chinghis Khan (Havell 1918: 368), Timur's conquests involved several genocidal massacres, including the conquest of Bhatnir, followed by the slaughter of everyone left in town, the piling up of a pyramid of 10,000 heads, setting fire to the houses, and the razing of the fortress (Havell 1918: 372). However, he had no intention of staying in India. He returned through Meerut, storming that city, and slaying everybody. Near Hardwar, where it was easy to cross the rivers, he left India as he had come, by the way of the Panjab, "leaving anarchy, famine, and pestilence behind him" (Smith 1958: 261).

Case 19: The Repeated Victimizations of Vijayanagar

The Bahmani sultans (1347–1482) attempted on several occasions to exterminate the Hindu population in the states of the Deccan or, failing in that aim, to forcibly convert the survivors to Islam. In the process they killed hundreds of thousands of men, women, and children. Remarkably, the population has remained largely Hindu (Smith 1958: 289–90). Vijayanagar was a large, flourishing city that had to bear the brunt of these efforts on several occasions (Havell 1918: 385). Muhammad Shah Bahmani distinguished himself in 1371 by swearing that he would not rest until he had killed 100,000 infidels. He defeated the Vijayanagar army and carried out that mission (Havell 1918: 385–86). In 1420 Sultan Firuz (1397–1422), after a mostly successful reign, suffered a major defeat at the hands of the Hindus. His brother Ahmad Shah (1422–1435) was so outraged by this reversal that he murdered his brother and his son, then ascended the throne in order to seek revenge for the losses suffered by the army of Islam in his brother's time. He conducted his campaign against Vijayanagar with great savagery, indiscriminately killing men, women, and children. "When the number of slain amounted to twenty thousand, he halted for three days, and made a festival in celebration of the bloody event" (Smith 1958: 283). In the sixteenth century the city was again victimized. On 23 January 1565 a major battle was fought between a coalition of Muslim sultans and an enormous Hindu army. The princes fled Vijayanagar with countless treasures and the proud capital lay at the mercy of the victors who occupied it almost immediately. They looted, pillaged, and massacred for five months and left the city in ruins (Smith 1958: 309).

Case 20: Babur's Style of Warfare

Babur, who through his Mongol mother was a descendant of Chinghis Khan, did not exalt in bloodshed as his savage ancestors did. However he continued the barbarous traditions of Tartar warfare as part of the business of the warlord; he himself notes down the wholesale butchery of prisoners in front of his royal pavilion and the building up of pyramids of human heads with the same faithfulness as he describes the conquest of Chanderi in 1527. After a brave defence the garrison was reduced to the traditional fate, accompanied by its terrible sacrifice of women and children (Havell 1918: 425).

Summary

These cases seem to support Havell's argument quoted above to the effect that conflicts in India were about wealth and power. However, Smith (in Part 2), deals with approximately the same period and includes a number of cases in which religious issues were important. But these religious issues appear not to have initiated these conflicts; instead they became relevant only after wealth and power considerations had become the primary motives.[2] Of course, in the literature of the perpetrators the religious motives loomed large because spreading the true faith, eradicating the infidels, and destroying the heathen temples contributed to their glory in this world as well as assuring them of rewards in the hereafter.

These are not the only cases that could have been extracted from Indian history. However, they suffice to illustrate the levels of cruelty and massacre that appear to have been commonplace in India. They also confirm the impression that genocides and genocidal massacres were acceptable modalities of conflict resolution that were mourned only by the victims. In addition, they illustrate how the same social inventions recur at different times in different places. The notion that defeated opponents are more valuable as slaves than as dead bodies occurred to Firuz Shah in the early fifteenth century (see chapter 2).[3] This reduced the incidence of genocide in India several thousand years after it had already done so in Egypt.[4]

Notes

1. Rock inscriptions of Asoka in Andhra Pradesh say that, "[i]n this war in Kalinga men and animals, numbering one hundred and fifty thousands were carried away captive from that country; as many as one hundred thousands were killed in action, and many times that number perished" (D. C. Sircar 1979, p. 47). These figures vastly exceed the probable population of Kalinga at that time.
2. This ought to be compared with other conflicts that were initiated by religious issues, like the Crusades, but were then dominated by considerations of power and wealth.
3. See "An Excursion on Varieties of Slavery" in part 1, chapter 2.
4. For additional information see also Goshale (1966) and Sircar (1975).

19

Perpetrators in China

Introduction

China is a very large and populous country with an ancient history and a long tradition of literacy. Like elsewhere, much of its recorded history ignored the fate of ordinary peasants and common people. This makes research on the origins and early history of genocidal events quite difficult. The following cases are not particularly early, but they indicate that China was no more immune to this scourge than other areas of the world.

Case 21: The Checkered Fate of the Ancient Capital at Lo-Yang

The earliest record of Lo-yang goes back to the eleventh century B.C. After the Chou conquerors had overthrown the Shang state, their legendary leader the duke of Chou decided to found a subsidiary capital there (Jenner 1981: 46). The Eastern Chou transferred their capital to Lo-yang in 770 B.C., and from then on it has intermittently been China's capital (Rodzinski 1984: 26). To protect itself against the periodic invasions by nomadic peoples from the central Asian steppes country, China began to build its famous wall in the third century B.C. (Rodzinski 1984: ch. 2). In 25 A.D. the Han dynasty shifted China's capital from Ch'ang-an, which had been completely destroyed, back to Lo-yang. In 190 A.D. Lo-yang was once again abandoned under pressure from military rivals. Everything within some fifty kilometers was burned, while the destruction within the city walls was total, including the homes of the people (Jenner 1981: 49). It was rebuilt and destroyed several more times as a result of wars between rival princes.

At the beginning of the fourth century Lo-yang was the capital of China. Then, in 311 A.D., it was sacked by the Huns whom the Chinese considered barbarians (Jenner 1981: 51). It was located in the northwest corner of Honan province and had a population of about 600,000. It was at that time the biggest, richest, and most cosmopolitan city in the Eastern world (Waley 1951: 7–10).

The Huns, remote cousins of the Western Huns who invaded Europe in the fifth century, had been given permission by the Chinese emperor to settle in northeastern China where they were expected to act as a buffer against the raids and invasion by other nomads. But the Chinese treated them so badly that they rebelled. They began by plundering northeastern China and in 307 sacked the great city of Yeh, northeast of Lo-yang. By 311 they were ready to take their revenge on Lo-yang. First they occupied much of the country around the city, so that food supplies within the city ran low and a famine began. After some reverses, the Hun armies entered the city. They ransacked the palace and carried off everything of value. The Huns seem to have considered making the city their own capital, but decided that it might be too difficult to hold. They pillaged its wealth and burned the whole city to the ground. But a large proportion of the official classes had fled before the city fell and made a new capital at Nanking. Lo-yang was so thoroughly destroyed that no considerable town stood there until the Wei Tatars made it their capital in 493. While we have no specific information on the fate of the population, it can be assumed as most likely that the Huns, in keeping with the traditions of the nomadic steppe peoples, massacred most or all of the population.

The new capital, founded in 493, was equally ill-fated. In 534 it was abandoned in favour of a new capital at Yeh. In the preceding fifteen years misrule and corruption had given rise to revolts and mutinies until a succession of civil wars led to its total destruction. The population of 400,000 families, perhaps 2,000,000 people, had to pack up and leave their homes in and around the city within three days and move about 150 miles to the new capital, in spite of it being the beginning of winter (Jenner 1981: 101). While a great many people perished on this long trek to Yeh, this abandonment of Lo-yang clearly was a major violation of human rights, though not a genocide.

Yang-ti (604–618) again chose to rebuild Lo-yang as his capital and embarked on a grandiose construction program (Rodzinski 1984: 87–88).

During the T'ang dynasty a peasant rebellion broke out which conquered Fukien in 878, Lo-yang in 880 and Ch'ang-an soon after. In 879 they captured Canton which had refused to surrender: "[I]ts capture in 879 was followed by a massacre of the population including, according to Arab sources, a prosperous 120,000-strong community of foreign merchants—Moslems, Zoroastrians, Christians and Jews" (Rodzinski 1984: 104).

During the founding of the Ch'ing (Manchu) empire Nanking refused to surrender (1662); it was then stormed and taken. For ten days the Manchus systematically massacred most of its inhabitants (Rodzinski 1984:105).

The reports on most of these destructions of cities leave us guessing as to the fate of their inhabitants. Very often the population was forced to move to the new capital, but in several of these cases we are dealing with either genocides or genocidal massacres.

Case 22: The Taiping Rebellion of 1850–1864

The Taiping Rebellion is often referred to as one of the bloodiest civil wars in history. It "raged in China for over fifteen years, ravaged two-thirds of that empire, caused incalculable material damage, and is said to have cost over ten million lives" (Cheng 1963: vii).

The Taiping Rebellion was an antimonarchical movement created in Kwangsi during a period of widespread social unrest. Its underlying cause was the inefficiency and corruption of the Manchu government and the weakness it had shown in its dealings with the Western powers. Widespread discontent with a system that exploited masses of people for the good of a small elite had been felt in China for some time. The Taipings sought recruits from the disaffected sections of the community, providing mutual protection against other groups.

What distinguished the Taiping movement from earlier rebellions was its distinct ideology involving the establishment of a new form of society. Its originator and leader was Hung Hsiu-ch'uan (1814–1864) who came from a poor family, failed the examinations that were necessary steps to a successful career, and became a village school teacher. He had visionary hallucinations that, under the influence of Protestant missionary tracts, grew into a creed whose main aim was the creation of a Heavenly Kingdom in China where all men would be brothers. This, of course, also meant an end to the Manchu regime. His preaching attracted enough followers by 1849 to allow him to plan for the implementation of his creed. Between 1850–1856 the Taipings conducted many successful campaigns against the Manchus, controlling more and more territory. They captured Hunan province in 1850 and within two years had advanced through Hunan and Hopeh provinces and then down the Yangtze river to Nanking. In 1853, after having destroyed much of the city's population, they captured Nanking and decided to make it their capital.

Once established in Nanking, the Taiping army continued to conquer more territory, almost reaching Tiensin in the north and establishing strongholds in Anhwei, Honan, Hupeh, and Kiansi provinces after having ravaged the countryside. The government that was established combined a rigidly enforced form of Christianity with many socialist features, but it was poorly organized and administered. What might have culminated in revolution degenerated into power struggles between rivals, resulting in a purge in 1856 in which thousands of people were killed, considerably weakening the movement.

In spite of their egalitarian creed they soon developed a very hierarchical social and governmental structure in which complex palace rivalries flourished. As a result their regime began to deteriorate. Both internal intrigues and military setbacks contributed to the decline of the movement. After 1860 the Taipings, in addition to being weakened by internal dissension and massacres, were increasingly threatened by the imperial army. The main reason for the desperate courage of the Taiping forces was the reputation of the imperial army for its plundering and massacring of civilians. This brutality was a calculated policy of Tseng Kuo-fan, their general, who clearly stated his aim of exterminating all of the Taipings in order to prevent recurrences of a peasant revolt. He was assisted in his campaign by foreign forces and advisors, both British and French, who supported the Manchu regime. Because they believed it was in their interest to support the Manchu dynasty they gave it unofficial aid by forming a corps of "foreign adventurers" in 1860—the Ever-Victorious Army under General Charles Gordon.

There is no doubt that the Manchu government and its allies intended to exterminate the Taipings. For example, in a letter entitled "Mopping-Up Operations in Kiangsu," Hung-Chang, one of the Manchu military leaders, states that, "[r]ecently Gordon has been quite reasonable, saying that the people of Kwangstung and Kwangsi within the city should be utterly exterminated, but that their conscripted followers willing to surrender may be spared...with the walls blown up, we could still not force our way in. The only thing to do is to surround the city for several months and wait for their starvation as a result of lack of provisions" (Cheng 1963: 133).

In 1864 Nanking fell and the soldiers as well as the civilian population that had not fled were massacred. The Taiping revolution resulted in enormous devastation in central China, in the destruction of hundreds of towns, and an estimated 15 to 20 million lives lost.

There is no question that both sides practiced unspeakable cruelties during their campaigns. But their aims were quite different. The Taipings wanted to replace the Manchu rule with a more egalitarian regime, while the Manchus wanted to exterminate the Taipings—a clear case of genocide.

Case 23: Famines

Famine has been one of the constants of Chinese history. One study arrives at a total of 1,828 famines that are known to have occurred between 108 B.C. and 1911 A.D. That means that one famine occurred nearly every year in some part of China (Kane 1988: 26). Ways of dealing with such disasters became institutionalized very early. The local magistrates maintained granaries that were controlled by the provincial governments. In addition, charitable and community granaries were established in each county (Kane 1988: 32). When famines affected more than a local area, the emperor would open the national granaries, permit transfer of grains from other provinces, and authorize imports from outlying regions. While these methods were usually adequate for dealing with local famines, they could not cope with widespread or national famines.

As far as we know, these recurring famines were caused by floods or droughts. Their effect was sometimes increased by incompetent or inefficient administration of relief measures. What was new in the twentieth century was that two kinds of man-made famines became common. The first kind was the unforeseen result of ill-conceived government policies. The second kind of man-made famine was the result of deliberate and planned government action. It is this second kind of famine that in most parts of the world and throughout history has been a method of perpetrating genocide. It is still in use because it requires neither high technology nor elaborate bureaucracy and it can be easily disguised as the result of natural events (see part 1, chapter 3).

In the twentieth century China has acquired the dubious distinction of having produced the most devastating famines. The massive famine that occurred between 1959 and 1962 is variously estimated to have caused 16 to 27 million deaths above those that would have been expected during those years under conditions of normal mortality (MacFarquhar and Fairbank 1987: vol.14, part 1).

The causes of this particular famine seem to have been located in a political system based on rigid adherence to an ideology, extreme centralization, and totalitarian intolerance of debate, criticism, and empirical facts. The government tried to consolidate agriculture into giant communes; it engaged in large-scale dam construction which often did more harm than good; it tolerated a disorganized information system based on wrong reporting due to the intolerance of correct reporting that diverged from Mao Tse Tung's industrialization program, the Great Leap Forward. Thus, it "insisted that the peasants leave the land fallow in 1959 to avoid losses from not having enough storage facilities to handle the anticipated surplus" (MacFarquhar and Fairbank 1987: 318–19). Of course, the anticipated surplus never materialized, but the land that was left fallow contributed to the famine.

This famine fell much more severely on rural than urban areas because agricultural procurement quotas continued to drain the countryside of available supplies; these quotas were even increased to support the intense mobilization of resources for accelerated industrialization. The famine was also aggravated because self-sufficiency, which was an integral part of the ideology of the commune movement, inhibited the traditional interprovincial flow that used to make up for local shortages. This was particularly hard on regions that specialized in nonfood crops, such as cotton. Distribution by the government broke down because nobody wanted to report local failures and also because transportation was disrupted by the Great Leap Forward (Lardy 1987: 376–78).

Based on the still-limited evidence available, it seems clear that originally there was no intent on the part of the government to decimate a specific group of victims. The government did want to implement its design for the Great Leap Forward, and it did enforce its new agricultural and industrial policies. Mao rejected critical reports from the field by insisting that the gains of the Great Leap Forward outweighed the costs (Kane 1988: 133). The most likely hypothesis is that the famine started out as the unintended consequence of a series of particularly inept political decisions, and that it was allowed to run its course because the government saw it as the punishment for an uncooperative peasantry.

Only a few years later, beginning in 1966, China was again ravaged by a major upheaval: the Cultural Revolution. The issue here was not hunger so much as the enforcement of orthodoxy to Mao's ideas of a permanent revolution. The intellectuals, in particular, were targeted.

Many of them were forced to give up their careers and were transported to agricultural communes for hard physical labor and intensive reeducation. The resulting disorganization and dislocation produced enormous hardship, including starvation. Chinese sources claim that 100 million intellectuals were victimized in a variety of ways, from loss of their occupation to forced labor, to beatings and killings. Scholarly estimates of the number of fatalities vary between one million and twenty million (White 1989: 7). No information is available on the proportion of the victims who died of disease, starvation, or at the hands of the Red Guards.

There was at the outset no intent to produce a famine. Rather it was the result of lack of planning and disorganization. But the anarchy of the Cultural Revolution was encouraged by Mao's regime, although it was not tightly coordinated (White 1989: 331). Since, for quite a long time, no attempt appears to have been made to stop the rising toll of the Cultural Revolution, we must assume that Mao thought that the victims deserved their fate. Thus, we must conclude that both of these cases started out as the unintended consequences of policies designed to produce radical change in Chinese society, but ended up as the welcome punishment of those groups that were perceived as being less than fully cooperative.[1]

Note

1. For additional information see also Curven (1977) and Teng (1971).

20

Perpetrators in Colonial Africa

Introduction

The European expansion into Africa began with the Portuguese in the early fifteenth century. Portugal was trying to establish a sea route to India and Asia and also to make direct contact with the gold producing areas of West Africa. Within a century of these explorations, the Atlantic slave trade was developed to meet demands for slave labor in the Americas. While there had always been a slave trade in parts of Africa, the trade across the Atlantic was to eclipse in scale anything of the kind that had happened before. Although Arabs and Africans alike participated in the Atlantic slave trade, the Portuguese had a monopoly over that trade for much of the sixteenth century. This monopoly was broken by the Dutch, particularly in West Africa. They were soon joined by the English, French, Swedes, and Danes. While Europeans organized the transatlantic slave trade, they did not make serious inroads into African territory until the nineteenth century.

The end of the nineteenth century marked the age of imperialism in Africa, as European nations scrambled for control over territory. African colonies were established by England, France, Belgium, Portugal, Germany, and Italy. Colonialism was never benevolent toward indigenous people: besides exploiting land and raw materials, the people themselves were often viewed as an exploitable resource or, just as often, dismissed as primitive, subhuman, and of little use. The European belief in their racial and moral superiority over Africans, coupled with a particular flavor of paternalistic missionary zeal, guaranteed that indigenous people would be brutally exploited and ruthlessly punished when they dared to rebel.

In *The History and Sociology of Genocide,* Frank Chalk and Kurt Jonassohn demonstrated that colonialists will sometimes resort to genocide when indigenous people block their access to wealth. This they illustrated by the genocides committed against the Pequot Indians by the Puritans, the Tasmanians by the British, and the Hereros by the Germans. Here we shall briefly look at how European colonial powers treated the indigenous people they encountered. It is safe to say that no colonial administration was distinguished by its fairness or benevolence. All were engaged in various forms of exploitation and brutalities. The latter ranged all the way from random violence to organized slaughter. It is not always easy to distinguish between massacres and genocides. The reader is invited to examine a few short examples from British, Belgian, French, German and Italian administrations.

Case 24: Britain in Matabeleland and Mashonaland, 1896–1897

"I come to ask why the white man brings war to my country, kills my people, and burns my villages?"—Nkosi Gomani, chief of a section of the Ngoni, before his arrest and execution by the British in 1895 (Rotberg 1967: 676)

Late in 1896 Matabeleland and Mashonaland (now Zimbabwe) suffered one of the worst famines in their history. This famine was a direct result of the Ndebele and Shona tribal rebellion against the British and its suppression. The revolt was started by the Ndebele March 20, 1896, several months before the harvest. Once the violence began they moved their women and children, their livestock, and grain stores from the previous year's harvest to strongholds in the Matopos Hills and other safe retreats. By holding the Europeans on the defensive in Bulawayo during April and the first half of May, Ndebele harvested and stored some standing crops, but much was still in the fields when European patrols regained the initiative in May.

To prevent the Ndebele and the Shona from harvesting was a vital military objective for the British South Africa Company. One missionary reported, "All native supplies of corn are destroyed throughout the eastern districts where the war has raged" (Iliffe 1990: 24). By August, the Ndebele had lost the initiative, were running short of food and were fighting amongst each other for the remaining supplies. The British were also facing a crisis: newly arrived imperial troops advanced toward the Matopos Hills, met sharp resistance, and were stuck in a terrain well-suited for guerilla warfare. Famine became the core of their strategy and proved very successful. Deaths from starvation and disease were reported from all corners of Matabeleland.

Mashonaland suffered less from famine, despite the fact that the war continued there longer. The Shona were more difficult to repress, mainly because they were more difficult to starve: their methods of storing grain were superior to those of the Ndebele, they had more experience in hiding their reserves from foraging enemies, and unlike the Ndebele, they delayed their rebellion until June 1896, after the harvest. By the time Imperial troops reached Salisbury in August, the Shona were already preparing their fields for the new season. Although active in destroying areas where Europeans had been killed or where overt resistance continued, the British believed the Shona wanted peace and were less eager to create another famine. The British did systematically destroy crops in dissident areas, particularly in March 1897 when the drying countryside made movement easier. This campaign put pressure on the hardcore rebels, but did not prevent the major chiefs from replenishing their stores. The Shona revolt lasted until July 1897, when the British captured the Mashayamombe's capital. With the need to prepare their fields once more imminent, most surviving rebels surrendered in the following weeks.

This case is interesting in that it not only demonstrates the use of force in suppressing native revolt, it also shows that colonial powers were willing to use food as a weapon in quashing such rebellions. It is clear that the British campaign caused widespread starvation and long-term impoverishment, ensuring that the Ndebele and the Shona would be incapable of rising up again in the future. Although there are no figures as to the exact number of dead, estimates are in the tens of thousands. It is said that this famine was "unquestionably the most terrible that Southern Rhodesia experienced" (Iliffe 1990: 29).

Case 25: The Belgian Congo (Léopoldville)

"The Congolese system was too viciously wasteful, too recklessly short-term in its conception, to deserve even the term of exploitation. It was no more than a prolonged raid for plunder."—Neal Ascherson (1963: 203)

The first European contact with the Congo took place in 1484 when the Portuguese sailed to the mouth of the Congo River. They did not penetrate beyond the rapids that blocked the river forty-five kilometres from the sea, but began to organize the first transatlantic slave trade in the late 1400s, which, together with the slave trade carried out by Arabs on the eastern coast, devastated the tribes of the interior for more than three centuries. At the time of the Belgian invasion in the late nineteenth century, the Congo's population was already considerably depleted.

The interior was not fully explored by Europeans until the latter half of the nineteenth century, when Sir Henry Morton Stanley and David Livingstone became the first Europeans to travel deep into the Congo. Stanley first offered this territory to Great Britain, but was rejected. Instead, he found a willing ally in Belgium, and in 1879 founded the Congo Free State at the service of King Leopold II of Belgium.

To understand the development of Leopold II's colonial policy, it is necessary to look at the early years of Belgium's history. In 1830 Belgium seceded from the Kingdom of the Netherlands and by doing so lost its access to world markets and the use of the Dutch merchant fleet. Belgium also suffered socially and economically during this period from the effects of the industrial revolution. The danger of social unrest was very much in evidence as, by 1845, one Belgian in three was living off charity. It was clear to Leopold I that Belgium needed to find new markets for her products and a fresh source of raw materials. The acquisition of a colony was perceived as the only solution to Belgium's economic problems. Leopold I made fifty-one attempts at acquiring a colony: Crete, Texas, various Caribbean islands, parts of Central and South America, parts of Africa and China were considered, but all without success (Emerson 1979: 24–25).

Twenty years after the death of his father, Leopold II succeeded in getting the Berlin conference of 1885 to entrust him personally with the management of the Congo Free State, a territory seventy-seven times the size of Belgium. One of Leopold's first acts as absolute ruler of the Congo was to claim possession of "unclaimed land." This measure, which did not define what sort of African occupancy might constitute a claim to land, formed a useful basis for what was to follow. A secret decree of September 1891 asserted the Congo Free State's right to the produce of the supposedly empty lands which now "belonged" to Leopold (Ascherson 1963: 196).

The Congo Free State was made into a set of closely interrelated monopolies which controlled the collection of wild rubber and ivory. The almost complete absence of competition and of imported goods which the African population could buy, meant that no money economy existed in these regions. In such conditions, forced labor and extortion were inevitable.

To most European colonial governments, taxation in money was one accepted way of forcing a native population to earn wages by productive labor on plantations or public works. The Congo Free State and its concession companies took the shorter and cheaper method of imposing a system of forced deliveries of wild rubber, copal (a form of resin used in varnishes), or food grains. Africans were forced to spend days in the forest searching for a steadily declining number of rubber vines, doing unpaid work as porters, or working as woodcutters for the river steamers. The amount of rubber levy varied greatly from region to region, but failure to deliver resulted in corporal punishment, collective fines in kind, imprisonment, or in punitive expeditions which burned villages and, on occasion, massacred their inhabitants. One consequence of such taxes in produce or labor was a severe restriction of movement and migration (Ascherson 1963: 202).

An enormous machine of exploitation by force had been erected and put in motion. But its efficient lifetime was necessarily very limited. Producing great wealth at first, for little cost beyond a high bill for rifle ammunition, the system rapidly wore itself out. The rubber vines grew rarer and rarer, mortally slashed for their latex by laborers who feared death if they did not deliver as much as the trunk contained. And as the search for wild rubber grew more difficult, the African population itself began to dwindle, through clandestine migration, massacre, epidemic and starvation, until there was a shortage of labor to seek it (Ascherson 1963: 202–3).

The first reports of atrocities committed in the Congo came from foreign missionaries, particularly those from the United States and Sweden. They described in the press the revolting results of the "rubber system" and spoke of the practice of bringing severed hands as evidence of a successful punitive raid against a village slow to deliver its rubber quota. British humanitarians and radicals, unable to use their own missionaries as a source of information because of a gag order on all British missionaries in Africa, relied on foreign sources to mount their campaign against the evils of the rubber trade (Ascherson 1963: 243).

The most pointed attack on Belgium's policy in the Congo came from Britain's Roger Casement, British consul in the Congo. After the campaign against Belgian misgovernment in the Congo became more widespread, Casement was asked in 1903 to tour the interior of the Congo and report his findings to Parliament. The report contained many examples of cruelty, torture, and widespread killings. For example, he witnessed women with their babies chained in sheds as hostages for the delivery of the rubber quota. At a rubber collection point, he watched Africans being detained or beaten for failure to produce a sufficient weight of latex. At second-hand, he was told of whole clans who had migrated across the Congo river to escape extortions, of mutilations by punitive raiders, and of mass executions by white officials (Ascherson 1963: 250).

What gave Casement credibility was the fact that he had been in the Congo in the late 1880s and was therefore able to compare conditions among the native population to a time before the Belgians had made a major impact on the region. Central to his report was the depopulation of the country which, he argued, could not be caused by sleeping sickness alone, as the Belgians had once suggested. He asserted that the native population had grown weak and unable to resist illness because of the excessive amount of energy used up in trying to comply with the state's demands and, in cases where resistance had been significant, the military expeditions which devastated their number.

The Casement Report had a great impact on British public opinion, resulting in demands that the British government pressure Belgium into cleaning up its act. The reaction from Leopold and the Congo secretaries-general was predictably hostile. The existence of forced labor was acknowledged but was said to be necessary in order to encourage a work habit among the natives. They claimed that evidence of atrocities was based on lies spread by certain Congolese and missionaries who were trying to further their own interests. However, Leopold and his supporters did admit that odd cases of cruelty may have occurred and promised they would looked into them (Emerson 1979: 247).

Leopold's position was severely weakened by the British government's continued insistence that he should take steps to investigate the accusations against him. Due to mounting pressure from his own parliament, he was forced to set up his own commission of enquiry. The commission was made up of a Belgian judge, an Italian judge and a Swiss jurist (Emerson 1979: 248). Their findings were not favorable, criticizing the system of forced labor and questioning the wisdom of allowing commercial companies to levy taxes without state supervision. The commission's findings resulted in mounting pressure against Leopold from within Belgium itself. Many Belgians had dismissed the findings of Roger Casement as anti-Belgian propaganda, but were unable to ignore the findings of the commission of enquiry. Parliamentarians, lawyers, professors and especially Belgium's socialist leaders called for fundamental reforms or the annexation of the Congo (Emerson 1979: 252). With mounting pressure from the

United States and from within his own government, Leopold was eventually forced into accepting the annexation of the Congo by the Belgian parliament.

Case 26: French "Pacification" of the Ivory Coast and the French Congo

The "pacification" of the Ivory Coast was the work of Governor Angoulvant, a so-called "apostle of strong-arm methods" in French-controlled Tropical Africa (Suret-Canale 1971: 95). Angoulvant felt a deep need to explain his actions in great detail, leaving historians with valuable accounts of French colonial expansion into Africa (Angoulvant 1916). The colony, established in 1893, bordered French Liberia to the west, the French Sudan to the north, and the British-controlled Gold Coast to the east. Most of the territory had been well-explored and covered with a network of posts by 1900; a poll tax was introduced the following year.

Between 1900 and 1906 the French faced considerable African resistance in the Ivory Coast, particularly in Baoulé county. The Baoulé were very adept at guerilla warfare, forcing the French into a pattern of repressing recurring revolts for more than six years without clear results. In 1908, when Governor Angoulvant took command of the region, the only areas that the French occupied were to the north, the coastal regions to the south and a narrow strip of territory in the east. Baouléland was only half occupied. To Angoulvant, the only way to achieve colonization was through the use of force. One of his first acts as governor was to destroy five villages close to his post and to take the stores of rice belonging to nearby farming villages. But it was not until January 1910, after the Abbey forest people rose up in rebellion because of high taxes and inhuman working conditions, that the governor was able to take full military control of the region. The settlers in the area, once content to trade with the natives without controlling them, now demanded "strong measures."

Angoulvant took action at once, sending out a punitive expedition that massacred those deemed responsible for attacks against Europeans:

[t]he losses suffered by the traders along the route...were so serious that the most terrible repressions were authorized and justified.... The villages taken were burnt down. No pity was shown to prisoners. The severed heads were put upon poles by the railway stations or in front of the huts in the village. (Angoulvant, quoted in Suret-Canale 1971: 100)

Angoulvant is not clear on how many Africans were massacred, or whether the victims included women and children, but what is clear is that this incident marked the beginning of a series of measures designed by the Governor to "pacify" the region. Among these measures were: the confiscation of guns, forcing the natives from the forests and into agricultural settlements; the arrest and internment of African leaders suspected of fomenting revolt; the imposition of high taxes which served to deplete the region of its wealth; the imposition of porterage and statute labor; and the destruction of remote camps and villages in favor of larger and more easily controlled settlements.

These measures created more unrest in the region, but it was soon quelled by Angoulvant. Any attempt at resistance resulted in the immediate destruction of villages. For example, a Captain Larroque, angered by what he perceived as an insolent reply by the Yansuas to his demand for porters, burnt down all the villages of the Niono. Four days later, he burnt down four more large villages (Suret-Canale 1971:103). There is no mention of the number of dead or whether the destruction of villages also involved the burning of crops, but judging from the previous record of the French in this region, where the burning or confiscation of food was commonplace, it is likely that Larroque's measures resulted in many deaths.

Similar conditions were imposed all over French-controlled Tropical Africa, particularly in the Congo, where villages were regularly burned when the population showed any signs of resistance. For example, during a discussion between lieutenant governor Dolisie and a local chief, Dolisie had one of the chief's followers disarmed for taking, in his opinion, a "threatening attitude." The chief demanded the restitution of the rifle and an indemnity, to which Dolisie replied by having the village burnt down and the palm trees felled. When the troops' porters were attacked, all the villages of the region were systematically burnt down (Suret-Canale 1971: 27).

The French began exploiting the Congo in 1898 after ousting Governor Pierre Savorgnan de Brazza. Brazza was the first European to explore this area of Equatorial West Africa, had founded Brazzaville and Franceville, and had acted as governor for the region from 1887 to 1897. Brazza had failed to appeal to French capitalists to invest in the region and had made an enemy of King Leopold of Belgium because of his benevolent treatment of Africans. His rule was a standing rebuke to the Belgians: missionaries reported that thousands of Africans were seeking refuge from Belgian troops by crossing the Congo river to French soil.

Leopold faced mounting criticism from Great Britain and the United States for atrocities committed in the Congo Free State. He believed that if the three big colonial powers were to unite in condemning these atrocities, his colony's wealth and sovereignty could be threatened. By inducing France to adopt similar policies of plunder and brutality, the king was able to deflect some of the mounting international criticism he was receiving. Through diplomacy, financial intrigue and the corruption of the press, Leopold was able to persuade the French to replace Brazza and introduce the Belgian system of plunder into the French Congo (West 1972:160).

In 1898, a commission drew up the plans and terms for dividing France's Equatorial colony into territories ruled by concessionary companies. Apart from a few native reserves and zones of free trade, the companies were given exclusive rights over all "agricultural, forest, and industrial" exploitation for thirty years. In return for which they would pay the state rents, as well as customs, military and police services. Borrowing from the Belgian experience, the French decreed that all "vacant lands" (namely all rubber-producing forests) belonged to the state, as did the rivers and river banks on which the natives depended for trade (West 1972: 166).

The concessionary system brought widespread misery to the French Congo. At first, most of the villages refused to hand over their own rubber to foreigners. At the request of the concessionary companies, the French government sent in squads of Senegalese troops, who burned down villages and pursued those who refused to cooperate (West 1972: 170). Father Daigre, a missionary in the Oubangui area, reported that "the natives did not try to resist, but several thousands, living near to the river, fled to the Belgian Congo. Others hid in the bush or in caves from which they were dislodged by hand-grenades" (Father Daigre, quoted in West 1972: 170).

As resistance to French rule became more widespread in the French Congo, its suppression also increased. The burning of villages and the massacring of civilians continued unabated. Men forced into the rubber plantations were rarely given enough food to survive and usually starved to death. Those who were allowed to return to their villages were given three months to plant a harvest. Feeling exhausted and discouraged, these men were convinced that they would not be given enough time to care for their fields and that their harvests would be plundered: they refused to do any planting. As a result of this refusal, the French labelled these men as lazy, stating that it was their own slothfulness that was responsible for the mass starvation in the area. Those who attempted to elude forced labor were arrested. Roped by the neck, and usually naked, they often died of starvation before they reached their work assignment.

In the river regions of the French Congo, the population was less exposed to the hardships of forced porterage, but was exposed instead to the hardships of river navigation (forced labor for cutting timber, requisitioning of paddlers, provisions and fowls rounded up for passenger consumption, etc.). Professor Auguste Chevalier noted during his mission the devastation on the river banks. At Isasa, he found the village three-quarters burnt down. The few remaining inhabitants fled the approach of the steamer *Dolisie*; and what remained of the village was immediately burnt down by troops.

> We watched a heart-breaking scene caused not by the natives but by the European army personnel travelling with us. From the indifference displayed by the officers who let it happen, I came to believe that such things must occur frequently. (Auguste Chevalier, quoted in Suret-Canale 1971: 33)

According to Chevalier, the French colonials, especially the concession holders, considered the natives as freely available for forced labor and proceeded to seize all their property, including cattle, under the pretext that the produce of soil was included in the concession. The few plantations still kept by the village people were "requisitioned" by the Europeans, their servants, or the Senegalese. Chevalier also quoted the opinion of the heads of trading stations and of army officers: "There is nothing to be got from these blacks here: the best thing to do is to exterminate them and so make the other regions more docile" (Auguste Chevalier, quoted in Suret-Canale 1971: 34).

The French also forcibly recruited laborers to build the railways on the Congo-Ocean line. Labor was brought in from areas as far as 300 kilometres from the railway construction sites to replace workers who had died on the job. Aside from the difficulties of making such a journey, epidemics broke out from overcrowding on barges, and the men suffered for many weeks almost without food and under extremely unhygienic conditions. The Sara and the Banda of the savannahs suffered the most, being accustomed to a dry climate and cereal food, and now being transferred naked to a damp equatorial climate and forced to eat food they were not accustomed to.

General Hilaire, at one time supreme commander in French Equatorial Africa, a man one can hardly suspect of being anti-colonial, wrote:

For some five or six years, the cruel problem of native labor has led to a disastrous solution, that of the intensive depletion—yet again!—of a population already sadly decimated by drastic cuts enforced blindly on its weakest elements, over the 500 kilometres of these homicidal construction sites!...After Bakongo, the Laongo, the Krèche, the Gabonese, the Souma, the Dagba, Baya, Yacoma and others; even the Sara, the ethnic elite of French Equatorial Africa, magnificent and supreme reserves of farmers and soldiers, have been successfully decimated, some of them even exterminated by the prison of the "machine"—as, in their language of fear, they call the deadly labor on the railway line. (General Hilaire, quoted in Suret-Canale 1971: 202)

It was Governor-General Antonetti, appointed in 1924, having decided to make the construction of the Congo-Ocean line the main achievement of his period of rule, who pushed for the completion of the railways. Not only was he frank about the human cost of such a project, he also believed that such a cost was necessary: "Either accept the sacrifice of six to eight thousand men, or renounce the railways" (Governor-General Antonetti, quoted in Suret-Canale 1971: 203). With even greater frankness, he stated, "I need 10,000 dead for my railways." Albert Londres believed the price in human lives was almost double that figure. According to official statistics there was a recorded "improvement" because the 45.20 percent mortality in the total labor force in 1927 fell to 39.18 percent in 1928 and to 17.34 percent in 1929 (Suret-Canale 1971: 203).

Case 27: The Graziani Massacre in Italian Ethiopia

Italy, which had gained a foothold in Northern Ethiopia in 1890, invaded the rest of Ethiopia in 1935 and occupied most of the country until 1941. The Italian colonial administration was consistently brutal toward the Ethiopian people. The most infamous example of Italian colonial brutality was the Graziani massacre of February 19, 1937. This occurred in Addis Ababa when Marshal Graziani, the Italian viceroy, announced that he would distribute Maria Teresa dollars to the poor outside the palace to celebrate the birth of the prince of Naples.

Resistance fighters hid amongst the crowd that had gathered and threw grenades into the group of presiding dignitaries, wounding thirty, including Graziani. Italian troops then opened fire on the crowd, much of it composed of women and children. Three days of terror in the capital ensued: Italian soldiers killed thousands of defenseless Ethiopians. Ethiopians were shot, bayoneted, beaten, or clubbed to death; their homes were set on fire, often with people still inside them. Extensive areas of every quarter of the city were ablaze and more than 4,000 huts were destroyed. Women, children, and priests received the same treatment as the resistance fighters. It was reported that whole quarters were destroyed with their inhabitants. This was reported in the Italian press as "cleaning up" sections of the city "suspected of harboring seditious elements." The Fascists who took part in these massacres were in large part not soldiers but civilian party members, some of them long-time residents of the country (Dugan and Lafore 1973: 321–22). The massacre went on for three days. One eye witness is quoted as saying that notices signed by Guido Cortese, the mayor of Addis Ababa, were posted on February 22 saying that "reprisals must cease at noon," evidence that the authorities had tacitly approved of the massacre (Del Boca 1965: 221). Participants in the massacre were awarded medals (Dugan and Lafore 1973: 322).

Graziani used the attempt on his life as an excuse to liquidate the entire Ethiopian intelligentsia, including anyone who held a high school diploma or university degree, every member of the Young Ethiopia Party, and all the officers and cadets of the imperial military academy. While the Mussolini government approved of these measures, it gave express orders that the executions be carried out in secrecy, an instruction that was never followed. Estimates of the number of people killed range from a few hundred to 6,000. The exact figure will never be known, but it is said that when the Italian regime ended, there were only two university graduates and twelve high school graduates alive in the entire country. Although the intelligentsia was very small, it is certainly evident that an entire generation of educated Ethiopians had been eradicated (Dugan and Lafore 1973: 323).

Following the attempt on his life, Graziani planned to destroy Addis Ababa and place its inhabitants in concentration camps, but Mussolini vetoed this measure for fear of negative world opinion. Instead, Mussolini, who feared a general Ethiopian uprising, ordered the execution of all prisoners. Thousands of Ethiopian soldiers who had fought against the Italians and had surrendered on condition that they be well-treated were executed and buried in mass graves. Graziani, who is said to have become increasingly paranoid after the attempt on his life, took a particular interest in eradicating traditional storytellers and soothsayers. He also ordered the execution of Coptic deacons and monks, resulting in the massacre of every monk at the Debra Libanos monastery (Del Boca 1965: 224).

The total number of dead resulting from the Graziani massacre has been variously estimated at between 1,400 and thirty thousand. It is impossible to get an accurate figure as records were not kept by the perpetrators.

Case 28: The War against the Hehe, 1891–1898, in German East Africa

Germany entered the imperialist stage rather late compared to other European nations, but proved itself as enthusiastic a supporter of colonial expansion in Africa as Great Britain and France. Bismarck paved the way for German intervention in Africa during the Berlin Conference in 1884–1885. The Anglo-German agreement, signed in 1890, divided much of the East African hinterland between them as spheres of influence, Germany taking on the region later known as Tanganyika.[1] In 1890 the Germans also purchased the rights to the coastal strip from the sultan of Zanzibar, stretching their territory to the Indian Ocean from British East Africa (now Kenya) in the north to Mozambique in the south. German East Africa (Tanganyika) bordered what are now Malawi and Zambia in the southwest; the Congo, Rwanda, and Burundi to the west; and Uganda to the northwest. In total, the Germans occupied an area covering roughly 360,000 square miles.

The region that became German East Africa was especially prone to drought and had few permanent rivers. Land suitable for German plantation was limited to the coastal areas, as the interior was densely covered in shrubbery and bush. The local population consisted of many diverse tribes, such as the Watutsi, the Hutu, the Masai, and the Matumbi, and the population was subject to many influences and new arrivals. Immigration to the region from many parts of Africa was common and continued even after German colonization had begun.

Throughout the nineteenth century, before the arrival of the Germans, East Africa was particularly hard hit by the Arabian slave trade and by civil wars. Although this had a devastating effect on the population, it has been argued that historians have, for a long time, exaggerated the magnitude of these events, portraying the African as a helpless victim or a war-crazed individual. Helge Kjekshus questions this traditional point of view, asserting that there is little evidence that Tanganyika's population was on the decline and, judging from the existence of a variety of work-intensive agricultural systems, there is an indication that it was, in fact, on the increase. Moreover, one must ask why African immigrants would continue to be drawn to an area plagued by civil war and slave traders.

Depopulation came to Tanganyika in the 1890s as a result of the sand flea plague and rinderpest, plagues which were previously unknown in that part of Africa. A smallpox epidemic also devastated many parts of the country during this period. These catastrophes had a devastating effect on the population. When the Germans arrived in Tanganyika, they found a people and an economy already in rapid decline. What guaranteed that East Africa would remain underdeveloped was the German enforcement of two administrative measures: population concentration and wildlife protection. These further weakened what control the Africans had over their environment. Local African controlled economies were devastated as the Germans brought a greater degree of foreign trade to the region, leading directly to the destabilization and eventual destruction of local social and economic structures.[2]

The people of East Africa not only lost their economic independence, they also lost control over their own affairs. German administrative methods at the time can only be qualified as brutal. The Germans ignored local customs, employed forced labor, and imposed heavy taxation, called the "hut tax." Armed conflicts between the Germans and a number of different tribes were fought throughout Tanganyika from 1888 onward. These attempts at resistance were met with brutal force by the Germans: besides the killing of rebellious tribesmen, German "pacification" measures also included the systematic destruction of houses, crops and storages, as well as the capture of livestock.

One example of such "pacification" measures taken by the Germans is the war against the Hehe (1891–1898). In the 1890s the Hehe (or Wahehe) had complete independent control over a vast area of the Iringa plateau in southeastern Tanganyika. Through bitter armed resistance, they had successfully delayed German encroachment into the Morogoro-Tabora trading route. During the next few years, they repeatedly stopped traffic on the trade route, raiding caravans and collecting tribute from subject peoples and itinerant merchants.

The Hehe had emerged as the most powerful tribe in southern Tanganyika after years of almost constant warfare. The Ngoni and Sangu tribes had clashed in the 1840s when the Ngoni migrated to this area from southern Africa. The Ngoni had learned their methods of warfare from the Zulus, particularly their regimental military system and their use of stabbing spears in combat, thus enabling them to easily defeat the Sangu. In turn, the Sangu were forced to retreat eastward where they waged an aggressive war against several small-scale societies. Two great leaders, Munyigumba and his son Mkwawa, emerged among the Ngoni and Sangu. They unified the various clans under the name "Hehe" and drove the Sangu out of the plateau in the 1870s. Between 1878 and 1882, the Hehe also waged war against the Ngoni, this time reaching a truce after years of bitter fighting.

In 1891, the Hehe ambushed and destroyed a German punitive expedition led by Captain von Zelewsky. Governor von Soden sent a telegram to Berlin stating:

> Zelewsky's expedition wiped out. Presumably 10 Europeans and 300 blacks killed. 300 Mausers all ammunition 2 Cannons 2 Maxims in enemy hands. Remaining 4 Europeans and 60 natives fled to Mounda. (von Soden, quoted in Stoecker 1986: 103)

This telegram indicates that at that time the Germans did not have a sufficient military presence to man their own army and that they used African soldiers from a different tribe than the one in revolt to quell any opposition to their rule. It also demonstrates that Mkwawa now had a sufficient amount of guns and ammunition to put up quite a fight.

For the following two years the Hehe had surrounded the town of Kalenga on the banks of the Ruaha river with twelve-foot stone walls that measured eight miles in circumference. It was not until late 1894 that the Germans made another attempt to crush the Hehe. A large German-officered force was able to break through a weak section of the walls and, after severe hut to hut fighting, occupied Kalenga, capturing numerous cattle and large supplies of guns and powder.

Mkwawa himself escaped, however, and refused for four years to accept the German conquest. He led the remainder of his followers in a series of guerrilla actions that, despite German efforts, retained the complete support of the Hehe population for several years. Meanwhile, the Germans were offering 5,000 rupees for Mkwawa, dead or alive, and ordered all Hehe warriors to be shot.

After three years the Hehe were unable to provide a unified front against the Germans: the pressure of being under siege resulted in a split within their ranks. Moreover, as the Germans gained better control of the Iringa district, they managed to severely restrict Mkwawa's activities. Harried from place to place, and in poor health, he committed suicide in 1898 to avoid being captured. His head was severed from his body and sent to Germany. With Mkwawa's death, the Hehe were indeed defeated: their lands were burned and their cattle driven away by mercenaries.

Case 29: The Maji Maji Uprising, 1905–1907

What separates the Maji-Maji uprising from earlier conflicts in Tanganyika, such as the Hehe war, is its magnitude and unprecedented intertribal cooperation. The Maji-Maji uprising, begun by the Matumbi in mid-1905, spread to a large part of the colony within weeks, covering an area of 26,000 square kilometres and involving over twenty different ethnic groups. German rule was still spread rather unevenly during this period. The Germans concentrated most of their efforts on the coast and in the northeast where resources were more plentiful and the land more arable. In contrast, the southern and western regions were neglected: the arid landscape was not an easy place to make a profit. Germany had reduced the defense forces in these areas and because there had been relative peace in that region, rumours of an impending revolt were not taken very seriously. Although this revolt was sparked by the introduction of forced labor, it is clear that African grievances against foreign domination ran very deep. Traditional tribal leaders were quick to motivate their people to revolt.

At Ngarembe, a man named Kinjikitile, regarded by many as a prophet, provided the unifying ideological force behind the rebellion. He believed that the unity and freedom of Africans was a fundamental right, that a war against the Germans was ordained by God, and that his followers' ancestors would return to life and assist in the insurrection. He also prescribed a magic water (*maji*) or potion that he claimed would turn German bullets into water and make the user of the potion virtually invincible. Although the *maji* did not protect the user from bullets, it did provide the courage needed to fight the Germans. As the movement spread to various regions under German control, messengers (called *hongo*) would carry and administer the potion to the people. The *hongo* also called on all black men to rise against European rule.[3] It is difficult to assess just how much faith the Africans had in this potion, but it is generally felt that groups who had not initially resisted the Germans were more likely to believe in the potion, as they were not aware of the superiority of German weaponry.

It has been suggested that the use of the *maji* was widely exaggerated by the Germans who were unable to explain the violence and scale of the uprising. Many preferred to blame the revolt on African superstition rather than the administrative abuses committed by the Germans themselves. Such brutal methods as were often employed in the collection of taxes, may have been at the root of the African insurrection.[4]

Although there are no exact figures as to the number of people involved in the uprising, it is obvious that it was large enough to pose a real threat to German rule in the region. At first the only victims of the uprising were Europeans, but within months, Arabs, Indians, coastal people, even Africans who wore European clothes, became targets. Anyone perceived as having cooperated with European colonialism became an enemy.

German authorities responded to the rebellion with brutal force. Reinforcements were quickly sent in to quash the rebellion. The method used was the systematic destruction of village after village: this was the same scorched earth policy the Germans had used earlier to fight rebellions in Tanganyika. This strategy was employed by the Germans because of the vastness of the war zone and the African's advantage in using guerrilla attacks rather than military confrontation. The Germans had clear orders to starve the population into submission. Villages were burned, food confiscated, and harvests destroyed. Tens of thousands were killed in fighting or massacres. An even larger number of people starved to death. For example, only 1,500 of the roughly 30,000 Pangwa living near Lake Nyasa survived after the revolt. Other tribes who participated in the revolt suffered similar fates. Whole areas of the south were completely depopulated. Estimates of the number of African dead as a result of the uprising, including those who died in battle and as a result of the scorched earth policy, are as high as 300,000.

The methods used and the scale of casualties seem to justify the inference that the aim was to exterminate the rebellious tribes. Therefore this case should be considered a genocidal massacre, if not an outright genocide.

Case 30: Revolt against the Germans in Kamerun, 1903–1908

Cameroun is a federal republic in West Africa covering an area of over 320,000 square kilometers. It borders Nigeria, Chad, Central African Republic, Congo, Gabon, and Guinea-Bissau. Eastern Cameroun comprises a former French administered United Nations trust (earlier a mandate), while western Cameroun, known as the Cameroons under the British, consists of the southern part of a former British administered trust (the northern region is now part of Nigeria). Much of this region consists of coastal plains, behind which lie thick tropical rain forests. Farther north are high grassland plateaux, and in the Chad basin, semi-desert savanna. Its main exports are cacao, bananas, palm kernels, coffee, and lumber. Cameroun became independent in 1960 and united with the southern part of the Cameroons as the Federal Republic of Cameroun in 1961. All of this territory (including that now in Nigeria) became part of the German protectorate of Kamerun in 1884. German rule ended in 1919 when the region was divided between France and Great Britain.

In the first decade of German rule in Kamerun, the Germans limited their control to its coastal regions. The first two governors, Julius von Soden and Eugen von Zimmerer, limited their activities to safeguarding the interests of two Hamburg based commercial firms, C. Woermann and Jantzen & Thormählen, at whose request the territory had been annexed.

Until the mid 1890s the Duala people retained a monopoly over inland trade, one which had been guaranteed by Germany. The Duala made it difficult for both of these firms to access raw materials in the interior. Because the administration did not have the necessary troops to open up the country by force the Germans could not break their agreement with the Duala (and they did want to break it) or coerce other natives to obey German rule. Both firms, dissatisfied with this state of affairs, began to lobby the Foreign Office to send in military forces to break up the network of native middlemen. Although Germany was slow to respond to the companies' request, it did eventually send in expeditionary forces to move into the interior. The first of such expeditions, undertaken in 1889, failed because of resistance by the Bakoko people. The interior of the country remained inaccessible because the coastal peoples continued to resist the Germans.

Such resistance was met with brutal force. When the Abo rose up in rebellion in 1891, Captain von Gravenreuth formed a "police force" from the 370 slaves he had bought. With the aid of this force, German junior barrister (*Gerichtsassessor*) Wehlan was able to subjugate the Bakoko and the Mabea through several military campaigns, ordering "villages to be burnt down, women, children and old people to be killed, and captives to be tortured to death" (Stoecker 1986, 64). Wehlan also gave orders not to use rifles; as a result, a number of prisoners were hacked to pieces with knives. Some members of this police force kept the heads of their dead opponents as "souvenirs."[5]

During the 1890s the administration finally succeeded in wresting the monopoly of access to inland trading from the Duala, but bloody campaigns by a small German mercenary force were still necessary before they could successfully penetrate the interior of the country. Hardly a year went by without open rebellion in some part of the colony. The Germans crushed these uprisings one after another by routinely burning down villages and killing prisoners.[6]

Notes

1. Tanganyika united with Zanzibar in 1964 and is now the Republic of Tanzania.
2. Kjekshus points out that these precolonial economies had greater control over their environment and were thus better equipped to combat such potential threats as the tzetze fly than they were under European rule. She demonstrates that earlier historical portrayals of East Africans were overshadowed by the colonial belief that Africans were incapable of achieving any level of economic success and by the fact that when these earlier historians looked at East Africa, they could not see past the devastating effects of the ecological and economic crisis brought on by colonialism. This analysis is particularly relevant in this case study as it calls into question the broad statements made by Stoecker which argue that the German suppression of the Maji Maji uprising was solely responsible for the long-term detrimental effects on the economy and population (Stoecker 1986: 113).
3. Gwassa and Iliffe suggest that the uprising had a millenial character in that it promised a unity and invincibility capable of eradicating the evils of witchcraft and European rule. They also maintain that millenial teachings were not uncommon in southern Tanzania before the uprising, and that what was different about this movement was the way it mobilized against the Germans (p.17).
4. Iliffe argues that it is unlikely that religious leaders could provoke an uprising in this area of Tanganyika, as religious and cultural ties between tribes were very fragmented. Moreover, when it became clear that the *maji* failed to protect the user from German bullets, the rebels returned to their established patterns of guerrilla warfare. The rebels were more inspired by a desire to end colonial rule than they were by a religious movement (Iliffe 1969: 21–25).
5. Stoecker notes that this police force, made up entirely of slaves, rebelled against the Germans. All captured members of this police force were executed (1986: 64–65).
6. For additional information see also Ascherson (1963), Austen (1968), Chilver (1967), Cobbing (1977), Cooke (1973), Emerson (19790, Gann and Duignan (1969), Grimal (1965), Ranger (1967), Rudin (1968), Sbacchi (1985), and West (1972).

21

More Twentieth-Century Cases

Case 31: Kazakhs in the USSR in the 1930s

There is no agreement as to how the nomadic Kazakh people were formed, largely due to a lack of contemporary source material. Before the eighteenth century, there were few European travellers going through the region of Asia now called Kazakhstan, and Eastern chroniclers were not generally interested in nomadic peoples and their origins. The oral history of the Kazakhs themselves does not give many clues. However, the general consensus is that the Kazakhs are descendants of the Mongols and originate from a split that took place in the mid-fifteenth century when the two sons of Barak Khan of the White Horde of the Mongol empire broke away from Aba'l Khayr, Khan of the Uzbeks. Their supporters increased in number and established themselves in the environs of Lake Balkhash and the lands immediately above and below the Syr Darya River. Kazahkstan now extends from the Caspian Sea on the southwest to the Chinese Sinkiang-Uigur region on the east.

Russian expansion into Kazakhstan began in 1731 when a Kazakh khan in the area south of the Urals acknowledged Russian suzerainty. Colonization in the south was very limited until 1905, when the Orenburg-Tashkent railroad was completed. In 1916 the Kazakhs revolted against the tsarist government, and when the Bolshevik revolution occurred, Kazakh leaders were in process of organizing an independent state on western models. A Kirghiz[1] Soviet Republic was set up in 1920, but the Soviets did not establish effective control until 1925. In 1936 Kazakhstan was raised to the status of a union republic, although its government continued to be ruled by that of Moscow. Under Stalin, Russian and Ukrainian colonization increased rapidly.

In 1928 Josef Stalin set up his first Five Year Plan. He believed that after the failure of Lenin's New Economic Plan, a new economic course had to be taken. Under his new system, assuming optimal conditions, the volume of production of various industrial commodities would rise tremendously. He believed that the peasants should not anticipate immediate improvements in their normal lives and that they should be willing to make sacrifices to bring about future goals. Stalin abolished trade unions and unemployment benefits, while also expecting workers to give a set amount of their earnings toward state loans to improve industrial development.

One of the most striking aspect of Stalin's first Five Year Plan was the theory of collectivization, under which small individual farms would be replaced by mechanized, state controlled, collective farms. These collective farms were intended to create places where workers would voluntarily pool their labor and capital while distributing their proceeds to the government. By the end of the first Five Year Plan, almost sixty percent of all Soviet farms were collectivized.

Kazakh society is traditionally nomadic, organized according to clan, sub-clan and village relationships. Kazakhs regarded the old clan system and their traditional leaders as offering stability through the continuation of their old way of life. Even when Stalin rose to power, clan, sub-clan and village authorities governed much as they had before, having simply reconstituted themselves as Soviets. Stalin's government found it very difficult to find Kazakhs willing to enforce the collectivization program. Few were willing to take livestock or land away from the elite classes who were usually both clan and local Soviet leaders. The Soviet government realized that alternative ways had to be found in order to enforce their economic plan.

The Kazakh Communist party was mostly composed of resettled Soviet citizens from Russia and the Ukraine. Few Kazakh males were attractive candidates to be moved into the higher levels of the party apparatus. In truth, the Kazakh Communist party was no more than a puppet of the Soviet government in Moscow. The traditional communist forms of government, such as the party itself and Soviet-style bureaucracy, were simply superimposed over the already functioning local social and political regimes. The traditional authorities in Kazakhstan were therefore allowed to remain in place. When the Soviet government demanded that, under their collectivization plan, agriculture had to become more efficient and that the peasants would have to make more sacrifices, some Kazakh government representatives protested. Their objections proved ineffective, however, as those who protested were removed from office and replaced by people the Soviets knew they could rely on.

By the early 1930s the Soviet government had almost complete control over the Kazakh government and party apparatus. Stalin did not trust the Kazakh leadership, believing that only through mass education and propaganda would a loyal Kazakh elite and supportive Kazakh public be created. A propaganda plan was designed to reinforce the idea of collectivization by indoctrinating children. It was also aimed at eradicating Islam and Kazakh cultural traditions. Among the first to be placed into camps or murdered were Kazakh schoolteachers, writers and poets thought to be disloyal to the state. As collectivization began, collectives were set up with a loyal party man in charge. He would be responsible for ensuring that production requirements were met.

Forced collectivization began in 1930, resulting in the creation of close to five thousand collective farms. Because these farms did not have the means of producing even close to what was expected of them, the economy plummeted and there was no food even for the peasants working on the collectives. Peasants who failed to produce the required amount were not allowed to take any grain to eat. What livestock was left was slaughtered for food or killed in protest against the collectivization drive. People began to starve.

The Soviets intended to settle 544,000 out of the 560,000 nomadic and semi-nomadic people by the end of the first year plan. After the first year, the government no longer held on to the pretext that the public would be voluntarily resettled. Forced resettlement brought more starvation, disease and death, primarily caused by inadequate shelter and food supplies, back-breaking labor and sparse technical assistance in the area of agriculture. It is estimated that more than one third of Kazakhstan's population, over one million people, died as a result of the man-made famine. "Loss of human life was proportionately greater in Kazakhstan than anywhere else in the Soviet Union" (Olcott 1987: 185).

"Shortly after the 1937 congress, mass arrests began; by the end of the year, a whole generation of Kazakh intellectuals, historians, journalists, poets and writers were found guilty and executed for the crime of dedication to the Kazakh people" (Olcott 1987: 218–19). The purges themselves were next; before another year had passed every member of the Kazakh bureau of that first congress was arrested and charged with "defamation and repression of party members" (Olcott 1987: 219). Almost an entire generation of Kazakh intellectuals, communists and non-communists alike, were wiped out during the purges.

There is no doubt that the deliberate starvation of the Kazakh people, coupled with the purges of Kazakh intellectuals and cultural leaders makes this a clear case of genocide. It was one of several genocides perpetrated during the Stalin period. Except for the Armenian genocide, these were the first cases of modern, ideological genocide in the twentieth century. The intent was to implement the regime's ideological imperatives, but the outcome was that they were not implemented. This failure was very costly in societal terms due to the destruction of lives, cultures, and agricultural resources.

Case 2: Chittagong Hill People in Bangladesh

Bangladesh (formerly East Pakistan) is a small country in South Asia on the Bay of Bengal, covering an area of 143,998 square kilometres. It is one of the most densely populated countries in the world, with 797 inhabitants per square kilometre. It is also one of the poorest. Its annual GNP per capita in 1994 was U.S.$ 234. It is an agricultural country with a tropical monsoon climate, prone to hurricanes and flooding. Since it established independence from Pakistan in 1971, Bangladesh has had a series of elected and military governments, all of which have been criticized by Amnesty International and the United Nations for gross abuses of human rights, mostly against the indigenous tribal peoples of the Chittagong Hill Tracts (CHT).

The majority of the population of Bangladesh is Muslim (over 87 percent), 12 percent is Hindu and less than 1 percent Buddhist. In June of 1988 Islam was declared the state religion of Bangladesh, causing tens of thousands of non-Muslims to flee to India. 50,000 aboriginal Chittagong refugees were already living in India at this time. The number of refugees from the Chittagong Hill Tracts continues to increase in India, even though it is widely known that they may never again return to their homeland. It has become increasingly difficult to repatriate to the Chittagong area.

The Chittagong District in Bangladesh is on the northeastern coast of the Bay of Bengal. Its capital, the city of Chittagong, is the largest and most industrially developed port in Bangladesh. Because rainfall is so heavy in this region, rice is the main crop of choice among farmers. Most of the Chittagong district is not farmland; a large area is taken up by low forested foothills close to the Burmese border. These foothills, the Chittagong Hill Tracts, are home to the aboriginal tribes of Bangladesh, namely the Chakma, the Marma (Mogh) and the Tippera, collectively known as the Jumma or the Chittagong. The Jumma are mostly Buddhist, but also have sizeable Animist and Christian populations.

The root of the problem between the Bengali government and the Chittagong lies in the encroachment by Bangladeshi immigrants, culture, and laws into the tribal, resource-rich lands of Chittagong. The Hill Tracts are also the least populated areas of Bangladesh, which makes it an attractive region for settling Bengalis; it is primarily for this reason that the Bengali government continues to follow a policy of genocide toward the Jumma. Bengali armed forces have been active participants in massacres of tribal men, women and children since early 1977.

Certain elements among the Jumma have also engaged in an insurgency movement, led by a group called the Shanti Bahini, against the Bengali government. This insurgency movement evolved out of the failure of tribal leaders to negotiate any level of political autonomy with the government of Bangladesh in the early 1970s, their subsequent loss of credibility, and the frustration of Jumma young people, many of whom are highly educated, with the increasing encroachment of Bengali settlers on Chittagong land. Thousands of Bengali settlers have been massacred at the hands of insurgents. Although the majority of the Jumma did not participate in these activities, the government used these events as justification for its repression of the Chittagong people.

The government passed a Disturbed Areas Bill in 1981, giving police and the army unrestricted powers to shoot anyone suspected of antistate activities. It has used this law against the Jumma time and time again, claiming that the tribal people pose an inner threat to the people of Bangladesh. The government is also surprisingly open about its policies. For example, in 1983 Brigadier Hannan and Lieutenant-Colonel Salam, speaking for the government, declared, "we want the soil and not the people of the Chittagong Hill Tracts" (Burger and Whitaker 1984: 61).

The massacres committed against the Jumma can be defined as genocidal. One example of such a massacre took place on March 3, 1980 when the army tricked leading tribal people into believing that they were to assemble to help repair a Buddhist temple. When they and other villagers lined up to work, they were "showered with bullets" (Mey 1984: 152). Of the three or four thousand inhabitants of the village, none survived. The amount of bloodshed continued to escalate in the early 1980s, reaching a peak in 1985 and 1986, as Bengali settlers, backed by the military, have also become engaged in the fighting. Shanti Bahini attacks on Bengali settlers were met with brutal indiscriminate reprisals. Not only did the Bengali para-military Ansars engage in a scorched earth policy, leaving the Jumma who had not been massacred starving, but they also engaged in a policy of mass rape. Mark Levene argues:

> ...the rape, particularly of young girls, was significant as a conscious, collective defilement and punishment of [J]umma communities; indeed mass rape had been similarly perpetuated on Bengalis by the Pakistani army in their 1971 genocide. As then, so in the CHT of the 1980s, defiled women could not be readmitted into their own families or communities. Taken to its logical conclusion this was genocide by other means, though it is worth noting that much of the military-sponsored rape in the CHT simply preceded mutilation and murder. (Levene 1997: 28)

Tens of thousands of Jumma have since become refugees, fleeing either to India or Burma. In a 1992 report, the U.S. Committee for Refugees estimated the number of refugees at 65,000. Although the Bengali government has recently made some cosmetic efforts at peace talks with the Jumma, the Chittagong Hill Tracts remains highly militarized and human rights violations against the Jumma continue unabated.

The absence of objective international observers and the lack of effective international pressure, despite a high level humanitarian and economic aid to the region, has enabled the Bengali government to continue with its genocidal policy toward the tribal peoples of the Chittagong with impunity. It has been argued that the very nature of the conflict between a nation which sees itself as ethnically homogeneous, and an indigenous people which sees itself outside that definition is potentially genocidal. What remains clear is that the situation for the tribal people of the Chittagong Hill Tracts has become critical.

Case 33: Myanmar (Burma)

Burma, as Myanmar was known until the military Saw Maung coup in 1988, is a country in South East Asia, covering a territory of 678,000 square kilometres (approximately the size of Thailand and Cambodia combined). It includes Burma proper and seven ethnic minority states. The population today stands at roughly 40 million, double the figure estimated in 1947, the year Burma became independent from Great

Britain. In 1987, Burma was named by the United Nations General Assembly as the "least developed country" in the world with annual incomes below US$ 200 per capita and a low level of literacy and industrial development.

Although there are no reliable statistics available with regard to Burma's ethnic minorities, most neutral estimates claim that the Karen, Burma's second largest minority group, have a population of some seven million with another 200,000 living across the border in Thailand. The Shan and the Mon are said to number some four million each, the Muslim Rohingyas in Arakan State one to two million, the Zo or Chin two to three million, the Kachin 1.5 million and the Palaung-Wa one to two million. Burma's official religion is Buddhist, professed by 84 percent of the population. There are also Animist, Muslim, Hindu, and Christian minorities. Non-Buddhists have always been regarded with great suspicion in Burma and the present government shows as little tolerance toward religious as to ethnic minorities.

Before the British took over Burma in 1885, the concept of a Burmese nation based on a Western concept of nationhood did not exist. The kingdom of Burma coexisted with, and was more often involved in wars against, the Mon, the Arakanese, the Shan, and the Karen kingdoms. Some of these conflicts, dating back to the eleventh century A.D., were marred by mass killings of civilians and brutal occupations practiced by all sides. These kingdoms were independent of Burma (Karen and Shan) or were overrun by the Burman[2] army in the latter half of the eighteenth century (Arakan and Mon). The British annexation of Burma united these states to form one nation. The roots of ethnic conflict in Burma stem from the fact that relations between what are now ethnic minority groups in Burma and the Burman government in Rangoon have rarely been congenial.

The first Anglo-Burman war (1824–1825) started when the Burman army penetrated Assam, a province in British colonial India, for the apparent purpose of overrunning Bengal. Within a year, British-Indian forces had advanced to the capital, Rangoon, forcing the Burman monarchy to cede control of both the Arakan and Tenasserim coasts to British India. Burma's royal Konbaung dynasty never recovered from this humiliating defeat and the morale of the army slowly disintegrated. As British and Indian traders began to exploit Burma's resources, friction between British and Burman officials continued to worsen.

By 1885, relations between British India and Burma had deteriorated to such a point that the Indian government took it upon itself to take complete control of the Burman government, moving the King and his court to India. Burma was thereafter placed under a British-Indian commissioner. During the span of complete British rule from 1885 to 1940, Burmans made few economic gains, while British, Indian and resident Chinese exploited Burman resources and labor.

The final British annexation did, administratively and politically, unify the Mon and Burman homelands which were put under direct rule. Although the Shan, Chin and Kachin homelands, and some Arakanese and Karen areas were administered separately, they were nevertheless governed by British authority and were considered part of Burma. It was the British who introduced the idea of creating a Burmese nation state and, contrary to the widely held views of the present Burman government, rejected the notion that minorities should have their own separate states.

Japan's conquest of Burma in 1942 destroyed British prestige. Many Burmans, who resented the British in the first place, accepted posts in and collaborated with the Japan-sponsored government of Premier Ba Maw. In return for military alliance, Japan granted a facade of independence in August of 1943. As the war progressed, Japan largely ignored the Burman government and appropriated whatever they needed. As a consequence, young nationalists within Ba Maw's regime, calling themselves the Anti-Fascist People's Freedom League (AFPFL), aided the returning British armies in the final weeks of the war, in spring of 1945, by attacking Japan's forces.

By 1947, the British had signed a treaty with Burman Premier U Nu, effective on January 4, 1948, granting independence to Burma. U Nu had taken over the leadership of the Burmese government and the AFPFL following the assassination of General Aung San in July of 1947. He believed, like Aung San, that Burma could remain unified by encouraging and tolerating its diversity. Within two years, the Burman government was involved in conflicts with certain communist and nationalist Karen separatists. However, the government remained popular with most minority groups by continuing to uphold democratic principles and maintaining certain socialist policies with regard to health and education.

Socialism has been strongly connected with Burman nationalism since the 1930s. Associated with the Burman nationalistic struggle against colonialism and domination of the economy by European, Indian, and Chinese business interests, all Burman governments since independence have been based on a socialist platform. While the interpretation of socialist dogma has differed over the years, it was the central key to political legitimacy in Burma.

On March 2, 1962, General Ne Win and the military seized power in Burma. The reason given for this act was that the Union was endangered, forcing the military to act in order to maintain unification. They imprisoned members of the elected government and imposed a brutal dictatorship. The Burman military, which has been in control ever since 1962, has made it clear that it rejects General Aung San's "unity in diversity" formula. It is under this regime that Burma has seen the most ruthless persecution and killing of minorities and of people in opposition to the government. There are no rights, no freedom, and no free press.

The 1948 constitution, although it was not a federal one, provided minorities with a degree of autonomy and internal authority. It also acted as a framework under which non-Burmans felt comfortable and which allowed adjustments in center-state relations. On the other hand, the 1978 constitution, drawn up and imposed by the military, has reduced the status of minority states and has effectively terminated relations between the central government and ethnic leaders. As a result of this change in government-ethnic relations, there has been continuing conflict between the center, dominated by the military, and other ethnic segments, namely the Rohingya, Shan, Karen and Mon minorities.

The Burman military government displayed a high level of xenophobia. From their point of view, Burma had been economically, culturally and politically colonized for the past two hundred years. Under the British, indigenous minorities were governed separately, and sometimes given preference in retaining their ruling elites and tribal culture, as well as in certain types of employment. Minorities who converted to Christianity were more likely to be supported by foreign states and were still perceived as having closer relations with foreigners than with their own central government.

The government also felt that Burman culture was under attack from Western influences. For example, General Ne Win was against the introduction of television into Burma until he was persuaded that it could be used for educational and propaganda purposes. Ne Win supported Burma's internal role as that of civilizing the "ruder peoples" on its frontiers and its external role as isolationist and neutral. The government often publicized the "loose morals" of Westerners, contrasting them with the purity of Burman ethics and life.

Foreigners and foreign governments were perceived as intent on exploiting Burma and its people. The public was urged to identify citizens with foreign sympathies "and eradicate them like maggots from the country's flesh" (Steinberg 1990: 62). The government used xenophobia as a means of promoting its ideology, of excusing its mistakes, and directing internal dissatisfaction toward the outside world. Burma today has some of the most restrictive citizenship laws in the world. Full citizenship is reserved for those who can prove they had ancestors resident in Burma before the first British annexation in 1824.

Case 34: The Rohingyas

The Rohingyas live in Arakan state, sharing a border with Bangladesh and separated from Burma proper by the Arakan Yoma mountains. Between one and two million Rohingyas live in Arakan, making up more than half of the state's population. The Rohingyas are the descendants of foreign traders and soldiers, most notably Arab, Mongol, Turkish, Portuguese, and Bengali, who began to settle in Arakan after the ninth century, mixing with different native tribes. The Rohingyas converted to Islam in the fifteenth century when Arakan was a feudatory of Bengal. It was during this period that the Rohingyas developed their own distinct culture and art.

In the following centuries, Arakan was subjugated at various times by the armies of Burma and Portugal, leaving the area depopulated and impoverished. Burman raids on Arakan were frequent and brutal. In 1785 over 30,000 Burman soldiers attacked Arakan, destroying mosques, libraries, and cultural institutions. 20,000 prisoners were captured and brought back to Burma as slaves. Besides profiting materially from the plunder, the Burman monarchy saw these raids as a way of breaking the spirit of a people they considered foreign. Massacres of civilians were encouraged. During one of these raids, Rohingya men, women, and children were driven into bamboo enclosures and "burned alive by the hundreds" (Harvey 1967: 161).

With the memory of Burman brutality fresh in their minds, the Rohingyas welcomed British rule in 1825, recognizing that they would be well-protected from further military invasion on the part of Burma. Moreover, under the British, the Rohingyas enjoyed a certain degree of political and cultural autonomy; by the 1930s the Rohingyas were actively campaigning for independence.

During World War II the Rohingyas remained loyal to the British, even when they retreated into India. They paid dearly for this choice: advancing Japanese and Burmese armies tortured, raped, and massacred thousands of Rohingyas and over 22,000 refugees fled to India. After reconquering the region in 1945, the British rewarded the Rohingyas for their loyalty by setting up a civilian administration for the Rohingyas in Arakan. The dream of Rohingya autonomy was rather short-lived, however, as Arakan state was incorporated into Burma in the 1948 treaty granting Burma her independence from Britain.

Burman-Rohingya relations, which were not very friendly to begin with, deteriorated rapidly. In 1948 Muslims were barred from military service. Muslim civil servants and policemen were replaced by Burman government and military officials; Rohingya leaders were arbitrarily placed under arrest. Rohingya refugees who had remained in India after the war were not permitted to return to Burma. Considered by the government as illegal immigrants, their properties were seized and resettled by Burman nationals.

Diplomatic negotiations having failed, the Rohingyas took up arms. The rebels made rapid progress, and by 1949 they occupied northern Arakan, having expelled the Burmans who had settled there. Although the government did respond militarily, the Rohingyas, even in rebellion, retained their rights to elect representatives to parliament and to appeal in the courts. In 1961 the rebellion in Arakan state was subdued and the area was placed under the administration of a number of experienced army officers.

General Ne Win's military takeover of the government in 1962 brought tighter military control to the area and also marked the beginning of a series of military operations designed to victimize Rohingya rebels and civilians. Being highly suspicious of non-Buddhists, Muslims were perfect targets for the new military regime. The Rohingya secessionist movement was met with brutal force on the part of the Burman military and Ne Win's troops were highly visible in Arakan state, particularly in the 1970s and 1980s.

In 1974, Rohingyas were denied the right to vote and jails in Akjab and Rangoon became places of detention for Rohingyas suddenly considered "illegal immigrants." After widespread unrest, the Burman government began its project "Naga Min" (Operation Dragon King). There were widespread reports of forced labor, torture, rapes, and mass killing in Arakan state as the Burman government set forth its plan to push the Rohingyas off its territory. Ne Win's government stated that the Rohingyas were not Burma's citizens (Burma had refused to give citizenship cards to Rohingyas after 1970) and asserted that the refugees leaving for Bangladesh were illegal immigrants. In 1979 Ne Win, despite his own mixed Burman-Chinese heritage stated:

> Today you can see that even people of pure blood are being disloyal to the race and country but are loyal to others. If people of pure blood act this way, we must carefully watch people of mixed blood. Some people are of pure blood, pure Burmese heritage and descendants of genuine citizens. Karen, Kachin and so forth, are of genuine pure blood. But we must consider whether these people are completely our race, our Burmese people. (General Ne Win, quoted in Smith 1991: 37)

Over 250,000 Rohingyas arrived in Bangladesh in 1978, but most were repatriated that same year after an agreement with Burma's government. Ne Win's government was apparently bowing to international pressure from the U.N. and the United States.

Oppression of the Rohingya did not stop in 1978, however. The Burman government became involved in a systematic campaign of genocide against the Rohingyas. Villages were destroyed, mass killings of civilians took place, including those of two hundred Rohingyas in prayer in a mosque, and children as young as seven were forcibly conscripted. Between 1991 and 1992, over 250,000 Rohingya fled to Bangladesh. Although Bangladesh has been hospitable to the Rohingyas, it is also one of the world's poorest countries. The area where these refugees were living is considered to be the most unsafe place in the world. This was the area where a cyclone hit in 1991, killing over 113,000 people. Voluntary and involuntary repatriation of the Rohingya began after Burma and Bangladesh signed a repatriation treaty in 1992. In November 1993, the Burman government agreed to permit the United Nations High Commission for Refugees (UNHCR) to assist and monitor returned refugees. However, the United States Committee for Refugees (USCR) has found that Bangladesh authorities coerced many Rohingya refugees into repatriating and that many of these refugees did not believe they could refuse to repatriate under the UNHCR program. By the end of 1995, fewer than 55,000 Rohingya refugees remained in Bangladesh. The USCR has indicated that the continuing reports about human rights abuses in Arakan, the small number of UNHCR workers, their reliance on interpreters provided by the Burman government, the lack of international NGO activity and the returnees being sent to hard-to-reach areas, make it very difficult

for the UNHCR to guarantee the safety of Rohingya refugees returning to Burma.

Case 35: Oppression of Other Minorities
and Political Opposition

The first pro-democracy demonstrations in Burma took place in 1987
when university students held mass demonstrations, burned portraits
of Ne Win, and sent threatening letters to the police. In 1988 these
protests were met with violence as the army and the police opened fire
on demonstrators, killing hundreds of students. Protests continued and
spread from campuses in Rangoon and Mandalay to other colleges and
universities in Pegu, Moulmein, and Prome and to factories. In that
same year, Amnesty International published a report saying that the
Burman army was responsible for the execution, torture and rape of
thousands of civilians in the frontier areas, and for forcing villagers to
walk ahead of troops as human mine detectors during campaigns against
ethnic insurgents. It is estimated that 5,000 to 10,000 anti-government
protestors were killed in Burma in 1988, with over 1,000 students killed
in Rangoon alone. Mass protests continued until 1990 when the Burman government bowed to pressure and announced that it would allow
elections to take place.

After nationwide elections in May 1990, when the National League
for Democracy was elected, Burma's military regime publicly con-
ceded defeat. Yet it was evident by August that it would not give up
power. On August 8, 1990, Burman security forces opened fire on protestors in Mandalay, killing at least four people. A State Law and Order Restoration Council (SLORC), headed by the chief of staff, General
Saw Maung, was formed to ensure "peace and tranquillity." Burma's
pro-democracy movement attempted to thwart the military take-over
of the election, but was met with gunfire. Thousands of students, monks,
women, and even schoolchildren were murdered by the military.
SLORC arrested Nobel Prize-winning dissident Aung San Suu Kyi,
who had returned from abroad and united Burma's fractious democracy movement.

In spite of Suu Kyi's release in 1994 and recent negotiations with
pro-democracy groups, the government has continued its policy of
thwarting pro-democracy activity. In May 1995, SLORC arrested over
250 key members of the National League for Democracy, indicating
that the government means to maintain its firm grip on power. Suu

Kyi's release from house arrest brought a surge in foreign investment from countries eager to take a share in Burma's national resources. Many of the investors who were previously unwilling to invest in a country holding under house arrest one of the most famous political dissidents, saw her release as a green light to start economic activity. Investors have also been willing to overlook the lack of any real progress with regard to democracy because the government's growing trade with China was seen as competing with their own interests. Most countries see their investment in Burma as a way of preventing China from gaining influence in the region.

However, some of the Western "dialogue partners" of ASEAN, including Canada, the United States, Australia, New Zealand, the European Union and Japan, have shown some opposition to investing in Burma. The United States has indicated that it may recommend reimposing sanctions if the government in Rangoon does not begin negotiating with the democrats. Australia has recently given Suu Kyi one of its highest awards, and has stated publicly that it is committed to working for the restoration of democracy and human rights in Burma. Trade may well be the deciding factor in international response to Burma's government. Britain, France, Malaysia, Singapore, Thailand, the United States, among others, have made major investments in Burma. Whether the conscience of the international community can overcome its greed remains to be seen.

What is certain is that the Burman government has committed genocide against its ethnic minorities. The suspected intent was not only to wipe out the last vestiges of resistance on the borders, but also to draw popular attention away from the pro-democracy movement. Among the victims were the Karen, an ethnic minority group who have been fighting a forty-year civil war with the government in Rangoon. The Shan, the Mon, the Palaung-Wa and the Rohingya in Arakan state have also been targeted by the government. The General Secretary of the Overseas Karen Organization, a refugee organization based in Thailand, reported:

> They've [the military government] injected their 280,000 soldiers with racist and distorted ideals, with the aim to have their killing machine exterminate our race—not just the Karens, but other ethnic minorities as well: the Shans, Mons, the Rohingyas, Kachins, Karennis and others. SLORC's policy is one of mass slaughter. (David Tharckabaw, quoted in Clements 1992: 78)

The military government has displayed its genocidal intentions by continuing to espouse xenophobic and racist policies toward its ethnic minorities, declaring that it must eradicate non-Burmans in order to save Burma from "inferior peoples." Political opponents are arrested or more often murdered. However, there have been some important changes in Burma that could bring more international attention to such offences. In a complete turnaround from its previous exclusionary policy, the government has adopted a new policy to bolster its trade and acquisition of hard currency. Foreigners are encouraged to invest and even tourists are now welcome. While these policies are having a considerable amount of success, they are also increasing publicity surrounding Burma's human rights record. Although there does appear to be an increase in awareness of the atrocities taking place in Burma, there is still no coordinated international pressure on Burma to change its brutal policies.[3]

Notes

1. The Kazakhs were known to the Russians as Kirguiz until 1925, as Kazaks from 1925 to 1936, and as Kazakhs since 1936–1937.
2. Silverstein (1977: 4) asserts that most scholars since World War II have used the terms Burman and Burmese as follows: Burman is used as an ethnic term referring to a particular group within Burma. Burmese is a political term referring to all inhabitants of the country (Burmans, Karens, Shans, Kachins, Chins, Palaung Wa and Mons). Not all scholars follow this rule, however.
3. For additional information see: Anti-Slavery Society (1981), Bahar (1981), Burger and Whitaker (1984), Clements (1992), Conquest (1986), Falla (1991), Harvey (1967), International Work Group for Indigenous Affairs (1981), Kabir (1980), Kolvig (1991), Lias (1956), Lintner (1990), Mey (1984), Silverstein (1989 and 1990), Tzang (1987 and 1989), U.S. Committee for Refugees (1988 to 1996).

22

The Relevance of History for the Case of the Former Yugoslavia

Introduction

The region to be examined here is the area of what was once the Socialist Federal Republic of Yugoslavia; this includes Serbia, Bosnia and Hercegovina, Croatia, Slovenia, Kosovo, Macedonia, and Montenegro. While we were flooded with a barrage of news of "ethnic cleansing" and mass slaughter in the former Yugoslavia, there has been little effort on the part of the media to place these events within a historic framework. Although current events are not examined in this paper, we hope that by exploring the history of this region we might shed some light on why it is currently experiencing such brutal conflicts. Whether these conflicts should be characterized as genocides or genocidal massacres will not become clear until they have run their course and fuller documentation becomes available.

The Influence of Geography

Situated in southeastern Europe on the eastern shores of the Adriatic Sea in the northwestern part of the Balkan peninsula, this region is bounded by Italy to the northwest, Austria and Hungary to the north, Romania and Bulgaria to the east, and Greece and Albania to the south. Its geography is open to entry from all directions: to the northwest the plains of the middle Danube afford a route from central Europe, to the northeast there is a wide corridor through Romania, Moldova, and the steppes of the Ukraine, to the east one can travel on land through Bulgaria and Turkey, and to the west the Adriatic offers an easy passage by sea.

While this area is so open to entry, it also has a diverse internal geography full of mountains, steep gorges, and narrow valleys. This natural environment helps account for a geopolitical setting whose ethnographic make-up is remarkably heterogeneous. Among the different ethnic and national groups living in this region in the twentieth century are Albanians, Bosnians, Croats, Gypsies, Hercegovinans, Hungarians, Jews, Macedonians, Montenegrins, Romanians, Serbs, Slovaks, Slovenes, and Turks. This diversity is further accentuated by the variety of religions adhered to among the population. In order to deepen our understanding of these cleavages it is useful to return to the past.

Antiquity

Because of its geography, this region has always been open to invasion from both east and west. This is demonstrated by the Roman invasion of the Balkan peninsula in antiquity and later by the Ottoman, Austro-Hungarian, and Nazi occupations. In antiquity, this region was inhabited by Thracians, Illyrians, and Celtic tribes. When the Romans first began to expand into the Balkans, they found several powerful Greco-Illyrian kingdoms occupying the Albanian coast. Although Roman attacks on these Illyrian tribes began as early as the third century B.C., it was not until the wars of Octavian in 35–33 B.C. that they were brought under Roman rule. Despite an attempt at rebellion, the Illyrians were completely subjugated by 9 A.D. Illyria became a Roman province in the first century B.C.

The Romans continued to extend their frontiers beyond the Danube and even to the banks of the Dniester throughout the first and second centuries A.D., but later the defenses in this region were fairly neglected and became thus prone to attacks by the Germanic tribes from the north and east. In 285 A.D. the emperor Diocletian, himself a native of Dalmatia, divided the empire into east and west. Although the emperor Constantine reunited the empire, a second division was made in 395 A.D. after the death of Theodosius in order to split the empire between his two sons. The dividing line ran north-south from the Sava near Sirmium (Sremska Mitrovica) to Lake Scutari (Skadar) on the present Montenegrin-Albanian border and deeply affected the historical development of Europe:

> This line became a permanent feature on the cultural line of Europe, separating Byzantium from Rome, the Greek from the Roman cultural heritage, the Eastern Orthodox from the Roman Catholic Church and the users of the Cyrillic script from those of the Latin (Singleton 1985: 11).

The internal weakening of the Roman empire, resulting from the recession of economic life and the slow decay of state organization, was also accompanied by persistent and growing attacks by different Germanic tribes on its borders. The Roman provinces in the Balkans were spared a direct attack by the Goths, who destroyed the boundary system along the lower Danube. However, the Goths were not able to withstand the Hun incursions from the steppes of Central Asia in 448 which brought widespread devastation to the area. Particularly hard hit were the towns in the northern regions, such as Sirmium (near present day Sremska Mitrovica), Singidunum (Belgrade), Naissus (Nis), Poetovio (Ptuj) and Emona (Ljubljana).

After the collapse of the Western Roman Empire in 476 A.D. and the establishment of the kingdom of the Ostrogoths under Theodoric in Italy, Dalmatia, Pannonia, and Noricum joined the kingdom. The Ostrogoths did not settle into the western Balkan provinces in any great numbers and had great respect for the old Roman system. Their rule brought a level of stability to the region, making it possible to repair the damage brought on by the Huns. Ostrogoth rule in the western part of the Balkan peninsula was interrupted by the emperor Justinian (527–565), the ruler of Byzantium. In 535 Justinian's fleet conquered Salona, the capital of Dalmatia. Within a short time all the Balkan provinces were ruled by the emperor. Justinian's rule was short lived, however. The emperor's massive military manoeuvres had left few troops to protect the territories bordering the Danube: the Huns had left the region sparsely populated and therefore more open to invasion.[1]

The Slavs took advantage of this situation by entering the Balkans. Basically an agricultural people, they were themselves frequently the victims of attacks by the nomadic hordes that swept across Eastern Europe. It was as vassals of such nomadic tribes that the Slavs spread into southern Russia and Pannonia from an area located in what is now central Poland. By 517 A.D. groups of Slavs were crossing the Danube to raid in Thrace, Macedonia, Thessaly, and Epirus. Slavs were also moving toward the Dalmatian coast. In an attempt to neutralize the threat caused by the Slavic invasion, imperial officials in Constantinople offered the Slavs on the lower Danube the status of foederati, in which status they would act as paid border guards for the empire. The Slavs, however, chose instead to become vassals of the Avars, a new Turkic horde of nomads who appeared on the southern Russian steppe.

The Avars had successfully driven the remaining Germanic tribes from the Pannonian plain where they established a state that loosely controlled the Slavic settlers. Both the Avars and their Slavic vassals plundered cities and towns throughout the Balkans. The devastation seems to have been very widespread. John of Ephesus, a contemporary, but not a witness, to the Avar invasions of the Balkans, stated:

> today they still are established and installed in Roman provinces, killing, burning, and pillaging, having learned to make war better than the Romans. (John of Ephesus, quoted in Fine 1983: 31)

Usually, the ravaging of territory was followed by permanent Slavic settlements being made in the devastated villages. Between 591 and 602, the Byzantines made several unsuccessful attacks on the Avar-Slavic armies. The Slavs moved without resistance through the Balkan peninsula, populating it anew.

Although it is true that much of the indigenous population was killed or forced into slavery, many continued to live among the Slavic settlers. Others withdrew to the mountains or to remote regions: their descendants today are Albanians. Most of the Greek and Latin speaking populations took refuge in fortified Byzantine cities. Nothing is known of the fate of the Thracian people.[2] There is considerable archaeological evidence that shows a cultural continuity from the pre-Slavic to the Slavic population and that, overall, the descendants of the indigenous population were assimilated into Slavic culture.

In 626 A.D. the Byzantines won a decisive victory, first against the Avars and then the Persians, marking the decline of both these empires. It was also at this point that the Byzantine emperor Heraclius invited the Croats and the Serbs, two strong tribes from beyond the Carpathian Mountains, to settle in land held by the Avars in the northwestern Balkans. As vassals of Byzantium, they took control of Dalmatia and then of territory that was thereafter called Croatia and Serbia.

The Schism between Greek and Latin Christendom

The Christian community in Europe had once been a united political entity, the Roman Empire, with one undivided church. Even before the founding of Constantinople in 330 A.D. certain cultural and linguistic differences emerged between the Greek (Eastern) and Latin (Western) halves of Christendom. The foundation of the German kingdoms in the West in the following centuries added an element of political disunity to Christian Europe. The political schism between East and West occurred in 800 when the pope crowned Charlemagne as the Holy Roman Emperor in denial of Byzantine claims.

What has traditionally been considered the definitive break between the Greek and Roman branches of the church occurred in 1054 when mutual excommunications took place of papal legates and of Patriach Cerularius at the Church of St. Sophia in Constantinople. But even this ecclesiastical schism and the mutual distrust engendered by the first crusades did not irreparably damage relations between East and West. Western travellers on their way to Jerusalem continued to be well received in the Greek East.

The mounting hostility between East and West became a permanent feature after the Fourth Crusade. In 1204, the Latin army, led by the Venetians, and under the guise of a holy crusade, sacked Constantinople and carved up the Byzantine Empire, forcibly imposing Roman Catholicism on the Greek people. The Venetians were undoubtedly motivated by greed and the desire to destroy their most competitive trading rival. In his book *Byzantine East & Latin West*, Deno John Geanakoplos states that the Fourth Crusade destroyed Greco-Latin relations:

> the growing animosity of the Greeks for the Latins was transformed into a mass revulsion, a permanent hostility that permeated every level of society and was to poison all subsequent relations between the two peoples. It is at this point, when the ecclesiastical schism became ethnic and political as well as religious in scope, that the break between the two churches may be said to have been truly consummated. (Geanakoplos 1966: 1–2)

As we shall demonstrate, the hostility between the Greek and Latin churches was to profoundly affect relations between the Croatian and Serbian peoples.

Medieval Croatia and Serbia

The demarcation line between the Roman and Byzantine civilizations, the Roman Catholic and Greek-Orthodox churches, and the Austro-Hungarian and Ottoman empires has separated Serbs and Croats for centuries. Although these two peoples speak the same language and came to the Balkans during the same period in history, they experienced quite separate historical developments.

Croatia was flourishing economically and culturally in the tenth and eleventh centuries, but began to experience serious difficulties when it found itself squeezed between the Hungarians advancing from the north to the Adriatic and the Venetians advancing from the south. In 1102 the Croats were forced to accept the suzerainty of the Hungarians and since then Croatia has embraced Catholicism and come under the influence of the Vatican. Despite the Hungarian occupation of Croatia, Croat nobles continued to govern their own internal affairs. When the Ottomans defeated the Magyars at Mahacs in 1526, seizing a good portion of Hungarian lands, the Croat nobility put the province under the protection of the Hapsburg Emperor.

Vienna viewed Croatia as a strategic military outpost against the Ottomans and crucial to its survival. Croatian independence was suppressed so as to serve the interests of the Holy Roman Empire. The authority of the Croatian parliament (or estates) was restricted in order to form the "military frontiers" over which the Emperor himself had sole authority. As the Hapsburg's war against the Ottomans pushed southeastward in the years after 1683, liberating Hungary and Slavonia-Srem, the border territories were settled by new Serb immigrants who had fled from the Ottomans in Serbia into Croatia and Voyvodina which were thus added to these "military frontiers."

Hundreds of thousands of Serbs moved out of the Ottoman Empire and into the regions of Krajina and Slavonia in the seventeenth century. They were well received by Austrian authorities, given free land, various privileges, and a high level of autonomy, with the obligation to defend the borders. They were ruled directly from Vienna and were never subordinate to any Croatian authorities. Serbia continued its existence and even expanded first under Stevan Nemanji and later under Dushan the Mighty, when in 1345 it became an empire that included Thessaly, Epirus, and Albania. After the death of Dushan, the Serbian state was unable to withstand an Ottoman invasion. Following defeat by the Ottomans at Marica (1371) and Kosovo (1389), Serbia endured five hundred years of vassalage under the Ottoman Empire. The battle of Kosovo was later to become a significant memory for Serbian nationalism. Serbian folk songs and poetry still emphasize a Serbian moral superiority over the Ottomans. Today Serbs still celebrate the battle of Kosovo as their national holiday.

The memory of the battle of Kosovo has played an important role in preserving Serbian national identity. The Serbian church romanticized Kosovo and would relate the story to their parishioners. The death of the Serbian prince Lazar, executed by the Ottomans after the battle, was used by the church to symbolize the atonement for all the sins of Serbia (those sins that had brought the wrath of God against Serbia and had made the Serbs lose their independence). By placing such a strong emphasis on the teaching of the battle of Kosovo, the church was able to maintain the memory of Serbian independence. In addition to teaching the legend of Prince Lazar and the battle of Kosovo in church, it was also expressed in Serbian epic poetry and continues to be taught in Serbian schools. By keeping this legend alive, the Serbians were not only able to hold onto their national identity, they were also being taught that it was acceptable to fight against tyranny (in this case represented by the Ottoman empire). Kosovo has become the symbol for all Serbian national movements, whether the movement be anti-Ottoman or anti-Croatian (Emmert 1990: 121).

Serbs have always had a strong sense of national unity, even under the Ottomans. Each Serbian village was governed directly by the traditional chief or knez and groups of villages elected representatives to deal with Ottoman authorities. The preservation of local government served to foster Serb rebellion, as did the various groups of outlaws who roamed the mountains and preyed on travellers. The Serbian church, with its patriarchate at Pec was also a reminder of national unity. The Serbs rose in rebellion several times during the Ottoman occupation. One major revolt took place in 1593 and was not quashed until 1606. The Serbian patriarchate was abolished by the Ottomans in 1766 and the Serbian church was put directly under the authority of the Greek patriarch in Constantinople.

The Ottoman Empire

The Ottoman Empire first established itself on the European mainland in 1354. As an active and aggressive military organization comprised of dedicated frontier warriors, the Ottoman armies took Adrianople (Edirne) in 1362, making it their capital. From this center the Ottoman armies moved up the Maritsa and Vardar valleys against the Christian states of the Balkans and marched into Europe virtually unchecked; in 1453 they took control of Constantinople. The empire then included most of Bosnia, Bulgaria, Greece, and Serbia. Although some isolated areas still resisted, no major center of opposition remained. Constantinople (Istanbul) became the capital of the empire.

It is important to emphasize that, in this case, the conquering power was a Muslim state. Ottoman leaders divided their peoples by religion and not nationality. An individual could join the ruling group by converting to Islam. A large proportion of the Slavic population converted to Islam during the centuries of Ottoman occupation (Burg 1983: 3).[3] Non-Muslims were divided into religious communities called millets: Orthodox, Gregorian Armenian, Roman Catholic, and Jewish. Each group was under the direction of its own religious head. Thus, for the Balkan people, the vast majority of whom were Orthodox, the titular leader was the patriarch of Constantinople. In practice, however, the Balkan Orthodox church organization became divided into its national components. For example, the Serbians had their own patriarchate at Pec and the Bulgarians had a metropolitanate at Ohrid. National separateness was preserved through ecclesiastical organizations.

The principal interest of Ottoman officials in the Balkans was the collection of taxes to pay for the military and civil administration of the empire. As only Muslims could hold office in the empire or serve in the military forces, many Balkan Christians converted, eventually forming a large part of the military and administrative apparatus of the state. However, the highest civil and military officials were the children of Christian subjects taken from the Balkan provinces through a tribute of children levied only in that part of the empire. Specially educated for the sultan's service, they depended on his favour for their advancement and could be discharged or executed at his will (Wolff 1986: 59).

The subordinate position of all non-Muslims was constantly emphasized. They were forced to carry an unequal share of the tax burden of the empire. Although non-Muslims were not subject to military conscription, they were assessed a special tax as a replacement. They also were liable to other services and payments which were attributes of their secondary status within the state, particularly in times of war. This secondary status was accorded only to Christians and Jews because they were considered "people of the book" and, thus, considered as superior to heathens. Despite these and other severe disabilities, there were relatively few examples of mass conversions, with the exception of those that occurred in Bosnia, Albania, and Crete.

Despite the long existence of the empire, signs of weakness appeared in its structure as early as the reign of Suleyman (1494–1566). The Ottoman system could not function well without good direction from the top. Until Suleyman, the state had been remarkably fortunate in its rulers, but among the seventeen sultans that followed, few were men of ability. With the lack of direction from the top, the administration became increasingly more inept and corrupt.

Christians, together with their Muslim neighbours, were directly affected by the decline of the Ottoman administration. Among the most severe consequences of the breakdown of the Ottoman government was the rise of lawlessness throughout the peninsula. As the central authority grew weaker, local Muslim leaders throughout the empire established what were in effect small principalities from which they were able to defy Istanbul and make war among themselves. Christian bands of robbers also existed in large numbers. Their activities, together with the destruction caused by the Ottoman wars of the eighteenth century, made certain areas uninhabitable for long periods. The Serbians, in particular, suffered from the corruption and lawlessness of the time. Their lands were the scene of repeated struggles between local Muslim leaders in addition to the Ottoman battles against the encroaching armies of Austria, Venice, Poland, and Russia.

The Rise of Balkan Nationalism

In Balkan history the French Revolution and the Napoleonic Wars mark the shift from the long period of Ottoman domination into the era of the national revolutions of the nineteenth century. To some extent, the stage had been set in the eighteenth century, when both Russia and Austria appealed to the Balkan subject populations for assistance against the Ottoman Empire. It was through these wars that the weakness of the Ottoman military became known. Moreover, Balkan nationals who had fought in these wars had learned modern military methods and were armed. Equally important, the period of war and internal upset had opened the area to outside influences. The national and liberal ideologies of revolutionary France provided a program that would allow Balkan leaders to combat not only Ottoman political control but also the stifling cultural influence of their Christian church hierarchies.

Balkans leaders did not receive the support of other European powers, however. After the Napoleonic Wars (1803–1815), the Great Powers (Austria, Russia, France, and Great Britain) desired social and political stability. Revolutionary methods and liberal-national programs were not encouraged. Subject Christian peoples could no longer expect aid or sympathy from abroad. At the same time, it was also apparent to the European powers that the Ottoman Empire was in a dangerous condition of internal decay and military weakness. The question of the fate of the Ottoman territories and of the control of that government became perhaps the most important single diplomatic problem for Europe in the century after the Congress of Vienna (1814–1815). This issue, the so-called "Eastern Question," was the direct cause of the

Crimean War and World War I. Despite a lack of support from abroad, the Balkan peoples rose in rebellion against Ottoman and Austro-Hungarian rule. At the beginning of the nineteenth century the Hapsburgs ruled the northwestern part of the Balkans, while the Ottomans dominated the main, central, and southern regions of the peninsula. The development of a national renaissance among the Balkan peoples varied according to the different political and social conditions prevailing in these areas: political development occurred under the Hapsburgs, and revolutionary upheavals predominated under the Ottomans.

Nationalist Ideology: Hegemony or Negation

At the end of the nineteenth century, South Slavic intellectuals believed it was their birthright to have their own state. They believed that speakers of various South Slavic dialects could be encompassed within the frame of a single literary language, variously called Serbo-Croatian, Croatio-Serbian, Croatian, or Serbian. The view that this common language identified areas that should be enveloped within a Serbian nation state was espoused by Vuk Stefanovic Karadzic (1787–1864), said to be the single most influential Serb in modern history, and whose work greatly contributed to Serbian and Croatian linguistic unity. Karadzic argued that everyone who used any of three variants of the Serbo-Croatian dialect was a Serb. He then identified the lands in which Serbs lived, namely in Serbia, northern Macedonia, Kosovo, Bosnia, Vojvodina, Slavonia, Croatia, Dalmatia, and Istria. In short, he argued against religion as a defining factor of national identity (Jelavich 1990: 31–33). Throughout the nineteenth century, the goal of the Serbian government, as well as of the politicians of all parties, religious leaders, military spokesmen, intellectuals, teachers, and peasants was to pursue the unification of the Serbian nation along the lines expressed in Vuk Karadzic's writings (Jelavich 1990: 38). Moreover, Serbian nationalist ideology merged with a concept of the expanded Serbian state that would include both Serbs and other South Slavs. The predominant Serbian assumptions about statehood therefore became hegemonic, following the model of nation-state building elsewhere in Europe (Denich 1994: 372).

The Serbian or pan-Yugoslav view was challenged in the late nineteenth century by Croatian nationalists who vehemently argued that Croatia constituted a separate nation entitled to its own state. The intellectual father of this Croatian nationalism, Ante Starcevic, constructed an ideological opposition between Croat and Serb that defined Croatian statehood in terms requiring the exclusion of Serbs (Denich 1994: 373). According to this view, "there could be only one political people in a given state, and the Croats, as the bearers of the individual Croat state right, were the sole political people on the territory of Starcevic's Great Croatia" (Banac 1984: 86).

In terms of language and shared history, Croats in ethnically mixed areas often had more in common with their neighbours of other religions than they did with more distant Catholics living under other rulers. In the absence of one unifying historical or cultural Croatian identity, Starcevic's attempts to establish conceptual boundaries were fraught with contradiction. Insofar as the primary marker at the folk level consisted of religious practice, the differentiation between Croat and Serb coincided with the Catholic/Orthodox distinction.

Since Starcevic's territorial aspirations also included Bosnia-Hercegovina, with its large Muslim population, he resolved that these Muslims were actually Islamized Croats. In contrast to the Serbs, the Muslims in Bosnia-Hercegovina had no national statehood ideology and were therefore not perceived as a threat to Croatian statehood ideology (Denich 1994: 373).

To further legitimize the claim that Croats constituted a distinct nation, entitled to their own state, Starcevic revived archaic usages and invented new words to artificially separate a Croatian literary language from the common Serbo-Croatian linguistic stock. It is interesting to note that Starcevic's ideas were later advocated by Ante Pavelic and the Ustashi.

After 1918, the domination of the new state of Yugoslavia by the Belgrade government provided a realistic basis for anti-Serbian sentiment on the part of Croats. But it is important to note that ideological anti-Serbianism had long antedated the legitimate grievances of non-Serbs in post-1918 Yugoslavia; the annihilative attitude toward Serbian cultural identity on territory coveted for an independent Croatia also predated the Yugoslav state (Denich 1994: 374).

A New Yugoslav State

With the fall of the Austro-Hungarian Empire at the end of World War I, it became possible for a Yugoslav state to be formed. This state was made up of different ethnic and religious groups, but had a definite Serbian majority. The constitutional structure of the new state was decided upon in 1921 by a constituent assembly that adopted a centralist constitution despite Croatian objections. The Croatian Peasant Party of Stjepan Radic, which emerged as the most powerful political group in Croatia after the introduction of universal male suffrage in the new state, refused to support the new constitution. Although he wanted a federated republican state, Radic was an opportunist, allowing Croatian Peasant Party deputies to sit in the Yugoslav parliament. At a turbulent session of parliament in 1928, Radic was shot and killed by a Montenegrin deputy.

It was at this point that Alexander I, the former prince regent of Serbia (1914–1921) and king of Yugoslavia, decided that parliamentary government had become impossible. In 1929 he set up a dictatorship, putting severe restrictions on the press and dissolving all political parties. In 1931 he divided the country into nine administrative provinces, with the object of breaking down old provincial loyalties. However, while visiting Marseilles in 1934 the king was assassinated. Alexander had believed that his rule would prevent political chaos in Yugoslavia; instead it contributed to the turmoil.

After 1933, as fascist and Nazi ideologies became widespread in neighbouring countries, fascists began to infiltrate the Croatian Peasant Party. In 1939, Radic's successor Vladimir Macek, undertook secret negotiations with Italy with the object of creating a separate Croatian state. The Yugoslav government thereupon reached an agreement with the Croatian Peasant Party, whose terms united Dalmatia, Croatia, and a small part of Bosnia into a single province called the banovina of Croatia. This agreement satisfied neither the Croats or the Serbs.

On March 25, 1941, Yugoslavia signed the Tripartite Pact, allying itself with Hitler. Two days later, a bloodless coup d'état took place in Belgrade, led by the Serbian general Dusan Simovic. In response, the Germans attacked Belgrade and the Italians attacked Dalmatia; Hungarian and Bulgarian troops also invaded the country. The Yugoslav army surrendered within two weeks.

Croatia welcomed the invading German armies and accepted Ante Pavelic as its leader. Pavelic had been espousing Croatian nationalism since the 1920s when he helped to form the Croatian National Movement. It was in the atmosphere of Serbian domination under King Alexander that the Croatian independence movement defined its program. Evidence of fascist influence was also very strong. While attending a conference in Paris, Pavelic was warmly received by representatives of Benito Mussolini who offered to support the military training of his Croat nationalist followers. Training camps for

Pavelic's Ustashi movement were set up in Bovigno, Vichetto, Borgotaro, San Fontecchio, and San Demetrio. The Ustashi were considered the paramilitary wing of the Croatian Nationalist Party. Pavelic also followed a racial ideology, believing the Croats were Aryan in origin, therefore having no place in a Pan-Slavic state.[4]

Besides being influenced by the Nazis' anti-Semitic and racist ideology, Pavelic was also fanatically anti-Serbian and pro-Catholic. Anti-Serbian sentiment had already been expressed throughout the nineteenth century when Croatian intellectuals began to make plans for their own national state. They viewed the presence of more than one million Serbs in Krajina and Slavonia as intolerable. While some Croats saw the solution in the creation of a common Yugoslav state with the Serbs and Slovenes, most believed that Orthodox Serbs must somehow be eliminated, either through converting them to Catholicism or by expelling them. As the leader of a Croatian nationalist party, Pavelic had inherited a rich tradition of extreme anti-Serbian sentiment (Dedijer 1992: 10).[5] The dominance of Pavelic's Ustashi and the Axis victory in Yugoslavia would spell disaster for both the Serbian and Jewish populations in Croatia.

By May 1941 Yugoslavia was divided among the Axis powers and ceased to exist as a state. Germany occupied Northern Slovenia, the Banat, and Serbia. Hungary acquired Backa and Baranja, the remaining two sections of the Voyvodina, and several smaller adjacent areas. Italy annexed Southern Slovenia and most of the Dalmatian littoral and also occupied a considerable portion of the interior regions in the south, bordering on Albania. Bulgaria acquired most of Macedonia. The remaining territory, including Bosnia-Hercegovina, was handed over to the Croatian nationalists and became the Independent State of Croatia.

The Killing of Jews in the Independent States of Croatia and Serbia, 1939–1945

In Serbia, Nazi authorities immediately set up their genocidal policy against the Jewish population. On May 30, 1941, German authorities in Belgrade issued a definition of who was a Jew, removed all Jews from public service and the professions, made it mandatory to register all Jewish property, introduced forced labour, forbade any citizen to hide Jews, and forced all Jews to wear a yellow star.

By July, Jews were being arrested and a number put to death in retaliation for Communist activities. In August several concentration camps were set up and a systematic round-up of Jewish men began all over Serbia and in the Banat. In October some 4,000 Jewish men were shot by the German army. Women and children were also rounded up and sent to Sajmiste, a concentration camp erected in Zemun across the river from Belgrade. During the spring and summer of 1942, more than 6,000 women and children were killed in gas vans. By August 1942 Serbia was declared *judenrein*.

In the Independent State of Croatia, it was the Ustashi who implemented anti-Jewish policies. Discriminatory regulations, similar to those in Serbia, were issued as early as April 30, 1941. The Ustashi began killing large numbers of Croatian and Bosnian Jews in the summer of 1941. Sarajevo's Jews disappeared by August 1942; Zagreb's in 1944. Most were sent to concentration camps, the most notorious being the torture camp of Jasenovac where Jews and other "undesirable elements" were interned and more often murdered. It was located in a small city in Slavonia near the Bosnian border and was the largest camp set up by the Croatian government. Those who did not die in Jasenovac were deported to Auschwitz or other death camps. By the end of 1944, the only Jews to remain on Croatian territory were those who were recognized as "honorary Aryans": Jewish partners in mixed marriages, and children of intermarriages.

Approximately 55,000 to 60,000 of Yugoslavia's Jews, nearly 80 percent of the region's prewar Jewish population, were murdered in the Holocaust (Freidenreich 1979: 190–93).

The Killing of Gypsies in Serbia and Croatia, 1941–1945

Gypsies had been living in the Balkans since the thirteenth century. By the twentieth century, the majority of Gypsies living in Croatia and Serbia had given up their nomadism in favour of a more sedentary lifestyle and were well-established in villages. When World War II broke out, many Gypsies in Croatia and Slovenia sought refuge in Italy, where they were interned and deported to Sardinia. Others were detained at Puglia, though many escaped, some choosing to join the partisans. Those who entered Italy after the creation of the Independent State of Croatia in 1941 were sheltered in detention camps by the Italians in order to keep them from recrossing into Yugoslavia in search of relatives. Many of them were given Italian identity cards to put them further beyond the reach of the Nazis and the Ustashi in 1943 (Reinhartz 1991: 84).

Like the Jews, Gypsies were also viewed by the Nazis and the Ustashi officials of the Independent State of Croatia as "racially inferior" and targeted for extermination. In Croatia, under the Decree No. 13–542 of the Ministry of the Interior, all Gypsies had to register with the police on 22–23 July 1941. Thereafter, Gypsy businesses and other property were confiscated and "Aryanized." Between 1941 and 1943 most of Croatia's Gypsies were put into Ustashi-manned concentration camps like Jasenovak, Tenje, and Satra Gradska (Reinhartz 1991: 88). By the summer of 1942, these Gypsies, like those in Serbia, were being transported to camps for "medical" experimentation and more systematic extermination at Auschwitz and other camps outside Yugoslavia.[6]

Many Gypsies were also executed in reprisal for Chetnik or Partisan activities within Croatia. Since Gypsies were often not welcome in the Chetnik organization, many joined the Partisans and sometimes formed their own resistance groups in the mountain regions. Approximately 26,000 Gypsies were murdered by the Ustashi in the Independent State of Croatia.

At the time of the German occupation of Serbia, over 100,000 Gypsies lived in Serbia, with 10,000 in Belgrade alone. Gypsies were defined by the Nazis as those having at least three Gypsy grandparents and were viewed as racially inferior. The local German commander Straatsrat Harald Turner, chief of civil administration and an SS Gruppenführer under General Franz Böhme, the commander of troops within Serbia, stated:

> The Gypsy cannot, by reason of his inner and outer makeup, be a useful member of international society.... As a matter of principle it must be said that the Jews and the Gypsies represent an element of insecurity and thus a danger to public order and safety. (Staatstrat Harald Turner, quoted in Reinhartz 1991: 89)

As in Croatia, Gypsies were targeted in reprisal for resistance activity. Others were put into concentration camps and forced to work as grave diggers. Over 20,000 Gypsies perished in the Semlin camp alone. Fortunately, the Germans only controlled about one third of the Gypsy population within Serbia, as the majority succeeded in fleeing the region or in joining the resistance (Reinhartz 1991: 88–89).

The Massacre of Serbs in the Independent State of Croatia

The establishment of the Independent State of Croatia in 1941 provided Croats with the opportunity to murder hundreds of thousands of Serbs. This was a genocide by Croatian Roman Catholics, often with Muslim support, against Serbian Orthodox Christians. The religious side to this genocide should not be underrated. Catholic priests took part in the killings and conducted ceremonies of forced conversion. Although Serbs could sometimes escape being killed if they converted to Catholicism, conversion was in no way a guarantee they would not be killed by the Ustashi. There is also evidence that these killings were condoned by high levels of the Catholic hierarchy.[7]

When Pavelic's government took power in Croatia, the Ustashi began mass arrests of Jews, Gypsies, and Serbs. In accordance with their ideas of racial purity and the nation, these groups were singled out for annihilation. Croats who had expressed an anti-fascist stance were also targeted and, like Serbs, Jews, and Gypsies, sent to concentration camps. Most Serbs were sent to Jasenovac death camp where hundreds of thousands of people, mostly Orthodox Serbs, were murdered.[8] The exact number of people murdered at Jasenovac will never be known. Besides the obvious problems of documentation and the fact that many of the victims were cremated so as not to leave evidence behind, most of the victims were buried in mass graves on the banks of the Save river, where their bones are being uncovered even today when water levels are low. Thousands were also murdered and then thrown directly into the Save which then carried the bodies down river into Belgrade and sometimes even into the Danube.

The Ustashi were not particular in their choice of weapons: they used revolvers, carbines, machine guns, knives, axes, hatchets, wooden hammers, iron bars, iron hammers, hoes, belts, and leather whips, hanging, burning, trampling, freezing, poison gas, suffocation and starvation to kill their victims (Dedijer 1992: 54–56). The killings were so bloody that German Nazis, not normally very sensitive in this regard, protested their brutality (Gottfried Niemietz, editor's preface, in Dedijer 1992: 27). The victims included men, women, and children.

There is evidence that the Nazis planned to use Serbia and Croatia as a place for repopulation by Germans, once having finished killing the Jewish and Gypsy population. Serbs would either be resettled elsewhere or annihilated. Serbs, as Slavs, were viewed by the Nazis as racially inferior. Although the Independent State of Croatia took an active role in the killing of Serbs, it was done with the approval and, often, with the active participation, of Nazi officials (Dedijer et al. 1974: 577–79).

The Resistance

The centuries-old Balkan tradition of guerilla warfare and banditry facilitated the transition from standing army to resistance fighters. For example, instead of facing surrender and internment, many Serbian officers and their men fled to the forests to await the moment when they could fight again. The region's geography is extremely suitable for guerilla warfare and accounts for much of the success that the resistance had against the occupying Axis powers. There were two resistance forces operating in Serbia and Croatia: the loyalist Chetniks and the communist Partisans. Both guerilla organizations were fighting the Axis powers, but they were too ideologically at odds to succeed in joining forces.

The Chetniks began their struggle as early as May 1941. Draza Mihailovich, with the support of the government-in-exile and the Allies, led the Chetniks into the mountains in Ravna Gora to wage war against the Nazis and the Ustashi. Mihailovich, a Serbian, was an ardent monarchist and his supporters tended toward an ultraconservative ideology. The Chetniks were most active in Nazi-occupied Serbia.

Within months, Josip Broz Tito, a leading member of the Communist party of Yugoslavia, emerged as the head of the Partisans. Backed by the Soviets and the Comintern, Tito and his followers sought a united socialist Yugoslavia where ethnic divisions would be erased in favor of the state. At first the Axis powers underestimated the numbers and skill of the resistance forces. By September of 1941, Chetnik and Partisan attacks had become such a threat that orders were issued for reprisals against the civilian population in response to Serb ambushes. For every German soldier killed, one hundred civilian hostages were to be executed; for every soldier injured, fifty civilians were to be killed. One particularly brutal reprisal took place in October 1941. In response to a Chetnik ambush, Nazi commander Major König rounded up the entire male population of Kragujevak, including several hundred schoolboys from grade five and up. 7,000 men and boys were gunned down by machine guns in a field just outside of town.

Ultimately, the Partisans were the more successful and aggressive of the two resistance groups, committed to a strategy of ceaseless struggle against the occupiers, no matter what the cost. Mihailovich, in addition to his obvious concern over Nazi reprisals, became increasingly convinced that the Partisans were an even worse enemy than the Nazis. The Chetniks even participated in joint actions with both the Germans and the Italians against the Partisans in 1942. Mihailovich lost British support for his cause in 1943 and was ultimately discredited; his Chetnik organization eventually disintegrated.

There is no doubt that the Partisans participated in the massacre of civilians during and after the war. Ustashi forces and anyone deemed a supporter of the Ustashi, including entire villages, were targeted by the Partisans. As the end of the war drew near, the number of such massacres increased alarmingly and tens of thousands of people were killed.[9]

Yugoslavia under Tito

When the Yugoslav communists took power under Tito in spring of 1945, they displayed a great degree of self-confidence in both their domestic and foreign policies. The Tito regime launched an ambitious industrialization program preceded by the most rapid and sweeping nationalization program in Eastern Europe. Tito also displayed independence from Soviet control in his foreign policy, most notably during the Greek civil war when he was the chief supporter of the communists.

Tito's confidence that he would continue to receive widespread internal support rested to a large degree on his knowledge that his own aims were in relative harmony with the nationalist aspirations of the peoples of Yugoslavia. What he offered was protection from traditional enemies: the Slovenes from Italy and Germany, the Croats from Italy and Serbia, and the Macedonians from Greece and Serbia, but also from Bulgaria. The Serbs, however, received less than the total dominance they had previously enjoyed in the prewar kingdom (Cviic 1991: 26–27).

The main reason for Tito's success in keeping peace in this region was his complete monopoly over the use of force and the constant threat of using that force should anyone dare to break with the union. But while Titoism embraced all ethnicities within an overarching ideology, it never actually replaced the nineteenth-century definition which equated "nation" with "people." Thus, the Serbs, Croats, and other "peoples" were ethnically defined, and each accorded an ambiguous hegemonic status within its own "republic." Since mixed populations prevail through much of Yugoslavia, the ideological definition of the republics as nation-states failed to recognize their multicultural realities (Denich 1994: 375–76).

The Titoist regime suppressed not only the nationalism of the past, but also any reminder of the Ustashi genocide against Serbs and the subsequent revenge killings of Croats in the immediate postwar period. The regime felt that the subject itself was too threatening to the social order.[10] However, the memory of past horrors did not disappear, but remained a hidden, ticking time bomb waiting for another opportunity to explode.

Many contemporary authors point to the Tito era as the root of the present-day conflict in the former Yugoslavia. We argue that the roots go, in fact, much deeper. While we agree that the Tito era must be included among the antecedents of the present conflict, a more in depth study of this period and its aftermath is not within the scope of this chapter.

The Abuse of History

In light of recent events in the former Yugoslavia, the history of this region may seem remote and unimportant. One must remember, however, that the players in this conflict justify their actions by looking to the past. History is regularly distorted and brought back to life as a means of fanning the flames of nationalism and ethnic hatred.

During a visit to Zagreb in 1992, Daniel Chirot came upon a book entitled *Historical Maps of Croatia*, published on behalf of the government of Croatia in 1992, that claims that Croatia was first mentioned in 500 B.C. on an inscription of Darius the Great of Persia (Chirot 1994: 423–25). In reality, Croatia does not appear in recorded history until more than a thousand years later. The claim that Croats are somehow descended from the Persians stems from the desire on the part of Croatian nationalists to separate themselves from the Serbs despite the fact that the two groups are linguistically almost identical. During World War II, the myth of Persian roots made it possible for Croatian fascists to identify themselves as Aryans, to ally themselves with the Nazis, and to provide a "pseudo-scientific basis" for the mass murder of hundreds of thousands of Serbs. It is also interesting that *Historical Maps of Croatia* omits any mention of the Croatian massacre of Serbs in World War II and chooses to cite only cases of massacres committed by Serbs.

Serbian extremists have exploited Croatia's insensitivity toward its fascist past and have used it to promote the idea that Serbs in Croatia would face another Jasenovac unless they fight back. Serbs have also been guilty of "historical mystification" based on distorted demographic and linguistic claims and calls for revenge. In both Croatia and Serbia these historical myths have been promoted, not by illiterate peasants, but by highly educated intellectuals. These myths are taught in schools and celebrated by national holidays (Chirot 1994: 423–25).

As we have demonstrated, this region has a long history of solving conflict with armed struggle. It also has an alarming tradition of massacring civilians in times of war. It is in such countries with a history of accepting violence as a means of solving conflict that further violations of gross human rights are likely to occur. Any efforts at prevention and intervention might well take cognizance of such historical roots of settling conflict by violent means.

Conclusion

At the time of writing, the fate of the former Yugoslavia has not yet been decided. However, what is already clear is that gross human rights violations have been committed by all sides. This paper has attempted to sketch, with broad strokes, some of the historical background against which current events must be understood. The news media do not usually supply such background information without which current events can only be misinterpreted. The burden of history hangs heavy over this beautiful country and, unfortunately, none of the ethnocentric and national movements will allow each other to forget it. Some of the massacres and starvation regimes, imposed on people once considered fellow citizens, certainly approached the level of genocidal massacres. Whether recent efforts at intervention and to negotiate peace will reestablish some semblance of normality in this region remains to be seen.

Notes

1. It is possible that the Hun attacks on the Balkan cities in Dalmatia were genocides or genocidal massacres, but there is not enough evidence to confirm this.
2. There is no evidence that adequately explains their fate, but it is possible that they were assimilated into Slavic society. Fine states that they simply "disappear from history" (Fine 1983: 37).
3. Burg states that, for the most part, Islamization was voluntary and peaceful.
4. Pavelic once explained to Hitler that the Croats "were not Slavs at all. They were Goths in origin, and the idea of them being Slavs had been forced upon them" (Pavelic, quoted in Dedijer et al. 1974: 577).
5. Dedijer also argues that this extreme anti-Serbianism played a large role in the nationalist Croatian mass movement in 1970–1971 and in the ruling Croatian Democratic Community of 1990.
6. For a description of the extermination of Gypsies within Auschwitz, see Hancock (1987: 74–78).
7. Dedijer gives countless examples of the Catholic clergy's direct involvement in organizing massacres and/or condoning these massacres. For example, he cites the case of Brale Bozidar, Roman Catholic pastor in

Sarajevo, who headed the Ustashi in that city. Brale acted with the approval of his superior, Archbishop Saric, who promoted him to the position of honourary head of the archbishopric of Upper Bosnia one month after he assumed leadership of the Ustashi. After the war, Brale was found guilty of war crimes by the High Court for Bosnia, having instigated, commanded and organized the arrest, torture, forced emigration, and transport of Serbs and Jews to concentration camps (Dedijer 1992: 176–79).

8. For more discussion of sources used to uncover Croatian atrocities at Jasenovac, see Dedijer (1992: 54–56).
9. For a discussion of atrocities committed by the Partisans, see Krarpandzich (1980: passim).
10. Denich (1994: 369–70) shows that when the Titoist regime acknowledged the horrors of the past, it did so only by identifying collective categories, such as "victims of fascism" on the one side, and "foreign occupiers and domestic traitors" on the other. Thus the monument erected at Jasenovac did not specifically identify the ethnic identities of either the perpetrator or the victims.

Afterword

In order not to conclude on a too depressing note, I am adding the following suggestions for a more humane future. Since the members of the international community are not willing to agree on an enforcement mechanism for all the noble instruments that they have passed, perhaps they can be convinced to collaborate on shaming campaigns. A theory of shaming has been developed by John Braithwaite although he has not extended it to apply to the international scene (Braithwaite 1989). That such shaming can be very effective has been shown by the case of Kurt Waldheim, the former United Nations secretary general, who was not even a major war criminal, but had merely lied about his war record. Although the Austrians elected him their president, his prestige was damaged to such an extent that he was unable to travel to most countries. He has since then disappeared into total obscurity. The major effect of such shaming would be that perpetrators would not be welcome in any other country. This assumes, of course, that potential host countries are able to withstand the blandishments of the ill-gotten fortunes that such perpetrators are often willing to bring with them. If such shaming is to have an effect, it will require the cooperation of the entire international community in refusing invitations and visas to perpetrators. Whether such persons will also be brought before an international court of justice will depend entirely on the international community's willingness to recognize such a court's jurisdiction and to establish an authority to carry out its sentences. These are among the questions currently being tested by the International Tribunal in The Hague.

However, in one important respect I have changed my mind. In my earlier writings about prevention and intervention I have placed far too much confidence in the good sense of the "powers that be" to support the implementation of the various human rights documents. I now believe that such a hope was naive and that many governmental and non-governmental organizations have quite different agendas. These agendas have a great deal more to do with money and power than most of them are prepared to admit in public. Individual human rights come very low on their agendas, in spite of the sanctimonious public relations efforts they sponsor when these are likely to accrue to their benefit.

To change such agendas will not be easy, as recent events have clearly demonstrated. Until the events in the former Yugoslavia gained momentum, many of us thought that there was now sufficient opposition to the perpetrators of gross violations of human rights to mobilize the signatories of the various international instruments against them. Many Holocaust scholars thought that the world did not interfere with the implementation of Hitler's plans for the Holocaust of the Jews and the operation of the death camps because of widespread, though latent, anti-Semitism. When Jewish refugees found most doors closed to them, and when the request to bomb the gas chambers and the crematoria in Auschwitz was refused, anti-Semitism seemed sufficient as an explanation. However, the terrible events in the former Yugoslavia have forced us to look reality in the eye and to acknowledge that anti-Semitism was, at most, a secondary issue. The unpalatable reality is that no major power bloc, nor the international community, cares enough about the victims of genocidal massacres to intervene on their behalf—unless it happens to further their power and/or financial interests.

Given this realization, further research ought to be guided by curiosity about the motivations of the perpetrators. Three important questions should deal with how they perceive their chances of increasing their domestic and/or international influence, how they define their economic goals, and what considerations determine their population policy.

The previous hopes that were placed on international law, international organizations, and their member countries' willingness to implement the instruments that they have signed with so much hypocrisy, turns out to have been entirely misplaced. The one hope that does remain is to place our confidence in the decency of ordinary people. Except for a few pathological types, ordinary people are not in favor of killings, massacres, and genocides. I like to think that one of these days these same ordinary people will become so outraged at the indifference of their governments that they will demand action with such unanimity that their governments will either act or face defeat at the next election. It often seems that people have become so inured to the continuing stream of bad news that they have ended up by ignoring it. However, that apathy may be a condition for maintaining one's sanity in the face of the media's daily concentration on horror stories from all parts of the world.[1] When this mechanism breaks down people are likely to turn on rulers who are willing to be either silent supporters or disinterested bystanders when perpetrators victimize their fellow citizens. The big question is when, where, and how such popular outrage will spill over into popular action. The potential for such action has been demonstrated in the past on several occasions; movements against the war in Vietnam, against the killing of the seals pups in the Canadian north, against the destruction of the few remaining rain forests in several parts of the world, etc. have demonstrated that the *vox populi* can make itself heard.

Another way in which the "voice of the people" has shown itself to be effective is in the widespread aversion toward the use of some of the more devastating methods of aggression. Such animus against biological and chemical warfare is undoubtedly one of the reasons they have not been used more frequently.

That there exists an enormous reservoir of good will and sympathy for victimized groups may be readily deduced from the number of volunteers that seem to be available to the various humanitarian organizations, as well as from the enormous amounts of money that people are willing to contribute to various aid efforts. Thus far, such efforts to assist victimized groups in several parts of the world have generally not been in conflict with domestic politics. This situation was possible because volunteers and donors have usually seen their contribution as supplementing whatever measures their own government was taking. This attitude may change as people become more aware of their governments' hidden agendas, of the misinformation that was made available to them, and the misuse to which their financial donations were sometimes put. Just one illustration will suffice to make the point: popular outrage is surely going to be wide-spread if ever the population at large becomes aware of the fact that there never was a shortage of food in either Ethiopia or Somalia and that the reported famines were manmade. There was plenty of food for the people with the guns and very little food for those without the guns. Clearly, such a situation requires prompt action, though shipping in additional food supplies hardly seems the most appropriate form of aid.

The voicing of popular outrage will occur when accurate and unbiased information becomes widely available. This can occur only in democratic societies, although even there we frequently observe powerful interest groups that attempt to prevent public access to such information. The defense of democratic governments is essential if access to information and the people's rights to express their opinions is to be preserved. That defense will not be very effective until we understand

294 Genocide and Gross Human Rights Violations

how democratic societies can, almost overnight, be transformed into totalitarian states.

This popular outrage can become widespread only in democracies. But it is also likely to spread to totalitarian and authoritarian societies when their people, unlike their governments, decide that they are no longer prepared to be passive bystanders when they or their fellow citizens are being victimized.

In totalitarian states there exists another process of social change that is not very well understood. This kind of change occurs when members of the establishment become disenchanted with the prevailing system and produce change from the top down; modern examples are Mao's China and the former Soviet Union. These totalitarian regimes exercised such total control over access to information that it remains unclear just how these bloodless revolutions have been accomplished.[2]

Notes

1. However, when citizens abstain from exercising their right to vote, this is not due to apathy—as has been alleged. Such abstaining is much more likely to be a refusal to vote for any one of several equally undesirable alternatives.
2. Perhaps the vast peaceful demonstrations in Belgrade, lasting for many weeks during the winter of 1996–1997, point not only to such popular expressions of outrage, but also point to a nonviolent method of systemic change.

Bibliography of Print Materials

African Rights. *Facing Genocide: The Nuba of Sudan.* African Rights, July 1995.

Aguirre, Luis Pérez. "The Consequences of Impunity in Society." pp. 107–20 in *International Meeting on Impunity of Perpetrators of Gross Human Rights Violations. Organized by The commission nationale consultative des droits de l'homme and the International Commission of Jurists and held under the auspices of the United Nations.* Geneva: Palais des Nations: 2 to 5 November 1992.

Ainsztein, Reuben. *Jewish Resistance in Nazi-Occupied Eastern Europe: With a Historical Survey of the Jew as Fighter and Soldier in the Diaspora.* New York: Barnes & Noble, 1974.

Allwood, John. *The Great Exhibitions.* London: Studio Vista, 1977.

Angoulvant, G. *La Pacification de la Côte d'Ivoire.* Paris: Larose, 1916.

Anti-Slavery Society, "Genocide in Bangla-desh." *Anti-Slavery Reporter,* December 1981.

Antonov-Ovseyenko, Anton. *The Time of Stalin: Portrait of a Tyrant.* George Saunders, trans. New York: Harper & Row, 1981.

Appianus of Alexandria. *Appian's Roman History.* Horace White, trans. London: William Heinemann Ltd.; Cambridge, Mass.: Harvard University Press, 1913.

Arad, Yitzhak. *Belzec, Sobibor, Treblinka: the Operation Reinhard Death Camps.* Bloomington: Indiana University Press, 1987.

Arad, Yitzhak. *Ghetto in Flames: The Struggle and Destruction of the Jews in Vilna in the Holocaust.* New York: Ktav, 1981.

Arendt, Hannah. *Between Past and Future: Eight Exercises in Political Thought.* New York: Penguin Books, 1993 (1961).

Arendt, Hannah. *The Origins of Totalitarianism.* New York: Harcourt Brace Jovanovich, 1951.

Armer, Micheal and Allen D. Grimshaw, eds. *Comparative Social Research: Methodological Problems and Strategies.* New York: John Wiley & Sons, 1973.

Ascherson, Neal. *The King Incorporated: Leopold II in the Age of Trusts.* London: George Allen & Unwin, 1963.

Astin, A.E. *Scipio Aemilianus.* Oxford: Clarendon Press, 1967.

Astin, A.E., F.W. Walbank, M.W. Frederiksen, and R. M. Ogilvie, eds. *The Cambridge Ancient History.* Second edition, vol. VIII. Cambridge: Cambridge University Press, 1982.

Austen, Ralph A. *Northwest Tanzania under German and British Rule: Colonial Policy and Tribal Politics.* New Haven, Conn.: Yale University Press, 1968.

Babeuf, Gracchus. *La guerre de la Vendée et le système de dépopulation.* Introduction, présentation, chronologie et notes par R. Secher et J. J. Brégeon. Paris: Tallander, 1987.

Bahar, A.T.M. *Dynamics of Ethnic Relations between the Burmese and the Rohingyas.* Windsor, Ontario: M.A. thesis, University of Windsor, Department of Sociology and Anthropology, 1981.

Baillet, Jules. *Le Régime Pharaonique dans ses rapports avec l'évolution de la morale en Egypte. Tome Premier.* Grande Imprimerie de Blois, 1912.

Balfour, Michael. *Withstanding Hitler in Germany 1933–45.* London: Routledge, 1988.

Ballhaus, Jolanda. "The Colonial Aims and Preparations of the Hitler Regime 1933–1939." in *German Imperialism in Africa: From the Beginnings until the Second World War.* Helmuth Stoecker, ed., Bernd Zöllner, trans. London: C. Hurst & Co., 1986.

Ball-Kaduri, Kurt Jakob. "Did the Jews of Germany Revolt?" *Yad Vashem Bulletin* 4/5 (1959).

Banac, Ivo. *The National Question in Yugoslavia.* Ithaca, N.Y.: Cornell University Press, 1984.

Barraclough, Geoffrey. *An Introduction to Contemporary History.* Hammondsworth, Middlesex: Penguin Books, 1967.

Bauer, Yehuda. *They Chose Life.* New York: American Jewish Committee, 1973.

Bauer, Yehuda, ed. *The Jewish Emergence from Powerlessness.* Toronto: University of Toronto Press, 1979.

Bauer, Yehuda. *Jewish Reactions to the Holocaust.* Tel Aviv: MOD Books, 1989a.

Bauer, Yehuda. "Jewish Resistance and Passivity in the Face of the Holocaust," in François Furet, ed. *Unanswered Questions: Nazi Germany and the Genocide of the Jews.* New York: Schocken, 1989.

Bauer, Yehuda. *Jews for Sale? Nazi-Jewish Negotiations, 1933–1945.* New Haven, Conn.: Yale University Press, 1994.

Becker, Jasper. *Hungry Ghosts: China's Secret Famine*. London: John Murray, 1996.

Bello, José Maria. *A History of Modern Brazil: 1889–1964*. James A. Taylor, trans. Stanford, Cal.: Stanford University Press, 1966.

Bennett, Benjamin. *Hitler Over Africa*. London: T. Werner Laurie, 1939.

Benz, Wolfgang, ed. *Die Juden in Deutschland 1933–1945: Leben unter nationalsozialistischer Herrschaft*. München: C. H. Beck, 1988.

Berger, Rainer and Reiner Protsch. "The Domestication of Plants and Animals in Europe and the Near East," pp. 214–227 in *Approaches to the Study of the Ancient Near East: A Volume of Studies Offered to Ignace Jay Gelb on the Occasion of his 65th Birthday, October 14, 1972*. Giorgio Buccellati, ed. Rome: Biblical Institute Press and Los Angeles: Undena Publications, 1973.

Berry, Brewton. *Race and Ethnic Relations*. Boston: Houghton Mifflin, 1965 (1951).

Bialystok, Frank. "The Holocaust: Official and Unofficial Memory in Poland and Germany," *Viewpoints*, vol. xxi, no. 4 (September 29, 1993).

The Bible. Translated out of the original tongues by the commandment of King James the first anno 1611. New York: AMS Press, 1967. Exodus, 17: 8–16; Deuteronomy, 25: 17–19; Samuel, 15: 2–8; Samuel, 30: 1–19.

Binder, David. "Anatomy of a Massacre." *Foreign Policy* 97 (Winter 1993–1994): 70–78.

Bley, Helmut. "German South West Africa after the Conquest 1904–1914," in *South West Africa: Travesty of Trust. The expert papers and findings of the International Conference on South West Africa, Oxford 23–26 March 1966, with a postscript by Iain MacGibbon on the 1966 Judgement of the International Court of Justice*. ed. Ronald Segal and Ruth First. London: Andre Deutsch, 1967.

Bley, Helmut. "Unerledigte Deutsche Kolonialgeschichte." (Unfinished German Colonial History) *Entwicklungspolitische Korrespondenz: Zeitschrift zu Theorie und Praxis der Entwicklungspolitik*. Hamburg, 5–6/77. Reprinted as 2–5 in Gerd Sudholt, *Die deutsche Eingeborenenpolitik in Südwestafrika; Von den Anfängen bis 1904*. Hildesheim, N.Y.: Georg Olms Verlag, 1975.

Bley, Helmut. *South-West Africa under German Rule 1894–1914*. English edition translated, edited and prepared by Hugh Ridley. London: Heinemann, 1971.

Bodley, John. *Victims of Progress*. Menlo Park, Cal.: Cummings Press, 1975.

Borkin, Joseph. *The Crime and Punishment of I.G. Farben.* New York: The Free Press, 1978.

Böttcher, Kurt, Karl Heinz Berger, Kurt Krolop, and Christa Zimmermann. *Geflügelte Worte: Zitate, Sentensen und Begriffe in ihrem geschichtlichen Zusammenhang.* VEB Bibliographisches Institut Leipzig, 1981.

Boucher, E.S. *Spain under the Roman Empire.* Oxford: B.H. Blackwell, 1914.

Bradford, E. *The Great Betrayal: Constantinople, 1204.* London: Hodder & Stoughton, 1967.

Braeckman, Collette. *Rwanda: Histoire d'un génocide.* Paris: Fayard, 1994.

Braithwaite, John. *Crime, Shame and Reintegration.* Cambridge: Cambridge University Press, 1989.

Brecht, Bertolt.*The Resistible Rise of Arturo Ui.* Adapted by George Tabori. New York: S. French, 1972. Epilogue.

Bridgman, Jon M. *The Revolt of the Hereros.* Berkeley: University of California Press, 1981.

Brock, Peter. "Dateline Yugoslavia: The Partisan Press." *Foreign Policy* 93 (Winter 1993–1994): 152–72.

Brundage, B. C. *A Rain of Darts: The Mexican Aztecs.* Austin: University of Texas Press, 1972.

Buccellati, Giorgio. *Cities and Nations of Ancient Syria: An Essay on Political Institutions with Special Reference to the Israelite Kingdoms.* Rome: Università di Roma, Istituto di Studi del Vicino Oriente, 1967.

Bullitt, Orville H. *The Search for Sybaris.* London: J. M. Dent & Sons, 1969.

Burg, Steven L. *The Political Integration of Yugoslavia's Muslims: Determinants of Success and Failure.* Pittsburgh: The Carl Beck Papers in Russian and East European Studies, University of Pittsburgh, 1983.

Burger, Julian and Alan Whitaker, eds. *The Chittagong Hill Tracts: Militarization, Oppression and the Hill Tribes.* London: Anti-Slavery Society, 1984.

Bury, J. B. "Dionysius of Syracuse." In *The Cambridge Ancient History,* vol. VI. Cambridge: Cambridge University Press, 1975: 108–36.

Calvert, F.C.S., Albert F. *South-West Africa: During the German Occupation 1884–1914.* New York: Negro Universities Press, 1969 (1915).

Calvocoressi, Peter, Guy Wint, John Pritchard. *Total War: The Causes and Courses of the Second World War.* New York: Viking Penguin, 1989 (1972).

The Cambridge Ancient History, vol. VI. Cambridge: Cambridge University Press, 1964.

Cameron, Alan. *Circus Factions: Blues and Greens at Rome and Byzantium.* Oxford: Clarendon Press, 1976.

Cazacu, Matei. "The Reign of Dracula in 1448," in *Dracula: Essays on the Life and Times of Vlad Tepes.* Kurt W. Treptow, ed. New York: East European Monographs, 1991.

Centre for Human Rights, Geneva. *Human Rights: A Compilation of International Instruments.* New York: United Nations, 1988.

Chalk, Frank and Kurt Jonassohn. *The History and Sociology of Genocide: Analyses and Case Studies.* New Haven, Conn.: Yale University Press, 1990.

Chandler, David P. and Ben Kiernan, eds., *Revolution and its Aftermath in Kampuchea: Eight Essays.* New Haven, Conn.: Yale University Southeast Asia Studies, 1983.

Cheng, J. C. *Chinese Sources for the Taiping Rebellion, 1850–1864.* Hong Kong: Hong Kong University Press, 1963.

Chickering, Roger. *We Men Who Feel Most German: A Cultural Study of the Pan-German League, 1886–1914.* Boston: George Allen & Unwin, 1984.

Chilver, Elizabeth M. "Paramountcy and Protection in the Cameroons: The Bali and the Germans, 1889–1913," pp.479–511 in *Britain and Germany in Africa: Imperial Rivalry and Colonial Rule.* P. Gifford and W.R. Louis, eds. New Haven, Conn.: Yale University Press, 1967.

Chirot, Daniel. *Modern Tyrants: The Power and Prevalence of Evil in Our Age.* New York: The Free Press, 1994.

Clari, R. de. *The Conquest of Constantinople.* Edgar Holmes McNeal, trans. New York: Octagon Books, 1966.

Clark, Lance. *Early Warning of Refugee Flows.* Washington, D.C.: Refugee Policy Group, December 1989.

Clay, Jason W. and Bonnie K. Holcomb. *Politics and the Ethiopian Famine: 1984–1985.* Second edition. Cultural Survival Report 20. Cambridge, Mass.: Cultural Survival, 1986.

Clements, Alan. *Burma: The Next Killing Fields?* Berkeley, Cal.: Odonian Press, 1992.

Cobbing, Julian. "The Absent Priesthood: Another Look at the Rhodesian Risings of 1896–1897." *Journal of African History.* vol. 18, no. 1 (1977): 61–84.

Cohen, John M. and David B. Lewis. "The Role of Government in Combatting Food Shortages: Lessons from Kenya 1984–85," pp. 269–96 in *Drought and Hunger in Africa: Denying Famine a Future*. Michael H. Glantz, ed. Cambridge: Cambridge University Press, 1986.

Cohen, Roberta. *Introducing Refugee Issues into the United Nations Human Rights Agenda*. Washington, D.C.: Refugee Policy Group, January 1990.

Cohen, Stanley. *Denial and Acknowledgement: The Impact of Information about Human Rights Violations*. Jerusalem: Center for Human Rights, the Hebrew University, 1995.

Cohn, Norman. *Cosmos, Chaos and the World to Come: The Ancient Roots of Apocalyptic Faith*. New Haven, Conn.: Yale University Press, 1993.

Conquest, Robert. "No Grain of Pity," pp. 291–300 in *The History and Sociology of Genocide: Analyses and Case Studies*. Frank Chalk and Kurt Jonassohn, eds. New Haven, Conn.: Yale University Press, 1990.

Conquest, Robert. *The Great Terror: Stalin's Purge in the Thirties*. New York: Macmillan, 1968.

Conquest, Robert. *The Harvest of Sorrow: Soviet Collectivization and the Terror-Famine*. Oxford: Oxford University Press, 1986.

Cooke, James J. *New French Imperialism, 1880–1910: The Third Republic and Colonial Expansion*. Hamden, Conn.: Archon Books, 1973.

Cooper, John M. "The Araucanians," pp. 687–760, in *Handbook of South American Indians*, vol. I. Julian H. Steward, ed. New York: Smithsonian Institution Bureau of American Ethnology, 1963.

Cooper, John M. "The Patagonian and Pampean Hunters," pp. 127–68 in *Handbook of South American Indians*, vol. I. Julian H. Steward, ed. New York: Smithsonian Institution Bureau of American Ethnology, 1963.

Cornevin, Robert. "The Germans in Africa before 1918." Chapter 12 in *The History and Politics of Colonialism 1870–1914*. eds. L. H. Gann and Peter Duignan, which is Volume 1 of *Colonialism in Africa 1870–1960*. Cambridge: Cambridge University Press, 1969.

Cortes, Hernando. *Five Letters, 1519–1526*. J. Bayard Morris, trans. New York: W.W. Norton & Company, Inc., 1962.

Coser, Lewis A. *Greedy Institutions: Patterns of Undivided Commitment*. New York: The Free Press, 1974.

Crawford, Robert. *Across the Pampas and the Andes.* London: Ballantine Press, 1884.

Crowl, James William. *Angels in Stalin's Paradise: Western Reporters in Soviet Russia, 1917–1937, A Case Study of Louis Fischer and Walter Duranty.* Washington, D.C.: University Press of America, 1982.

Curwen, J. C. *Taiping Rebel: The Deposition of Li Hsiu-ch'eng.* Cambridge: Cambridge University Press, 1977.

Cviic, Christopher. *Remaking the Balkans.* London: The Royal Institute of International Affairs. Pinter Publishers, 1991.

D'Souza, Frances and Jeff Crisp. *The Refugee Dilemma.* London: Minority Group, Report No. 43, 1985.

da Cunha, Euclides. *Rebellion in the Backlands.* Os Sertoes, trans. Chicago: The University of Chicago Press, 1944 (1902).

Dadrian, V.N. "The Role of Turkish Physicians in the World War I Genocide of Ottoman Armenians," *Holocaust and Genocide Studies,* vol. 1, no .2 (1986).

Dadrian, Vahakn N. "Genocide as a Problem of National and International Law: The World War I Armenian Case and its Contemporary Legal Ramifications." *Yale Journal of International Law,* vol.14, no. 2, (Summer 1989): 221–334.

Dando, William A. "Biblical Famines, 1850 B.C.–A.D.46: Insights for Modern Mankind." *Ecology of Food and Nutrition,* vol. 13 (1983): 231–49.

Dando, William A. "Man-Made Famines: Some Geographical Insights from an Exploratory Study of a Millennium of Russian Famines." *Ecology of Food and Nutrition,* vol. 4 (1976): 219–34.

Dando, William A. *The Geography of Famine.* London: Edward Arnold, 1980.

Davis, Harold E. *History of Latin America.* New York: The Ronald Press Company, 1968.

Davison, Roderic H. *Reform in the Ottoman Empire, 1856–1876.* Princeton, N.J.: Princeton University Press, 1963.

Dawson, Raymond. *The Chinese Chameleon: An Analysis of European Conceptions of Chinese Civilization.* London: Oxford University Press, 1967.

Dawson, W. H. Letter to the Editor of *The Times* of November 4th, 1936.

de Castro, Josué. *The Geopolitics of Hunger.* New York and London: Monthly Review Press, 1977.

de Madariaga, Salvador. *Hernan Cortes: Conqueror of Mexico*. London: Hodder & Stoughton, 1942.

de Sahagun, Fr. Bernardino *The War of the Conquest: How It Was Waged Here in Mexico*. The Aztecs own story as given to Fr. Bernardino de Sahagun. Arthur O. Anderson and Charles E. Dibble, trans. Salt Lake City: The University of Utah Press, 1978.

de Waal, Alexander. *Famine That Kills: Darfur, Sudan, 1984–1985*. Oxford: Clarendon Press, 1989.

de Waal, Alexander. "The Politics of Information: Famine in Ethiopia and Sudan in the 1980s," in *Starving in Silence: A Report on Famine and Censorship*. London: Article 19, 1990.

Dedijer, Vladimir, Ivan Bozic, Sima Cirkovic, and Milorad Ekmecic. *History of Yugoslavia*. New York: McGraw-Hill Book Company, 1974.

Dedijer, Vladimir. *The Yugoslav Auschwitz and the Vatican*. Harvey L. Kendall, trans. Buffalo, N.Y.: Prometheus Books, 1992.

Del Boca, Angelo. *The Ethiopian War, 1935–1941*. P.D. Cummins, trans. Chicago: The University of Chicago Press, 1965.

Delbrueck, Hans. *History of the Art of War.* Westport, Conn.: Greenwood Press, 1975 (original German edition, 1920). Volume 1: *Antiquity.*

Denich, Bette. "Dismembering Yugoslavia: Nationalist Ideologies and the Symbolic Revival of Genocide," *American Ethnologist* 21, 2 (1994): 367–90.

Deutscher, Irwin. "Asking Questions Cross-Culturally: Some Problems of Linguistic Comparability." In Donald P. Warwick and Samuel Osherson, eds., *Comparative Research Methods*. Englewood Cliffs, N.J.: Prentice-Hall, 1973.

Devine, Albert. "Alexander the Great," pp. 105–29 in John Hackett, ed., *Warfare in the Ancient World.* New York: Facts on File, 1990.

Diaz, Bernal del Castillo. *The Conquest of New Spain*. J.M. Cohen, trans. Baltimore, Md.: Penguin Books, 1963.

Dieng, Adama. "Opening Speech," pp. 19–26 in *International Meeting on Impunity of Perpetrators of Gross Human Rights Violations. Organized by The commission nationale consultative des droits de l'homme and the International Commission of Jurists and held under the auspices of the United Nations.* Geneva: Palais des Nations: 2 to 5 November 1992.

Dobson, Brian. "The Empire," pp. 192–221 in John Hackett, ed., *Warfare in the Ancient World.* New York: Facts on File, 1990.

Donat, Alexander. *Jewish Resistance*. New York: Warsaw Ghetto Resistance Organization (WAGRO), 1964.

Donat, Alexander. *The Death Camp Treblinka: A Documentary.* New York: Holocaust Library, 1979.

Doyle, William. *The Oxford History of the French Revolution.* Oxford: Clarendon Press, 1989.

Dragnich, Alex N. "The Rise and Fall of Yugoslavia: The Omen of the Upsurge of Serbian Nationalism." *East European Quarterly,* vol. XXIII, no. 2 (June 1989): 183–98.

Dragnich, Alex N. and Slavko Todorovich. *The Saga of Kosovo: Focus on Serbian Albanian Relations.* Boulder, Col.: East European Monographs, 1984.

Drechsler, Horst. *"Let Us Die Fighting": The Struggle of the Hereros and the Nama Against German Inperialism (1884–1915).* Bernd Zollner, trans. London: Zed Press, 1980; Akademie-Verlag, 1966.

D'Souza, Frances and Jeff Crisp. *The Refugee Dilemma.* London: Minority Rights Group, 1985 (1980).

DuBois Jr., Josiah E. in collaboration with Edward Johnson. *Generals in Grey Suits: The Directors of the International "I.G.Farben" Cartel, Their Conspiracy and Trial at Nuremberg.* London: The Bodley Head, 1953; first published as *The Devil's Chemists: 24 Conspirators of the International Farben Cartel who Manufacture Wars.* Boston: Beacon Press, 1952.

Dugan, James, and Laurence Lafore. *Days of Emperor and Clown: The Italo-Ethiopian War, 1935–1936.* New York: Doubleday, 1973.

Duggan, A. *He Died Old: Mithradates Eupater, King of Pontus.* London: Faber and Faber, 1958.

Duraczinski, Eugeniusz. "Polish Resistance during the Second World War." in *Unesco Yearbook on Peace and Conflict Studies, 1985.* Paris: Unesco and New York: Greenwood, 1987: 101–24.

Eckman, Lester Samuel and Chaim Lazar. *The Jewish Resistance: the History of the Jewish Partisans in Lithuania and White Russia during the Nazi Occupation, 1940–1945.* New York: Shengold, 1977.

Edelheit, Abraham J. and Hershel Edelheit. *Bibliography on Holocaust Literature.* Boulder, Colo.: Westview, 1986. (*Supplement 1:* 1990. *Supplement 2:* 1993).

Edelman, Marek. *The Ghetto Fights.* London: Bookmarks, 1990. First Polish edition in Warsaw, 1945.

Elkins, Michael. "Not Like Sheep." *The Jerusalem Report,* February 25, 1993.

Emerson, Barbara. *Leopold II of the Belgians: King of Colonialism.* London: Weidenfeld and Nicolson, 1979.

Emmert, Thomas A. *Serbian Golgotha: Kosovo, 1389.* Boulder, Colo.: East European Monographs, 1990.

Engelmann, Bernt. *Germany Without Jews.* D. J. Beer, trans. Toronto: Bantam Books, 1984.

Eschwege, Helmut. "Resistance of German Jews against the Nazi Regime," in Micheal Marrus, ed. *Jewish Resistance to the Holocaust,* volume 7 of *The Nazi Holocaust: Historical Articles on the Destruction of European Jews.* London: Meckler, 1989: 385–428.

Etcheson, Craig. *The Rise and Demise of Democratic Kampuchea.* Boulder, Colo.: Westview Press, 1984.

Eusebius, *Ecclesiastical History.* R.J. Deferrari, ed. and trans. New York: Fathers of the Church, Inc., 1953.

Fair, Jo Ellen. "Are We Really the World? Coverage of U.S. Food Aid in Africa, 1980–1989," in *Africa's Media Image*, Beverly G. Hawk, ed. New York: Praeger, 1992.

Falla, Jonathan. *True Love and Bartholomew: Rebels on the Burmese Border.* Cambridge: Cambridge University Press, 1991.

Feig, Konnilyn G. *Hitler's Death Camps: The Sanity of Madness.* New York: Holmes & Meier, 1979.

Fein, Helen. "Accounting for Genocide After 1945: Theories and Some Findings," *International Journal of Group Rights* 1 (1993): 79–106.

Fein, Helen. "Genocide, Terror, Life Integrity and War Crimes: The Case for Discrimination." In *Genocide: Conceptual and Historical Dimensions.* George Andreopoulos, ed. Philadelphia: University of Pennsylvania Press, 1994.

Fein, Helen. *Genocide: A Sociological Perspective.* London: Sage, 1993.

Fein, Helen. "Genocide: A Sociological Perspective." *Current Sociology,* vol.18, no.1 (Spring 1990).

Fine, John V.A. *The Early Medieval Balkans: A Critical Survey from the Sixth to the Late Twelfth Century.* Ann Arbor: The University of Michigan Press, 1983.

Fleming, Gerald. *Hitler and the Final Solution.* Berkeley: University of California Press, 1984 (1982).

Foot, M. R. D. *Resistance: An Analysis of European Resistance to Nazism 1940–1945.* London: Eyre Methuen, 1976.

Fox, Robin Lane. *Pagans and Christians.* New York: Alfred A. Knopf, 1987.

Freidenreich, Harriet Z. P. *Belgrade, Zagreb, Sarajevo: A Study of Jewish Communites in Yugoslavia Before World War II.* Ph.D. Diss. Columbia University, 1973.

Freidenreich, Harriet Z. P. *The Jews of Yugoslavia: A Quest for Community.* Philadelphia: The Jewish Publication Society of America, 1979.

Frelick, Bill. "Refugees: A Barometer of Genocide," in *World Refugee Survey: 1988 in Review,* 13–17. Washington: U.S. Committee for Refugees, 1989.

Frend, W.H.C. *Martyrdom and Persecution in the Early Church.* New York: New York University Press, 1967.

Furet, François and Denis Richet. *French Revolution.* Stephen Hardman, trans. London: Weidenfeld and Nicolson, 1970.

Furet, François. *Unanswered Questions: Nazi Germany and the Genocide of the Jews.* New York: Schocken, 1989.

Galtung, Johan. "On the Meaning of "Nation" as a variable," in Manfred Niessen and Jules Peschar, eds., *International Comparative Research: Problems of Theory, Methodology and Organization in Eastern and Western Europe.* Oxford: Pergamon Press, 1982.

Gann, L. H. and Peter Duignan. *The Rulers of German Africa 1884–1914.* Stanford, Cal.: Stanford University Press, 1977.

Gann, L. H., and P. Duignan. *Colonialism in Africa.* Cambridge: Cambridge University Press, 1969.

Garnsey, Peter. *Famine and Food Supply in the Graeco–Roman World.* Cambridge: Cambridge University Press, 1988.

Geanakoplos, Deno John. *Byzantine East & Latin West: Two Worlds of Christendom in Middle Ages and Renaissance. Studies in Ecclesiastical and Cultural History.* New York: Harper Torchbooks, 1966.

Gibson, C. *Spain in America.* New York: Harper & Row, 1966.

Gilbert, Martin. *Final Journey: The Fate of the Jews in Nazi Europe.* New York: Mayflower Books, 1979.

Giurescu, Constantin C. "The Historical Dracula," in *Dracula: Essays on the Life and Times of Vlad Tepes.* Kurt W. Treptow, ed. New York: East European Monographs, 1991: 13–28.

Glenny, Misha. *The Fall of Yugoslavia: The Third Balkan War.* New York: Penguin, 1992.

Glickman, Yaacov and Alan Bardikoff. *The Treatment of the Holocaust in Canadian History and Social Science Textbooks.* Downsview, Ont.: League for Human Rights of B'nai Brith, 1982.

Goldblatt, I. *History of South West Africa from the Beginning of the Nineteenth Century.* Cape Town: Juta, 1971.

Golkin, Arline T. *Famine: A Heritage of Hunger. A Guide to Issues and References.* Claremont, Cal.: Regina Books, 1987.

Gordenker, Leon. "Early Warning of Forced Migration," in Lydio F. Tomasi, ed., *In Defense of the Alien, vol. vii of Immigration Reform and Refugee Policy Developments: Proceedings of the 1984 Annual National Legal Conference on Immigration and Refugee Policy.* New York: Center for Migration Studies, 1985.

Goshale, Balkrishna Govind. *Asoka Maurya.* New York: Twayne Publishers, 1966.

Graham, R. B. Cunnimghamme. *The Conquest of the River Plate.* New York: Greenwood Press, 1968.

Graham, Stephen. *Ivan the Terrible: Life of Ivan IV.* Hamden, Conn.: Archon Books: 1968.

Gray, Andrew. *The Amerindians of South America.* London: Minority Rights Group, 1987.

Grey, Ian. *Ivan the Terrible.* Philadelphia: J.P. Lippincott Company, 1964.

Grey, Jerry. "2 Nations Joined By A Common History of Genocide," *New York Times*, April 9, 1994: I6.

Grimal, Henri. *Decolonization: The British, French, Dutch and Belgian Empires, 1919–1963.* Stephan De Vos, trans. London: Routledge & Kegan Paul, 1965.

Grimm, Hans. *Suchen und Hoffen: aus meinem Leben 1928 bis 1934.* (Seeking and Hoping: from my life 1928 until 1934) Lippoldsberg: Klosterhaus-Verlag, 1960.

Grimm, Jacob and Wilhelm Grimm, eds. *Deutches Wörterbuch*, vol. 26 Leipzig: Verlag von Hirzel, 1854.

Gulbekian, Edward V. "The Poles and Armenians in Hitler's Political Thinking," *Armenian Review,* vol. 41, no.3/163 (Autumn 1988): 1–14.

Gutman, Israel. ed. *Encyclopedia of the Holocaust,* four vols. New York: Macmillan, 1990.

Gutman, Yisrael and Efraim Zuroff, eds. *Rescue Attempts during the Holocaust.* Proceedings of the Second Yad Vashem International Historical Conference, Jerusalem, April 8–11, 1974. Jerusalem: Yad Vashem, 1977.

Gutman, Yisrael. *The Jews of Warsaw, 1939–1943: Ghetto, Underground, Revolt.* Ina Friedman, trans. Bloomington: Indiana University Press, 1982.

Gwassa, G.C.K. "The German Intervention and African Resistance in Tanzania," in *A History of Tanzania.* I.N. Kimambo and A.J. Temu, eds. Nairobi: East African Publishing House, 1969.

Hachten, William. "African Censorship and American Correspondents," in *Africa's Media Image*. Beverly G. Hawk, ed. New York: Praeger, 1992.

Hackett, John, ed. *Warfare in the Ancient World.* New York: Facts on File, 1990.

Hæstrup, Jørgen. *European Resistance Movements, 1939–1945: A Complete History.* Westport, Conn.: Meckler, 1981.

Haffner, Sebastian. *The Meaning of Hitler.* Ewald Osers, trans. New York: Macmillan, 1979.

Hancock, Ian. *The Pariah Syndrome: An Account of Gypsy Slavery and Persecution.* Ann Arbor, Mich.: Karoma Publishers, Inc., 1987.

Hannum, Hurst. "International Law and Cambodian Genocide: The Sounds of Silence." *Human Rights Quarterly* 11, 1 (February 1989): 82–138.

Harris, David. *Britain and the Bulgarian Horrors of 1876.* Chicago: University of Chicago Press, 1939.

Harrison, Paul and Robin Palmer. *News Out of Africa.* London: Hilary Shipman, 1986.

Harvey, G.E. *The History of Burma: From the Earliest Time to the Beginning of the English Conquest.* New York: Octagon Books, 1967.

Havel, Václav. *Disturbing the Peace.* New York: Vintage Books, 1990.

Havell, E. B. *The History of Aryan Rule in India: From the Earliest Time to the Death of Akbar.* London: George G. Harrap, 1918.

Hawk, Beverly G. "Introduction: Metaphors of African Coverage," in *Africa's Media Image*. Beverly G. Hawk, ed. New York: Praeger, 1992.

Hay, Malcolm. *Europe and the Jews: The Pressure of Christendom on the People of Israel for 1900 Years.* Chicago: Academy Chicago Publishers, 1992 (1950).

Helbig, Ludwig. "Der Koloniale Früfaschismus." in *Ein Land, eine Zukunft: Namibia auf dem Weg in die Unabhängigkeit.* eds. Nangolo Mbumba, Helgard Patemann, Uazuvara Katjivena. Wuppertal: Peter Hammer Verlag, 1988 (Ein Terre des Hommes Buch).

Henze, Paul. "Behind the Ethiopian Famine: Anatomy of a Revolution." Three-part article in *Encounter,* vol. 67, no.1 (June 1986): 5–17; no.2 (July-August 1986): 15–27; no.3 (Sept.-Oct. 1986): 20–31.

Hess, Stephen. "Media Mavens," *Society*, vol. 33, no. 3 (March-April 1996): 70–78.

Hilberg, Raul. *Exécuteurs, Victimes, Témoins. La catastrophe juive, 1943–1945.* Paris: Gallimard, 1994.

Hilberg, Raul. *Perpetrators, Victims, Bystanders: The Jewish Catastrophe 1933–1945.* New York: Harper Collins, 1992.

Hilberg, Raul. *The Destruction of the European Jews.* New York: Harper & Row, 1979 (1961).

Hitler, Adolf. *Mein Kampf.* Boston: Houghton Mifflin, 1971 (1924).

Horowitz, Helen H. "Animal and Man in the New York Zoological Park," *New York History,* 4 (Oct. 1975): 426–55.

Horowitz, Irving Louis. *Taking Lives: Genocide and State Power.* Fourth edition. New Brunswick, N.J.: Transaction Publishers, 1997.

Hozier, Sir Henry Montague. *The Russo-Turkish War: Including An Account of the Rise and Decline of the Ottoman Power and the History of the Eastern Question,* vol. II. London: William Mackenzie, n.d.

Huguet, Edmont. *Dictionnaire de la Langue Française du Seizième Siècle,* Tome Cinquième. Paris: Librairie M. Didier, 1961.

Human Rights Watch/Africa. "Genocide in Rwanda, April-May 1994", *Human Rights Watch/Africa,* vol. 6, no. 4.

Iliffe, John. *Famine in Zimbabwe, 1890–1960.* Gweru, Zimbabwe: Mambo Press, 1990.

Iliffe, John. "The Effects of the Maji Rebellion of 1905–1906 on German occupation Policy in East Africa," pp. 557–75, in *Britain and Germany in Africa: Imperial Rivalry and Colonial Rule.* P. Gifford and W.R. Louis, eds. New Haven, Conn.: Yale University Press, 1967.

Iliffe, John. *Tanganyika Under German Rule, 1905–1912.* London: Cambridge University Press, 1969.

"In Brief." *Manchester Guardian Weekly.* January 21, 1996: 11.

Institoris, Heinrich and J. Sprenger, *Malleus Maleficarum.* Translated with an Introduction, Bibliography and Notes by the Rev. Montague Summers. London: The Hogarth Press, 1949 (1928).

International Conference on the History of the Resistance Movements. First: Liège, 1958. *European Resistance Movements, 1939–1945: Proceedings.* London: Pergamon, 1960. Second, Third and Fourth conferences were held in Italy, Poland, and Austria.

International Work Group for Indigenous Affairs, "Bangladesh: Tribal Fight for Land in the Chittagong Hill Tracts." *International Work Group for Indigenous Affairs Newsletter,* no. 27, June 1981.

James, Selwyn. *South of the Congo.* New York: Random House, 1943.

Jelavich, Charles. "Serbian Nationalism and the Croats: Vuk Karadzic's Influence on Serbian Textbooks." *Canadian Review of Studies in Nationalism,* XVII, 1–2 (1990): 31–42.

Jenner, W. J. F. *Memoirs of Loyang: Yang Hsüan-chih and the lost capital (493–534).* Oxford: Clarendon Press, 1981.

Johannsen, G. Kurt and H. H. Kraft. *Germany's Colonial Problem.* London: Thornton Butterworth, 1937.

Jones, A.H.M. *A History of Rome through the Fifth Century,* vol. II. New York: Walker and Company, 1970.

Joshi, Rekha. *The Reign of Sultan Balban.* Delhi: Ravi Publishers, 1982.

Jungk, Robert. *Brighter than a Thousand Suns: A Personal History of the Atomic Scientists.* New York: Harcourt Brace Jovanovich, 1958.

Jurés, Jean. *Histoire Socialiste de la Révolution Française,* vol. VII. Paris: Édition de la Librairie de l'Humanité, 1924.

Kabir, Muhammad Ghulam. *Minority Politics in Bangladesh.* New Delhi: Vikas, 1980.

Kahn, Paul. *The Secret History of the Mongols: The Origin of Chingis Khan: An Adaptation of the Yuan Ch'ao Pi Shih, Based Primarily on the English Translation by Francis Woodman Cleaves.* San Francisco: North Point Press, 1984.

Kamphausen, Erhard. "Namibia im Kolonialen Zeitalter: Weisse Herrschaft—Schwarzer Widerstand." *Entwicklungspolitische Korrespondenz: Zeitschrift zu Theorie und Praxis der Entwicklungspolitik,* (Hamburg) vol.8, no.5–6 (1977): 20–29.

Kane, Penny. *Famine in China, 1959–61: Demographic and Social Implications.* London: Macmillan, 1988.

Kates, Robert W. and Sara Millman. "On Ending Hunger: The Lessons of History." Chapter 15 in Lucile F, Newman, ed. *Hunger in History.* Cambridge, Mass.: Basil Blackwell, 1990.

Katjavivi, Peter H. *A History of Resistance in Namibia.* London: James Currey; Addis Ababa: OAU; Paris: UNESCO Press, 1988. Chapter 2. "German Conquest and Namibian Resistance."

Katz, Barbara Goody. *A Quantitative Evaluation of the Economic Aspect of the Great Purges of the Soviet Union.* Ph.D. Diss. in Economics and History. Pittsburgh: University of Pennsylvania Press, 1973.

Katz, Steven T. *The Holocaust and Mass Death before the Modern Age,* volume 1 of *The Holocaust in Historical Context.* New York: Oxford University Press, 1994.

Keay, S.J. *Roman Spain.* London: British Museum Publications Ltd., 1988.

Kennedy, William V. *The Military and the Media: Why the Press Cannot Be Trusted to Cover a War.* Westport, Conn.: Praeger, 1993.

Kenney, George. "The Bosnia Calculation," *The New York Times Magazine.* April 23, 1995: 42–43.

Keppie, Lawrence. "The Roman Army of the Later Republic," pp. 169–91 in John Hackett, ed., *Warfare in the Ancient World.* New York: Facts on File, 1990.

Kjekshus, Helge. *Ecology Control and Economic Development in East African History: The Case of Tanganyika, 1850–1950.* London: Heinemann Educational Books, 1977.

Klein, Lisa. "The Social Construction of Racism and Sexism: A Study of the New York Times Media Reporting of the Famine and Civil War in Somalia, 1990 to the Present." Research report submitted to the School of Social Work, Faculty of Graduate Studies and Research, for Master's of Social Work, McGill University, November 1994.

Knightley, Philip. *The First Casualty, from the Crimea to Vietnam: The War Correspondent as Hero, Propagandist, and Myth Maker.* New York: Harcourt Brace Jovanovich, 1975.

Kolski, John and David Crow, eds. *The Gypsies of Eastern Europe.* Armonk, N.Y.: M. E. Sharpe Inc., 1991.

Kolvig, Eric. *Burma Today: Land of Hope and Terror.* Washington, D.C.: International Burma Campaign, 1991.

Koslov, Jules. *Ivan the Terrible.* London: Alden University Press, 1961.

Kowalski, Isaac, comp. and ed. *Anthology on Armed Jewish Resistance 1939–1945.* 3 vols. Brooklyn, N.Y.: Jewish Combatants Publishers House, 1985, 1986.

Krakowski, Shmuel. *The War of the Doomed: Jewish Armed Resistance in Poland, 1942–1944.* Orah Blaustein, trans. New York: Holmes and Meier, 1984.

Krarpandzich, Birivoje M. *The Bloodiest Yugoslav Spring, 1945: Tito's Katyns and Gulags.* New York: Carlton Press, 1980.

Kuper, Leo. *Genocide: Its Political Use in the Twentieth Century.* New Haven, Conn.: Yale University Press, 1981; New York: Penguin, 1981.

Kurtz, Howard. *Media Circus: The Trouble with America's Newspapers.* New York: Random House, 1993.

Kurzman, Dan. *The Bravest Battle: The Twenty-eight Days of the Warsaw Ghetto Uprising.* New York: G. P. Putnam's, 1976.

Lactantius. *De Mortibus Persecutorum.* J. L. Creed ed. and trans. Oxford: Clarendon Press, 1984.

Lacville, Robert. "Breeze of politics is refreshing Africa." *Guardian Weekly,* July 28, 1991.

Lane-Poole, Stanley. *Medieval India under Mohammedan Rule (A.D. 712–1764).* New York: Haskell House, 1970 (1903).

Langbein, Hermann. "Genocid im 20. Jahrhundert: Protocol einer Podiums Diskussion" (Genocide in the 20th Century: Transcript of a Panel Discussion), *Frankfurter Hefte* (West Germany), vol. 31, no. 5 (1976): 21–34.

Langbein, Hermann. *...nicht wie die Schafe zur Schlachtbank: Widerstand in den nationalsozialistischen Konzentrationslagern.* Frankfurt am Main: Fischer Taschenbuch Verlag, 1980.

Lardy, Nicholas R. "The Chinese Economy Under Stress, 1918–1965," pp. 360–97, in MacFarquhar and Fairbank, eds. *The Cambridge History of China*, vol. 14: *The People's Republic,* part 1: *The Emergence of Revolutionary China 1949–1965.* London: Cambridge University Press, 1987.

Larner, Christina. *Enemies of God: The Witch-Hunt in Scotland.* London: Chatto & Windus, 1981.

Laska, Vera, ed. *Women in the Resistance and the Holocaust: the Voices of Eyewitnesses.* Westport, Conn.: Greenwood, 1983.

Laska, Vera. *Nazism, Resistance and Holocaust in World War II: A Bibliography.* Metuchen, N.J.: The Scarecrow Press, 1985.

Lau, Brigitte. "Uncertain certainties: The Herero-German war of 1904." *Migabus,* no. 2 (April 1989): 4–5, 8.

Lau, Brigitte. Letter to the Editor, *Southern African Review of Book* (June/July 1990): 31.

Lavergne, Bernard and Herve Lauriere. "Genocide in the Puppet State of Croatia." *Contemporary Review* 224, no. 1301 (June 1974): 291–98.

Lea, Henry Charles. *The Inquisition of the Middle Ages,* vol. 1. New York: Russell & Russell, 1955.

Lemkin, Raphael. *Axis Rules in Occupied Europe: Law of Occupation, Analysis of Government, proposals for Redress.* Washington, D.C.: Carnegie Endowment, 1944.

Lenski, Gerhard. "Societal Taxonomies: Mapping the Social Universes," pp. 1–22, in John Hagan and Karen S. Cook, eds., *Annual Review of Sociology*, vol. 20. Palo Alto, Cal.: Annual Reviews Inc., 1994.

Leon-Portilla, M., ed. *The Broken Spears: The Aztec Account of the Conquest of Mexico.* Spanish trans. from Nahuatl by Angel Maria Garibay and Lysander Kemp, trans. Boston: Beacon Press, 1962.

Letter to the Editor, *Manchester Guardian Weekly*, vol. 151, no. 21 (November 20, l994), 2.

Leutwein, Dr. Paul, ed. *Kämpfe um Afrika: Sechs Lebensbilder.* Lübeck: Charles Coleman, 1936.

Levene, Mark. *"We Want the Land not the People" The Chittagong Hill Tracts as a Case study in the Political Economy of 'Developmental' Genocide.* Paper Presented at the Association of Genocide Scholars Conference, June 11–13, 1997, Concordia University, Montreal.

Levin, D. *Fighting Back: Lithuanian Jewry's Armed Resistance to the Nazis, 1941–1945.* Moshe Kohn and Dina Cohen, trans., foreword by Yehuda Bauer. New York: Holmes and Meier, 1985.

Levin, Nora. *The Holocaust: The Destruction of European Jewry, 1939–1945.* New York: T. Y. Crowell, 1968.

Levin, Nora. *The Holocaust Years: The Nazi Destruction of European Jewry, 1933–1945.* Malabar, Fla.: R. E. Krieger Publ. Co., 1990.

Lias, Godfrey. *Kazakh Exodus.* London: Evans Bros., 1956.

Liebenow, J. Gus. "Food self-sufficiency in Malawi: are successes transferable?" Chapter 16 in *Drought and Hunger in Africa: denying famine a future.* Michael H. Glantz, ed. Cambridge: Cambridge University Press, 1987.

Lintner, Bertil. *Outrage: Burma's Struggle for Democracy.* London: White Lotus, 1990.

Littré, Emile. *Dictionnaire de la langue française.* Paris: Gallimard-Hachette, 1962.

Livy. *Livy's Summaries.* Alfred C. Schlesinger, trans. The Loeb Classical Library, vol. XIV. London: William Heinemann Ltd., 1959.

Llorente, Juan A. *History of the Spanish Inquisition*, abridged from the original work of M. Llorente by Leonard Gallois. New York: G. C. Morgan, 1826.

Lloyd, Clem. "The Case for the Media," in *Defense and the Media in Time of Limited War.* Peter R. Young, ed. London: Frank Cass, 1992.

Lorch, Donatella. "Anarchy Rules Rwanda's Capital and Drunken Soldiers Roam City," *New York Times*, April 14, 1994: A1, A12.

Lustiger, Arno. "Täter, Opfer, Zuschauer." *Der Spiegel,* vol. 47, no. 7 (15 February 1993): 54, 58–59, 61.

Mace, James E. "Genocide in the U.S.S.R," chapter 6 in Israel W. Charny, ed., *Genocide: a Critical Bibliographic Review.* London: Mansell, 1988.

Mace, James E., "The Man-Made Famine of 1933 in the Soviet Ukraine: What Happened and Why," chapter 5 in Israel Charney, ed. *Toward an Understanding and Prevention of Genocide.* Boulder, Colo.: Westview, 1984.

MacFarquhar, Roderick and John K. Fairbank, eds. *The Cambridge History of China,* vol. 14: *The People's Republic,* part 1: *The Emer-*

gence of Revolutionary China 1949–1965. London: Cambridge University Press, 1987.

Magie, D. *Roman Rule in Asia Minor to the End of the Third Century After Christ,* vol. 2. Princeton, N.J.: Princeton University Press, 1950.

Mallory, Walter H. *China, Land of Famine.* New York: American Geographical Society, 1926.

Mark, Ber. "The Warsaw Ghetto Uprising," pp. 92–115 in Yuri Suhl, ed. *They Fought Back: the Story of Jewish Resistance in Nazi Europe.* New York: Schocken Books, 1975 (1967).

Marrus, Michael R. *The Nazi Holocaust: Historical Articles on the Destruction of European Jews,* 15 vols. Westport, Conn.: Meckler, 1989 (vol.7, *Jewish Resistance to the Holocaust*).

Marshall, S. L. A. "Preface" in Eschel Rhoodie, ed. *South West: The Last Frontier in Africa.* New York: Twin Circle Publishing Co., 1967.

Maspero, G. *History of Egypt, Chaldea, Syria, Babylonia, and Assyria,* 13 vols. London: The Grolier Society, n.d. (1906–1908).

Matas, Carol. *Lisa's War.* New York: Scribners, 1989 (1987).

McCarthy, Richard D. *The Ultimate Folly: War by Pestilence, Asphyxiation, and Defoliation.* New York: Alfred A. Knopf, 1970.

McDougal, Myres S., Harold D. Lasswell and Lung-chu Chen. *Human Rights and World Public Order: The Basic Policies of an International Law of Human Dignity.* New Haven, Conn.: Yale University Press, 1980.

McFarlane, Bruce. *Yugoslavia: Politics, Economics and Society.* London: Pinter Publishers 1988.

McGing, B.C. *The Foreign Policy of Mithradates VI Eupator, King of Pontus.* Leiden: E.J. Brill, 1986.

McNally, Raymond T. *Dracula, Prince of Many Faces: His Life and His Times.* Boston: Little, Brown and Company, 1989.

McNally, Raymond T. and Radu R. Florescu. *Dracula: A True History of Dracula and Vampire Legends.* Greenwich, Conn.: New York Graphic Society, 1972.

McNeill, William H. *The Pursuit of Power: Technology, Armed Force, and Society since A.D. 1000.* Oxford: Basil Blackwell, 1982.

Medvedev, Roy A. *Let History Judge: the Origin and Consequences of Stalinism.* New York: Vintage Books, 1973 (1971).

Melber, Henning, Mary Melber, and Werner Hillebrecht, eds. *In Treue fest, Südwest! Eine ideologiekritische Dokumentation von der Eroberung Namibias über die deutsche Fremdherrschaft bis zur Kolonialapologie der Gegenwart.* Bonn: edition südliches afrika 19 (1984), 187–88.

Melber, Henning. "Kontinuitäten totaler Herrschaft: Völkermord und Apartheid in 'Deutsch-Südwestafrika': Zur kolonialen Herrschaftspraxis im Deutschen Kaiserreich," pp. 91–116 in *Jahrbuch für Antisemitismusforschung 1*. Wolfgang Benz, ed. Frankfurt: Campus Verlag, 1992.

Melson, Robert. *Revolution and Genocide: On the Origins of the Armenian Genocide and the Holocaust.* Chicago: University of Chicago Press, 1992.

Mey, Wolfgang. "The Road to Resistance: Politics in the Bloody Triangle," pp. 123–74 in *Genocide in the Chittagong Hill Tracts, Bangledesh,* Wolfgang Mey, ed. Copenhagen: International Work Group for Indigenous Affairs, 1984.

Michel, Henri. *The Shadow War: Resistance in Europe, 1939–1945.* Richard Barry, trans. London: Deutsch, 1972 (1970).

Milazzo, Matteo J. *The Chetnik Movement and the Yugoslav Resistance.* Baltimore, Md.: Johns Hopkins University Press, 1975.

Millman, Sara and Kates, Robert W. "Toward Understanding Hunger," chapter 1 in Lucile F. Newman, ed. *Hunger in History.* Cambridge, Mass.: Basil Blackwell, 1990.

Milton, Sybil, trans. *The Stroop Report: The Jewish Quarter of Warsaw Is No More.* London: Secker & Warburg, 1980.

Montville, Joseph V., ed. *Conflict and Peacemaking in Multiethnic Societies.* Lexington, Mass.: D. C. Heath and Company, 1990.

Morgenthau, Henry. *Ambassador Morgenthau's Story.* New York: Doubleday, 1918.

Mudge, George Alfred. "Starvation as a Means of Warfare." *International Lawyer,* vol.4, no.2 (1969–70): 228–68.

Mufson, Steven. "Move to Curb Financial News Firms," *Manchester Guardian Weekly,* January 28, 1996.

Müller-Hill, Benno. *Murderous Science: Elimination by Scientific Selection of Jews, Gypsies, and Others, Germany 1933–1945.* George R. Fraser, trans. Oxford: Oxford University Press, 1988.

Muszkat, M., ed. *Jewish Fighters in the War Against the Nazis.* Tel Aviv: Moreshet, 1974.

Myrdal, Gunnar. "The Beam in Our Eyes," pp. 89–99 in Donald P. Warwick and Samual Osherson, eds. *Comparative Research Methods.* Englewood, N.J.: Prentice-Hall, 1973.

Nash, Gary, et al. *The American People: Creating a Nation and a Society.* New York: Harper and Row, 1986.

Newman, Lucile F., ed. *Hunger in History.* Cambridge, Mass.: Basil Blackwell, 1990.

Nohrstedt, Stig A. "Ruling by Pooling," in *Triumph of the Image: The Media's War in the Persian Gulf: A Global Perspective.* Hamid Mowlana, George Gerbner and Herbert I. Schiller, eds. Boulder, Colo.: Westview Press, 1992.

Novitch, Miriam. *Sobibor: Martyrdom and Revolt: Documents and Testimonies presented by Miriam Novitch,* preface by Léon Poliakov. New York: Holocaust Library, 1980 (Anti-Defamation League of B'nai Brith).

Nowak Jan. *Courier from Warsaw.* Detroit: Wayne State University Press, 1982.

O'Brien, Connor Cruise. "A Lost Chance to Save the Jews?" *The New York Review of Books,* vol.30, no.7, April 27, 1989: 27–28, 35.

Olcott, Martha Brill. "The Collectivization Drive in Kazakhstan," *The Russian Review* 40, 2 (April 1981): 122–42.

Olcott, Martha Brill. *The Kazakhs.* Stanford, Cal.: Hoover Institution Press, 1987.

Oldenbourg, Zoé *Massacre at Montségur.* New York: Pantheon, 1961.

Orlinsky, Harry M. "The New Jewish Version of the Torah: Toward a New Philosophy of Bible Translation," *Journal of Biblical Literature,* vol.82, 1963: 249–64.

Oxford, Duden. *Standardwörterbuch English, Englisch-Deutsch, Deutsch-Englisch,* edited by the Editorial Department of Duden and Oxford University Press. Mannheim: Dudenverlag, 1991.

Øyen, Else. *Comparative Methodology: Theory and Practice in International Social Research.* London: Sage, 1990.

Pawelczynska, Anna. *Values and Violence in Auschwitz: A Sociological Analysis.* Catherine S. Leach, trans. Berkeley: University of California Press, 1979 (1973).

Pears, Sir E. *The Fall of Constantinople, Being the Story of the Fourth Crusade.* New York: Harper & Bros., 1886.

Perlman, Fredy. *The Continuing Appeal of Nationalism.* London: Phoenix Press, 1984.

Perry, Richard O. "Warfare in the Pampas in the 1870s," *Military Affairs* 36 (April 1972), 52–58.

Peters, F. E. *Jerusalem: The Holy City in the Eyes of Chroniclers, Visitors, Pilgrims, and Prophets from the Days of Abraham to the Beginning of Modern Times.* Princeton, N.J.: Princeton University Press, 1985.

Picard, G.C. and Colette Picard. *The Life and Death of Carthage: A Survey of Punic History and Culture from its Birth to the Final Trag-*

edy. Dominique Collin, trans. New York: Taplinger Publishing Co., 1969.

Platonov, S. F. *Ivan the Terrible.* J. Wieczynski, trans. Gulf Breeze, Fl.: Academic International Press, 1974.

Poewe, Karla. *The Namibian Herero: A History of their Psychosocial Disintegration and Survival.* Lewiston: The Edwin Mellen Press, 1985.

Porter, Jack Nusan, ed. *Jewish Partisans: A Documentary of Jewish Resistance in the Soviet Union during World War II.* Washington, D.C.: University Press of America, 1982.

Prunier, Gérard. *The Rwanda Crisis: History of a Genocide.* New York: Columbia University Press, 1995.

Queller, D. E. *The Fourth Crusade: The Conquest of Constantinople, 1201–1204.* Philadelphia: University of Pennsylvania Press, 1977.

Ra'anan, Uri. "The Nation-State Fallacy," in Joseph Montville, ed., *Conflict and Peacemaking in Multiethnic Societies.* Lexington, Mass.: D.C. Heath and Company, 1990.

Ranger, T.O. *Revolt in Southern Rhodesia, 1896–7: A Study in African Resistance.* London: Heinemann, 1967.

Reed, A M. *The Ancient Past of Mexico.* New York: Crown Publishers, Inc., 1966.

Refugee Policy Group Issue Paper. *Refugees and Human Rights: A Research and Policy Agenda.* Washington, D.C.: Refugee Policy Group, May 1989.

Reinhartz, Dennis. "Damnation of the Outsider: The Gypsies of Croatia and Serbia in the Balkan Holocaust, 1941–1945," pp. 81–92, in David Crowe and John Kolski, eds. *The Gypsies of Europe.* Armonk, N.Y.: M.E. Sharpe Inc. 1991.

Rennie, Ysabel. *The Argentine Republic.* New York: Macmillan, 1945.

Rhoodie, Eschel. *South West: The Last Frontier in Africa.* New York: Twin Circle Publishing Co., 1967.

Riasanovsky, N.V. *A History of Russia.* New York: Oxford University Press, 1984.

Richburg, Keith B. "Rwanda Wracked by Ethnic Violence." *Washington Post.* April 8, 1994: A1.

Ridley, R.T. "To Be Taken With A Grain of Salt: The Destruction of Carthage." *Classical Philology* 81 (April 1986): 140–46.

Riskin, Carl. "Food, Poverty, and Development Strategy in People's Republic of China," in Lucile F Newman, ed. *Hunger in History.* Cambridge, Mass.: Basil Blackwell, 1990.

Rock, David. *Argentina 1516–1982: From Spanish Colonization to the Falklands War.* Los Angeles: University of California Press, 1985.

Rodd, Sir R. *The Princes of Achaia and the Chronicles of Morea,* vol. I. London: Edward Arnold, Publisher to the India Office, 1907.

Rodzinski, Witlod. *The Walled Kingdom: A History of China from Antiquity to the Present.* New York: The Free Press, 1984.

Rostovtzeff, M. and H. A. Ormerod. "Pontus and Its Neighbours." In *The Cambridge Ancient History,* vol. IX. Cambridge: Cambridge University Press, 1932: 211–59.

Rotberg, Robert R. "Resistance and Rebellion in British Nyasaland and German East Africa, 1888–1915: A Tentative Comparison," pp. 667–90 in *Britain and Germany in Africa: Imperial Rivalry and Colonial Rule.* Prosser Gifford and W. M. Roger Louis, eds. New Haven, Conn.: Yale University Press, 1967

Roth, Cecil. *The Spanish Inquisition.* New York: Norton, 1964.

Rückerl, Adalbert. *The Investigation of Nazi Crimes 1945–1978: A Documentation.* Derek Rutter, trans. Hamden, Conn.: Archon Books, 1980.

Rudin, H.R. *Germans in the Cameroons, 1884–1914: A Case Study in Modern Imperialism.* Hamden, Conn.: Archon Books, 1968.

Rüger, Adolf. "The Colonial Aims of the Weimar Republic" in *German Imperialism in Africa: From the Beginnings until the Second World War.* Helmuth Stoecker, ed. Bernd Zöllner, trans. London: C. Hurst & Co., 1986.

Rummel, R.J. *China's Bloody Century: Genocide and Mass Murder since 1900.* New Brunswick, N.J.: Transaction Pubishers, 1991.

Rummel, R.J. *Death by Government,* chapters 2 and 3. New Brunswick, N.J.: Transaction Publishers, 1994.

Rummel, R.J. "Power Kills; Absolute Power Kills Absolutely," *Internet on the Holocaust and Genocide* 38 (June 1992): 1–10; republished as "Megamurders," *Society* 29 (September/October 1992): 47–52.

Sable, Martin H. *Holocaust Studies: a Directory and Bibliography of Bibliographies.* Greenwood, Fl.: Penkevill Publication Co. 1987.

Sansom, George B. *A History of Japan: 1615–1867.* Stanford, Cal.: Stanford University Press, 1963.

Sawyer, P.H. *Kings and Vikings: Scandinavia and Europe,* A.D. 700–1100. London: Methuen Publishers, 1982.

Sbacchi, Alberto. *Ethiopia Under Mussolini: Fascism and the Colonial Experience.* London: Zed Books Ltd., 1985.

Schiller, Herbert I. "Manipulating Hearts and Minds," in *Triumph of the Image: The Media's War in the Persian Gulf: A Global Perspec-*

tive. Hamid Mowlana, George Gerbner, and Herbert I. Schiller, eds. Boulder: Colo.: Westview Press, 1992.

Schmitt-Egner, Peter. *Kolonialismus und Faschismus: Eine Studie zur historischen und begrifflichen Genesis faschistischer Bewusstseinsformen am deutschen Beispiel.* Giessen/Lollar: Verlag Andreas Achenbach, 1975.

Schmokel, Wolfe W. *Dream of Empire: German Colonialiam, 1919–1945.* New Haven, Conn.: Yale University Press, 1964.

Schnee, Dr. Heinrich. *German Colonization Past and Future: The Truth About The German Colonies,* with an introduction by William Harbutt Dawson. London: George Allen & Unwin, 1926.

Schneider, Karl Max, ed. *Vom Leipziger Zoo: aus der Entwicklung einer Volksbildungsstätte.* Leipzig: Akademische Verlagsgesellschaft Geest & Portig K.-G., 1953.

Schulten, Adolf. "The Romans in Spain," in *The Cambridge Ancient History,* vol. VIII, S.A. Cook, F.E. Adcock, and M.P. Charlesworth, eds. Cambridge: Cambridge University Press, 1930: 306–25.

Scobie, James R. *Revolution in the Pampas.* Austin: University of Texas Press, 1964.

Scullard, H.H. *A History of the Roman World: From 753 to 146 BC,* fourth edition. London: Methuen & Co. Ltd., 1980.

Secher, Reynald. *Le génocide franco-français: la Vendée-Vengé.* Paris: Presses Universitaires de France, 1986.

Segal, Ronald and Ruth First, eds. *South West Africa: Travesty of Trust. The expert papers and findings of the International Conference on South West Africa, Oxford 23–26 March 1966, with a postscript by Iain MacGibbon on the 1966 Judgement of the International Court of Justice.* London: Andre Deutsch, 1967.

Sen, Amartya. *Poverty and Famines: An Essay on Entitlement and Deprivation.* Oxford: Oxford University Press, 1981.

Shannon, R.T. *Gladstone and the Bulgarian Agitation, 1876.* Sussex, England: The Harvester Press Ltd.; Hamden, Conn.: Archon Books, 1975.

Shapiro, Gershon, compiler. *Under Fire: Jewish Heroes of the Soviet Union.* Jerusalem: Yad Vashem, 1988.

Shawcross, William. *The Quality of Mercy: Cambodia, Holocaust and Modern Conscience.* New York: Simon and Schuster, 1984.

Shimoni, Gideon, ed. *The Holocaust in University Teaching.* Oxford: Pergamon, 1991.

Shub, Boris. *Starvation Over Europe (Made in Germany): A Documented Record.* New York: The Institute of Jewish Affairs, 1943.

Shub, Boris., ed. *Hitler's Ten-Year War on the Jews*. New York: Institute of Jewish Affairs of the American Jewish Congress, September 1943.

Silverstein, Josef. *Burma: Military Rule and the Politics of Stagnation*. Ithaca, N.Y.: Cornell University Press, 1977.

Singleton, Frederick Bernard. *A Short History of the Yugoslav Peoples*. New York: Cambridge University Press, 1985.

Sircar, D. C. *Asokan Studies*. Calcutta: Indian Museum, 1979.

Sircar, Dineschandra. *Inscriptions of Asoka*. New Delhi: Publications Division, Ministry of Information and Broadcasting, Government of India, 1975.

Sivard, Ruth Leger. *World Military and Social Expenditures 1996*. Washington, D.C.: World Priorities, Inc., 1996.

Smith, Anthony D. *The Ethnic Origin of Nations*. Oxford: Basil Blackwell, 1986.

Smith, Martin. *Burma: Insurgency and the Politics of Ethnicity*. London: Zed Books, 1991.

Smith, R. Boswarth. *Carthage and the Carthaginians*. London: Longmans, Green & Co., 1878.

Smith, Vincent A. *The Oxford History of India*, third edition, Percival Spear, ed. Oxford: Clarendon Press, 1958.

Smith, Woodruff D. *The German Colonial Empire*. Chapel Hill: The University of North Carolina Press, 1979.

Smith, Woodruff D. *The Ideological Origins of Nazi Imperialism*. New York: Oxford University Press, 1986.

Sordi, Marta. *The Christians and the Roman Empire*. London: Croom Helm, 1983.

Speer, Albert. *The Slave State: Heinrich Himmler's Masterplan for SS Supremacy*. London: Weidenfeld and Nicolson, 1981.

Spohr, Otto H. comp. *German Africana: German Publications on South and South West Africa*. Pretoria: State Library, 1968.

Spraul, Gunter. "Der 'Völkermord' an den Herero: Untersuchungen zu einer neuen Kontinuitätsthese." *Geschichte in Wissenschaft und Unterricht* 12 (1988): 713–39.

Staehelin, Balthasar. *Völkerschauen im Zoologischen Garten Basel 1879–1935*. Basel: Basler Afrika Bibliographien, 1993.

Stanton, Gregory H. "Blue Scarves and Yellow Stars: Classification and Symbolization in the Cambodian Genocide." Montreal: Montreal Institute for Genocide and Human Rights Studies, Occasional Paper, April 1989.

Steering Committee of the Joint Evaluation Emergency Assistance to Rwanda. "The International Response to Conflict and Genocide:

Lessons from the Rwanda Experience." *Journal of Humanitarian Assistance* (http://131.111.106.147/policy/pb020b.htm), March 1996.

Steinberg, David I. *The Future of Burma: Crisis and Choice in Myanmar.* Lanham, Md.: University Press of America, 1990.

Steinberg, David I. "Neither Silver nor Gold: The 40th Anniversary of the Burmese Economy," in *Independent Burma at Forty Years: Six Assessments.* Josef Silverstein, ed. Ithaca, N.Y.: Cornell University Southeast Asia Program, 1989.

Steinberg, Lucien. *The Jews Against Hitler. (Not as a Lamb)* London and New York: Gordon & Cremonesi, 1978 (first French edition, 1970).

Steiner, Jean-François. *Treblinka.* London: Weidenfeld & Nicolson, 1967.

Stoecker, Helmuth, ed. *German Imperialism in Africa: From the Beginnings until the Second World War.* Bernd Zollner, trans. Atlantic Highlands, N.J.: Humanities Press International, 1986.

Strayer, Joseph R. *The Albigensian Crusades.* New York: Dial, 1971.

Sudholt, Gerd. *Die deutsche Eingeborenenpolitik in Südwestafrika: von den Anfägen bis 1904.* Hildesheim, New York: Georg Olms Verlag, 1975.

Suhl, Yuri, ed. *They Fought Back: the Story of Jewish Resistance in Nazi Europe.* New York: Schocken Books, 1975 (1967).

Suret-Canale, Jean. *French Colonialism in Tropical Africa, 1900–1945.* Till Gottheiner, trans. New York: Pica Press, 1971.

Sutherland, C. H. V. *The Romans in Spain: 217 B.C.–117 A.D.* London: Methuen & Co. Ltd., 1939.

Swan, Jon. "The Final Solution in South West Africa: The confrontation between Germans and native Africans had mortal consequences not only for blacks but, ultimately, for Europe's Jews," *The Quarterly Journal of Military History* (1991): 36–55.

Syrkin, Marie. *Blessed is the Match: The Story of Jewish Resistance.* Philadelphia: The Jewish Publication Society of America, 1976 (1947).

Szonyi, David M. *The Holocaust: An Annotated Bibliography and Resource Guide.* Hoboken, N.J.: Ktav, 1985.

Tanakh: A New Translation of The Holy Scriptures According to the Traditional Hebrew Text. Philadelphia: The Jewish Publication Society, 1965.

Tatz, Colin. *Reflections on the Politics of Remembering and Forgetting.* The First Abraham Wajnryb Memorial Lecture, 1 December

1994. North Ryde, NSW, Australia: Centre for Comparative Genocide Studies, 1995: 26–31.

Taylor, A. J. P. *Germany's First Bid for Colonies 1884–1885: A Move in Bismarck's European Policy.* Hamden, Conn.: Archon Books, 1967 (1938).

Taylor, James and Warren Shaw. *The Third Reich Almanac.* London: Grafton Books, 1987.

Taylor, Simon. *Prelude to Genocide: Nazi Ideology and the Struggle for Power.* New York: St. Martin's Press, 1985.

Taylor, S.J. *Stalin's Apologist: Walter Duranty, The New York Times' Man in Moscow.* New York: Oxford University Press, 1990.

Teitelbaum, Joshua. "If You Can't Beat 'em, Buy'em." *Jerusalem Report.* November 16, 1995.

Teng, Szu-yu. *The Taiping Rebellion and the Western Powers: A Comprehensive Survey.* Oxford: Clarendon Press, 1971.

Ternon, Yves. *Enquête sur la négation d'un génocide.* Marseilles: Editions Paranthèses, 1989.

Ternon, Yves. *L'état criminel: Les génocides au XXe siècle.* Paris: Editions du Seuil, 1995. Cinquième Partie, "Problématique de l'intervention."

"This Week" *Manchester Guardian Weekly,* vol. 141, no. 25 (December 24, 1989): 6.

Thompson, Mark. *Forging War: The Media in Serbia, Croatia and Bosnia-Hercegovina.* London: Article 19, International Centre Against Censorship, 1994.

Todorov, T. *The Conquest of America, The Question of the Other.* Richard Howard, trans. New York: Harper & Row, 1984.

Totten, Samuel. *First-Person Accounts of Genocidal Acts Committed in the Twentieth Century: An Annotated Bibliography.* New York: Greenwood Press, 1991.

Townsend, Mary Evelyn. *The Rise and Fall of Germany's Colonial Empire 1884–1918.* New York: Howard Fertig, 1966 (1930).

Troyat, Henri. *Ivan the Terrible.* Joan Pinkham, trans. New York: E.P. Dutton Inc., 1984.

Trumpener, Ulrich. *Germany and the Ottoman Empire: 1914–1918.* Princeton, N.J.: Princeton University Press, 1968.

Tzang Yawnghwe, Chao. "The Burman Military: Holding the Country Together?" in *Independent Burma at Forty Years: Six Assessments.* Josef Silverstein, ed. Ithaca, N.Y.: Cornell University Southeast Asia Program, 1989.

Tzang Yawnghwe, Chao. *The Shan of Burma: Memoirs of a Shan Exile.* Singapore: Local History and Memoirs, Institute of Southeast Asian Studies, 1987.

Ullrich, Volker. "...deutsches Blut zu rächen!" *Die Zeit,* no. 3 (21 January 1994).

Union of South Africa. *Report on the Natives of South-West Africa and Their Treatment by Germany.* Prepared in the Administrator's Office, Windhuk, South-West Africa, January 1918. Presented to both Houses of Parliament by Command of His Majesty, August 1918. London: His Majesty's Stationery Office, 1918.

The U.S. Committee for Refugees. *World Refugee Surveys.* Washington, D.C.: Immigration and Refugee Services of America, Annual Reports from 1988 to 1996.

United Nations, Commission on Human Rights, Sub-Commission on Prevention of Discrimination and Protection of Minorities, *Summary of Information Relating to Bangladesh,* (Study of the Problem of Discrimination against Indigenous Populations: Special Rapporteur, Mr. José Martinez Cobo).

Van Creveld, Martin L. *Technology and War: From 2000 B.C. to the Present.* New York: The Free Press, 1989.

Verschave, François Xavier. *Complicité de génocide, La politique de la France au Rwanda.* Paris: La Découverte, 1994.

Vigne, Randolph, Henning Melber, Brigitte Lau, Letters to the Editor, *Southern African Review of Book* (August/October 1990): 23.

Vigne, Randolph. "Shark Island" *Southern African Review of Books* (February / May 1990): 31.

Villehardouin, G. de *Memoirs of the Crusades.* Frank Marzials, trans. London: J.M. Dent & Sons Ltd.; New York: E.P. Dutton & Co., 1908.

Voeltz, Richard A. *German Colonialism and the South West Africa Company, 1884–1914.* Athens: Ohio University Center for International Studies, Monographs in International Studies, Africa Series, no. 50, 1988.

Wakefield, W. L. *Heresy, Crusade and Inquisition in Southern France, 1100–1250.* London: Allen & Unwin, 1974.

Waley, Arthur. "The Fall of Lo-yang," *History Today,* (April 1951): 7–10.

Walford, Cornelius. *Famines of the World: Past and Present.* New York: Burt Franklin, 1970. (Reprinted papers from the *Journal of the Statistical Society of London,* 1878, 1879.)

Waliszewski, K. *Ivan the Terrible.* Lady Mary Lloyd, trans. Hamden, Conn.: Archon, 1966.

Warner, Philip. *Sieges of the Middle Ages.* London: G. Bell & Sons, 1968.

Watkins, Trevor. "The Beginnings of Warfare," pp. 15–35, in John Hackett, ed. *Warfare in the Ancient World.* New York: Facts on File, 1990.

Weinreich, Max. *Hitler's Professors.* New York: YIVO, 1946.

Weiss, Thomas G. in "UN Responses in the Former Yugoslavia: Moral and Operational Choices." *Ethics And International Affairs,* vol. 8 (1994).

Wellington, John H. *South West Africa and its Human Issues.* Oxford: Clarendon Press, 1967.

Wertheimer, Mildred S. *The Pan-German League 1890–1914.* New York: Octagon Books, 1971 (1924).

West, Richard. *Brazza of the Congo: European Exploration and Exploitation in French Equatorial Africa.* London: Jonathan Cape, 1972.

Westington, Marc McClelland. *Atrocities in Roman Warfare to 133 B.C.* Chicago: private edition, distributed by the University of Chicago Libraries, 1938.

Wharton, Jr., Clifton R. "The Nightmare in Central Africa." *New York Times.* April 9, 1994: A21.

Whitaker, Ben. *Revised and Updated Report on the Question of the Prevention and Punishment of the Crime of Genocide.* United Nations Economic and Social Council, Commission on Human Rights (E.CN.4. Sub. 2. 1985. 6: 2 July 1985).

Whitaker, Benjamin C. G., et al. *The Biharis in Bangladesh.* London: Minority Rights Group Report, no. 11, 1982.

White III, Lynn T. *Politics of Chaos: the Organizational Causes of Violence in China's Cultural Revolution.* Princeton, N.J.: Princeton University Press, 1989.

Wiener Library. *Persecutions and Resistance under the Nazis.* London: Institute of Contemporary History, 1978.

Wilken, Robert L. *The Christians as the Romans Saw Them.* New Haven, Conn.: Yale University Press, 1984.

Williams, Robin M. "The Sociology of Ethnic Conflicts: Comparative International Perspectives." In John Hagan and Karen S. Cook, eds., *Annual Review of Sociology,* vol. 20. Palo Alto, Cal.: Annual Reviews, Inc., 1994: 49–79.

Williams, Steven. *Diocletian and the Roman Recovery.* London: B.T. Batsford, 1985.

Wilson, James. *The Original Americans: US Indians*. London: Minority Rights Group, report no. 31, 1986.

Wiseman, F.J. *Roman Spain: An Introduction to the Roman Antiquities of Spain and Portugal*. London: G. Bell & Sons Ltd., 1956.

Wiseman, J. D. "The Assyrians," pp. 36–53, in John Hackett, ed. *Warfare in the Ancient World*. New York: Facts on File, 1990.

Woldegabir, Semena. *Amharic for Foreigners*, fifth edition. Addis Ababa: n.p., 1994.

Wolff, Robert Lee. *The Balkans in Our Time*. Cambridge, Mass.: Harvard University Press, 1986.

World Food Conference. *Universal Declaration on the Eradication of Hunger and Malnutrition: Adopted on 16 November 1974 by the World Food Conference convened under General Assembly resolution 3180 (XXVIII) of 17 December 1973; and endorsed by General Assembly resolution 3348 (XXIX) of 17 December 1974*, pp. 392–97 in Centre for Human Rights, Geneva. *Human Rights: a Compilation of International Instruments*. New York: United Nations, 1988.

Yad Vashem International Historical Conference (5th: 1983: Jerusalem) *The Historiography of the Holocaust Period: Proceedings*. Jerusalem: Yad Vashem, 1988.

Yad Vashem Studies on the European Jewish Catastrophe and Resistance. Jerusalem: Yad Vashem, vol. 1, 1957.

Yad Vashem. *Proceedings of the Conference on Manifestations of Jewish Resistance during the Holocaust, Jerusalem, April 7–11, 1968*. Moshe M. Kohn, ed. Jerusalem: Yad Vashem,1971.

Yates, Robin D. S. "War, Food Shortage, and Relief Measures in Early China," chapter 6 in Lucile F. Newman, ed. *Hunger in History*. Cambridge, Mass.: Basil Blackwell, 1990.

Yavner, Robert Simon. *I. G. Farben's Petro-Chemical Plant at Auschwitz*. M. A. thesis. Old Dominion University, 1984.

Zimmerman, A. F. "The Land Policy of Argentina, with particular reference to the conquest of the Southern Pampas," *Hispanic American Historical Review* 25 (Nov 1945), 3–26.

Zolberg, Aristide R. "The Formation of New States as a Refugee- Generating Process," *The Annals of the American Academy of Political and Social Science* 467 (May 1983): 24–38.

Zolberg, Aristide R., Astri Suhrke, and Sergio Aguayo. *Escape from Violence: Conflict and the Refugee Crisis in the Developing World*. New York: Oxford University Press, 1989.

Zuckerman, Isaac, ed. *The Fighting Ghettos*. New York: Belmont-Tower, 1971.

Bibliography of Internet Materials

Introduction

The following list of Internet Web Sites is included here in the hope that it will be useful to readers who are interested in pursuing some of the issues raised in this book—especially where up-to-date information is relevant. While this is a very small list that is obviously quite incomplete, each of these web sites contains many links to other relevant sites.

The user of these internet resources should realize that anyone with access to a computer and the appropriate software can set up a web site. There are no restrictions. This means that materials can appear without the time delays involved in hard copy publishing and also without the usual economic and editorial restraints. However, it also means that readers will have to use their judgement in deciding what information is accurate and reliable and what bias has informed it. In other words, the cautions discussed in part 2 above certainly apply here.

http://www.umn.edu/humanrts/africa/index.html
African Human Rights Resource Center: many links, including a bibliography.
http://www.africanews.org/
AfricaNews Online: provides continent-wide coverage that is updated on a continuous basis.
http://www.freeworld.it/peacelink/afrights/homepage.html
African Rights: Africa's problems seen by the African perspective.
http://www.umn.edu/humanrts/africa/africanlinks.html
Links to other WWW resources relating to Africa: has over 60 links to useful sites.
http://heiwww.unige.ch/humanrts/links/alphalinks.html
Alphabetical Listing of Links by Category: an invaluable guide of over 600 links relating to human rights. Its 19 pages are worth downloading for use as a guide even though it takes a few minutes.

http://www.amnesty.org
Amnesty International
http://www.umd.umich.edu/dept/armenian/facts/gen_bibl.html
The Armenian Genocide: A Bibliography: is fairly complete up to
1992 and features notes with very complete publication details.
http://www.umd.umich.edu/dept/armenian/facts/gen_bib2.html
The Armenian Genocide: A Supplemental Bibliography, 1993–1996:
see above.
http://users.aol.com/BalkanInst/home.html
The Balkan Institute Home Page. The Balkan Institute is a nonprofit
organization dedicated to educating the public, the media and
policymakers about the conflict in the Balkans, providing up-to-
date news and analysis.
http://www.spfo.unibo.it/spolfo/ILMAIN.htm
*University of Bologna, Research Guide to International Law on the
Internet*: is organized into several specialties, of which the most
useful are "Peace and Security," "Current Conflicts and Humanitarian Crisis," "Peacekeeping Operations," and "Human Rights." Each
is organized into subheading listing many annotated links.
http://www.tue.nl:80/aegee/hrwg/exyu/
*Bosnia-Herzegovina, Croatia, Macedonia, Slovenia and FR Yugosla-
via*: this web page is produced by the Association des Etats Généraux
des Etudiants de l'Europe and provides some very useful information.
http://sunsite.unc.edu/freeburma/ba/ba.html
Burma Alert Online: gives access to the monthly *Burma Alert.*
http://www.sunsite.unc.edu
Free Burma Bulletin Board Service: a subscription service.
http://www.sas.upenn.edu/African_Studies/Country_Specific/
Burundi.html
Burundi Page: in addition to country information, contains a map.
http://www.intr.net/cpss/index.html
The Center for Post-Soviet Studies: has useful sites not otherwise
too often covered, such as Central Asia and Caucasus.
http://www.columbia.edu/~slc11/
Coalition Against Slavery in Mauritania and Sudan, Inc. CASMAS.
http://www.igc.org/igc/conflictnet/
ConflictNet.
http://www.ichr.org/xlines/index.html
*Crosslines Global Report: an Independent Newsjournal on Humani-
tarian Action, Development and World Trends*, is an internet journal
that keeps content from back issues available.

http://www.igc.org/desip/
Demographic, Environmental, and Security Issues Project (DESIP) is very much structured by the editor's interests, but has some links relevant to wars, conflicts, and demography.

http://www.yale.edu/dianaweb/about.htm
Diana: A Human Rights Database, claims that it "will be the most comprehensive global source of human rights materials available electronically."

http://www.peg.apc.org/~etchrmel/
East Timor Human Rights Centre in Melbourne, Australia is "An independent centre for the promotion of Human Rights in East Timor" that is kept very up to date.

http://shell.ihug.co.nz/~calliope/Nettalk.html
East Timor International News: in addition to English this web site covers news in French, Italian, Portuguese and Spanish.

http://www.uc.pt./Timor/TimorNet.html
East Timor, *timorNET,* is an information service located at the University of Coimbra in Portugal that has many good links and includes news updates.

http://www.educ.com/ejournal/
e.journal: is a listing of electronic and print publications on the internet and has a search feature.

http://www.ids.ac.uk/eldis/eldis.htlm
Electronic Development and Environment Information System (ELDIS) is a project in the British Library for Development Studies at the Institute for Development Studies, Sussex, UK. It lists over 3,500 items covering 60 broad subject areas. Each link provides addresses, key words, and related subjects.

http://www.ids.ac.uk/eldis/disast/dis_gbib.html
ELDIS select bibliography on Gender and Humanitarian Assistance

http://www.ids.ac.uk/eldis/disast/dis_lele.html
ELDIS sources list for disasters and refugees.

http://www.ids.ac.uk/eldis/eldis2.html
Alphabetical 50-page list of sources described in *ELDIS*.

http://www.partal.com/ciemen/ethnic.html
Ethnic World Survey, provides "information on ethnic, native and nationalistic affairs all over the world." It is organized into sections for the five continents and then by countries.

http://www.aber.ac.uk/~inpwww/res/femin.htm
Feminism Resources on the WWW is assembled by the Department of International Politics of the University of Wales and contains sev-

eral links dealing with human rights, including a "Gender and Humanitarian Assistance Bibliography."

http://www.gdn.org/proposal.html

The Global Democracy Network.

http://www.hamp.hampshire.edu/~ratS88/romani/

A Compendium of Gypsy Resources on the Internet: includes among other items the "Romani Rights Watch" and an "Annotated Bibliography."

http://www.hrw.org/about/about.html

Human Rights Watch: "includes five divisions covering Africa, the Americas, Asia, the Middle East, as well as the signatories of the Helsinki accords. It also includes three collaborative projects on arms transfers, children's rights, and women's rights."

http://www.soros.org/burma/burmrigh.html

Human Rights and Burma: this is a very good site with many interesting and useful links.

http://www.umn.edu/humanrts/

Human Rights Library at the University of Minnesota has many useful categories with many extensive, sometimes quirky, links. See esp. the next item listed.

http://www.umn.edu/humanrts/links/links.htm

Human Rights and Related Sources Available Through the Internet: has many links worth following.

http://www.columbia.edu/cu/humanrights/index.html

Center for Human Rights at Columbia University, under the heading "human rights & related resources on the web," lists a number of quite fascinating links.

http://www.brown.edu/Departments/Watson_Institute/H_W/index.html

The Humanitarianism and War Project is one of the initiatives of the Thomas J. Watson Jr. Institute for International Studies at Brown University: reports current activities and publications

http://www.brown.edu/Departments/World_Hunger_Program/

Hungerweb: has an index to all their links.

http://www.incore.ulst.ac.uk/

Internet Service on Conflict Resolution and Ethnicity (INCORE) is a joint initiative of the University of Ulster and the United Nations University and it is best used by going to the "country guides."

http://www.oneworld.org/index_oc/index.html

Index on Censorship: a journal that also accepts subscriptions.

http://www.incore.ulst.ac.uk/ods/metadata/intalert.html

International Alert: "is a non-governmental alliance for the resolution of conflicts within countries."

http://www.ichrdd.ca/

International Center for Human Rights and Democratic Development.

http://www.ichr.org/related.html

The International Centre for Humanitarian Reporting's "Other related Web Sites" lists quite a number of them.

http://www.icrc.org/

International Committee of the Red Cross.

http://www.cij.org/tribunal/

International Criminal Tribunals: this web page is also available in French. It provides information about the Tribunals for the Former Yugoslavia (ICTY) and for Rwanda (ICTR) and includes links to related subjects.

http://www.cfcsc.dnd.ca/links/intrel.confli.html

International relations: Conflict and conflict resolution is produced by the Information Resource Centre of the Canadian Armed Forces and has useful links to bibliographies, archives, organizations and programs.

http://www.isn.ethz.ch/wwwl_ism.html

International Relations and Security Network, includes peace and conflict research, is very comprehensive and is updated daily.

http://www.link.no/ips/eng/last.html

IPS (Inter Press Service): "Founded in 1964 in Rome as a communications bridge between the countries of the North and South.... IPS is a non-governmental organization structured as a non-profit International Association of Journalists." It is available in five languages and news is delivered daily to this site.

http://131.111.106.147/jha.html

Journal of Humanitarian Assistance: an internet journal edited at Cambridge University, publishes not only excellent scholarly papers, but also reports from various NGOs within a day or two of receipt.

http://www.afnews.org/ans/liblinks.html

Liberia: News & Resources.

http://www.unicc.org/unrisd/wsp/blocks1.htm

Links to Internal and External Actors has a quite complete list of Global International Organizations.

http://www.oneworld.org/news/index.html

OneWorld News Service: provides " human rights and development coverage from 90 organizations and 124 countries, updated every day and cross-indexed by country and by theme."

http://www.soros.org/osiny.html
Open Society Institute: see esp. links to Burma Project, Forced Migration Project, Southern Africa Project.
http://www.phrf.org/index.html
Parliamentary Human Rights Foundation.
http://www.igc.org/igc/peacenet/
"PeaceNet/IGC is the only unionized Internet service provider in the United States."
http://www.reliefweb.int/
ReliefWeb: is a project of the United Nations Department of Humanitarian Affairs (DHA). It disseminates information on prevention and disaster response. It has over 500 links and is updated twice a day. Also see under:
http://www.info.usaid.gov/ofda/reliefweb/related.html
which is the *Relief Web's* listing of Related Sites.
http://www.rwanda.net/
Rwanda Information Exchange: "this is a forum and a network for the exchange of information."
http://www.soros.org/
Soros Foundation Network has an extensive list of "related sites."
http://www.survival.org.uk/
Survival International: "is a worldwide organization supporting tribal peoples."
http://www.manymedia.com/tibet/TibetSupportGroupFactIndex.html
Tibet Support Group Fact Sheets: while not very up to date, it has several useful links.
http://coombs.anu.edu.au/WWWVL-TibetanStudies.html
Tibetan Studies WWW Virtual Library, is the best site on Tibet, not only because it is up-dated almost daily and has 165 links, but also because links are inspected and evaluated before being added.
http://www.vita.org/
Volunteers in Technical Assistance (VITA) is a long established organization dedicated to helping developing countries by providing useful information. Its "Emergency Information Service" has links to many humanitarian disaster situations that are frequently updated from official sources. See esp. "Humanitarian Response."
http://www.w3.org/vl/
The WWW Virtual Library. Its subject listings are an inexhaustible source of information. If you have ever enjoyed a trip to your library, this is a new high.

Name Index

This index includes the names of individuals, organizations, and international documents that appear in the text and the notes. It does not include material that appears in the two bibliographies.

For locating subjects in this volume, the reader is invited to consult the detailed table of contents.

S. P. Oliner